Byzantium in Eastern European Visual Culture in the Late Middle Ages

East Central and Eastern Europe in the Middle Ages, 450–1450

General Editors

Florin Curta and Dušan Zupka

VOLUME 65

The titles published in this series are listed at *brill.com/ecee*

Byzantium in Eastern European Visual Culture in the Late Middle Ages

Edited by

Maria Alessia Rossi
Alice Isabella Sullivan

BRILL

LEIDEN | BOSTON

Cover illustration: From left to right, details of in-text Figs. 10.1, 8.1, 6.6, 2.2, and 5.6.
Figure 10.1 The Veglia Altar Frontal, ca. 1358, Victoria and Albert Museum, London, 2016 (photograph by Danijel Ciković, by permission of Victoria and Albert Museum).
Figure 8.1 Church of the Annunciation, 1532–37, view from southeast, Moldoviţa Monastery, Moldavia, Romania (photograph by Alice Isabella Sullivan).
Figure 6.6 Baptism of Christ, approx. date 1327–35, Church of Christ Pantokrator, Dečani Monastery, south portal (photograph by Platoneum Publishing).
Figure 2.2 Crown attributed to Monomakh, The Moscow Kremlin State Historical and Cultural Museum and Heritage Site (photograph by S. V. Baranov).
Figure 5.6 Marriage at Cana, detail of the two newlyweds, 1320–21, fresco. Monastery of Gračanica, *naos*, west wall (photograph provided by BLAGO Fund, USA/Serbia, www.srpskoblago.org).

Library of Congress Cataloging-in-Publication Data

Names: Rossi, Maria Alessia, editor. | Sullivan, Alice Isabella, editor.
Title: Byzantium in Eastern European Visual Culture in the late Middle Ages
   / edited by Maria Alessia Rossi, Alice Isabella Sullivan.
Description: Leiden ; Boston : Brill, [2020] | Series: East Central and
   Eastern Europe in the Middle Ages, 450-1450, 1872-8103 ; volume 65 |
   Includes bibliographical references and index.
Identifiers: LCCN 2020022163 (print) | LCCN 2020022164 (ebook) | ISBN
   9789004421363 (hardback) | ISBN 9789004421370 (ebook)
Subjects: LCSH: Art, Medieval—Europe, Eastern—Byzantine influences. |
   Art, European—Europe. | Art and society—Europe, Eastern—History—To 1500. |
   Europe, Eastern—Civilization—Byzantine influences.
Classification: LCC N6750 .B99 2020 (print) | LCC N6750 (ebook) |
   DDC 709.02—dc23
LC record available at https://lccn.loc.gov/2020022163
LC ebook record available at https://lccn.loc.gov/2020022164

Typeface for the Latin, Greek, and Cyrillic scripts: "Brill". See and download: brill.com/brill-typeface.

ISSN 1872-8103
ISBN 978-90-04-42136-3 (hardback)
ISBN 978-90-04-42137-0 (e-book)

Copyright 2020 by Koninklijke Brill NV, Leiden, The Netherlands.
Koninklijke Brill NV incorporates the imprints Brill, Brill Hes & De Graaf, Brill Nijhoff, Brill Rodopi, Brill Sense, Hotei Publishing, mentis Verlag, Verlag Ferdinand Schöningh and Wilhelm Fink Verlag.
All rights reserved. No part of this publication may be reproduced, translated, stored in a retrieval system, or transmitted in any form or by any means, electronic, mechanical, photocopying, recording or otherwise, without prior written permission from the publisher. Requests for re-use and/or translations must be addressed to Koninklijke Brill NV via brill.com or copyright.com.

This book is printed on acid-free paper and produced in a sustainable manner.

*Dedicated to Robin and Christian,
with love and gratitude*

∴

Contents

Acknowledgments IX
List of Illustrations X
Notes on Contributors XVI

Introduction 1
   Maria Alessia Rossi and Alice Isabella Sullivan

1   The Allegory of Wisdom in Chrelja's Tower Seen through Philotheos Kokkinos 14
   Justin L. Willson

2   How Byzantine Was the Moscow Inauguration of 1498? 36
   Alexandra Vukovich

3   Intellectual Relationships between the Byzantine and Serbian Elites during the Palaiologan Era 71
   Elias Petrou

4   An Unexpected Image of Diplomacy in a Vatican Panel 91
   Marija Mihajlovic-Shipley

5   Byzantine Heritage and Serbian Ruling Ideology in Early 14th-Century Monumental Painting 119
   Maria Alessia Rossi

6   Dečani between the Adriatic Littoral and Byzantium 143
   Ida Sinkević

7   Triconch Churches Sponsored by Serbian and Wallachian Nobility 167
   Jelena Bogdanović

8   Moldavian Art and Architecture between Byzantium and the West 200
   Alice Isabella Sullivan

9   The Byzantine Tradition in Wallachian and Moldavian Embroideries 232
   Henry David Schilb

10   Rethinking the Veglia Altar Frontal from the Victoria and Albert
     Museum and Its Patron   248
       Danijel Ciković and Iva Jazbec Tomaić

     Indices   281

Acknowledgments

This volume stems from two sessions organized at the 44th Byzantine Studies Conference (4–7 October 2018; San Antonio, Texas) and titled "North of Byzantium: Art and Architecture at the Crossroads of the Latin, Greek, and Slavic Cultural Spheres, c.1300–c.1550 (I) and (II)." We are grateful to the audience members at the conference for the thoughtful comments, questions, and the lively discussion, and to the Mary Jaharis Center for Byzantine Art and Culture for sponsoring the sessions and for making possible this project from beginning to end. We have also received individual and joint support, as well as generous financial assistance for the research, writing, and revising stages of this volume from the following institutions and organizations: The Index of Medieval Art at Princeton University, a Getty/ACLS Postdoctoral Fellowship in the History of Art from the American Council of Learned Societies, generously supported by the Getty Foundation, as well as the VolkswagenStiftung and the Andrew W. Mellon Foundation.

In addition to the session speakers at the Byzantine Studies Conference, and in efforts to enrich the topics and issues under consideration, we invited other authors to contribute to this publication. We would like to thank all of the contributors for their enthusiasm toward this project, and for their hard work in bringing their individual essays to fruition. We also greatly appreciate the unfailing support from the staff and editors at Brill, and in particular Florin Curta and Dušan Zupka for accepting this volume for inclusion in the series *East Central and Eastern Europe in the Middle Ages, 450–1450*. A special thanks to the anonymous reviewer for the thorough comments and sound advice that helped improve the individual contributions and the volume as a whole. Finally, we are deeply indebted to our copyeditor, Joseph Hannan, for his invaluable assistance in helping us bring this project to completion and to our indexer, Sever J. Voicu, for his time and effort.

This edited volume is the first publication to arise from our joint initiative—*North of Byzantium* (NoB)—through which we aim to explore the rich history, art, and culture of the northern frontiers of the Byzantine Empire in Eastern Europe between the thirteenth and seventeenth centuries. We are very grateful to all of the mentors, scholars, and friends who have greeted us with encouragement from the very beginning, and to the Mary Jaharis Center for Byzantine Art and Culture for believing in this project and supporting it with an initial three-year grant.

Illustrations

Figures

0.1 Map of the Byzantine, Ottoman, and Serbian empires and their neighboring states, 1355 (image from William R. Shepherd, *Historical Atlas* [New York: Henry Holt and Company, 1911], 89, provided by Wikimedia Commons) 2

0.2 Map of Europe with the Iron Curtain Trail (image courtesy of the Iron Curtain Trail) 5

1.1 Chrelja's Tower, Rila Monastery, 1335 (photograph by Mark Ahsmann, provided by Wikimedia Commons, published under the Creative Commons license CC-BY-3.0) 15

1.2 Vertical cross section of Chrelja's tower (drawing by Georgi Stoikov. Reproduced after Prashkov, *Khrel'ovata kula*, fig. 7) 16

1.3 Floor plan of upper level of Chrelja's tower, east is to the left (drawing by Stefan Boiadzhiev, repr. after Prashkov, *Khrel'ovata kula*, fig. 8) 18

1.4 Drawing of frescoes in upper registers, chapel of Chrelja's tower (drawing by M. Reynolds; based partially on Prashkov, *Khrel'ovata kula*, annotation figs. 7, 21–23, repr. in Kirin, "Vistas of Piety," 129, fig. 42) 20

1.5 Allegory of Wisdom, fresco, chapel of Chrelja's tower (photograph by Ivan Vanev) 21

1.6 Wisdom, fresco, chapel of Chrelja's tower (photograph by Ivan Vanev) 23

1.7 Allegory of Wisdom, fresco, narthex, *katholikon* of Markov Monastery, 1376–77 or 1380–81 (photograph by Marka Tomić Đurić) 24

1.8 Allegory of Wisdom, fresco, nave, *katholikon* of Dečani Monastery, 1348 (photograph provided by BLAGO Fund, USA/Serbia, www.srpskoblago.org) 26

2.1 Cathedral of the Dormition, Kremlin, Moscow, 1479 (photograph by S. V. Bardanov) 44

2.2 Crown attributed to Monomakh, The Moscow Kremlin State Historical and Cultural Museum and Heritage Site (photograph by S. V. Baranov) 45

2.3 Barmy attributed to Aleksei Mikhailovich (photograph provided by Wikimedia Commons / Shakko) 46

2.4 Portrait of Tsar Aleksei Mikhailovich Romanov (1629–76), The State Hermitage Museum, St. Petersburg (photograph by Vladimir Terebenin, provided by The State Hermitage Museum) 47

3.1 John Argyropoulos teaching at the Xenon of the Kral, folio 33v, Oxon. Barocci 87, Bodleian Library (Digital reproduction by the Bodleian Library; reproduced with permission) 76

ILLUSTRATIONS XI

3.2 The note on the upper-right part of the folio by John Chortasmenos for the restoration of the codex, folio 1r, Vind. Med. gr. 1, Österreichische Nationalbibliothek (Austrian National Library) (Digital reproduction by the Austrian National Library; reproduced with permission) 77

3.3 The fortifications of Smederevo along with the Jerinina Kula (Tower of Irene) next to the main gate, Smederevo, Serbia (Photograph by Dragan Bosnic; reproduced with permission) 83

3.4 The note on the lower-right part of the folio by Demetrios Lascaris Leontares for George Palaiologos Cantacouzenos, folio 232r, GKS 6 folio, the Royal Danish Library (Digital reproduction by the Royal Danish Library; reproduced with permission) 85

4.1 Exact copy of panel of St. Peter and St. Paul, second half of 13th century, egg tempera on wood, 29–1/8 × 19–1/4 in. (74 × 49 cm) from the Vatican Treasury. The copy was commissioned by the National Museum in Belgrade and was made by Zdenka Živkovic in 1967 (photograph provided by National Museum of Belgrade) 93

4.2 Detail of icon of St. Paul, Jacob the Elder, Stephen, Lawrence, Martin of Tours, and Leonard of Limoges, second half of the 12th century, egg tempera on wood, 13–1/8 × 9–3/8 in. (33.3 × 23.7 cm) (reproduced with permission of Saint Catherine's Monastery, Sinai, Egypt; photograph provided by Michigan-Princeton-Alexandria Expeditions to Mount Sinai) 102

4.3 Fresco of St. Peter and St. Paul in the Church of St. Achillius, Arilje, 1296 (photograph by Marija Mihajlovic-Shipley) 103

4.4 Panel of triptych depicting St. Nicholas, second half of 13th century, egg tempera on wood, h. 22–3/4 in. (57.8 cm) (reproduced with permission of Saint Catherine's Monastery, Sinai, Egypt; photograph provided by Princeton University, Michigan-Princeton-Alexandria Expeditions to Mount Sinai) 104

4.5 Jacopo Torriti, detail of apse mosaic showing Pope Nicholas IV with St. Peter and St. Paul, 1290–95. Santa Maria Maggiore, Rome (reproduced with permission of the Conway Library, The Courtauld Institute of Art, distributed under a CC BY-NC 4.0 license) 105

4.6 Queen Jelena depicted with Stefan the First-Crowned and King Uroš I as monks, 1296, fresco. Church of St. Achillius, Arilje (photograph by Marija Mihajlovic-Shipley) 109

4.7 The brothers King Milutin and King Dragutin depicted in identical attire, 1283–85, fresco. Dragutin's Chapel in the church Tracts of St. George, Novi Pazar (photograph by Marija Mihajlovic-Shipley) 113

5.1 Church of St. George at Staro Nagoričino, 1316–17, interior view toward west, with frescos by Michael Astrapas (photograph by Maria Alessia Rossi) 125

5.2 Michael Astrapas, Christ calling Zacchaeus, 1316–17, fresco. Church of St. George at Staro Nagoričino, *naos*, west wall (photograph by Maria Alessia Rossi) 128

5.3 Christ calling Zacchaeus, 1320–21, fresco. Monastery of Gračanica, *naos*, west wall (photograph provided by BLAGO Fund, USA/Serbia, www.srpskoblago.org) 130

5.4 Attributed to Michael Astrapas, Christ calling Zacchaeus, ca. 1321, fresco. Church of St. Nikita, near Čučer, *naos*, south wall (photograph by Maria Alessia Rossi) 131

5.5 Marriage at Cana, 1320–21, fresco. Monastery of Gračanica, *naos*, west wall (photograph provided by BLAGO Fund, USA/Serbia, www.srpskoblago.org) 133

5.6 Marriage at Cana, detail of the two newlyweds, 1320–21, fresco. Monastery of Gračanica, *naos*, west wall (photograph provided by BLAGO Fund, USA/Serbia, www.srpskoblago.org) 134

5.7 Portrait of Simonis, 1302–21, fresco. Monastery of Gračanica, *naos*, west wall (photograph provided by BLAGO Fund, USA/Serbia, www.srpskoblago.org) 135

6.1 Interior of the Church of Christ Pantokrator, Dečani Monastery, mid-14th century, east view (photograph by Platoneum Publishing) 144

6.2 Church of Christ Pantokrator, Dečani Monastery, 1327–35, southwest view (photograph by Platoneum Publishing) 145

6.3 Axonometric view of the Church of Christ Pantokrator Dečani Monastery (from Slobodan Ćurčić, *Architecture in the Balkans*, p. 661, fig. 773) 149

6.4 Sculpture from the portal between the narthex and the *naos*, approx. date 1327–35, Church of Christ Pantokrator, Dečani Monastery (photograph by Platoneum Publishing) 151

6.5 The Ascension of Christ, approx. date 1327–35, Church of Christ Pantokrator, Dečani Monastery, west portal (photograph by Platoneum Publishing) 155

6.6 Baptism of Christ, approx. date 1327–35, Church of Christ Pantokrator, Dečani Monastery, south portal (photograph by Platoneum Publishing) 157

6.7 The Tree of Life, approx. date 1327–35, Church of Christ Pantokrator, Dečani Monastery, north portal (photograph by Platoneum Publishing) 159

7.1 A typical example of the triconch Morava churches: Church of the Holy Protomartyr Stephen (Lazarica), Serbia, ca. 1375–78, sponsored by Prince Lazar Hrebeljanović of Serbia (r. 1373–89), exterior view and floor plan (photograph courtesy Ivan Krstić; drawing by Jelena Bogdanović) 170

ILLUSTRATIONS XIII

7.2   Floor plans of monastic Morava churches: Ravanica (1375–78), Ljubostinja (ca. 1389), and Resava (Manasija, 1407–18), Serbia (drawings by Jelena Bogdanović)   171
7.3   Development of triconch churches from cross-in-square Middle Byzantine type: a) in the region of Skopje by showcasing the churches at Šiševo, Matka and Andreaš (after Ćurčić and Bogdanović, drawings by Jelena Bogdanović), b) on Mt. Athos based on the Great Lavra Monastery (after Mylonas, drawing by Paulos Mylonas)   174
7.4   Serbian and Wallachian triconch churches in the territories of Byzantine Greece: a) Serbian Monastery Hilandar, Mt. Athos, Greece, established 1196–98, rebuilt ca. 1300–11; b) Wallachian Monastery Koutloumousiou, Mt. Athos, Greece, established 1350s–60s, rebuilt ca. 1540; c) Transfiguration of Christ, Great Meteoron Monastery, Kalabaka, Greece, 1356–72, established by St. Athanasios and king and later monk Ioannis-Ioasaph Uroš Palaiologos (r. 1370–73, d. 1387/8), remodeled in the 1540s (drawing by Jelena Bogdanović)   181
7.5   Comparative analysis of typical examples of triconch churches in Serbia and Wallachia, with exterior views and floor plans: a) Church of the Holy Protomartyr Stephen (Lazarica), Serbia, ca. 1375–78, sponsored by Prince Lazar Hrebeljanović of Serbia (r. 1373–89) (photograph courtesy Ivan Krstić, drawing by Jelena Bogdanović); b) Holy Trinity Church at Cozia Monastery, Wallachia, ca. 1387–91, built by Voivode Mircea I of Wallachia (r. 1386–95; 1397–1418) (photograph by Cristian Chiriță, drawing by Tianling (Rusty) Xu)   183
7.6   a) Monastic, "mausolea" triconch churches: Hilandar, Mt. Athos, ca. 1300–11, and Ravanica, Serbia, ca. 1375–78; b) urban, "court" triconch churches: Lazarica, Serbia ca. 1375–78, and Cozia, Wallachia, ca. 1387–89 (drawings by Jelena Bogdanović and Tianling (Rusty) Xu)   184
7.7   Church of St. Nicholas, Lapušnja Monastery, Serbia, 1500–10, sponsored and built by Voivode Radu cel Mare (r. 1495–1508), Princess Katalina Crnojević of Zeta, Joupan Gergina, Prince Bogoje and his family, Hieromonks Gelasios (ca. 1500), and Theodor (ca. 1510) (photograph by Jelena Bogdanović)   192
8.1   Church of the Annunciation, 1532–37, view from southeast, Moldovița Monastery, Moldavia, Romania (photograph by Alice Isabella Sullivan)   202
8.2   Church of the Annunciation, 1532–37, view from southwest, Moldovița Monastery, Moldavia, Romania (photograph by Alice Isabella Sullivan)   206
8.3   Church of the Annunciation, 1532–37, view from northwest, Moldovița Monastery, Moldavia, Romania (photograph by Alice Isabella Sullivan)   206

8.4 Moldovița Monastery, 1532–37, aerial view, Moldavia, Romania (image from Tereza Sinigalia and Oliviu Boldura, *Monumente Medievale din Bucovina* [Bucharest: ACS, 2010], 171)   208

8.5 Elevation and layout, Church of the Annunciation, 1532–37, Moldovița Monastery, Moldavia, Romania (image from *Bucovina: A Travel Guide to Romania's Region of Painted Monasteries* [Helsinki and Iași: Metaneira, 2006], 401)   209

8.6 Menologium, 1535–37, interior mural, *pronaos*, Church of the Annunciation, Moldovița Monastery, Moldavia, Romania (photograph by Alice Isabella Sullivan)   216

8.7 The Akathistos Hymn, the Siege of Constantinople, the Tree of Jesse, 1537, exterior mural, south wall, Church of the Annunciation, Moldovița Monastery, Moldavia, Romania (photograph by Alice Isabella Sullivan)   219

8.8 Pantokrator, 1535–37, interior mural, *naos*, Church of the Annunciation, Moldovița Monastery, Moldavia, Romania (photograph by Alice Isabella Sullivan)   223

9.1 *Epitaphios* of Stephen III, 1490, 8 ft. 3 in. × 5 ft. 5 in. (252 × 166 cm). Putna Monastery, Romania (photograph provided by Putna Monastery)   234

9.2 *Epitaphios* of Jefimija, ca. 1405, 67 × 43–3/4 in. (170 × 111 cm). Putna Monastery, Romania (photograph provided by Putna Monastery)   236

9.3 *Aër* or *Epitaphios* from Wallachia, 1535, 26–4/5 × 21–1/4 in. (68.1 × 54.1 cm). Burton Y. Berry Collection, Eskenazi Museum of Art, Indiana University Bloomington 72.2.6 (photograph by Kevin Montague)   238

9.4 *Epitaphios* from the Cozia Monastery, 1396, 69–3/4 × 56–3/4 in. (177 × 144 cm). National Museum of Art of Romania, Bucharest (photograph provided by National Museum of Art of Romania)   242

9.5 *Epitaphios Threnos*, 15th–16th century, 43–3/4 × 26–1/2 in. (111 × 67.5) cm. National Museum of Art of Romania, Bucharest (photograph provided by National Museum of Art of Romania)   244

9.6 *Epitaphios* of Șerban Cantacuzino, 1681, 74 × 51–1/4 in. (188 × 130 cm). National Museum of Art of Romania, Bucharest (photograph provided by National Museum of Art of Romania)   245

10.1 The Veglia Altar Frontal, ca. 1358, Victoria and Albert Museum, London, 2016 (photograph by Danijel Ciković, by permission of Victoria and Albert Museum)   249

10.2 The Veglia Altar Frontal at *The First Istrian Regional Exhibition*, 1910, Koper, Civici Musei di Storia ed Arte di Trieste, inv. F77194 (photograph provided by Civici Musei di Storia ed Arte di Trieste)   249

10.3　The Veglia Altar Frontal, detail of donor, Bishop Ivan II, ca. 1358, Victoria and Albert Museum, London, 2016 (photograph by Iva Jazbec Tomaić, by permission of Victoria and Albert Museum)　251

10.4　The Veglia Altar Frontal, detail of St. Quirinus and St. Peter, ca. 1358, Victoria and Albert Museum, London, 2016 (photograph by Iva Jazbec Tomaić, by permission of Victoria and Albert Museum)　253

10.5　The Veglia Altar Frontal, detail of the choir of angels, ca. 1358, Victoria and Albert Museum, London (photograph by Danijel Ciković, by permission of Victoria and Albert Museum)　254

10.6　The Zadar Altar Frontal, ca. 1340, Permanent Collection of Sacred Art (SICU), Zadar, 2009 (photograph by Natalija Vasić)　260

10.7　The Dobrinj Altar Frontal, ca. 1360–70, Collection of Sacred Art of the Parish Church of St. Stephen, Dobrinj (Island of Krk), 2003 (photograph by Damir Krizmanić)　262

Table

7.1　Comparative list of triconch churches sponsored by Serbian and Wallachian nobility (drawings by Jelena Bogdanović and Tianling [Rusty] Xu; photographs by Ivan Krstić [Lazarica], Dekanski [Ravanica], Andrei Stroe [Cozia], Jelena Bogdanović [Lapušnja], Razvan Sokol [Govora], Jelena Bogdanović [Great Meteoron], and Adriaticus [Koutloumousiou])　177

Notes on Contributors

Jelena Bogdanović
(PhD, Princeton University) specializes in architecture in the Balkans and the Mediterranean region. She is an associate professor of architecture at Iowa State University and author of *The Framing of Sacred Space: The Canopy and the Byzantine Church*.

Danijel Ciković
(PhD, University of Zadar) is a postdoctoral researcher at the Academy of Applied Arts, University of Rijeka. He has published articles on medieval and Renaissance liturgical furnishings in the Adriatic region.

Marija Mihajlovic-Shipley
(PhD candidate, Courtauld Institute of Art) works on artistic production and female patronage in medieval Serbia and the Adriatic region between the second half of the 13th century and the beginning of the 14th century.

Elias Petrou
(PhD, University of Ioannina) works as a Research Associate Specialist at the Thesaurus Linguae Graecae project at the University of California, Irvine. His areas of expertise include Greek scholarship and education in Byzantium in the 15th century.

Maria Alessia Rossi
(PhD, Courtauld Institute of Art) is an Art History Specialist at the Index of Medieval Art at Princeton University. She specializes in Byzantine artistic production and patronage in the 13th and 14th centuries, the role of the miraculous in text and image, and the artistic and iconographic exchanges between the Byzantine Empire, the Balkans, and the Latin West.

Henry David Schilb
(PhD, Indiana University Bloomington) is an Art History Specialist in Byzantine art at the Index of Medieval Art, Princeton University. His own research focuses on Palaiologan and post-Byzantine embroidered liturgical veils.

Ida Sinkević
(PhD, Princeton University) is the Arthur J. '55 and Barbara Rothkopf Professor of Art History at Lafayette College, in Easton, Pennsylvania. Her research is

focused on Byzantine art and on the impact of medieval visual culture on later periods. Her publications include a number of articles, a book on the Church of St. Panteleimon at Nerezi in the Republic of North Macedonia, and an edited volume, *Knights in Shining Armor: Myth and Reality, 1450–1650*.

Alice Isabella Sullivan
(PhD, University of Michigan) is an art historian specializing in the art, architecture, and visual culture of East-Central Europe and the Byzantine-Slavic cultural spheres during the medieval and early modern periods. Her current projects focus on the history, art, and culture of Moldavia and regions of the Carpathian Mountains between ca. 1300 and ca. 1700.

Iva Jazbec Tomaić
(PhD, University of Zagreb) is a teaching assistant at the Academy of Applied Arts, University of Rijeka. She has published articles on early modern textiles preserved on the eastern coast of the Adriatic.

Alexandra Vukovich
(PhD, University of Cambridge) is a British Academy Research Fellow in medieval history at St Edmund Hall, University of Oxford, where she works on the political culture of early Rus and Muscovy through chronicles and other artifacts.

Justin L. Willson
(PhD candidate, Princeton University) works on Byzantine and early Russian art and has published in *RES: Anthropology & Aesthetics, Studies in Iconography*, and *Journal of the History of Ideas*.

Introduction

Maria Alessia Rossi and Alice Isabella Sullivan

The recent global turn in medieval studies and art history has incited various conversations about the geographic and temporal parameters of the study of Western medieval and Byzantine art, architecture, and visual culture.[1] In efforts to expand the study of Byzantine art in particular, this collection of essays challenges understanding of the artistic production of late medieval Eastern Europe by tackling aspects of the little-studied and at times neglected regions situated at the northern fringes of the Byzantine Empire. Parts of the Balkan Peninsula, the Carpathian Mountains, and areas of early modern Russia were in contact with the empire during the Palaiologan period (1259–1453), and took on prominent roles in the continuation and refashioning of Byzantine artistic and cultural models after the fall of Constantinople in 1453 (Fig. 0.1).

At the heart of this volume is a more nuanced understanding of Byzantium in Eastern European visual culture during the late medieval period. Although the "influence" of Byzantium in Eastern Europe has been addressed in scholarship, and in particular by two influential thinkers, Nicolae Iorga and Dimitri Obolensky, their respective cultural histories did not tackle the art, architecture, and visual culture of the Balkans and the Carpathians in a thorough and nuanced manner.[2] At the core of their publications stood the idea that the fall of Constantinople did not put an end to Byzantium. Rather, from that point onward, Byzantium's legacy, both directly and indirectly, played a key role in

---

1 This volume builds upon a new worldwide interest in the global Middle Ages. The new global medieval art history initiative of the International Center of Medieval Art (ICMA) stands out, allowing for new platforms to discuss and research the significance and importance at this moment in time of areas outside the traditional geographic and temporal parameters of the study of medieval art. Similarly, the Index of Medieval Art at Princeton University organized a conference in November 2018 titled "Out of Bounds: Exploring the Limits of Medieval Art." Annual events have chosen to focus on the global turn in Byzantine and Medieval Studies, among them the 50th Spring Symposium of Byzantine Studies in the UK (2017) and the 2019 Medieval Academy of America Annual Conference. See also Alicia Walker, "Globalism," in "Medieval Art History Today—Critical Terms," special issue, *Studies in Iconography* 33 (2012): 183–96.

2 Nicolae Iorga, *Byzance après Byzance: Continuation de la vie Byzantine* (Bucharest: A l'Institut d'études byzantines, 1935), trans. Laura Treptow as *Byzantium after Byzantium* (Iași: Center for Romanian Studies, 2000); and Dimitri Obolensky, *The Byzantine Commonwealth: Eastern Europe, 500–1453* (New York and London: Praeger, 1971).

FIGURE 0.1 Map of the Byzantine, Ottoman, and Serbian empires and their neighboring states, 1355
IMAGE FROM WILLIAM R. SHEPHERD, *HISTORICAL ATLAS* [NEW YORK: HENRY HOLT AND COMPANY, 1911], 89, PROVIDED BY WIKIMEDIA COMMONS

shaping the cultural, religious, and political life of regions in Eastern Europe. Iorga underscored the important relations between the Romanian principalities of Wallachia and Moldavia and parts of the former Empire, like Mount Athos, and focused his attention on the role of Byzantine ideology in the north-Danubian principalities during the post-Byzantine period (16th–18th centuries). His ideas inspired at least two generations of Romanian historians looking at, for example, the architecture and decoration of 16th-century churches in the principality of Moldavia. On the other hand, Obolensky's "Byzantine Commonwealth"—spreading geographically from Constantinople to the Balkans, the Carpathians, and medieval Russia—was the space of the international community of Eastern Orthodox Christians under the superior influence, whether direct or indirect, of the Byzantine emperor, and stood in direct opposition to Western Europe. This model emphasizes the political and ideological superiority of Byzantium, while relegating to a lesser status those regions under the "influence" of the "center."

In recent years, scholars have problematized the center-periphery dynamics outlined by Iorga and Obolensky, and in particular the concept of the "Byzantine Commonwealth" across Eastern Europe.[3] On the one hand, Anthony Kaldellis has been highly critical of the concept from an "inner" perspective, arguing for the central role that Hellenism (classical tradition) played in the development of Byzantine culture up to the 14th century.[4] On the other hand, for the regions north of the Carpathian Mountains, especially medieval Kievan Rus', Christian Raffensperger has put forward a similarly constructed criticism about the concept of the "Byzantine Commonwealth." He has argued for the development of medieval Rus' at the crossroads of Byzantium and the West between the 10th and the 12th centuries.[5] Instead of a "Byzantine Commonwealth," Raffensperger proposes the concept of the "Byzantine ideal" in the context of which Byzantine models were appropriated in order to draw connections and forms of legitimacy with the Roman past.[6]

However, in the important contributions of these scholars, visual culture plays a small role, if any at all. Art historians ought to have a voice in these debates, as the art, architecture, and visual culture of Eastern Europe has much to offer. The textual sources considered in dialogue with the material evidence in the form of secular and religious buildings, painted images, manuscripts, metalwork, and embroideries, as well as liturgical and paraliturgical performances, reveal more dynamic facets of cultural contact and relations with Byzantium among the regions of the Balkans, the Carpathians, and early modern Russia that developed under the spiritual power of Orthodoxy. Indeed, in-depth examinations of the visual and material evidence, as revealed by the essays in this volume, problematize the concepts and arguments outlined by Iorga and Obolensky, which had held sway in scholarship for far too long, and enhance the scholarly contributions already made by Kaldellis, Raffensperger, and others.

---

3   See Antony Eastmond, "Art and Periphery," in *The Oxford Handbook of Byzantine Studies*, ed. Elizabeth Jeffreys with John F. Haldon and Robin Cormack (Oxford, UK, and New York: Oxford University Press, 2008), pp. 770–76; and Eastmond, "The Limits of Byzantine Art", in *A Companion to Byzantium*, ed. Liz James (Oxford, UK: Wiley, 2010), pp. 313–22.

4   Anthony Kaldellis, *Hellenism in Byzantium: The Transformations of Greek Identity and the Reception of the Classical Tradition* (Cambridge, UK: Cambridge University Press, 2007), pp. 109–10.

5   Christian Raffensperger, *The Kingdom of Rus'* (Kalamazoo: Medieval Institute Publications, 2017); Raffensperger, "Reimagining Europe: Discussing Rus' in a Wider Context," *Russian History* 42, no. 2 (2015): 204–16; and Raffensperger, "The Place of Rus' in Medieval Europe," *History Compass* 12, no. 11 (2014): 853–65.

6   Christian Raffensperger, *Reimagining Europe: Kievan Rus' in the Medieval World* (Cambridge, MA: Harvard University Press, 2012).

The essays in this volume engage with issues of cultural contact and patronage, as well as the transformation and appropriation of Byzantine artistic, cultural, theological, and political forms alongside local traditions as evident in architecture, monumental painting cycles, icons, sculpture, textiles, written texts, and ceremonies. Specifically, in discussing the regions of Croatia, Republic of North Macedonia, Serbia, Bulgaria, Romania, and Russia between the 14th and 16th centuries in their own right and in relation to developments especially in the Byzantine cultural sphere, this volume challenges earlier assumptions about their artistic production.

The interconnected lands that constitute modern-day Eastern Europe have developed within and beyond the borders of Byzantium. For much of the medieval period, the Balkans, the Carpathians, and further north in Russia experienced shifting political borders, at times some under Byzantine rule. Although the north-Danubian principalities and early modern Russia were never part of the empire, they were certainly under its influence. Eastern Orthodoxy has had a profound impact on the development of artistic, religious, political, economic, and ideological facets in these territories that have for far too long remained marginal in scholarship.

Often referred to as the "Slavic world," Eastern Europe has long been relegated to the margins of scholarly inquiry and regarded to have little to offer.[7] Inconsistencies in the definition of what constitutes Eastern Europe, as well as 20th-century politics, have contributed to the marginalization.[8] These regions that once formed kingdoms and empires are now part of many different countries.[9] History and politics have traced these lands, and communication and cooperation have been impossible at times, let alone comparative art historical analyses. For one thing, the Iron Curtain created actual and ideological barriers to the study of much of Eastern Europe, rendering relevant literature

---

7 On the marginalization of Eastern Europe in scholarship and classifications, see Robert Nelson, "The Map of Art History," *The Art Bulletin* 79, no. 1 (1997): 28–40, esp. 29–33.

8 See Maria Alessia Rossi and Alice Isabella Sullivan, "Late Medieval Visual Culture in Eastern Europe," in *Encyclopedia of the Global Middle Ages*, Thematic Overview, online resource, Bloomsbury Medieval Studies (London: Bloomsbury Academic, 2020); and Gábor Klaniczay, "Von Ostmitteleuropa zu Westmitteleuropa: Eine Umwandlung im Hochmittelalter," in *Böhmen und seine Nachbarn in der Přemyslidenzeit*, ed. Ivan Hlaváček and Alexander Patschovsky (Ostfildern: Jan Thorbecke Verlag, 2011), pp. 17–48.

9 These include Croatia, Bosnia and Herzegovina, Slovenia, Czech Republic, Slovakia, Serbia, Montenegro, Kosovo, Republic of North Macedonia, Romania, Bulgaria, Albania, Greece, Hungary, Poland, Lithuania, Ukraine, Moldova, Russia, and still others. See Florin Curta, ed., *Borders, Barriers, and Ethnogenesis: Frontiers in Late Antiquity and the Middle Ages* (Turnhout: Brepols, 2005).

INTRODUCTION 5

FIGURE 0.2 Map of Europe with the Iron Curtain Trail
IMAGE COURTESY OF THE IRON CURTAIN TRAIL

inaccessible and the study of actual objects and monuments impossible (Fig. 0.2). Much has changed since then, and much more remains to be done.

The specificities of each region, and in modern times, politics and nationalistic approaches, have reinforced the tendency to treat them separately, preventing scholars from questioning whether the visual output could be considered as an expression of a shared history. The artistic production of Eastern Europe could also help us reveal larger connections between the Byzantine cultural sphere and regions beyond the empire's margins, while challenging earlier assumptions about these lands, and the notion of "decline" generally associated with late Byzantine and post-Byzantine art, architecture, and visual culture.[10] Moreover, instead of being places of "influence" from elsewhere, these territories reveal dynamic networks of contact and interchange that may allow scholars to paint richer pictures of the development of local artistic and cultural forms, the shared traditions of these Eastern European lands, and their indebtedness to Byzantine models.[11] The art, architecture, and visual culture of these regions invite current and future generations of scholars to unravel their prismatic dimensions and chart the multitude of connections with Byzantium and still other traditions.

Each of the ten essays in this volume focuses on how the heritage of Byzantium was continued, transformed, and deployed alongside local developments and other models, in order to shape notions of identity in the artistic and cultural traditions of Eastern European centers. The authors are all specialists whose research examines the innovative visual and cultural production of the Balkan Peninsula, the Carpathian Mountains, and early modern Russia. Their contributions examine key objects, monuments, texts, and rituals in efforts to make them better known among the scholarly community, but also in order to introduce new questions and approaches that could serve as models for future studies within different disciplines, ranging from archeology and material culture to art and architectural history.

In Chapter 1, JUSTIN L. WILLSON examines Byzantine-Slavic relations by analyzing an early-14th-century fresco of Solomon's Allegory of Wisdom from Bulgaria in light of Philotheos Kokkinos's discourse on Wisdom. The essay argues in favor of the framework of the "commons" instead of "influence" with regard to cross-cultural contact between Byzantium and regions of the Balkans. ALEXANDRA VUKOVICH, in Chapter 2, tackles the same complex issue by examining the image of Muscovy as the north of Byzantium in the 15th century. Through the exploration of the rite of investiture, she discusses the multilayered relationship among Byzantine models, the local landscape of

---

10   See Andrea Mattiello and Maria Alessia Rossi, eds., *Late Byzantium Reconsidered: The Arts of the Palaiologan Era in the Mediterranean* (Abingdon, UK: Routledge, 2019).
11   On the topic of "influence" and its ramifications, see Kirk Ambrose, "Influence," in "Medieval Art History Today—Critical Terms," special issue, *Studies in Iconography* 33 (2012): 197–206.

power, and other cultural contacts, in this case with the Mongols. Particular emphasis is given to the performative part of the ceremony of investiture that allows for invented traditions, ancient objects, well-known rituals, and new idioms to come together in order to give shape to a new Muscovite image of power. For Vukovich, textual sources are the primary catalysts for the transfer and subsequent transformations of knowledge. This is a facet central to the study of ELIAS PETROU as well. Chapter 3 outlines the cultural and intellectual relationships that extended between the Serbian and Byzantine elites from the 13th to the 15th centuries. Two case studies illuminate Serbian patronage in Constantinople and the movement of people and objects from the Byzantine capital to regions of the Balkans.

The next chapters move deeper into the Serbian milieu to demonstrate the cultural connections and new visual forms, iconographies, and styles indebted to Byzantine and Western models that emerged in a local context. In Chapter 4, MARIJA MIHAJLOVIC-SHIPLEY addresses the sociopolitical issues, cultural interactions, and biconfessional circumstances in the Adriatic region during the 13th century by means of the icon of Sts. Peter and Paul in the Vatican Treasury. Mihajlovic-Shipley explores the possible reasons for a diplomatic gift from a Serbian queen to a Latin pope, placing the Serbian Kingdom at the crossroads between Eastern and Western Christendom during the second half of the 13th century. Chapter 5 focuses on the newly developed family ties between the Byzantine Empire and the Serbian Kingdom at the beginning of the 14th century by focusing on Christ's miracle cycle in monumental decorations in the Serbian lands in contrast to Byzantine models. MARIA ALESSIA ROSSI discusses similarities and differences in image cycles of Christ's miracles, showing how this iconography was transmitted, exchanged, and altered in a Serbian context in order to prove a shared Byzantine heritage as well as a need for innovation as a means to express a newly developing identity for the Serbian state.

The dynamics of patronage and identity in 14th-century Serbia are also central to Chapter 6. IDA SINKEVIĆ reveals the multiple factors—geopolitical, social, artistic, and religious—that contributed to the unique combination of Byzantine, Romanesque, and Gothic forms in the building of the main church, or *katholikon*, of Dečani Monastery in particular, and in Serbian medieval ecclesiastical architecture in general. Chapter 7 continues to explore the architectural history of the region and sheds new light on the connections between Serbia and Wallachia in the late Palaiologan and post-Byzantine periods. JELENA BOGDANOVIĆ examines the long lives of Middle Byzantine triconch churches to the south and north of the Danube River, arguing for vibrant processes of architectural development in Serbia and Wallachia that ought not to be discussed separately and in isolation due to national divides, but rather in dialogue, in order to reveal facets of the interconnectedness of these territories and their shared Byzantine models.

Moving further north and deeper into the multifaceted artistic production of the Carpathian Mountain regions, ALICE ISABELLA SULLIVAN, in Chapter 8, examines the distinctive architecture and iconographic programs of the Moldavian monastic churches built in the century after the fall of Constantinople in 1453. These monuments express complex social and religious politics, as well as elucidate processes of image translations, the transfer of artistic ideas, and the particular dynamics of cultural contact in the principality of Moldavia, which developed at the crossroads of different traditions, and which took on a central role particularly in the continuation and refashioning of Byzantine forms after 1453. In Chapter 9, HENRY SCHILB looks at the respective and distinct embroidery traditions of Wallachia and Moldavia, which developed along different avenues of cultural contact with the Slavic and Byzantine cultural spheres, and may reflect and illuminate aspects of the social, political, and even economic differences between these two north-Danubian Romanian principalities.

The final essay examines east-west relations across the Adriatic Sea. Chapter 10 presents another case study of the artistic contacts and patronage that extended across the Adriatic Sea during the 14th century. DANIJEL CIKOVIĆ and IVA JAZBEC TOMAIĆ focus on an embroidered altar frontal made for the Krk Cathedral in Croatia by Paolo Veneziano, exploring its production against the tense political situation that unfolded between the Hungarian-Croatian King Louis I of Anjou and the Venetian Republic.

The individual chapters and the volume as a whole, foster cross-disciplinary dialogues and offer examples of how scholars and future researchers may begin to expand the temporal and geographic parameters of the study of medieval and Byzantine art, architecture, and visual culture to the little-studied yet visually and culturally rich spheres of Eastern Europe. The essays offer a selection of case studies questioning any rigid understanding of the complex and stratified cultural production of these regions during the late Middle Ages.

The territories of Eastern Europe have been treated in scholarship within limited frameworks, or discussed within narrow geographic and chronological parameters, or excluded altogether from conversations. For example, certain studies continue to frame the artistic production of particular Eastern European centers with strong nationalistic undertones, dismissing the rich

INTRODUCTION

effects of cross-cultural contact on the development of local art, architecture, and visual culture. By allowing for an interdisciplinary discussion, Eastern European history, archaeology, art, and architecture can begin to be visualized in their entirety through a variety of case studies in dialogue with one another, as demonstrated by the fifty-seven volumes published so far by Brill in the series *East Central and Eastern Europe in the Middle Ages, 450–1450*.[12]

For the Balkans as a whole, Slobodan Ćurčić was the first to emphasize and research the common roots and parallel strands of cultural production, focusing on architecture. In his massive volume *Architecture in the Balkans from Diocletian to Süleyman the Magnificent*, Ćurčić analyzed both secular and religious structures, and traced the architectural developments of particular regions in the Balkans over many generations, up to the middle of the 16th century.[13] But while his noteworthy contribution treated the architectural history of the Balkan Peninsula as a whole, the architecture of the north Danubian principalities—much indebted to the artistic innovations of the Balkans and Byzantium—received little attention. The Danube River served as the main northern geographic divide for Ćurčić's study, but the famed river was in fact a much more fluid and porous border during the medieval period.[14] We now know that artists and masons trained in Serbian, Bulgarian, Greek, and Athonite workshops worked at the Wallachian and Moldavian courts during the 15th century, for example. Considerations of the transfer of visual forms and ideas between the territories north and south of the Danube River would enrich our picture of the cultural contacts that extended in Eastern Europe during the later Middle Ages, and the central role played by Byzantium and Mount Athos in shaping local artistic styles.[15] Bogdanović's essay in this volume offers an exploration of the architectural production of Eastern Europe, by putting in conversation materials and visual traditions to the north and south of the Danube

---

12   Florin Curta and Dušan Zupka, eds., *East Central and Eastern Europe in the Middle Ages, 450–1450* (Leiden: Brill, 2007–20).
13   Slobodan Ćurčić, *Architecture in the Balkans from Diocletian to Süleyman the Magnificent* (New Haven: Yale University Press, 2010).
14   The Danube River served as the main line of defense for the territories to the north and south, whose tributary status relative to the Ottoman Empire, especially for Wallachia and Moldavia, was in flux during the 15th and 16th centuries. See Liviu Pilat and Ovidiu Cristea, *The Ottoman Threat and Crusading on the Eastern Border of Christendom during the 15th Century* (Leiden: Brill, 2017); and Viorel Panaite, *The Ottoman Law of War and Peace: The Ottoman Empire and Its Tribute-Payers from the North of the Danube*, 2nd rev. ed. (Leiden: Brill, 2019).
15   See Graham Speake, *A History of the Athonite Commonwealth: The Spiritual and Cultural Diaspora of Mount Athos* (Cambridge, UK: Cambridge University Press, 2018).

River that have been treated separately. Most recently, Robert Ousterhout's volume *Eastern Medieval Architecture: The Building Traditions of Byzantium and Neighboring Lands* offers a different model, treating regional differences within larger traditions.[16] With a broad geographic and chronological focus, Ousterhout's book traces the developments in medieval architecture across the eastern Mediterranean from early Christian times and through the century after the fall of Constantinople in 1453, including also discussions of regional styles indebted to Byzantium in Croatia, Republic of North Macedonia, Serbia, Bulgaria, the Romanian principalities north of the Danube River, and Russia.

For regions of the Carpathian Mountains, and in particular the principalities of Wallachia, Moldavia, and Transylvania, a great deal of art historical work remains to be done. Although scholarship in Romanian has addressed the Byzantine heritage in the Carpathians, the studies tend to offer overarching pictures of the development of Romanian art relative to Byzantium and not in-depth examinations that could reveal the regional distinctions and specificities.[17] By and large, Romanian historians and archaeologists have studied the art and architecture of the medieval principalities that form the modern-day country of Romania largely from specific, somewhat limiting viewpoints. In scholarship in the languages of Western Europe, in particular English, art historians have begun to incorporate aspects of the late medieval artistic production of the Carpathian territories into their individual considerations of large issues centered on Byzantine visual culture.[18] A recent exhibition at the Louvre Museum looked at Romanian Byzantine embroideries from the 15th to the 17th centuries: *Broderies de tradition byzantine en Roumanie* (April 18–July 29, 2019). Current work is also beginning to examine the medieval artistic production of the Carpathian regions through cultural connections, historically grounded methodologies, and more nuanced interpretative strategies, offering comprehensive models for future studies.[19] Schilb's essay brings to the forefront Wallachian embroidery, until now overshadowed by

---

16   Robert Ousterhout, *Eastern Medieval Architecture: The Building Traditions of Byzantium and Neighboring Lands* (Oxford, UK: Oxford University Press, 2019).

17   One example is Adela Văetiși, *Arta de tradiție bizantină în România* (Bucharest: NOI Media Print, 2008).

18   See, for example, Warren Woodfin, *The Embodied Icon: Liturgical Vestments and Sacramental Power in Byzantium* (Oxford, UK: Oxford University Press, 2012).

19   See Alice Isabella Sullivan, "The Painted Fortified Monastic Churches of Moldavia: Bastions of Orthodoxy in a Post-Byzantine World" (PhD diss., University of Michigan, 2017); and Sullivan, "Visions of Byzantium: *The Siege of Constantinople* in Sixteenth-Century Moldavia," *The Art Bulletin* 99, no. 4 (December 2017): 31–68.

the Moldavian production. The chapter discusses the differences between the traditions of these two principalities that shared adjacent liminal conditions with the post-Byzantine sphere. Moving deeper into the east Carpathian territory, Sullivan's essay examines how Moldavian art and architecture developed with respect to Byzantium and Western Gothic models adapted alongside local forms, underscoring the eclectic visual character of the artistic production of the post-1453 world.

Indeed, the regions under scrutiny in this volume developed at the crossroads of the Latin, Greek, and Slavic traditions in the later medieval period, that is, between the 14th and the 16th centuries.[20] Cultural contact and interchange resulted in local assimilations of selected elements from distinct traditions but especially from Byzantium, reshaping the cultural and artistic landscapes of the Balkans and the Carpathians. The essay by Ciković and Tomaić demonstrates this development with respect to liturgical embroideries produced in the Croatian cultural context. Moving further north, Vukovich looks at the transfer of Byzantine rituals and regalia at the Muscovite court, suggesting the transformation and invention of Byzantine artifacts and models alongside other examples for local aims and contexts. Building on these dynamics of cultural exchange, the contributions by Mihajlovic-Shipley and Sinkević discuss the negotiations between Serbia and the West and the ways in which the former, through its visual and architectural output, sought to represent itself in the Mediterranean.

To date, several important scholarly studies in English have brought to the fore the art historical and architectural specificities of medieval Serbia. The artistic production of Serbia has been treated, most recently, in a three-volume publication.[21] The second volume, edited by Dragan Vojvodić and Danica Popović, explores the Byzantine heritage in Serbian art of the Middle Ages.[22] The work of Ivana Jevtić, Ivan Drpić, Ida Sinkević, Ivan Stevović, and Jelena Erdeljan has also offered nuanced insights into the history, culture, and artistic production of this region in connection to the late Palaiologan monumental tradition, to the Orthodox architectural heritage, and to the significance

---

20 See Maria Alessia Rossi and Alice Isabella Sullivan, eds., Eclecticism at the Edges: Late Medieval Visual Culture at the Crossroads of the Latin, Greek, and Slavic Cultural Spheres (Berlin: De Gruyter), forthcoming.
21 The series is titled *Byzantine Heritage and Serbian Art*, and the three volumes develop chronologically.
22 Dragan Vojvodić and Danica Popović, eds., *Sacral Art of the Serbian Lands in the Middle Ages* (Belgrade: Serbian National Committee of Byzantine Studies: P.E. Službeni Glasnik: Institute for Byzantine Studies, Serbian Academy of Sciences and Arts, 2016).

of the choice of media in structuring sacred space.[23] In addition to Sinkević and Mihajlovic-Shipley, Rossi builds upon this scholarship, examining issues of diplomacy, ruling ideology, and the meaning of distinctive local features in 14th-century Serbian artistic production. Rossi suggests an original reading of miracle cycles that speaks to a fluid, multicultural, and multifaceted relationship between Byzantium and Serbia, where the latter wants to partake in the Byzantine cultural sphere as well as showcase its independence.

The contributions in this volume also tackle different ways to approach the concept of influence and transmission, which has often been tainted by the center-periphery dichotomy. Once one acknowledges that there is nothing inferior about the artistic output of less "central" regions, the next step is to question how indebted to Byzantine models, in this case, were the creativity and autonomy in developing visual vocabularies of these cultural centers, such as those of Eastern Europe. The essays of Willson and Petrou build upon this thinking and look at alternative ways to examine the issue: the former by discussing the contemporary presence in Byzantium and the Slavic world of shared works of art that are not necessarily traceable to one or the other tradition;[24] the latter, by pinpointing actual cases of intellectual exchange in Constantinople and the Balkans that stand at the crossroads. Indeed, the medieval world was not static; people, goods, objects, and knowledge traveled across empires, contributing to the rich visual cultures so characteristic, in this case, of the regions of Eastern Europe.

---

23 Ivana Jevtić, "Art in Decline or Art in the Age of Decline? Historiography and New Approaches to Late Byzantine Painting" in *Late Byzantium Reconsidered: The Arts of the Palaiologan Era in the Mediterranean*, ed. Andrea Mattiello and Maria Alessia Rossi (Abingdon, UK, and New York: Routledge, 2019), pp. 31–52; Ida Sinkević's contribution in the present volume as well as her pioneering work *The Church of St. Panteleimon at Nerezi: Architecture, Programme, Patronage* (Wiesbaden: Reichert, 2000); Ivan Stevović, *The Monastery of Kalenić* (Belgrade: Institute for the Protection of Cultural Monuments of the Republic of Serbia, 2007); and Jelena Erdeljan, *Chosen Places: Constructing New Jerusalems in "Slavia Orthodoxa"* (Leiden and Boston: Brill, 2017). Ivan Drpić is currently working on a project on the economy, technology, and aesthetics of gilded murals in medieval Serbia.

24 Medieval Bulgaria is the topic of two recent collections of essays that highlight the art, history, literature, and culture of the region in dialogue with the Byzantine cultural spheres. The first volume, *State and Church: Studies in Medieval Bulgaria and Byzantium*, ed. Vasil Gjuzelev and Kiril Petkov (Sofia: American Research Center, 2011), centers on the medieval history and historiography of Bulgaria. The articles of the second volume, *Medieval Bulgarian Art and Letters in a Byzantine Context*, ed. Elka Bakalova, Margaret Dimitrova, and M.A. Johnson (Sofia: American Research Center, 2017), examine the cultural contacts between Bulgaria and the Byzantine Empire during the medieval period with a focus on art, philosophy, theology, and philology.

INTRODUCTION 13

What emerges from these contributions—read in sequence, or each on its own, or paired in various configurations—are issues of cultural contact, local translations, patronage, diplomacy, and ruling ideology, as well as modern politics and their effects on scholarship. But above all, the indebtedness of local specificity to artistic models adopted from elsewhere, and especially from Byzantium, takes center stage. The spiritual power of Byzantium left its mark across the Balkan Peninsula, the Carpathian Mountains, and areas of early modern Russia for many centuries, during and after the empire's collapse. But in efforts to expand and nuance the artistic landscapes of Eastern Europe during the late medieval period, the culture and artistic production of individual centers must be considered individually *and* as part of a larger network, thus revealing the shared heritage of these lands that formed a cultural sphere extending beyond medieval, Byzantine, and modern borders. This volume considers aspects of how the heritage of Byzantium was deployed to shape notions of identity and visual rhetoric in Eastern European visual culture and in regions that developed at the crossroads of different traditions. It is our hope that this volume will encourage current and future students and researchers to explore the nuances of cultural contact and interchange and to further the research of the rich and varied art, architecture, and visual culture of Eastern Europe during the medieval period.[25]

---

25   This volume is the first of a series of publications meant to bring attention to the rich artistic and cultural traditions of Eastern Europe. These efforts are part of *North of Byzantium* (www.northofbyzantium.org), an initiative primarily funded by the Mary Jaharis Center for Byzantine Art and Culture.

CHAPTER 1

The Allegory of Wisdom in Chrelja's Tower Seen through Philotheos Kokkinos

Justin L. Willson

1   Chrelja's Tower: The Setting of the Frescoes

In 1335 the Serbian general Stefan Chrelja Dragovol (d. 1342) erected a military tower on the grounds of the Monastery of St. John of Rila in southwestern Bulgaria (Fig. 1.1).[1] Similar in design to structures built on Mount Athos in the Palaiologan period, the tower overlooked a string of valleys cascading down from the peaks of the Rila mountains. Dedicated to the Mother of God Osianovitsa and St. John of Rila, the tower consisted of six stories, standing almost twenty-four meters (seventy-eight feet) high, and measuring roughly eight meters (twenty-six feet) square.[2] On the upper elevation an ambulatory enclosed a narthex which led into a chapel at the tower's eastern end (Figs. 1.2 and 1.3). While the builders equipped the lower floors with outlooks and fortified recesses, to serve military enterprise, they designed the upper story to open into a communal space of worship, echoing the layout of a cross-in-square Byzantine church.[3]

Likely under the patronage of Chrelja, the narthex and chapel were decorated with frescoes. Damaged by fire in the late 18th century, they underwent repainting and subsequently were uncovered and restored in the 1960s by a team under Liuben Prashkov's direction.[4] In the narthex, frescoes of

---

1 On Chrelja, see M.C. Bartusis, "Chrelja and Momčilo: Occasional Servants of Byzantium in Fourteenth Century Macedonia," *Byzantinoslavica* 41 (1980): 201–21. On the tower, see Asen Kirin, "Contemplating the Vistas of Piety at the Rila Monastery Pyrgos," *Dumbarton Oaks Papers* 59 (2005): 95–138.
2 On the southern wall of the tower a brick and mortar inscription states: "During the rule of the most exalted master King Stefan Dušan, master Protosebast Chrelja, with great effort and expense, built this tower dedicated to the Holy Father John of Rila and to the Mother of God called Osianovitsa in the year 6843 indiction 5 [i.e., 1335]." Translation in Kirin, "Vistas of Piety," p. 102 n. 14. The monks later rededicated the chapel to the Transfiguration.
3 Kirin, "Vistas of Piety," pp. 99, 122.
4 The fundamental study of the frescoes remains Liuben Prashkov, *Khrel'ovata kula: Istoriia, arkhitektura, zhivopis* (Sofia: Bŭlgarski khudozhnik, 1973); summarized in "Khreleva bashnia Rilskogo monastyria i ee stenopis'," in *Drevnerusskoe iskusstvo: Zarubezhnye sviazi*, ed.

FIGURE 1.1 Chrelja's Tower, Rila Monastery, 1335
PHOTOGRAPH BY MARK AHSMANN, PROVIDED BY WIKIMEDIA COMMONS, PUBLISHED UNDER THE CREATIVE COMMONS LICENSE CC-BY-3.0

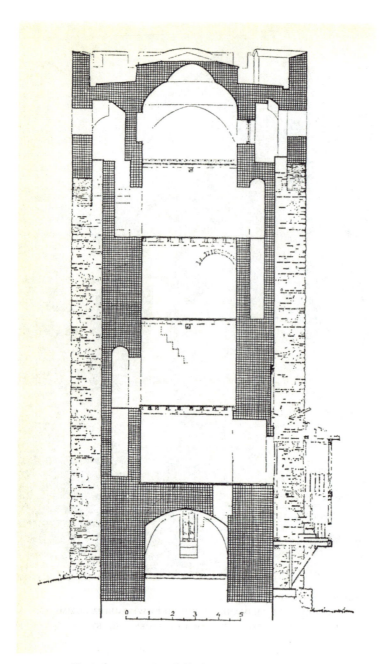

FIGURE 1.2 Vertical cross section of Chrelja's tower
DRAWING BY GEORGI STOIKOV. REPRODUCED AFTER
PRASHKOV, *KHREL'OVATA KULA*, FIG. 7

singers and musicians (after Psalms 148, 149, and 150), a melismos, and a Christ Pantokrator in the dome survive in fragments.[5] Unfortunately, the relation between this suite of images and that in the chapel is difficult to ascertain, given the fragmentary state of the narthex decoration. Nevertheless, Asen Kirin has proposed reading the psalm imagery in conjunction with the design of the ambulatory where windows overlooking the valley provided the monks with an opportunity to contemplate nature. For Kirin, these images guided the viewer out of nature into the chapel filled with images of saints and a single window facing east.[6]

Entering the small space of the chapel one is enveloped by a sophisticated program. Over the altar in the east stands a now-damaged Mother of God Platytera. Three fragmentary scenes from the life of St. John of Rila (876/80–946), the founder of the monastery, hang on the western wall in the adjacent conchs.[7] Due to their poor condition, very little can be said about the relation of either of these sets of images to the fresco in the dome overhead (Figs. 1.4–1.6). Measuring 1.8 meters (six feet) in diameter and standing almost four meters (thirteen feet) high, the scalloped, six-part surface portrays Solomon's Allegory of Wisdom. While abraded, the image provides a clear indication of the talent and inventiveness of the Rila painter.[8]

The use of the chapel during the 14th century remains uncertain. No documents exist to shed light on how the monks interacted with the space, nor

---

G.V. Popov (Moscow: Nauka, 1975), pp. 147–71. Several important remarks on Prashkov can be found in Patrick Lecaque, "The Monastery of Rila during the XIV Century and the Wall-Paintings of the Tower of Hreljo," *Macedonian Studies* 5, no. 3–4 (1988): 3–49, esp. 8–19. Color reproductions of the frescoes are printed in Mikhail Enev, *Rila Monastery* (Sofia: Balkan Pub. Co., with the assistance of the European Centre for Education and Training, 1997), pp. 115–25.

5 See D. Piguet-Panayotova, "La chapelle dans la tour de Khrelju au monastère de Rila," *Byzantion* 49 (1979): 363–84; and Lecaque, "The Monastery of Rila," pp. 24–37.
6 Kirin, "Vistas of Piety," pp. 130–31.
7 See Elka Bakalova, "Zur Interpretation des frühesten Zyklus der Vita des hl. Ivan von Rila in der bildenden Kunst," in *Festschrift für Klaus Wessel zum 70. Geburtstag: In memoriam*, ed. Marcell Restle (Munich: Editio Maris, 1988), pp. 39–48; Lecaque, "The Monastery of Rila," pp. 19–24; and Patrick Lecaque, "Représentations de Saint Jean de Rila dans les peintures de la tour de Hrel'o au monastère de Rila (XIVe siècle)," *Revue des études slaves* 60, no. 2 (1988): 513–17.
8 In speaking of the painter's "inventiveness," I am aware that originality bore a different valence in Byzantium. On artists in the medieval East, see *L'artista a Bisanzio e nel mondo cristiano-orientale*, ed. Michele Bacci (Pisa: Edizioni della Normale, 2007). For a discussion of originality in Byzantium, see Justin Willson, "A Meadow that Lifts the Soul: Originality as Anthologizing in the Byzantine Church Interior," *Journal of the History of Ideas* 81, no. 1 (2020): 1–21.

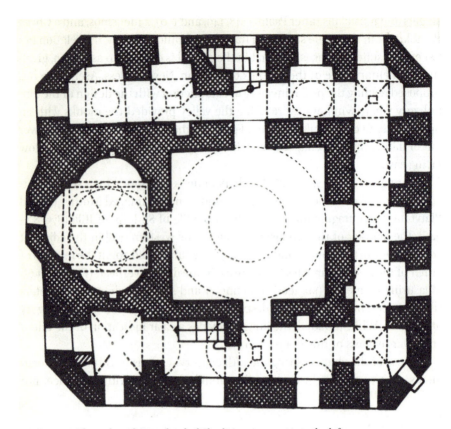

FIGURE 1.3   Floor plan of upper level of Chrelja's tower, east is to the left
DRAWING BY STEFAN BOIADZHIEV, REPR. AFTER PRASHKOV, *KHREL'OVATA KULA*, FIG. 8

are there any surviving monuments contemporary with the tower to situate the chapel within the monastery's early built environment. That said, given that the top floor replicates church architecture, one can probably assume a liturgical setting. Chrelja likely recruited painters from Serbia rather than Constantinople, because throughout the 1330s he was serving as a general under the Serbian king Stephen Dušan.[9] However, nothing in his life suggests a special interest in the theme of Wisdom. In this light, considering that the fresco in the dome skillfully overlays an unprecedented iconography onto a scalloped surface, as discussed below, one can imagine that the painter,

---

9   Chrelja defected around 1340, allying himself with the future Byzantine emperor John Kantakouzenos (r. 1347–54).

builders, and monks must have worked together on the form and layout of the chapel program.

In the present discussion I shall propose that we can read the elaborate iconography of Solomon's allegory in conversation with Greek writers who dealt with the same Biblical text. Pairing a visual witness from the Slavic context with a Greek thinker working in Constantinople—Patriarch Philotheos Kokkinos (r. 1353–54; 1364–76)—allows us to fully appreciate the common investment that both had in a shared Biblical teaching. Crucially, this teaching involved a theory of spiritual community. Conveyed through the mediums of paint and architecture, this allegory tells us about the Byzantine relationship to built space. Imbuing the tower with a didactic function, the Rila monks sought to inspire a form of life through a prophetic vision of community: a vision that became concrete in this house of worship.

2   The Iconography of the Chapel Frescoes

Importantly, the Rila dome marks a new iconography of the Wisdom allegory. Lev Lifshits has classified the iconography of Wisdom into incremental stages of development. In the 10th-century miniatures in the Paris Psalter and in later frescoes at St. Sophia in Ohrid (1295) as well as in the *katholika* at Gračanica Monastery (1321) and Dečani Monastery (1348), Wisdom personifies the knowledge of kings and serves as a member of the heavenly court.[10] In the *katholikon* at Sopoćani Monastery (1260s) and in the later Church of the Dormition on Volotovo Field in Novgorod (1380s), she inspires scriptural authors, including the four evangelists, to write eloquently.[11] Finally, during the

---

10   Lev I. Lifshits, "Premudrost'" v russkoi ikonopisi," *Vizantiiskii vremennik* 61 (2002): 138–50. On the Wisdom cycles in these churches, see Karl Christian Felmy, "'Die unendliche Weisheit, des Lebens Allgrund und Erschafferin': Die Ikonen der Weisheit und die Göttliche Liturgie," in *'Die Weisheit baute ihr Haus': Untersuchungen zu hymnischen und didaktischen Ikonen*, ed. Karl Christian Felmy and Eva Haustein-Bartsch (Munich: Deutscher Kunstverlag, 1999), pp. 43–68, esp. 43–44; Jean Meyendorff, "L'iconographie de la Sagesse divine dans la tradition byzantine," *Cahiers archéologiques* 10 (1959): 259–77, esp. 270–73; and Svetozar Radojčić, "La table de la Sagesse dans la littérature et l'art serbes depuis le début du XIIe jusqu'au début du XIVe siècles," *Zbornik radova Vizantološkog instituta* 16 (1975): 215–24.

11   Lifshits, "Premudrost'," 141. On the Wisdom cycle in the Novgorodian church, see T.A. Sidorova, "Volotovskaia freska 'Premudrost' sozda sebe dom' i ee otnoshenie k novgorodskoi eresi strigol'nikov v XIV v.," *Trudy otdela drevnerusskoi literatury* 26 (1971): 212–31. On Wisdom as a fountain of inspiration, see Christopher Walter, *Art and Ritual of the Byzantine Church* (London: Variorum, 1982), pp. 111–15; and Vladimir D. Sarabianov,

FIGURE 1.4 Drawing of frescoes in upper registers, chapel of Chrelja's tower
DRAWING BY M. REYNOLDS; BASED PARTIALLY ON PRASHKOV, *KHREL'OVATA KULA*, ANNOTATION FIGS. 7, 21–23, REPR. IN KIRIN, "VISTAS OF PIETY," 129, FIG. 42

Palaiologan era, she features as the hypostasis of the Trinity and the bestower of God's seven spirits, two roles that the Rila painter combines in his depiction of her.[12] Only one other instance of this previously unattested iconography is known from the medieval period: in the *katholikon* at Markov Monastery, in a

"Scenes of the 'Sources of Divine Wisdom' within the Iconographical Program of the Church of the Savior in the Monastery of Euphrosynia, Polotsk (Belarus)," Δελτίον της Χριστιανικής Αρχαιολογικής Εταιρείας 36 (2015): 49–64.

12   Erich Schilbach, "Ein eigenwilliger Maler aus der Spätzeit von Byzanz," in *Zwischen Polis, Provinz und Peripherie: Beiträge zur byzantinischen Geschichte und Kultur*, ed. Lars M. Hoffmann and Anuscha Monchizadeh, Mainzer Veröffentlichungen zur Byzantinistik 7 (Wiesbaden: Harrassowitz, 2005), pp. 895–925, esp. 918–22.

FIGURE 1.5   Allegory of Wisdom, fresco, chapel of Chrelja's tower
PHOTOGRAPH BY IVAN VANEV

cycle dating to the early 1380s. Unlike at Rila, where the painter has placed the scene over the main altar, at Markov the artist has tucked it away in a wing of the narthex (Fig. 1.7).[13]

The Rila painter depicts Wisdom with hands outstretched, seated on a rainbow as she dispatches seven spirits, symbolized as infant boys with individualized gestures.[14] They descend onto several groups of apostles, Old Testament kings, martyrs, church fathers, and angels (Figs. 1.4–1.5).[15] At the western end of the drum a handsome, young king Solomon stands conversing with two older monarchs, one of whom may be his father David. Dressed in the imperial *loros* and wearing a luxurious crown, Solomon points with his right hand to

13   Gabriel Millet and Tania Velmans, *La peinture du moyen âge en Yougoslavie (Serbie, Macédoine et Monténégro)*, vol. 4 (Paris: De Boccard, 1969), pls. 103–4, nos. 187–88.
14   The individualized gestures are noted by Priscilla Hunt, "The Intellectual Vision in the Fresco at Hrelyo's Tower: 'Wisdom Builds Her House,'" in *Fruits of Devotion: Essays in Honor of Predrag Matejic*, ed. M.A. Johnson and Alice Isabella Sullivan, *Ohio Slavic Papers* 11 (Columbus, OH: Department of Slavic and East European Languages and Cultures, 2020), forthcoming.
15   The exact identity of the martyr figures remains open to debate.

the majestic figure of Wisdom overhead, while he holds in his left hand a scroll bearing the opening verse of his celebrated proverb: "Wisdom has built her house and carved out her seven pillars" (Proverbs 9:1).

The text of the proverb continues around the base of the drum on several scrolls. Curling over the southern end of the ceiling is the second scroll with the next verse of the proverb: "She has sent forth her maidens, crying from the high places" (v. 3).[16] Beneath this scroll, three apostles approach an angel who serves them wine in a shallow vessel. Continuing into the eastern quadrant of the sanctuary is the next scroll, which reads: "She has summoned them to her cup, saying, 'Whoever is without reason, turn in to me'" (v. 4). Below, two angels tend to an altar table set with wine, bread, and a spoon. Finally, the last scroll, which unfurls over the northern end of the chapel, reads: "Drink the wine that I have mixed for you" (v. 5). Below, an angel serves wine to three church fathers who may be Chrysostom, Basil, and Gregory Nazianzos.

Intriguingly, the painter has chosen not to represent Wisdom's house, as was done at Dečani, in a fresco completed in 1348 and showing a temple with seven pillars (Fig. 1.8), but to solicit the architecture of the chapel to *be* that house. Differing from the smooth, convex curve of the vaulted narthex, the scalloped dome of the chapel, divided into six equal wedges, enables the painter to complete the iconography by treating the surfaces of the ceiling as if they *were* the very pillars of Wisdom's house. Allocating one spirit to each of the six faces of the dome, the painter portrays the spirits descending onto the saints, while he depicts the seventh reclined on the western radius of the ceiling, perched over Solomon's pointing index finger (Figs. 1.4–1.5).[17] Incorporating the structural design of the chapel into his medium, he is able to erect Wisdom's house in three dimensions. The painter sweeps worshipers up into the visionary mode of the allegory even as he concretizes, in this very chapel, the building Solomon foresaw.

---

16   For a transcription of the inscriptions, see Prashkov, *Khrel'ovata kula*, p. 30.

17   On these spirits, see D.S. Golovkova, "'Bogomater' neopalimaia kupina': Ikonografiia i simvolika," in *Iskusstvo khristianskogo mira. Sbornik statei 7*, ed. A.A. Saltykov (Moscow: Pravoslavnyi Sviato-Tikhonovskii Bogoslovskii Institut, 2003), pp. 205–20, who discusses their appearance on icons of the Mother of God of the Burning Bush; and Ivan M. Đorđević, "Darovi Svetog Duha u proskomidiji Bogorodičine crkve u Morači," in *Manastir Morača*, ed. Branislav Todić and Danica Popović (Belgrade: Balkanološki institut, Srpska akademija nauka i umetnosti, 2006), pp. 195–211, esp. 200–2, who likens them to angels and classical *erotes*.

FIGURE 1.6   Wisdom, fresco, chapel of Chrelja's tower
PHOTOGRAPH BY IVAN VANEV

FIGURE 1.7 Allegory of Wisdom, fresco, narthex, *katholikon* of Markov Monastery, 1376–77 or 1380–81
PHOTOGRAPH BY MARKA TOMIĆ ĐURIĆ

3 Kokkinos and the Byzantine and Slavic Commons

I would suggest that Byzantine literature on the allegory offers a way of interpreting these artistic choices. In the Slavic tradition, only a few texts on the allegory were available, and none of them sheds much light on the question of the possible intentions of the painter.[18] On the other hand, a discourse,

---

18 A commentary on the allegory by Hippolytus of Rome (d. 235) appears in the 1073 *sbornik* of Sviatoslav. See V.G. Briusova, "Tolkovanie na IX pritchu Solomona v Izbornike 1073 g.," in *Izbornik Sviatoslava 1073 g.*, ed. B.A. Rybakov (Moscow: Nauka, 1977), pp. 292–306. The Greek is in M. Richard, "Les fragments du commentaire de S. Hippolyte sur les *Proverbes de Salomon*," *Muséon* 79 (1966): 61–94, at p. 82 (= PG 89, col. 593). As Richard observes, the text was often attributed to Anastasios Sinaites (7th century). For the Greek, see Richard, "Fragments," 82–84. There also existed an ode for Great Thursday by Kosmas the Hymnographer (675–752), which is found in many Slavic manuscripts. For the Greek, see W. Christ and M. Paranikas, eds., *Anthologia Graeca Carminum Christianorum* (Leipzig: B.G. Teubner, 1871), p. 190 (ll. 7–13); and for a translation, Meyendorff, "Sagesse," p. 261. Relevant for the present study's focus on building, the allegory also featured in the liturgy for the dedication of churches (the enkainia). On the feast liturgy in Byzantium,

penned in the late 14th century by Philotheos Kokkinos, presents a far lengthier analysis of the Biblical text and offers a literary parallel for the Rila painter's handling of the allegory.[19] While Kokkinos's discourse has long been known to scholars and has been cited in passing in the context of visualizations of the allegory, no art historian has ever given it sustained attention.[20] In part, this is because medieval Slavic bookmen never translated the Greek text and because many of the images only appear in the Slavic world. Consequently, scholars have judged the text as only tangentially related to artworks outside Constantinople. I would, however, like to propose another way of looking at the situation. While it is true that one cannot claim a direct, or even indirect, influence on the Rila painter for Kokkinos (who wrote nearly a half century later), still one can understand the two as giving voice to a shared understanding of the allegory. This conceptual affinity should not surprise. Viktor Lazarev and others have demonstrated the remarkable amount of conversation and exchange between Greek and Slavic artistic and literary milieus.[21] But, at a deeper level, one can view this parity as an instance of what Cesare Casarino

see Robert Ousterhout, "New Temples and New Solomons: The Rhetoric of Byzantine Architecture," in *The Old Testament in Byzantium*, ed. Paul Magdalino and Robert Nelson (Washington, DC: Dumbarton Oaks, 2010), pp. 223–53, at 251; and in the Slavic world, Iu.K. Begunov, *Tvorcheskoe nasledie Grigoriia Tsamblaka* (Veliko-Turnovo: PIK, 2005), pp. 450–65, esp. 451, 452. See also an early Slavic hymnbook in V.G. Briusova, *Sofiia premudrost' bozhiia v drevnerusskoi literature i iskusstve* (Moscow: Belyi gorod, 2000), pp. 61–63.

19   B.S. Pseftonkas, ed., Φιλοθέου Κοκκίνου λόγοι καὶ ὁμιλίαι, Thessalonian Byzantine Writers 2 (Thessalonica: Centre for Byzantine Research, 1981). Kokkinos's discourse was edited twice in the 19th century: Triantaphyllès (Venice, 1874); and Episkop Arsenii (Ivashenko) (Novgorod, 1898), with a facing Russian translation.

20   On the text with special attention to artworks, see Meyendorff, "Sagesse," p. 262; G.M. Prokhorov, "Poslanie Titu-ierarkhu Dionisiia Areopagita v slavianskom perevode i ikonografiia 'Premudrost' sozda sebe dom,'" *Trudy otdela drevnerusskoi literatury* 38 (1985): 7–41, esp. 10; L.M. Evseeva, "Dve simvolicheskie kompozitsii v rospisi XIV v. monastyria Zarzma," *Vizantiiskii vremennik* 43 (1982): 134–46, esp. 138–41; Priscilla Hunt, "Confronting the End: The Interpretation of the Last Judgment in a Novgorod Wisdom Icon," *Byzantinoslavica* 65 (2007): 275–325, esp. 276 n. 3, 279 n. 15, 280, 282 n. 25, 287 n. 35, 291 n. 45, 300 n. 79, 312 n. 108, and 313 n. 109; Sidorova, "Volotovskaia freska," pp. 220–21; and L.M. Evseeva, "Pir Premudrosti," in *Sofiia premudrost' bozhiia: Vystavka russkoi ikonopisi XII–XIX vekov iz sobranii muzeev Rossii*, ed. O.A. Chernova, exh. cat. (Moscow: Radunitsa, 2000), pp. 194–97.

21   See Victor N. Lazarev, "Verbreitung der byzantinischen Vorlagen und die altrussische Kunst," in *Évolution générale et développements régionaux en histoire de l'art. Actes du XXIIᵉ Congrès international d'histoire de l'art*, Budapest, 1969, 3 vols. (Budapest: Akadémiai Kiadó, 1972), vol. 1, pp. 111–17; Viktor Lazarev, "La méthode de collaboration des maîtres byzantins et russes," in *Studies in Early Russian Art*, trans. Katharine Judelson (London: Pindar, 2000), pp. 427–40; and M.A. Makhan'ko, "Greki i moskovskaia Rus' XVI v. po materialam izobrazitel'nogo iskusstva i khudozhestvennoi kul'tury," in *Kapterevskie*

FIGURE 1.8   Allegory of Wisdom, fresco, nave, *katholikon* of Dečani Monastery, 1348
PHOTOGRAPH PROVIDED BY BLAGO FUND, USA/SERBIA, WWW.SRPSKOBLAGO.ORG

and Antonio Negri have called the "commons."[22] The commons, in Casarino's words, is "no more a dialogue than it is a monologue ... [but] that which is always at stake in any conversation: there where a conversation takes place ... there where we are in common."[23] Said differently, the commons can be theorized as the bedrock identity underlying any cultural give-and-take. Before representational strategies can be appropriated and the play of similarity and difference can occur, there has to be a shared sense of value. Contributing a cultural artifact to the system, the producer anticipates how others will identify with it. Consequently, in the artifact, the values of the maker merge with those of the receiver who is present at the object's conceptualization and material articulation. Representation is this moment of delay within the cause—a plurality that defines the artwork. This is what the "commons" captures. Quite simply, it draws our attention to the agency of all involved: the afterthought of production which yet has a foothold in the foreground of social capital—as a

---

  chteniia—7. *Sbornik statei*, ed. M.V. Bibikov (Moscow: Institut vseobshchei istorii Rossiiskoi akademii nauk, 2009), pp. 258–302.
22 Cesare Casarino and Antonio Negri, *In Praise of the Common: A Conversation on Philosophy and Politics* (Minneapolis: University of Minnesota Press, 2008).
23 Ibid., 1.

co-innovator, and a fellow enabler of a prized commodity. To stipulate this as a methodology is to ask whether an artifact that achieves wide success might not depend on the basic need for recognition that we all share, as finite creatures. In this spirit, I shall resist interrogating the "geography" of the Wisdom allegory or framing a "dialogue" between two locales of representation—a chapel in Bulgaria and a text from Constantinople—to ask about a far more expansive cultural landscape: a social totality in which the allegory's theory of architecture was invested at a very elemental level. With this heuristic in mind, we can explore the larger cultural "we" inhabited by Kokkinos and the fresco.

4   The Wisdom Fresco Seen through Kokkinos

Kokkinos addresses his discourse to a certain Bishop Ignatios (1353–76) who may have presided over the see of Panion/Thrace and have signed documents condemning the anti-Palamites.[24] In the first part of the discourse Kokkinos discusses the nature of Solomon's wisdom, distinguishing it from other wisdoms. In part two, he opens an analysis of Solomon's allegory. It is the latter section that bears relevance for a discussion of the Rila fresco.

Inquiring into how the seven pillars should be understood, Kokkinos writes:

> If you were to understand the building of the universal church of believers as the house of God's Wisdom, in the way mentioned [above], transferring the concept, that is, from what is partial and singular to what is general and universal, and thus you were to understand the seven pillars too, I think that this would be most excellent and entirely fitting. For, the seven pillars which support Wisdom's house, and the unshakeable foundation, we understand properly, before anything else, as the seven great activities of the Spirit, which the wonderful Zechariah calls "the seven eyes of God that cast their gaze over the entire earth" (Zechariah 4:10). And the great Isaiah calls these the seven spirits divinely reposed on the branch sprouting from David's root, which is evidently Christ (Isaiah 11:1–2). For, "in him," says the divine apostle, "the fullness of the godhead dwells bodily" (Colossians 2:9). Whence flowing abundantly, as if from an

---

[24]   In some manuscripts the scribe records the addressee as τῷ συνεπισκόπῳ Ἰγνατίῳ. Pseftonkas, *Κοκκίνου λόγοι*, p. 69. See *Prosopographisches Lexikon der Palaiologenzeit*, ed. Erich Trapp et al. (Vienna: Verlag der Österreichischen Akademie der Wissenschaften, 1976–1996), [nos.] 8013/14 for a Palamite bishop named Ignatios who oversaw the see of Panion/Thrace.

eternal spring, by an unlimited, as a certain writer says, grace, onto the evangelists and apostles through a variety of signs and miracles, so these firmly established and unmoving pillars have assembled and fastened together the universal church of believers [2:5].[25]

Kokkinos here describes Wisdom's pillars as the seven spirits reposed on the son of David.[26] Next, mixing metaphors, he adds that these spirits "flow" down onto the apostles and evangelists like a "spring," which, curiously, has "assembled" and "fastened together" the church of believers. In a similar way, the Rila painter mixes metaphors. Representing the "pillars" of Wisdom as spirits reclined on a holy power that manifests itself to the saints, he suggests that the monks below are a foundation enabling God's house to be built marvelously from the top down.

Kokkinos develops this thought later where he plays with a pun from the apostle Paul:

> Once again, the apostle, continuing his previous remark and teaching about the edification of the church and its means [τὴν οἰκοδομὴν τῆς ἐκκλησίας καὶ τὴν ὕλην], (says): "On the other hand, he who prophesies speaks to men for their edification and encouragement and consolation. He who speaks in a tongue edifies himself, but he who prophesies edifies the church ['Ο λαλῶν γλώσσῃ ἑαυτὸν οἰκοδομεῖ, ὁ δὲ προφητεύων, ἐκκλησίαν οἰκοδομεῖ]. Now, I want all of you to speak in tongues, but even more to prophesy. He who prophesies is greater than he who speaks in tongues, unless someone interprets, so that the church may be edified

---

25   Pseftonkas, *Κοκκίνου λόγοι*, pp. 95–96: Εἰ δὲ καὶ τὴν καθόλου τῶν πιστῶν ἐκκλησίαν ὁμοῦ τὸν οἶκον τῆς τοῦ θεοῦ σοφίας νοήσεις, ὑπ' αὐτῆς ἐκείνης, ὃν εἴρηται τρόπον, οἰκοδομούμενον, ἀπὸ τῶν μερικῶν δηλαδὴ καὶ καθένα πρὸς τὰ καθόλου τε καὶ κοινὰ μεταφέρων τὸν λόγον, καὶ οὕτω τοὺς ἑπτὰ στύλους ἐκλήψῃ, κάλλιστα τῶν πάντων οἶμαι καὶ προσφυέστατα. Στύλους γὰρ ἑπτά, τὸν τῆς σοφίας ὑπερείδοντας οἶκον, καὶ θεμελίους ἀρραγεῖς πρός γε τῶν ἄλλων ἀκριβῶς ἴσμεν τὰς μεγάλας ἑπτὰ τοῦ πνεύματος ἐνεργείας, ἃς ὁ μὲν θαυμαστὸς Ζαχαρίας « ἑπτὰ φησιν ὀφθαλμοὺς τοῦ κυρίου, ἐπιβλέποντας ἐπὶ πᾶσαν τὴν γῆν ». Ἡσαΐας δ' αὖθις ὁ μέγας πνεύματα ταύτας ἑπτὰ καλεῖ, τῷ ἐκ ῥίζης τοῦ Δαυὶδ ἀνατείλαντι ἄνθει, δηλαδὴ τῷ Χριστῷ, θεοπρεπῶς ἐπαναπεπαυμένα. « Ἐν αὐτῷ » γάρ, φησὶν ὁ θεῖος ἀπόστολος, « κατῴκησε πᾶν τὸ πλήρωμα τῆς θεότητος σωματικῶς ». Κἀκεῖθεν ὡς ἐξ ἀενάου πηγῆς εἰς εὐαγγελιστὰς καὶ ἀποστόλους διὰ ποικίλων σημείων τε καὶ θαυμάτων δαψιλῶς ἐκχυθέντα, κατὰ ἀπειρόδωρον, ὥς τίς φησι, χάριν, οἱονεί τινες ἑδραῖοι καὶ ἀπερίτρεπτοι στύλοι τὴν καθόλου τῶν πιστῶν συνεκρότησάν τε καὶ ἥδρασαν ἐκκλησίαν.

26   Prashkov, *Khrel'ovata kula*, p. 23, suggests that the spirits are "flying," but it seems that they are reclined.

[ἵνα ἡ ἐκκλησία οἰκοδομὴν λαμβάνῃ]" (1 Corinthians 14:3–5) ... This is how one should understand these things [2:5].[27]

Kokkinos here singles out prophecy as the foremost gift of the seven spirits. Classifying all of these gifts as, metaphorically, "house-building," or "edification," Kokkinos quotes apostle Paul who asserts that prophecy is the activity that "builds up" Wisdom's house. Comforting one another, teaching, encouraging, forging unity—these are the mighty pillars of Wisdom's house.

Kokkinos's interest in prophecy, and his metaphorical alignment of it with the building of Wisdom's house, is understandable: for the allegory was based on a vision of Solomon, and authors commonly discussed Solomon's prophecy by way of figurative language involving architecture. For example, writing about Solomon's divine foresight, the 15th-century Bulgarian theologian Gregory Tsamblak said: "And this wise man (i.e., Solomon) reveals another prophetic image [of the Mother of God]: 'Wisdom,' he says, 'hath built her house.' But with what stones? With what wood? The cedars of Lebanon? With what builder's craft? It is through none other than the purity of this young girl [that she builds]."[28] In Gregory's view, Solomon spoke of a house that the saints embody instead of a structure built with natural materials. Foremost among these saints, in his eyes, is the Mother of God—whose image notably hung over the altar in the apse of the chapel and whose body Gregory describes as the domicile of God.

5 The Figure of Wisdom

The Rila monks and painter intended this allegory to inspire a love of wisdom, or philosophy. The builder-prophet Solomon signaled the way to a true understanding of God by pointing to the figure of Wisdom, the embodiment of

---

27 Pseftonkas, *Κοκκίνου λόγοι*, pp. 96–97: Καὶ πάλιν ὁ ἀπόστολος τοῖς προρρηθεῖσιν ἐπεξιὼν καὶ τὴν οἰκοδομὴν τῆς ἐκκλησίας καὶ τὴν ὕλην διδάσκων, « ὁ προφητεύων, φησίν, ἀνθρώποις λαλεῖ οἰκοδομὴν καὶ παράκλησιν καὶ παραμυθίαν. Ὁ λαλῶν γλώσσῃ ἑαυτὸν οἰκοδομεῖ, ὁ δὲ προφητεύων, ἐκκλησίαν οἰκοδομεῖ. Μείζων γάρ φησιν ὁ προφητεύων ἢ ὁ λαλῶν γλώσσῃ, ἐκτὸς εἰ μὴ διερμηνεύοι, ἵνα ἡ ἐκκλησία οἰκοδομὴν λαμβάνῃ » ... Καὶ τοῦτο μὲν οὕτως. In the ellipsis Kokkinos cites two more instances of this pun from Paul's letters: 1 Cor. 14:26; 1 Thess. 5:11.

28 Gregory Tsamblak, *Homily on the Birth of the Bogoroditsa*, edited in *Velikiia Minei Chetii, sobrannyia vserossiiskim mitropolitom Makariem. Sentiabr,' dni 1–15* (St. Petersburg: Tipografiia Imperatorskoi akademii nauk, 1868), col. 413: Но и другій образъ пророчества премудрый сей являеть мужъ: премудрость, глаголя, созда себѣ храмъ. Отъ которыхъ каменій? отъ которыхъ древъ, ливановехъ и кедровыхъ? которыми хитростьми зиздца? ни отъ которыхъ, развѣ отъ чистыя сея отроковица.

knowledge (Figs. 1.4–1.6). The painter portrayed Wisdom's hands extended out to the edge of the sphere encircling her. Once again, Kokkinos opens an avenue for interpreting the iconography. Speaking of Wisdom, Kokkinos says:

> If someone were to say that by the hypostatic wisdom of the Father, the only-begotten Son of the Father and God, the creator and lord of the visible and invisible world, is meant the one *enacting* the aforementioned *divine drama* [ἐνεργεῖν ... τὰ θεῖα δράματα], building a house for himself, preparing a table and everything else stated before (for he is wisdom, the hypostatic power, and the Word of the Father [see 1 Corinthians 1:30; John 1:1]), we would not disagree. For, he *enacts* everything discussed just now, possessing the appointed wisdom, activity, and power together in common with the Father and Spirit, God equal in honor and substance, and with them in equal honor and in common distributing the godly gifts in proportion to their (i.e., the saints') desiring. For he is "the *choragos* of wisdom and the director of the wise," according to the wise man that we have just cited (Wisdom 7:15) [3:4].[29] (author italics)

Conflating Wisdom with the Son of God, Kokkinos says that she directs the heavenly *drama*. Kokkinos's name for her—*choragos*—which he has taken from Solomon, bears several valences. Referring to the director of the chorus in classical theater, and to the "bestower" of the divine gifts in Komnenian debates over the *Filioque*, its reciprocal valence bridging earthly and heavenly realms bespeaks a sense of dwelling as philosophy.[30] In the fresco, Wisdom sets the circular life cycle into motion insofar as she choreographs the movements of the heavenly spheres. In so doing, she directs the viewer's eye to the spirits who come to rest upon the saints in a manifestation of the heavenly drama on earth, the liturgy. Her hands signal the point of contact between these two worlds, God's relation to himself and intervention in the created

---

29 Pseftonkas, *Κοκκίνου λόγοι*, p. 131: Εἰ δὲ καὶ τὴν ἐνυπόστατον τοῦ πατρὸς σοφίαν, τὸν μονογενῆ δηλαδὴ τοῦ πατρὸς υἱὸν καὶ θεόν, τὸν τῆς ὁρωμένης ἅμα καὶ ἀοράτου κτίσεως δημιουργόν τε καὶ κύριον εἴποι τις ἐνεργεῖν ἐκεῖνα τὰ θεῖα δράματα, οἶκον ἑαυτῷ οἰκοδομοῦντα καὶ τράπεζαν ἑτοιμάζοντα καὶ τἄλλα πάντα τὰ προειρημένα φημί (σοφία γὰρ καὶ δύναμις ἐνυπόστατος καὶ Λόγος ὁ αὐτός ἐστι τοῦ πατρός), οὐ διαφερόμεθα. Ἐνεργεῖ καὶ γὰρ πάντα τοῖς ἀποδοθεῖσι λόγοις κατὰ ταὐτὰ κοινὴν τὴν ῥηθεῖσαν σοφίαν καὶ τὴν ἐνέργειαν καὶ τὴν δύναμιν κεκτημένος μετὰ πατρός τε καὶ πνεύματος, οἷα δὴ καὶ θεὸς ὁμότιμός τε καὶ ὁμοούσιος, καὶ κοινῶς καὶ ὁμοτίμως ἐκείνοις τὰς θεοπρεπεῖς δωρεὰς διανέμων ἀναλόγως τοῖς χρῄζουσιν, ἐπειδὴ καὶ τῆς « σοφίας αὐτός ἐστι χορηγὸς καὶ διορθωτὴς τῶν σοφῶν », κατὰ τὸν εἰπόντα πρὸ βραχέος σοφόν.

30 On the Komnenian discussions, see Alessandra Bucossi, "The Six Dialogues by Niketas 'of Maroneia': A Contextualizing Introduction," in *Dialogues and Debates from Late Antiquity to Late Byzantium*, ed. Averil Cameron and Niels Gaul (New York: Routledge, 2017), pp. 137–52, esp. 147.

universe, even as the hand of the prophet Solomon signals the seam between history and the present.

Wisdom's house, built through philosophy, returned thought to the everyday tools that habilitate theological knowledge. The Rila painter acknowledges this aspect of the allegory. He portrays the two angels serving the saints from shallow vessels—bespeaking the finitude of human reason—rather than from the deep *krater* of wine standing on the altar—bespeaking unmediated contemplation of God. Kokkinos explains this feature of Solomon's allegory:

> What do the words that Wisdom speaks to those who are poor in reason mean: "Drink the wine that I have mixed for you?" (Proverbs 9:5). She says, "My wine, as well as my bread, I have set before you as food. But for you partaking of it I have mixed this. Because all of my things are pure, and the divine mysteries are free from mixture with any human and earthly word and deed [ἀμιγῆ τὰ θεῖα μυστήρια παντὸς ἀνθρωπίνου καὶ γεώδους καὶ λόγου καὶ πράγματος]. For, searching out all things, just as you have heard, even the deep things of God (see 1 Corinthians 2:10), I have also now descended into human frailty, and I am mixing the wine with water for you in order that it might delight your heart and not shake your enfeebled mind, having filled it with a swell and swooning through an onslaught of power (see Psalms 103:15)." For this reason, when Moses told God that he wished "to see him clearly," God replied: "I will put you in a cleft of the rock while my glory passes by, and I will cover you with my hand. Then I will take away my hand, and you shall see my backside, but my face you shall not see. For no man can see my face and live" (Exodus 33:13, 22–23, 20) ... Here, Wisdom, as it were, has mixed and diluted the *krater* of transcendental contemplation with these human-loving things, along with the words and deeds of an angel [2:16].[31]

---

31 Pseftonkas, *Κοκκίνου λόγοι*, pp. 108–9: Τί δὲ καὶ τὸ « πίετε οἶνον, ὃν κεκέρακα ὑμῖν » πρὸς ἐκείνους τοὺς ἐνδεεῖς φρενῶν ὁμοίως λεγόμενον ὑπ' ἐκείνης; Ἐμὸς μέν φησιν ὁ οἶνος, ὥσπερ δὴ καὶ ὁ ἄρτος, ὃν ὑμῖν εἰς βρῶσιν προτέθεικα· ἀλλὰ τοῖς δαιτυμόσιν ὑμῖν τοῦτον κεκέρακα. Ἐμοὶ μὲν γὰρ ἄκρατα πάντα καὶ ἀμιγῆ τὰ θεῖα μυστήρια παντὸς ἀνθρωπίνου καὶ γεώδους καὶ λόγου καὶ πράγματος. Ἐρευνῶν γάρ, καθάπερ ἠκούσατε, πάντα, καὶ τὰ βάθη τοῦ θεοῦ, τῇ δ' ἀνθρωπίνῃ συγκατιοῦσα καὶ νῦν ἀσθενείᾳ, καὶ ὕδατι κιρνῶ τὸν οἶνον ὑμῖν, ἵν' εὐφράνῃ καρδίαν, μὴ τὸν ἐγκέφαλον ἀσθενοῦντα διασείσῃ, σάλου τινὸς καὶ ἰλίγγου πληρώσας τῷ τῆς δυνάμεως περιόντι, οὕτω πρὸς τὸν Μωϋσὴν ἔλεγεν ὁ θεός, ἐπιζητοῦντα « γνωστῶς ἐκεῖνον ἰδεῖν », ὅτι « θήσω σὲ εἰς ὀπὴν τῆς πέτρας, ἡνίκα δ' ἂν παρέλθῃ ἡ δόξα μου, καὶ σκεπάσω σὲ τῇ χειρί μου· καὶ ἀφελῶ τὴν χεῖρά μου καὶ ὄψει τὰ ὀπίσω μου, τὸ δὲ πρόσωπόν μου οὐκ ὀφθήσεταί σοι. Οὐ γὰρ μὴ ἴδῃ ἄνθρωπος τὸ πρόσωπόν μου καὶ ζήσεται » ... Ὡσανεὶ τὸν κρατῆρα τῶν ὑπερφυῶν θεωρημάτων τῆς σοφίας ἐνταῦθα κιρνώσης τε καὶ ἀναμιγνύσης τοῖς φιλανθρώποις τουτοισὶ καὶ πράγμασι καὶ ῥήμασι τοῦ ἀγγέλου.

In these sentences Kokkinos indicates that even the prophets were unable to pierce the veil separating mortals from divinity. And so the cup of wisdom must be diluted, which is to say, the wine must be served mixed with water. Kokkinos understands this water to be "human" and "earthly" words and deeds: the lover of wisdom will aspire to emulate the prophets who brought the divinity into the mediacy of experience through language and demonstration. In a similar way, the painter focuses on the tactile instruments of understanding, the shallow vessels served to the saints. In this way, the fresco draws the monks' attention to the limits of sensory experience even as it exalts the sapiential tradition. These handmade vessels are the artifacts of a constructivist epistemology. They are the humble containers of everyday life: the objects in which a philosophical mind discovers humanity, the ritual equipment over which community gathers.

This shared understanding of the allegory demonstrates that the Rila painter and Kokkinos indeed inhabited a commons, one that subtended geographical, social, and linguistic locales. On the same count, the allegory invites a methodological reflection horizontally, deep into the Balkans, beyond the closed horizon of the Byzantine capital during the Palaiologan centuries. In turn, the fresco itself, opening into the inhabited space of the chapel, offers a plea for beginning scholarly conversations afresh about the antecedent whole of verbal, visual, and architectural testimonies, which too often are studied as discrete media. In the case of the commons, the lesson is less about patterns of influence, modes of exchange, and copying, and more about the conditions for understanding ideas shared by all. In this light, it would be worthwhile, before investigating the creation and transference of ideas and objects, to consider narratives concerned with the concretization of community—the discourses in which ideas and objects were understood and came to bear value—narratives such as the Allegory of Wisdom. When it comes to such a fundamental concern as dwelling, it is not surprising to find common ground, because without this, few meaningful exchanges of any sort could have occurred.

Acknowledgements

I am grateful to Maria Alessia Rossi and Alice Isabella Sullivan for inviting me to participate in the panels "North of Byzantium: Medieval Art, Architecture, and Visual Culture in Eastern Europe" at the 2018 Byzantine Studies Conference in San Antonio. The panels were generously sponsored by the Mary Jaharis Center for Byzantine Art and Culture at Hellenic College Holy Cross. Beatrice Kitzinger, Charles Barber, and the audience in San Antonio discussed various aspects of the project with me. Rossi and Sullivan, the anonymous reviewer, and Joe Hannan provided helpful feedback on drafts of this paper. Unless otherwise noted, all translations are my own.

Bibliography

Primary Sources

Christ, W. and M. Paranikas. *Anthologia Graeca Carminum Christianorum.* Leipzig: B.G. Teubner, 1871.

Hippolytus of Rome. *Fragmenta in Proverbia*, in M. Richard, "Les fragments du commentaire de S. Hippolyte sur les *Proverbes* de Salomon." *Muséon* 79 (1966): 82–94.

Kokkinos, Philotheos. *Three Discourses on Divine Wisdom*, in Φιλοθέου Κοκκίνου λόγοι καὶ ὁμιλίαι, ed. B.S. Pseftonkas, Thessalonian Byzantine Writers 2. Thessalonica: Centre for Byzantine Research, 1981.

Tsamblak, Gregory. *Homily on the Birth of the Bogoroditsa*, in *Velikiia Minei Chetii, sobrannyia vserossiiskim mitropolitom Makariem. Sentiabr,' dni 1–15.* St. Petersburg: Tipografiia Imperatorskoi akademii nauk, 1868. cols. 409–17.

Secondary Sources

Bacci, Michele. *L'artista a Bisanzio e nel mondo cristiano-orientale.* Pisa: Edizioni della Normale, 2007.

Bakalova, Elka. "Zur Interpretation des frühesten Zyklus der Vita des hl. Ivan von Rila in der bildenden Kunst." In *Festschrift für Klaus Wessel zum 70. Geburstag: In memoriam*, ed. Marcell Restle, 39–48. Munich: Editio Maris, 1988.

Bartusis, M.C. "Chrelja and Momčilo: Occasional Servants of Byzantium in Fourteenth Century Macedonia." *Byzantinoslavica* 41 (1980): 201–21.

Begunov, Iu.K. *Tvorcheskoe nasledie Grigoriia Tsamblaka.* Veliko-Turnovo: PIK, 2005.

Briusova, V.G. "Tolkovanie na IX pritchu Solomona v Izbornike 1073 g." In *Izbornik Sviatoslava 1073 g.*, ed. B.A. Rybakov, 292–306. Moscow: Nauka, 1977.

Briusova, V.G. *Sofiia premudrost' bozhiia v drevnerusskoi literature i iskusstve.* Moscow: Belyi gorod, 2000.

Bucossi, Alessandra. "The Six Dialogues by Niketas 'of Maroneia': A Contextualizing Introduction." In *Dialogues and Debates from Late Antiquity to Late Byzantium*, ed. Averil Cameron and Niels Gaul, 137–52. New York: Routledge, 2017.

Casarino, Cesare and Antonio Negri. *In Praise of the Common: A Conversation on Philosophy and Politics.* Minneapolis: University of Minnesota Press, 2008.

Đorđević, Ivan M. "Darovi Svetog Duha u proskomidiji Bogorodičine crkve u Morači." In *Manastir Morača*, ed. Branislav Todić and Danica Popović, 195–211. Belgrade: Balkanološki institut, Srpska akademija nauka i umetnosti, 2006.

Enev, Mikhail. *Rila Monastery*. Sofia: Balkan Pub. Co. with the assistance of the European Centre for Education and Training, 1997.

Evseeva, L.M. "Dve simvolicheskie kompozitsii v rospisi XIV v. monastyria Zarzma." *Vizantiiskii vremennik* 43 (1982): 134–46.

Evseeva, L.M. "Pir Premudrosti." In *Sofiia premudrost' bozhiia: Vystavka russkoi ikonopisi XII–XIX vekov iz sobranii muzeev Rossii*, ed. O.A. Chernova, exh. cat., 194–97. Moscow: Radunitsa, 2000.

Felmy, Karl Christian. "'Die unendliche Weisheit, des Lebens Allgrund und Erschafferin': Die Ikonen der Weisheit und die Göttliche Liturgie." In *'Die Weisheit baute ihr Haus': Untersuchungen zu hymnischen und didaktischen Ikonen*, ed. Karl Christian Felmy and Eva Haustein-Bartsch, 43–68. Munich: Deutscher Kunstverlag, 1999.

Golovkova, D.S. "'Bogomater' neopalimaia kupina': Ikonografiia i simvolika." In *Iskusstvo khristianskogo mira. Sbornik statei 7*, ed. A.A. Saltykov. Moscow: Pravoslavnyi Sviato-Tikhonovskii Bogoslovskii Institut, 2003, 205–20.

Hunt, Priscilla. "Confronting the End: The Interpretation of the Last Judgment in a Novgorod Wisdom Icon." *Byzantinoslavica* 65 (2007): 275–325.

Hunt, Priscilla. "The Intellectual Vision in the Fresco at Hrelyo's Tower: 'Wisdom Builds Her House'." In *Fruits of Devotion: Essays in Honor of Predrag Matejic*, ed. M.A. Johnson and Alice Isabella Sullivan, *Ohio Slavic Papers* 11. Columbus, OH: Department of Slavic and East European Languages and Cultures, 2020, forthcoming.

Kirin, Asen. "Contemplating the Vistas of Piety at the Rila Monastery Pyrgos." *Dumbarton Oaks Papers* 59 (2005): 95–138.

Lazarev, Victor N. "Verbreitung der byzantinischen Vorlagen und die altrussische Kunst." In *Évolution générale et développements régionaux en histoire de l'art. Actes du XXIIe Congrès international d'histoire de l'art*; Budapest, 1969, 3 vols. Budapest: Akadémiai Kiadó, 1972, 1:111–17.

Lazarev, Viktor. "La méthode de collaboration des maîtres byzantins et russes." In *Studies in Early Russian Art*, trans. Katharine Judelson, intro Jana Howlett, 427–40. London: Pindar, 2000.

Lecaque, Patrick. "Représentations de Saint Jean de Rila dans les peintures de la tour de Hrel'o au monastère de Rila (XIVe siècle)." *Revue des études slaves* 60, no. 2 (1988): 513–17.

Lecaque, Patrick. "The Monastery of Rila during the XIV Century and the Wall-Paintings of the Tower of Hreljo." *Macedonian Studies* 5, no. 3–4 (1988): 3–49.

Lifshits, Lev I. "Premudrost' v russkoi ikonopisi." *Vizantiiskii vremennik* 61 (2002): 138–50.

Makhan'ko, M.A. "Greki i moskovskaia Rus' XVI v. po materialam izobrazitel'nogo iskusstva i khudozhestvennoi kul'tury." In *Kapterevskie chteniia—7. Sbornik statei*, ed. M.V. Bibikov, 258–302. Moscow: Institut vseobshchei istorii Rossiiskoi akademii nauk, 2009.

Meyendorff, Jean. "L'iconographie de la Sagesse divine dans la tradition byzantine." *Cahiers archéologiques* 10 (1959): 259–77.
Millet, Gabriel and Tania Velmans. *La peinture du moyen âge en Yougoslavie (Serbie, Macédoine et Monténégro)*, vol. 4. Paris: De Boccard, 1969.
Ousterhout, Robert. "New Temples and New Solomons: The Rhetoric of Byzantine Architecture." In *The Old Testament in Byzantium*, ed. Paul Magdalino and Robert Nelson, 223–53. Washington, DC: Dumbarton Oaks, 2010.
Piguet-Panayotova, D. "La chapelle dans la tour de Khrelju au monastère de Rila." *Byzantion* 49 (1979): 363–84.
Prashkov, Liuben. *Khrel'ovata kula: Istoriia, arkhitektura, zhivopis.* Sofia: Bŭlgarski khudozhnik, 1973.
Prashkov, Liuben. "Khreleva bashnia Rilskogo monastyria i ee stenopis'." In *Drevnerusskoe iskusstvo: Zarubezhnye sviazi*, ed. G.V. Popov, 147–71. Moscow: Nauka, 1975.
Prokhorov, G.M. "Poslanie Titu-ierarkhu Dionisiia Areopagita v slavianskom perevode i ikonografiia 'Premudrost' sozda sebe dom.'" *Trudy otdela drevnerusskoi literatury* 38 (1985): 7–41.
Prosopographisches Lexikon der Palaiologenzeit, ed. Erich Trapp et al. Vienna: Verlag der Österreichischen Akademie der Wissenschaften, 1976–1996.
Radojčić, Svetozar. "La table de la Sagesse dans la littérature et l'art serbes depuis le début du XIIe jusqu'au début du XIVe siècles." *Zbornik radova Vizantološkog instituta* 16 (1975): 215–24.
Sarabianov, Vladimir D. "Scenes of the 'Sources of Divine Wisdom' within the Iconographical Program of the Church of the Savior in the Monastery of Euphrosynia, Polotsk (Belarus)." Δελτίον της Χριστιανικής Αρχαιολογικής Εταιρείας 36 (2015): 49–64.
Schilbach, Erich. "Ein eigenwilliger Maler aus der Spätzeit von Byzanz." In *Zwischen Polis, Provinz und Peripherie: Beiträge zur byzantinischen Geschichte und Kultur*, ed. Lars M. Hoffmann and Anuscha Monchizadeh, 895–925. Mainzer Veröffentlichungen zur Byzantinistik 7. Wiesbaden: Harrassowitz, 2005.
Sidorova, T.A. "Volotovskaia freska 'Premudrost' sozda sebe dom' i ee otnoshenie k novgorodskoi eresi strigol'nikov v XIV v." *Trudy otdela drevnerusskoi literatury* 26 (1971): 212–31.
Walter, Christopher. *Art and Ritual of the Byzantine Church.* London: Variorum, 1982.
Willson, Justin. "A Meadow that Lifts the Soul: Originality as Anthologizing in the Byzantine Church Interior." *Journal of the History of Ideas* 81, no. 1 (2020): 1–21.

CHAPTER 2

How Byzantine Was the Moscow Inauguration of 1498?

Alexandra Vukovich

Byzance après Byzance is the paradigm that has often described the perceived continuation of Byzantine imperial culture (religious, political, or intellectual) in the centuries after the 1453 fall of Constantinople.[1] The Byzantine inheritance, reception, or transfer of Byzantine style and culture to Rus and Muscovy has received attention, and scholars have pointed to the vast array of Byzantine texts, objects, and people who eventually arrived in the Eurasian north in the early modern period. By the fall of Constantinople, a state centered around Moscow had begun to emerge in the north from one of the Rus principalities.[2]

---

1 Initially coined by Nicolae Iorga in his book *Byzance après Byzance: Continuation de l'histoire de la vie byzantine*, the term *Byzance après Byzance* described the historical and cultural context of Romania's place in Europe, as a transmitter of Byzantine culture after the empire had ceased to exist. Iorga saw the role of Southeastern Europe as both a bridge between the "East" and the "West" and as possessing distinct national histories within the paradigm of the spiritual, and institutional continuity of the Byzantine Empire within separate Balkan states. The concept itself relies on articulating continuity (through religion and cultural transmission) rather than revival or appropriation, even though this process began in the later years of the Ottoman period and during the period of nation-building in the 19th- and early 20th-centuries. The project of Byzantinization occurred at different points in the regions of the former Byzantine Empire and the Byzantine cultural sphere with Romania expressing its autonomy from the Ottoman Empire through a national architectural style that obscured obvious Ottoman influences and Byzantinized local features. However, *Byzance après Byzance* as a process, was seen to have deeper historical roots with the translation of Byzantine spiritual and cultural authority to Russia as well as the survival of Eastern Christian religion and religious communities across the Eastern Mediterranean which, to some degree, stultifies discussion of innovation, change, and transformation by insisting on continuity through endless comparison with Byzantine protypes, whether in art, letters, architecture, or even practice. For an analysis of *Byzance après Byzance*, see Diana Mishkova, *Beyond Balkanism. The Scholarly Politics of Region Making* (New York: Routledge, 2018), pp. 117–18, 285–87; Ada Hajdu, "The Search for National Architectural Styles in Serbia, Romania, and Bulgaria from the Mid-nineteenth Century to World War I," in *Entangled Histories of the Balkans*, ed. Roumen Daskalov and Tchavdar Marinov (Leiden: Brill, 2013), pp. 394–440, 420–28.

2 This *translatio imperii* from Kiev to Moscow was developed in the 16th century with the shaping of information about early Rus and Byzantium (and, to a lesser extent, medieval Serbia)

Over the preceding century, a *Pax Mongolica* had reigned in Rus (until about the 1350s), offering stable trade networks from Central Asia to the Baltic, across several khanates of the Chinggisid Dynasty.[3] The role of commercial networks in the political economy of early Muscovy is often overlooked in studies of its cultural production, but the transfer of texts, artifacts, people, and technical knowledge (from the former Byzantine lands, as well as other places) was made possible by the advantageous place of Muscovy as a thoroughfare in trade, the

---

as direct precursors to the nascent Muscovite principality, bypassing both the polycentric organization of the principalities of Rus and the more recent Mongol Empire. For an early and quite substantial evaluation of the phenomenon of *translatio imperii* in the 15th century, see Vladimir Savva, *Moskovskie tsari i viszantiiskie vasilevsy. k voprosu o vliianii Vizantii na obrazovanie idei tsarskoi vlasti Moskovskikh gosudarei* (Kharkov: M. Zilberberg, 1901), pp. 110–57 (on inauguration). See also Gustav Alef, *The Origins of Muscovite Autocracy: The Age of Ivan III* (Wiesbaden: Harrassowitz, 1986), pp. 90 note 131, and 206; and, for the general background on the transfer of Byzantine political culture to the north, Francis Dvornik, "Byzantine Political Ideas in Kievan Russia," *Dumbarton Oaks Papers* 9 (1956): pp. 73–121; and Sergei Ivanov, "The Second Rome as Seen by the Third: Russian Debates on 'the Byzantine legacy,'" in *The Reception of Byzantium in European Culture since 1500*, ed. Przemsław Marciniak and Dion Smythe (Abingdon: Ashgate, 2016), pp. 55–81.

From the mid-19th century, scholars in Russia began to offer an alternate vision to the theory of an unbroken and exclusive historical continuity from Kiev to Moscow. Nikolay Kostomarov postulated that Rus bequeathed a democratic heritage to Ukraine and an autocratic heritage to Russia via Muscovy, while Alexander Herzen depicted Novgorod as heir to Kiev's communal republican tradition. Kostomarov, a historian and proponent of Pan-Slavism, outlined his position in an academic article, "The Two Rus' Nationalities", published in 1861 in the journal *Osnova*. There, Kostomarov (following the ethnographer Mykhailo Maksymovych) asserted that Rus had been divided into two separate entities with the northern favoring authoritarianism and collectivism and the southern (following Poland) favoring individual freedom and federalism, see: Serhii Plokhy, *Lost Kingdom: The Quest for Empire and the Making of the Russian Nation* (New York: Hachette, 2017), pp. 138–40. Aleksander Herzen, Russian philosopher, polymath, and socialist, skirted the 19th-century Slavophile/Westernizer debate by viewing the popular assemblies (veche) of Old Novgorod and Pskov as autonomous institutions brutally centralized by the Muscovite grand princes in the 15th- and 16th-centuries. His view, following that of the Decembrists, saw Old Novgorod and Pskov as models for a national revival based on a pan-Slavic phenomenon. However, in the Slavophile/Westernizer debate, Herzen admonished both sides. On Herzen's use of history, see Alexander Ivanovich Herzen, *Sobranie sochinenii v tridtsati tomakh* (Moscow: Akademiia nauk SSSR, 1954–66), vi 164–65, vii 113–14, 33; Aileen Kelly, *The Discovery of Chance. The Life and Thought of Alexander Herzen* (Cambridge, MA: Harvard University Press, 2016), pp. 19, 98–100, 138–41 (for Herzen's argument with Chaadaev on the philosophy of history), pp. 230–32.

3   See Donald Ostrowski, *Muscovy and the Mongols* (Cambridge, UK: Cambridge University Press, 1998), pp. 29–36.

expansion of settled territory, and the overall stability of the *Pax Mongolica*.[4] Moreover, the dynastic politics of the princes of Rus fluctuated throughout the 14th century, but saw the conservation of power within the princely clan by means of alliances via intra-princely marriage, such as the 1367 union between Dmitrii Donskoi of Moscow (r. 1359–89) and Evdokiia, the daughter of Dmitrii Konstantinovich of Tver. The role of these alliances, most of which translated to military assistance, created a set of blocs that saw the rise of a Northern Coalition, which would be tested at Kulikovo.[5] Throughout the 14th century Moscow pushed the boundaries of Mongol power, expanded into the western Chernigov region and the Oka river to the east, and neutralized opposition via a series of strategic alliances with its neighbors.[6] The disaggregation of the Golden Horde in the first half of the 15th century saw previous attempts to gain ascendency come to fruition in a power vacuum, during which Moscow was bolstered by a new trade corridor connecting it with Italian colonies on the Black Sea.[7]

---

4   There were several axes of trade crossing Rus, from Novgorod to the Black Sea (under Italian control), from Moscow and Tver to Sarai joining the "silk road" across the Caspian Sea to Central Asia and India, or south to the Ottoman Empire and Mamluk Egypt. See Janet Martin, *Medieval Russia, 980–1584* (Cambridge, UK: Cambridge University Press, 1995), pp. 225–27. On the expansion of settled territory, the "Life of St. Stefan of Perm" describes the emergence of Perm via the conversion of the Vychegda Permians to Christianity and the monastic colonization of the Vologda area. See Jukka Korpela, "Stefan von Perm': Heiliger Täufer im politischen Kontext," *Jahrbücher für Geschichte Osteuropas* 49 (2001): 481–99.

5   For example, Nizhny Novgorod was subordinated in 1392. See Nancy Shields Kollmann, "The Principalities of Rus' in the Fourteenth Century," in *The New Cambridge Medieval History*, ed. Michael Jones (Cambridge, UK: Cambridge University Press, 2000), pp. 764–94.

   The Northern Coalition included Suzdal, Nizhny Novgorod, Iaroslavl, Kostroma, and Beloozero; it defeated Khan Mamai at the battle of Kulikovo Field in 1380. On the battle, see Anton Anatolevich Gorskii, "K voprosu o sostave Russkogo voiska na Kulikovom Pole," *Drevniaia Rus': Voprosy medievistiki* 6 (2001): 1–9; Gorskii, *Moskva i Orda* (Moscow: Nauka, 2000), p. 214; and Kati Parppei, *The Battle of Kulikovo Refought: The First National Feat* (Leiden: Brill, 2017), pp. 19–26.

6   On the Mongol border, Khan Mamai formed a coalition against Moscow (which had been withholding tribute), and the two sides clashed in three sieges between 1368 and 1382; see Martin, *Medieval Russia*, pp. 233–39.

   The Grand Duchy of Lithuania joined Moscow in a marriage alliance when Sofia, the daughter of Vytautas, married the Grand Prince of Moscow, Vasilii I Dmitrievich (r. 1389–1425), in 1391; see Robert Frost, *The Oxford History of Poland-Lithuania*, vol. 1, *The Making of the Polish-Lithuanian Union, 1385–1569* (Oxford: Oxford University Press, 2015), p. 80; and Stephen Christopher Rowell, *Lithuania Ascending: A Pagan Empire within East-Central Europe, 1295–1345* (Cambridge, UK: Cambridge University Press, 1994), pp. 19–25.

7   Martin, *Medieval Russia*, pp. 358–63.

Discussions of the transfer of knowledge, political and cultural power, and imperial legitimacy from Constantinople to Moscow (the "Third Rome") have often failed to take into account the unique set of political and economic circumstances that concentrated military and economic power in the hands of the Muscovite princes.[8] In the 15th century, the politico-territorial entity known as the Moscow Grand Principality was just beginning to emerge. The reign of Ivan III (r. 1462–1502) reflected a political program that sought both to promote the Grand Principality internationally and to secure power at home.[9] Ivan III's cultural program, developed over his long reign, was aided by the extension of his international diplomacy, one result of which was his 1472 marriage to Zoe/Sofiia Palaiologina.[10] The marriage project with Zoe/Sofiia has been viewed by historians as the source for the appearance of a set of Byzantine cultural and political symbols and sources in Muscovy. However, when reading the chronicle account of Ivan III's long reign, one is struck by the single-mindedness and diplomatic tenacity of the prince, who cultivated support within the Church, in the court, and through diplomacy to promote his rule and to give prominence to Muscovy as a (re)emergent player on the international scene, rather than an arriviste principality hewn from within the Mongol superpower. Ivan III and his supporters within the court and the Church used whatever means at their disposal to cultivate an image of power that was both remote while comprehensible to those whom it was meant to impress, and ancient while entirely constructed from spoliated references, Byzantine or other. Whether in his diplomatic dealings or the ambitious building program in Moscow, Ivan III and his court actively sought to delineate the power of the prince and his entourage in that city and to demarcate the site of princely power via a built landscape meant to impress residents and visitors alike.[11] This newly formed (or rebuilt, in the case of the Dormition Cathedral)

---

8   On the "Third Rome" theory, see Marshall Poe, "Moscow, the Third Rome: The Origins and Transformations of a 'Pivotal Moment,'" *Jahrbücher für Geschichte Osteuropas* 49 (2001): 412–29; and Daniel Rowland, "Moscow—The Third Rome or the New Israel?" *Russian Review* 55, no. 4 (1996): 591–614.

9   See Nancy Shields Kollmann, *The Russian Empire 1450–1801* (Oxford: Oxford University Press, 2017), pp. 12–13.

10 On Zoe/Sofiia's arrival at the Muscovite court, see Silvia Ronchey, "Orthodoxy on Sale: The Last Byzantine, and the Lost Crusade," in *Proceedings of the 21st International Congress of Byzantine Studies (London 21–26 August 2006)*, ed. Elizabeth Jeffreys (Aldershot: Routledge, 2006), pp. 313–42. On the princess's life in the Muscovite court, see Paul Bushkovitch, "Sofia Palaiologina in Life and Legend," *Canadian-American Slavic Studies* 52 (2018): 158–80.

11 Moscow was not an original fortified town of "old Rus," it only appears in the sources in the mid-12th century. See Kollmann, *The Russian Empire*, pp. 141–44.

15th-century landscape provided the setting for what would become an elaborate ceremonial, orchestrated by the court and elevated by the Church.[12] Ceremonies of *adventus*, religious celebrations and feast days, and rituals of allegiance all benefited from a new histrionic setting, but none more so than the newly reconfigured ceremony of inauguration that deployed a remote set of references, real and invented, and brought the princely art of prestidigitation pageantry to the forefront of court ceremonial in Moscow.

1 The Rite of Inauguration of Dmitrii Ivanovich

The major ritual that has been attributed to the reign of Ivan III is the rite of inauguration developed for the especially performative enthronement/coronation of his grandson, Dmitrii Ivanovich (r. 1498–1502) in 1498.[13] The rite, which is described in several chronicles, includes an array of sources and reflects the concertation of the court and the Muscovite Church.[14] The study of

---

12   See Michael Flier, "Political Ideas and Ritual," in *Cambridge History of Russia*, vol. 1, *From Early Rus' to 1689*, ed. Maureen Perrie (Cambridge, UK: Cambridge University Press, 2006), pp. 387–408.

13   I have reproduced the text from the Patriarchal/Nikon's Chronicle, with a translation, at the end of this chapter.

14   For the chronicle, see *Polnoe sobranie russkikh letopisei*, vol. 12 (Moscow: Izd. vostochnoi literatury, 1901/2000), pp. 246–48 (Patriarchal/Nikon Chronicle). The series title is hereafter abbreviated as PSRL. The text from the Nikon Chronicle (probably the oldest extant redaction, from the 1520s) is reproduced in several other chronicles, both in its long form (e.g., Voskressenskii Chronicle: PSRL 8 (1901/2001), pp. 234–36) and in a shorter form (e.g., Russkii Khronograf: PSRL 22, part 2 (1914/2005), pp. 512–13). The shorter form (reproduced below as the "First Account") may have been taken from an earlier chronicle, as George Majeska discusses in "The Moscow Coronation of 1498 Reconsidered," *Jahrbücher für Geschichte Osteuropas* 26, no. 3 (1978): 353–61, 360–61.

Nikon's Chronicle is compilatory in character and quite lengthy. Globally, for the late 15th century, there is a shared account for the Nikonian, Patriarchal, and Voskressenskii chronicles. The narrative is shared until about 1520. However, already for the account of events in the late 15th-century, there are variations, including which events are related and how information is shaped and conveyed, which will be discussed further on. As with previous chronicles, Nikon's Chronicle interpolates a variety of sources (including other chronicles) and types of narrative, and its manuscript tradition dates to later than the period in which it was compiled. On textology, see Iakov Solomonovich Lur'e, "Iz istorii russkogo letopisaniia kontsa XV veka," *Akademiia Nauk SSSR, TODRL* 11 (1955): pp. 156–86, 180–86; Boris Mikhailovich Kloss, *Nikonovskii svod i russkie letopisi XVI–XVII vekov* (Moscow: Nauka, 1980), pp. 190–95; and Iakov Solomonovich Lur'e, "Genealogicheskaia schema leteopisei XI–XVI vv.," *Akademiia Nauk SSSR, TODRL* 40 (1985): pp. 190–205, esp. 193–96. On the relationship between chronicle textology and the rite of enthronement of Dmitrii Ivanovich, see Majeska, "The Moscow Coronation of 1498 Reconsidered," 356.

the 1498 rite of enthronement has displayed the common tension in the study of ritual, that between particularism and generalization.[15] From this perspective, the 1498 rite of inauguration can be viewed as a composite entity, featuring a series of highly specific ritual elements (the cap of Monomakh, singing, interpolated scripts, and so forth), and as a snapshot, one element of an overall recuperation of Byzantine court culture.[16] Exploring court practices from this angle upholds the commonly held notion that most advances in the formation of Muscovite (and Russian) culture and representation were mainly derivative and delayed, new to Muscovy, but old elsewhere, overlooking the spontaneous power of ritual to structure political life, to signal social change, and to invent tradition.[17] Furthermore, the pageantry and display of collective effervescence during the ceremony must be read against the surrounding events, all of which suggest court conflict and contestation of Ivan III's rule. Thus, the ceremony of 1498 mobilized Byzantine notions of cosmic order and transcendental hierarchy, featuring new symbols of power, while masking conflict and the actual workings of the Muscovite court.

---

15   See David Cannadine and Simon Price, eds., *Rituals of Royalty Power and Ceremonial in Traditional Societies* (Cambridge, UK: Cambridge University Press, 1987), pp. 1–12.

16   The inauguration of Ivan III has often been evoked as a step in Muscovy/Russia's path to "autocracy," a specter of "oriental despotism" that drew its sources from Byzantine (sometimes Mongol) sources. This framing is very much an artifact of the nineteenth and twentieth centuries, hence the tendency toward generalizations about Muscovite political culture. See Alef, *The Origins of Muscovite Autocracy*, pp. 55–95, esp. 90–91; and Konstantin Vasilievich Bazilevich, *Vneshniaia politika russkogo tsentralizovannogo gosudarstva: Vtoraia polovina XV veka* (Moscow: Moscow University Press, 1952), pp. 72–88. More recently, studies of Muscovy and early modern Russia have taken a comparative approach to situate Muscovy within the paradigms of the formation of early modern empires, while also looking at the local circumstances governing the emergence of Muscovy, i.e., Mongol suzerainty. For the former, see Kollmann, *The Russian Empire*, pp. 2–7 (for a discussion of "oriental despotism"), pp. 130–35. For the latter, see Donald Ostrowski, "The Mongol Origins of Muscovite Political Institutions," *Slavic Review* 49, no. 4 (1990): 525–42; on trends in Muscovite "state-building" historiography, see Valerie Kivelson, "Culture and Politics, or the Curious Absence of Muscovite State Building in Current American Historical Writing," *Cahiers du Monde russe* 46, no. 1–2 (2005): 19–28.

17   The inauguration of Dmitrii Ivanovich should be seen as an "invented tradition" according to Eric Hobsbawm's parameters: "It includes both 'traditions' actually invented, constructed and formally instituted and those emerging in a less easily traceable manner within a brief and dateable period—a few years perhaps—and establishing themselves with great rapidity ... 'Invented tradition' is taken to mean a set of practices, normally governed by overtly or tacitly accepted rules and of a ritual or symbolic nature, which seek to inculcate certain values and norms of behaviour by repetition, which automatically implies continuity with the past." Eric Hobsbawn and Terrence Ranger, eds., *The Invention of Tradition* (Cambridge, UK: Cambridge University Press, 1983), p. 1.

The coronation of Dmitrii Ivanovich by his grandfather was an innovation in very real terms: it was the first event of its kind recorded in the chronicles of Rus/Muscovy to deploy this particular set of mixed symbols, accoutrements, choreographed movements, and dialogue.[18] However, it can be characterized neither as an outlier nor as the ultimate evolution of the Rus ceremony of inauguration, as most ceremonies of inauguration respond more to immediate political demands and circumstances than to ritual requirements.[19] The princely elite adopted certain rituals for its inauguration ceremonies; however, none of the attendant elements (such as enthronement on the princely seat) determined the success or failure of a ceremony.[20] Rather, the ceremony, whether grandiose or humble, rendered a *de facto* situation *de jure*. Thus, in the case of Ivan III, the ceremonial of investiture deployed for his grandson can be read as a manifestation of his ability to rule and impose his candidate on the throne in Moscow. The deployment of ceremonial was an effect, an externalization of his puissance, but it was no substitute for the concurrence of good economic and political fortunes, which represented the real basis of his authority over the court.

George Majeska portrayed the schema of a Kievan enthronement, in comparison with that of Dmitrii Ivanovich in 1498, thusly: "Prince (or Grand Prince)

---

18   Previous inaugurations, beginning in the 10th century, featured several ritual mainstays (including enthronement), but were relatively disparate and included a variety of rituals; for a chronological overview, see Fedir Androshchuk, "K istorii obriada intronizatsii drevnerusskikh kniazei ('sidenie na kurganakh')," in *Druzhnni starozhitnosti tsentral'no-skhidnoi Evropi VIII–X st. Materiali Mizhnarodnogo pol'ovogo arkheologichnogo seminaru* (Chernihiv: Siverians'ka dumka, 2003), pp. 5–10; Alexandra Vukovich, "Enthronement in Early Rus: Between Byzantium and Scandinavia," *Viking and Medieval Scandinavia* 14 (2018): 211–39; Vukovich, "The Enthronement Rituals of the Princes of Vladimir-Suzdal in the 12th and 13th Centuries," *FORUM University of Edinburgh Journal of Culture and the Arts* 17 (2013): 1–15; and Vukovich, "Le Prince et son épée dans le Rous' du Nord à la suite de l'exil byzantin de Vsévolod Iourevich," in *Byzance et ses voisins*, ed. Élisabeth Yota (Bern: Peter Lang, 2020), forthcoming.

19   For example, the 1206 enthronement of Konstantin Vsevolodich in Novgorod is especially elaborate compared with other medieval princely enthronements. Prince Konstantin is enthroned by his father, Prince Vsevolod Iurevich of Vladimir, and the ceremony includes biblical exegesis, the participation of the full clergy and people of Novgorod bearing crosses and standards, a focus on the princely sword (which I have posited as a Byzantine-inspired innovation), and enthronement at the Novgorod church of St. Sophia. See Vukovich, "Le Prince et son épée"; and Dvornik, "Byzantine Political Ideas in Kievan Russia," pp. 118–21.

20   See Oleksiy Petrovich Tolochko, *Kniaz' v drevnei Rusi: Vlast, sobstvennost, ideologiia* (Kiev: Naukova dumka, 1992), pp. 35–67, 127–50. For the overall ideological basis of the ceremony within the context of medieval Rus, see Igor Sergeevich Chichurov, *Politicheskaia ideologiia srednevekov'ia Vizantiia i Rus* (Moscow: History Institute SSSR, 1990).

blank came to *blank* and sat (*sede*) on the throne of his forefathers."[21] Though not as pithy as Majeska claims, the enthronement ceremonies of early Rus received none of the *ordines* or theoretical exegeses that defined analogous ceremonies in Byzantium, the Latin kingdoms, and, later on, Muscovy.[22] In general, the chronicles of Rus include consistent details about ceremonies of inauguration through enthronements at the church of St. Sophia in Kiev or at analogous churches in other polities, a ritual that is absent in the 1498 inauguration ceremony. Enthronements in Rus designated new princes and invested them with seniority (in the case of sole rule) or higher status (in the case of co-rule with a senior prince). Representations of Church prelates, monks, notables, lay people, and foreign dignitaries as participants and witnesses to the enthronements of certain princes of Rus suggest that the authors or compilers of the chronicles of Rus were concerned with the externalization of symbols of authority both to demonstrate hierarchy within the dynasty and to distance members of the dynasty from others.[23] Although there does appear to have been a steady evolution in the ceremonial of investiture, particularly in the northeast of Rus with the 1206 investiture of Konstantin Vsevolodich by his father in Novgorod representing a point of departure, information (or lack thereof) about the ceremonial of investiture varies from prince to prince, depending on context (of both the event and its depiction) and, most likely, the conservation of source material.[24] The enthronement of Dmitrii Ivanovich, as described in chronicle accounts, represents a real ceremonial innovation, especially compared to that of Ivan III himself, described as part of the testament of Vasilii II and stating simply that he ascended the throne, without further detail.[25]

The narrative about the coronation of Dmitrii Ivanovich at the Dormition Cathedral of the Kremlin (Fig. 2.1) described in the Patriarchal/Nikon Chronicle can be broken down into approximately ten parts:

1. [First Account] Assembly of the clergy of all of Rus and the laying out of vestments, the cap (of Monomakh) and *barmy* (Figs. 2.2–2.4), and seats on a platform

---

21 Majeska, "The Moscow Coronation of 1498 Reconsidered," p. 355.
22 See Janet Nelson, "Symbols in Context: Rulers' Inauguration Rituals in Byzantium and the West," in *Politics and Ritual in Early Medieval Europe* (London: Bloomsbury Publishing, 1986), pp. 259–83.
23 On the process of "role distancing" to create elite group identity, see Pierre Bourdieu, *La Distinction: Critique sociale du jugement* (Paris: Éditions de Minuit, 1979), pp. 1–23.
24 For the 1206 investiture, see PSRL 1 (1962/2001), cols. 421–24.
25 PSRL 12 (1901/2000), p. 115; PSRL 8 (1901/2001), p. 150.

FIGURE 2.1 Cathedral of the Dormition, Kremlin, Moscow, 1479
PHOTOGRAPH BY ALEXANDRA VUKOVICH

II. Arrival of the princes wherein Dmitrii Ivanovich is thrice showered with gold and silver coins[26]
III. [Second Account] Assembly at the Dormition Cathedral with singing; the Metropolitan, Ivan III, and Dmitrii Ivanovich assemble on a platform before the clergy, boyars, and other spectators
IV. Ivan III's speech in which he mentions primogeniture[27]

---

26 George Majeska suggested that this was possibly a misinterpretation of the distribution of largesse following the coronation of Emperor Manuel II in 1392 wherein the emperor is "showered with *staurata*/small silver coins." Ignatius of Smolensk, 'The Journey of Ignatius of Smolensk' in George Majeska, ed. and trans., *Russian Travelers to Constantinople in the Fourteenth and Fifteenth Centuries* (Washington, DC: Dumbarton Oaks Studies, 1984), pp. 76–113.

27 *PSRL* 12 (1901/2000), p. 246: "отци наши великие князи сыномъ своимъ первымъ давали великое княжство" (Our forefathers, the Grand Princes, would give the Great Principality to their firstborn son). The "tradition of primogeniture" finds its first clear articulation in this passage and continued to be contested well into the 16th century; see Sergei Bogatyrev, "Reinventing the Russian Monarchy in the 1550s: Ivan the Terrible, the Dynasty, and the Church," *Slavonic and East European Review* 85, no. 2 (2007): 271–93, 283.

FIGURE 2.2 Crown attributed to Monomakh, The Moscow Kremlin State Historical and Cultural Museum and Heritage Site
PHOTOGRAPH BY S. V. BARANOV

v. Metropolitan's blessing and prayer featuring veterotestamentary examples and common topoi about kingship[28]
vi. Ivan III vests his grandson with *barmy* and the cap of Monomakh while the Metropolitan prays
vii. Litanies
viii. Metropolitan's speech featuring an injunction for princes to care for "all Orthodox Christians"
ix. Liturgy

---

28   Including elements from: Math. 25:4, 35, 36, 40; Ps. 111–112:5; Ps. 40–41:1, 2; and II Cor. 9:6.

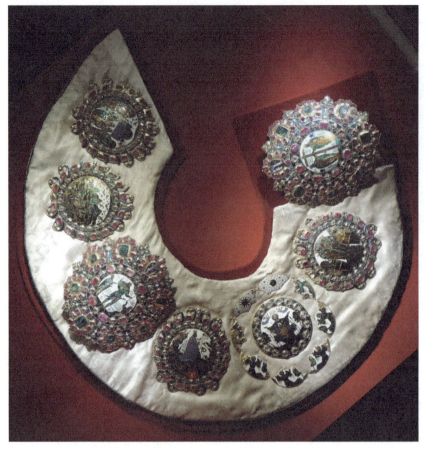

FIGURE 2.3 Barmy attributed to Aleksei Mikhailovich
PHOTOGRAPH PROVIDED BY WIKIMEDIA COMMONS / SHAKKO

x. Ivan III and "Grand Prince" Dmitrii Ivanovich are again showered with gold and silver coins

The ceremony of investiture is composed of several elements that interpolate past and present features of the symbolic landscape of Rus. The constitutional significance of enthronement and acclamation in a particular church remains in the first account and is included in the Patriarchal/Nikon Chronicle, but is superseded by new regalia and endorsement by the Metropolitan of Rus.[29] Far from Wortman's assertion of "foreignness" for these ritual developments,

---

29   Note that this particular church, the Moscow Dormition Cathedral, was one of Ivan III's foundations, heavily rebuilt during his reign, and with input from the Italian architects Ivan III invited to his court.

FIGURE 2.4 Portrait of Tsar Aleksei Mikhailovich Romanov (1629–76),
The State Hermitage Museum, St. Petersburg
PHOTOGRAPH BY VLADIMIR TEREBENIN, PROVIDED BY
THE STATE HERMITAGE MUSEUM

the overall ceremony reflects a composite reconstruction of past events and artifacts, reordered and enhanced to promote Ivan III's current political needs and program.[30] This reconstruction of the past becomes especially salient in

30   Richard Wortman, *Scenarios of Power: Myth and Ceremony in Russian Monarchy from Peter the Great to the Death of Nicholas I*, vol. 1 (Princeton: Princeton University Press, 1995), p. 6:

Muscovite chronicles, which reflect new ideological programs, including linearity of descent for Rus (as with Ivan III's historicization of primogeniture as a traditional feature of princely succession) or the mythic regalia of the Muscovite princes.[31]

The regalia featured in the ceremony has received the most attention due to its emphatically constructed and Byzantinized elements. The *barmy* (of Monomakh) and cap (of Monomakh) appear here in their inchoate forms. Both pieces descend from the "Legend of Monomakh," comprising a long tradition of items of "ancient" Byzantine regalia that were transferred to early Rus for princely coronations.[32] According to the legend, Vladimir Monomakh (r. 1113–25 in Kiev) received imperial regalia from the Emperor Constantine IX Monomachos (r. 1042–55), his supposed grandfather, as a diplomatic gift. The regalia of Monomakh included the "life-giving cross," a pectoral cross with a piece of the wood from the cross of the Crucifixion; the *barmy*, a counterpart to the Byzantine emperors' shoulder pieces; and the crown, "Monomakh's cap" (*shapka Monomakha*), which was very likely of Tatar origin.[33] The earliest

---

"The princes of Moscow who consolidated power over a unified Russian state in the 15th and 16th centuries understood sovereignty in terms of foreign images. Their forebears had looked to the Byzantine emperor and the Mongol khan as sovereign ... The expansion of empire confirmed the image of supreme power and justified the unlimited authority of the Russian emperors. The religious, eschatological element enhanced their moral dominion." Wortman's substantial work on Russian ceremony features generalizations about early Rus and Muscovite "customs" and "traditions," which are largely constructs of the early modern period.

31 An example of the new Muscovite historiography is the *Book of Degrees* (Stepennaia Kniga), see Nikolai Nikolaevich Pokrovskii and Gail Lenhoff, eds., *Stepennaia kniga tsarskogo rodosloviia po drevneishim spiskam. Teksty i kommentarii v trekh tomakh* (Moscow: Iazyki slavianskikh kul'tur, 2007–12). Piotr Stefanovich has recently explored the Muscovite construction of the Christianization of Rus as a "national event" and the favoring of a Varangian descent for Rus (Voskressenskii Chronicle); see Stefanovich, "Kreshchenie Rusi v istoricheskhikh sochineniiakh XVI–XVII vv.," in *Narrativy Rusi kontsa XV–serediny XVIII vv.: V poiskakh svoei istorii*, ed. Andrei Doronin (Moscow: Politicheskaia entsiklopediia, 2017), pp. 80–102; and Stefanovich, "Legenda o prizvanii Variagov v istorografii XVI–XVII vv.: Ot srednevekovykh mifov k rannemodernym," in *Dreviaia Rus' posle Drevnei Rusi: Diskurs vostrochnoslavianskogo (ne)edinstva*, ed. Andrei Doronin (Moscow: Politicheskaia entsiklopediia, 2017), pp. 326–44.

32 It should be noted that coronation was not part of the inauguration rituals of early Rus; see note 16.

33 The bibliography on the regalia of Monomakh is substantial. For a general outline, see Sergei Bogatyrev, "Shapka Monomakha i shlem naslednika: Reprezentatsiia vlasti i dinasticheskaia politika pri Vasilii III i Ivane Groznom," *Studia Slavica et Balcanica Petropolitana* 1 (2011): 171–200; Bogatyrev, "Eshche raz o shapke Monomakha i kazne moskovskikh kniazei," *Studia Slavica et Balcanica Petropolitana* 2 (2011): 251–54; Guzel' Fuadovna Valeeva-Suleimanova, "Shapka Monomakha—Imperskii symbol tatarskogo

mention of it is from 1341, in the "Testament of Ivan Kalita," where it is called the *shapka zolotaia* (golden crown). It continues to be mentioned as the golden crown in the testaments of Ivan II, Dmitrii Donskoi, Vasilii I, and Vasilii II.[34] Information about the regalia is sparse and appears intermittently in the chronicles; for example, the cap and *barmy* are mentioned at the investiture of Dmitrii Ivanovich, but not at that of his grandfather, and it is unclear, based on chronicle accounts, whether they should be attributed to Monomakh or not. The chronicle traditions for the investiture account do not agree on the Monomakh attribution, whereas they overlap otherwise. The designation of "Monomakh's cap" in the Patriarchal/Nikon Chronicle or "Monomakh's *barmy*" in the Voskressenskii Chronicle could be 16th-century projections onto the past, to strengthen historical claims about the regalia.[35] In effect, the most

---

proiskhozhdeniia," in *Zolotoordynskaia tsivilizatsiia*, ed. Il'nur Midkhatovich Murzaleev (Kazan: Institut istorii, 2008), pp. 22–29; and Ostrowski, *Muscovy and the Mongols*, pp. 174–76.

34 See Ostrowski, *Muscovy and the Mongols*, p. 175.

35 Majeska discusses the ideology of 16th-century chronicles and argues against a later attribution, in "The Moscow Coronation of 1498 Reconsidered," pp. 360–61. Although some scholars (Lur'e and Zimin) accepted the "cap of Monomakh" reading as older, the disparate attributions of the vestments "of Monomakh" and their absence in previous enthronements, as well as in the first version of Dimitrii Ivanovich's enthronement, suggest a later interpolation for the first account. On the relative relationships between the chronicles and their later emendation for specific political ends, see Aleksandr Aleksandrovich Zimin, *Russkie letopisi i khronografy kontsa XV–XVI vv.* (Moscow: MGIAI, 1960), 6–9. Lur'e describes this transitional period between the reigns of Ivan III (d. 1505) and Vasilii III (d. 1533) as a time of "fierce political struggle" that is reflected in the chronological boundaries of late 15th-century codices. In Lur'e's view there was a "re-working" of chronicles under Vasilii III with a possible emendation of Vasilii's removal from the line of succession and Ivan III's promotion of his grandson, Dmitrii. However, the shaping of information about the beginning of the reign of Dmitrii Ivanovich appears to have either remained unaffected (after all, Vasilii's place was restored and preserving the semblance of normalcy may have superseded the settling of scores) or may be a later interpolation to cohere the narrative of succession. As Lur'e saw it, the narrative of the rehabilitation of Vasilii, beginning in 1499, suggests that an editorial event took place during his reign. Therefore, it is curious that the chronicler kept (or inserted) both version(s) of Dmitrii Ivanovich's enthronement, affording him additional legitimacy, while at the same time shaping a narrative that downplayed the court conflict that led to Sofiia and Vasilii's disgrace and distancing from the court and line of succession. Lur'e saw this as a form of engaged (or journalistic/ публицистические) authorship that becomes obvious in the treatment of information about the restoration of Vasilii around 1500–5 that reworked information about his disgrace without suppressing it entirely. Due to the ambivalent and dismissive view taken by the recension/свод of 1539 of Dmitrii Ivanovich, Lur'e concluded that any positive readings of the former and negative readings of Vasilii Ivanovich had to be the result of a late 15th-century redaction completed under Ivan III. Therefore, it is possible that the amplified reading of the enthronement of Dmitrii Ivanovich (mentioning the crown of Monomakh, etc.) was part of a late 15th-century redaction that has

substantial information about the regalia, including its provenance, only appears in the first half of the 16th century in the *Skazanie o kniaz'iakh vladimirskikh* (Tale of the Princes of Vladimir).[36] The *Skazanie* connected Muscovy to a double Roman and Hellenic heritage via early Rus and asserted that the Muscovite princes received their authority from Byzantine emperors and that they also descended from the family of Augustus Caesar. Proof of this Byzantine provenance included the "ancient" regalia of the grand princes. However, *shapka Monomakha* (cap of Monomakh) is obviously of Central Asian manufacture and most likely had no connection with Constantine Monomachos or Vladimir Monomakh, even if it already existed (in whatever form) prior to the period of Mongol suzerainty. It is difficult to state with certainty whether the attribution to Monomakh predates the appearance of the *Skazanie*, and it is possible that the *Skazanie* only provided documentary evidence for what had become a commonly acknowledged provenance for the regalia in courtly circles.

The role of the Church in the promulgation of this tale was twofold: in the recording of the tale to provide textual evidence and in the sourcing of analogous texts, throughout the 16th century, to multiply the sites of legitimacy. In the 16th century, the cap is mentioned as the "crown of Monomakh" in the Epiphany Ritual of 1558; it appears in the testament of Ivan IV the Terrible; it featured on the murals on the ceiling of the Throne Room in the Kremlin's *Zolotaia palata* (Golden Palace), which depict the transfer of the regalia;[37] and the regalia are further depicted on the tsar's throne (which becomes the "throne of Monomakh") in the Kremlin's Dormition Cathedral.[38] From this perspective, the investiture of 1498 fits in with a set of nodal points of the

---

come down to us. See Lur'e, "Iz istorii russkogo letopisaniia kontsa XV veka," pp. 180–86. On the succession crisis, see John V.A. Fine, "The Muscovite Dynastic Crisis of 1497–1502," *Canadian Slavonic Papers/Revue canadienne des slavistes* 8 (1966): 198–215.

36 For discussion of the *Skazanie*'s date of composition, see Ostrowski, *Muscovy and the Mongols*, pp. 170–78, who writes: "This complex of texts plays fast and loose with historical accuracy and is unconcerned with chronological impossibilities" (p. 171). See also David Miller, "Once Again about the Dating and Provenance of the *Skazanie o Kniaz'iakh Vladimirskikh*," *Russian History/Histoire Russe* 25, no. 1–2 (1998): 65–77.

37 See Ekaterina Boltunova, "Imperial Throne Halls and Discourse of Power in the Topography of Early Modern Russia (Late 17th–18th Centuries)," in *Palaces from Augustus to the Age of Absolutism*, ed. Michael Featherstone et al. (Berlin: De Gruyter, 2015), pp. 341–53, 341; and Daniel Rowland, "Architecture, Image, and Ritual in the Throne Rooms of Muscovy, 1550–1650: A Preliminary Survey," in *Rude and Barbarous Kingdom Revisited: Essays in Russian History and Culture in Honor of Robert O. Crummey*, ed. Chester Dunning, Russell Martin, and Rowland (Bloomington: Slavica Publishers, 2008), pp. 53–71.

38 See Michael Flier, "The Throne of Monomakh: Ivan the Terrible and the Architectonics of Destiny," in *Architectures of Russian Identity: 1500 to Present*, ed. James Cracraft and Daniel Rowland (Ithaca: Cornell University Press, 2003), pp. 21–33.

cooperation between the Church and court, resulting in the reshaping of information about the past. The appropriation of Byzantine symbols in Muscovy went hand in hand with the transformation (Byzantinization) of texts and artifacts of local manufacture.

The symbiotic relationship between tsar and Church reflected the late Byzantine concept of the "symphony" between secular and ecclesiastical spheres, as elaborated in the Byzantine book of canons, *Kormchaia Kniga*.[39] The rhetorical complementarity between ruler and prelate is conveyed in the "speeches" of Ivan III and the Metropolitan (see below), in which the Grand Prince begins the proceedings by expounding on the patrilineal nature of princely rule in Muscovy, the Grand Prince's authority to invest his chosen heir, and the extent of his patrimony. After the Grand Prince lays out the parameters for rule over Muscovy, the Metropolitan elevates princely rule, investing it with a sacred and eternal character by invoking veterotestamentary kingship in the form of King David, with Ivan III compared to King Saul. The ensuing exposition of a ruler's duties includes the *topoi* of the ruler as justiciar, defender of Orthodoxy, and protector of the meek. The evocations of anointment with myrrh, of a "crown from the stone of honor," and of the "scepter of Tsardom" are all rhetorical amplifications copied from the source text, and the Metropolitan's speech is followed by the vesting of the prince with the *barmy* and princely cap. All of the *topoi* are standard for a ceremony of investiture. However, the modalities of rule conveyed by the ceremony (primogeniture, concentration of authorities, subordination to the primacy of Moscow) all point to a moment of state (re)formation and elite consciousness, an incipient Mucovite hegemony.

Efforts to realize the imperial vision of Ivan III and, more ostentatiously, of Ivan IV included the adoption of new and foreign symbols in the articulation of princely power. The investiture account, while featuring clear examples of Byzantine *realia*,[40] deploys them as befits local requirements and understanding. The most obvious example is the showering of the newly inaugurated ruler with gold and silver coins, which happens six times on two occasions, before and after the ceremony of investiture. As mentioned above, this mostly likely occurred in imitation of Ignatius of Smolensk's mistaken impression of the

---

39 Dvornik made the connection between chronicle texts and texts like the *Kormchaia Kniga*, which functioned as normative texts to represent rulership: see Dvornik, "Byzantine Political Ideas in Kievan Russia," pp. 89–94.
40 In reference to real Byzantine artifacts. What was manufactured in Muscovy was both an approximation of real objects and also an innovation according to local ideas of how a ruler/rulership should look.

symbolic largesse thrown to the people of Constantinople to celebrate the imperial coronation of Manuel II in 1392.[41]

2 Byzantine Antiquities, Real and Invented

The most persuasive argument for Byzantine *realia* appears in the articulation of the second account of the ceremony of investiture. In this account, the ceremony follows on from *rituals* contained in a 15th-century manuscript known as the "Synodal Ritual," with the addition of elements not mentioned in Byzantine texts.[42] The chronicle text differs from the "Synodal Ritual" (as

---

41 See Majeska, *Russian Travelers to Constantinople*, pp. 111–13; and Stephen Reinert, "Political Dimensions of Manuel II Palaiologos' 1392 Marriage and Coronation," in *Novum Millennium: Studies on Byzantine History and Culture Dedicated to Paul Speck*, ed. Claudia Sode and Sarlota Takacs (Aldershot: Ashgate, 2001), pp. 291–302, 291. However, this might not necessarily have been the case, since the account book of the Genoese colony in Pera, recounting the arrival of Manuel II's bride just days before the ceremony, indicates that the *podestà*, Leonardo de Rosio, and his entourage attended the arrival of the bride and showered her with gold coins. It is entirely possible that Ignatius of Smolensk could have witnessed this event as well as the coronation and mixed up the two coin-throwing spectacles.

42 Barsov reproduces an ideal text for the ceremony based on both ceremonial books (*trebniki*) and chronicle accounts. However, the general elements (reproduced below) are consistent in all of the accounts. See Elpidifor Vasilievich Barsov, *Drevnerusskie pamiatniki sviashchennogo venchaniia tsarei na tsarstvo* (Moscow: Imperial University Press, 1883), pp. 32–38. The original manuscript is held at the Trinity Lavra of St. Sergius in Russia, MS 304.I. Служебник и Требник (1474).

The attribution of the *rituals* to medieval Serbia may be overdetermined and deserves separate research. There is definite evidence for the transmission and interpolation of South Slavonic sources, about the Nemanjid Dynasty, in 15th- and 16th-century chronicles (the *Litsevoi Svod* contains a life of Stefan Nemanja, d. 1199), but there are consistent mentions of ceremonies of inauguration in medieval South Slavonic literature. The ceremonies of enthronement of the Nemanjid kings were developed from the time of the earliest Nemanjids, and the description of regalia in the transfer of power from Stefan Nemanja to his son Stefan Prvovenčani (the first-crowned) includes a crown that was sent from Rome and placed on his head by an papal legate, or a locally sourced (or papal, depending on the account) crown that was placed on his head by St. Sava. Enthronement at one of the religious foundations of the Nemanjids is a further ceremonial feature described in a similar way to those of early Rus princes, e.g., "и по благословенїю светааго Сїмеона прѣдрьже ѿ оу ѥмоу прѣстолъ дѣдинь и отьчинь" (and with the blessing of holy Simeon he took over the throne of his father and grandfather from him), in Domentijan's *Life of SS Simeon and Sava*; see Aleksandar Solovjev, "Pojam države u srednjovekovnoj Srbiji," *Godišnjica Nikole Ćupića* 42 (1933): 123. Compare with the 1176 account of Mikhailko Iurevich: "и седе на столе деда своего и отца своего" (and he sat upon the throne of his forefathers and his father), *PSRL* 2, col. 602. See Smilja

published by Barsov) in ways already outlined by Majeska.[43] Moreover, the text of the Patriarchal/Nikon Chronicle is a departure from what has been posited as its prototype, the coronation of Manuel II in 1392, described by Ignatius of Smolensk who traveled to Constantinople in 1389–92.[44] The coronation of Manuel is described in a Byzantine source referred to as the "Anonymous Tract" and found in a 15th-century compendium.[45] This source roughly depicts what Ignatius of Smolensk noted, with the addition of specific prayers, which suggests that it was influenced by a liturgical source (perhaps Byzantine *ordines*

Marjanović-Dušanić and Sima Ćirković, *Vladarske insignije i državna simbolika u Srbiji od XIII do XV veka* (Belgrade: Serbian Academy, 1994), pp. 23–37; and Jovanka Kalić, "Pretece Žice: Krunidbena mesta Srpskikh vladara," *Istorijski Časopis* 44 (1997): 77–87.

However, despite the basic similarities of the inaugurations, for the 1498 enthronement in Moscow, it is the potential overlap between medieval Serbian *ordines*, sermons, and prayers for investiture that is most intriguing. These *ordines* are not interpolated into medieval Serbian hagio-biographies and are preserved separately (Marjanović-Dušanić, 36). The *ordines/službe* (much like the princely hagio-biographies) contain disquisitions on the nature of princely rule as representative of the heavenly kingdom and hierarchy on earth and its symphony with the Church. It would need to be further studied whether the sermons/prayers of the 1498 enthronement are interpolated (i.e., feature intertextual elements) from a medieval Serbian source, or if there is merely thematic overlap.

43 Majeska, "The Moscow Coronation," p. 361. Here, Majeska was careful in delineating the differences found in 16th-century chronicle narratives that reflect the notion of princely autocracy, a departure from 15th-century practice. I am not entirely convinced that a purely "ideological" approach can dispel inconsistencies in the manuscript tradition for this passage. As I have pointed to above, the regalia, separate rituals, and discourse of investiture based on ancestry are all close enough to previous accounts. Furthermore, the attribution of already-known regalia to Monomakh may well be a 15th-century development that came to full fruition in the first half of the 16th century, so only about twenty to forty years after the 1498 inauguration account. Moreover, it should be noted that the first and second accounts are not mutually exclusive and, in the case of the Patriarchal/Nikon Chronicle, complement each other well, which is perhaps why both accounts were kept: one as the bare bones, a typical chronicle-style account of the ceremony; the second, a rite and an interpolation from another source, supplying the content for a future restaging.

44 The Byzantine ceremony for 1392 contains both of the wedding rituals for the marriage between Jelena Dragaš (the grand-niece of Tsar Stefan Dušan) and Manuel II Palaiologos. The marriage alliance and the conclusion of a pact with Sultan Bayezid I were attempts to thwart his nephew's ambitions to take Constantinople. Reinert writes, "Placing Manuel's marriage and the ensuing coronations against these background developments, scholars have surmised that their underlying logic entailed not only conformity with tradition, but at least some degree of political calculation" (the same could be written for Ivan III). Reinert, "Political Dimensions," p. 292.

45 See Peter Schreiner, "Hochzeit und Krönung Kaiser Manuels II. im Jahre 1392," *Byzantinische Zeitschrift* 60, no. 1 (1967): 70–85, 76–79.

that no longer exist) interpolated by the author, who may have been a member of the clergy at St. Sophia.[46]

A disambiguation of the source overlap, in terms of both interpolation and inspiration, demonstrates the scale of the problem. The narrative of the investiture of 1498 is loosely based on a Byzantine ceremony of investiture from 1392 that exists in both a Byzantine text (very likely unknown in Muscovy) and an eyewitness Slavonic version that was known in the 15th century. The eyewitness text for the Byzantine ceremony is not interpolated into the investiture of 1498 but inspires it. However, there are intertextual elements in the form of the Byzantine-style sermon of investiture pronounced by the Metropolitan. This sermon has been attributed to a Byzantine source, perhaps via medieval Serbian *rites*. However, there is no consensus or definitive proof that this is the case, and it is further possible that, as with the eyewitness text for the Byzantine ceremony, it may be a question of inspiration and interpretation rather than intertextuality. The ceremonial overlap between Byzantine practice, as recorded by a Rus traveller, and the 1498 investiture is undeniable, but it should not be overdetermined.

The link between the 1498 ceremony of investiture in Moscow and the 1392 Byzantine ceremony has repeatedly been made, largely because the text of the Byzantine coronation rite was available in Rus.[47] However, looking more closely at the content of the Byzantine ceremony, it becomes clear that it is not a template for the 1498 rite of investiture, rather, that particular elements from the Byzantine ceremony and the order of proceedings are loosely borrowed. The 1498 ceremony includes the following elements from the Byzantine ceremony described by Ignatius of Smolensk:[48]

- the arranging of congregants ahead of the proceedings
- the singing of hymns at the commencement of the ceremony
- the presence of two thrones on a platform (note that the platform in the Byzantine ceremony is located in a separate chamber, the *metatorion*)
- the patriarch vests the emperor on the *ambo* before the thrones (note that unlike in the 1498 ceremony, the patriarch does not have a throne), giving

---

46 Ibid., 76.
47 On the manuscript transmission of Ignatius of Smolensk's account, see Majeska, "Russian Travelers," pp. 67–73.
48 Majeska, "Russian Travellers," pp. 105–13. There are several points of divergence between Ignatius of Smolensk's report and Byzantine sources, including the 'Anonymous Tract,' and Byzantine accounts also diverge from each other.

him a cross and placing the crown on his head (in the 1498 investiture, it is the Grand Prince who does this)[49]
- the liturgy is celebrated, and the emperor is showered with gold coins

The overlapping elements are fairly schematic, and even in terms of language, the 1498 account does not appear to interpolate any significant portion of Ignatius of Smolensk's report. Furthermore, the most significant interpolation appears to be the text of a prayer attributed to the Constantinopolitan coronation and preserved in the chronicle account of Ignatius of Smolensk's journey, which is not mentioned in any known Byzantine source.[50] And yet, this sermon is the only clearly interpolated element attributed to the 1392 coronation of Manuel II and is preserved in the *rites* for Muscovite inauguration ceremonies.[51] Thus, it appears that the most often reproduced Byzantine artifact preserved from Ignatius of Smolensk's account of Manuel II's coronation was created by churchmen in Rus/Muscovy.[52]

3   Conclusion

Ceremonies of inauguration, whether in Constantinople or in Moscow, were usually very public affairs, meant to advertise the new ruler and fashion consensus. These ceremonies had to be both familiar and remote, and their performance had to be practicable within the built landscape. The 1498 ceremony in Moscow mixed both well-known rituals and new idioms for the expression of power, it featured invented traditions and ancient artifacts, and, like its Byzantine predecessor, it responded to a broader political program and imperative. Searching for the template of the 1498 inauguration, whether in Byzantine sources or normative Church texts (such as *trebniki*/liturgical books) misses the most common feature of this type of ceremony, namely, its constant reinvention. Certain characteristics are consistently repeated; in the case of Rus these include enthronement, elevated seating, and churches of dynastic significance. However, the shifting significance of any one or all of these constituent parts of the ceremony and the interpolation of words and acts from

---

49   Manuel II does crown his consort himself, so the 1498 Muscovy coronation of a co-ruler may have used this as its model.
50   See Majeska, "Russian Travelers," p. 433 note 114.
51   See Barsov, *Drevnerusskie pamiatniki*, pp. xxix–xxxi, discussed below.
52   See Majeska, "Russian Travelers," pp. 433–34; Savva, *Moskovskie tsari*, p. 153; Barsov, *Drevnerusskie pamiatniki*, pp. xxix–xxxi; and Khrisanf Mefodievich Loparev, *O chine venchaniia russkikh tsarei* (St. Petersburg: V.S. Balasheva, 1887), pp. 312–19.

disparate source material expose a key feature: tradition is generated through performance. Rather than viewing this ritual as a demonstration of Muscovite antiquarianism, a compilation of Byzantine sources, we should view the inauguration of Dmitrii Ivanonvich as a political action that performed the new political and social order.

When Iorga coined the term *Byzance après Byzance*, he also referred to the fixedness of the transmission of Byzantine artifacts across space and time with the phrase "l'immuable pérennité byzantine."[53] The phrase, which can be roughly translated to *the sempiternal permanence* (or *persistence*) *of Byzantium*, conveys the long-term durability and solidity of Byzantine ideas and material culture. This paradigm has been useful for its descriptive quality, making salient the numerous appropriations by the groups that entered the Byzantine cultural sphere via the adoption of Eastern Christianity. The notion of the immutability of Byzantine inheritance, whether via text, image, or idea, anchors the received artifact in space and time and estranges the possibility of adaptation and interpretation.[54] The case of court rituals in Rus/Muscovy and the Byzantine Empire demonstrates that court actors themselves undertook an excavation and, failing that, an invention of rituals and ritual elements. It should be remembered that Byzantine books of ceremonies were created both to document extant ceremonies and to compile sources for ceremonial practices based on previous examples (whatever traces were left) to inform and shape contemporary procedures.[55] In the case of Rus, the 1498 investiture of Dmitrii Ivanovich and ensuing ceremonies of inauguration also attempted to excavate and create a series of practices that featured appropriations from preceding ceremonies, the disappearance of some elements, and the adoption or adaptation of both existing and new practices, as well as the interpolation of new source material based on need and availability. In each case, the ritual element and the overall ceremony were meant to appear ancient, remote, and authentic. Certain factors were obfuscated, such as the Mongol origins of the cap/ crown of Monomakh, and others promoted, such as Byzantine connections or

---

53 Nicolae Iorga, *Byzance après Byzance: Continuation de l'histoire de la vie byzantine* (Bucharest: Institut d'études byzantines, 1971), p. 9.

54 See Simon Franklin, "The Reception of Byzantine Culture by the Slavs," in *Byzantium— Rus—Russia: Studies in the Translation of Christian Culture* (Variorum Collected Studies Series 754) (Aldershot: Ashgate, 2002), pp. 383–97. Franklin discusses pitfalls of terminology in describing the Byzantine heritage of Rus, stating that language is not aesthetically or socially neutral, which necessitates an alternative imagery for an alternative culture, and that the notion of cultural translation could also be applicable to the Byzantines' treatment of their own past.

55 See András Németh, *The* Excerpta Constantiniana *and the Byzantine Appropriation of the Past* (Cambridge, UK: Cambridge University Press, 2019), pp. 1–20, 77–88.

ancestral Rus practice. Furthermore, as with most court ceremonial, there is an immediacy of adoption and improvisation based on need.

Byzantine ceremonies of investiture, which have been thoroughly studied by historians, have been shown to be melanges of ritual arrangement, histrionic setting, and accoutrements used.[56] In effect, practically every recorded ceremony of investiture differed slightly, or radically, from its predecessor. Likewise, the 1498 investiture of Dmitrii Ivanovich was both a radical departure from Rus/Muscovite practice (if such a thing existed) and an innovation of Byzantine ritual elements. The immediacy of ritual is thus emphasized as a practice or set of practices generated based, first and foremost, on the aims of those in power. The content could be excavated or invented based on current ideological requirements, thereby demonstrating the active role of Muscovite bookmen and princely entourage in shaping the social, cultural, and political life of the court and its practices.

The paradigms of Moscow as "Third Rome" or of *Byzance après Byzance* are both as attractive as they are grandiose, but both obfuscate the sparse and select elements of verifiable Byzantine provenance that appeared in 15th-century Muscovite court culture. Furthermore, these paradigms conceal the degree of invention and originality fostered at the Muscovite court. The deployment of past fictions, staged as present facts in the form of the inauguration sermon, and the invention of regalia and incorporation of new spaces were all part of a strategy of rule and a result of recent economic and political fortunes in the Muscovite north.[57] The image of Muscovy as a "Byzantium of the North" is mostly a result of the reign of Ivan IV in the 16th century, which achieved a process of appropriation and transformation of court culture that had begun almost a century before.[58] The reigns of Vasilii II (r. 1425–62) and Ivan III saw innovations on several fronts, the concertation of political and

---

56   See George Ostrogorsky, "Evoliutsiia vizantiiskogo obriada koronovaniia," in *Vizantiia iuzhnye Slaviane i Drevniaia Rus' zapadnaia Evropa: Iskusstvo i Kul'tura; Sbornik statei v chest' V.N. Lazareva*, ed. Vladimir N. Grashchenkov, Tatiana B. Kniazevskaia, et al. (Moscow: Nauka, 1973), pp. 32–43.

57   A compelling corollary can be found in the 1953 coronation of Queen Elizabeth II. Tom Nairn writes that "the hearers were invited to revere … that moment itself [the coronation] as the culmination of a communal collectivity which had endured since … well, the paterfamilias of Britannic clichés, 'time immemorial.' In the cinema film which followed, after a decontaminatory blast from Shakespeare, Sir Laurence Olivier's script (by Christopher Fry) went on to describe the moment of anointing—'the hallowing, the sacring'—as so old that 'history is scarce deep enough to contain it.'" Nairn, *The Enchanted Glass: Britain and Its Monarchy* (London: Verso, 1989), pp. 124–25.

58   See Pierre Gonneau, *Ivan le Terrible ou le métier de tyran* (Paris: Tallandier, 2014); Andrei Pavlov and Maureen Perrie, *Ivan the Terrible* (London: Longman, 2003); Isabel de

religious authorities, the claim to protection over Eastern Orthodoxy, a marriage strategy with a scion of the Palaiologan clan, the deployment of new symbols (like the double-headed eagle), inchoate centralization of power around the prince and principality of Moscow, the construction of a new built landscape within the precincts of the Moscow Kremlin, and the development of a new court culture focused on Byzantine cultural artifacts.[59] Zoe/Sofiia and her entourage could not have been the sole agents for the development and importation of Byzantine practices and symbols (e.g., the double-headed eagle). After all, the princess had been a ward of the Pope and had grown up in Rome, which was not known as a site for the preservation of late Byzantine court culture. It should be noted further that by the time Ivan III concocted the investiture ceremony for his grandson, he had fallen out with his Palaiologan wife, who had been estranged from the court along with her partisans. In spite of the innovations presented here, certain customs remained, such as collective dining with the boyars and avowal of mutual fealty and rule by consent, which were central to the preservation of peace.[60] In this respect, the inauguration ceremony of 1498 was not a display of autocratic power, but a mask for political weakness at a time of strained relations between Ivan III and his wife, his eldest son's illness and death, and increasing factionalism within the court. Thus, it was in a time of political crisis that an impressive Byzantine-style coronation ceremony was orchestrated and heightened ritual thereafter increasingly became a feature of the Grand Prince's rule.

4 Text and Translation of the 1498 Inauguration of Dmitrii Ivanovich in Moscow

According to the Patriarchal/Nikon Chronicle[61]

[*First Account*] Тоя же зимы Февраля 4, въ неделю, князь великий Иванъ Васильевичь благословилъ и посадилъ на великое княжение Владимерское и Московское и всея Руси внука своего князя Дмитрия Ивановича, а посажение его бяше въ церкви Пречистыя на Москве. По благословению Симона митрополита всея Руси, и архиепископа Тихона

Madariaga, *Ivan the Terrible: First Tsar of Russia* (New Haven: Yale University Press, 2005); and Sergei Bogatyrev, "Ivan IV (1533–84)," in *The Cambridge History of Russia*, pp. 240–63.

59   See Robert Oliver Crummey, *The Formation of Muscovy* (London: Longman, 1987), pp. 133–35.
60   See Kollmann, *The Russian Empire*, p. 137.
61   PSRL 12 (1901/2001), pp. 246–48.

Ростовскаго, и епископовъ Нифонта Суздалскаго, Васиана Тверскаго, Протасия Рязанскаго, Авраамия Коломенскаго, Евфимия Сарского и всего освященнаго собора, возложиша на него бармы Мономоховы[62] и шапку, и осыпа его князь Юрьи Ивановичъ, дядя его, златомъ и сребромъ трижды: предъ Пречистою, и предъ Архангеломъ и предъ Благовещением.

[*Second Account*] В лето 7006 Февраля 4, в неделю о Мытари и Фарисеи сие бысть.

О поставлении внучне на великое княжение.

Среди церкви уготовиша место болшее, на чемъ святителей ставятъ, и учиниша на томъ месте три стулы: великому князю Ивану, да внуку его Дмитрию, да митрополиту. И егда приспе время, и облечеся митрополитъ и архиепископъ и епископы и архимандриты и игумены и весь соборъ во священныа ризы. И повелеша посреди церкви поставити налой, и на немъ положиша шапку Манамахову и бармы. Егда же вниде въ церковь князь великий со внукомъ, и митрополитъ со всемъ соборомъ начаша молебенъ пречистой Богородици и святому чюдотворцу Петру. И после Достойно есть и Трисвятаго и по тропарехъ митрополитъ и князь великий вшедъ, седоша на своихъ местехъ, а внукъ сталъ предъ ними у места на вышней степени, не восходя на место.

И князь великий Иванъ рече: « Отче митрополитъ! Божиимъ изволениемъ отъ нашихъ прародителей великихъ князей старина наша, то и до сехъ местъ, отци наши великие князи сыномъ своимъ первымъ давали великое княжство и язъ былъ своего сына перваго Ивана при себе же благославилъ великим княжством; Божя пакъ воли сталася, сына моего Ивана не стало въ животе, а у него остался сынъ первой Дмитрей, и язъ его ныне благославляю при себе и опосле себя великим княжством Володимерскимъ и Московскимъ и Новгородскимъ; и ты бы его, отче, на великое княжество благословилъ ».

И после речи великого князя велелъ митрополитъ внуку въступити на место и, въставъ, благославилъ его крестомъ, и поставляемому преклоншу главу. И митрополитъ положилъ руку свою на главу его.

---

62   In the Voskressenskii Chronicle this is given as "и Манамахову шапку" (Monomakh's cap) in PSRL 8 (1901/2001), p. 235.

И рече молитву сию во услышавше свемъ:[63] « Господи Боже нашь, Царь царствующимъ и Господь господствующимъ, иже Самуиломъ Пророкомъ избравъ раба своего Давида и помазавъ того въ царя надъ людми своими Израиля. Святый, ныне услыши молитву нашу недостойныхъ и виждь отъ святаго жилища твоего, и верна Ти раба Дмитрия, еже благоволилъ еси въздвигнути царя во языце твоемъ святомъ. Егоже стяжалъ еси честною кровию Единороднаго ти Сына, помазати сподоби[64] елеомъ въ здравие; одей того силою свыше, положи на главе его венець отъ камени честна, даруй тому длъготу дний, дай же въ десницу его скипетръ царствия, посади того на престоле правды, огради того всеоружествомъ Святаго ти Духа, утверди того мышцу, покори ему вся варварския[65] языки, всей въ сердце его страхъ твой и еже къ послушнымъ милостивное, съборныя церкви веления ихъ, да судя люди твоя правдою и нищихъ твоихъ, спасетъ сыны убогыхъ и наследникъ будетъ небеснаго ти царствия. » Възгласъ: « яко твоя есть дръжава и твое есть царствие и сила и слава Отца и Сына и Святаго Духа ныне и присно и въ веки векомъ, аминь. »

По молитве велелъ къ себе митрополитъ съ налоя принести бармы двема архимандритомъ, да вземъ ихъ далъ великому князю, и знаменалъ митрополитъ внука крестомъ, и князь великий положилъ бармы на внука.

Молитва втай: « Господи Боже Вседержителю и царю векомъ, иже земный человекъ тобою царемъ сътвореный поклони главу свою тебе помолитися, Владыко всехъ! Съхрани того подъ кровомъ твоимъ, удержави того царство, благоугодная ти творити всега того сподоби, възсияй въ днехъ его правду и множество мира, да въ тихости его тихо и безмлъвно житие поживемъ въ всякомъ благочестий и чистоте. » Възгласъ: « ты бо еси Царь мирови и Спасъ душамъ нашимъ. » По « амине ».

Велелъ къ себе митрополитъ приснести съ налоя шапку двема архимандритомъ да вземъ ее далъ великому князю, и знаменалъ митрополитъ внука крестомъ, глаголя: « въ имя Отца и Сына и Святаго

---

63 As Barsov demonstrated, the Metropolitan's sermon is an interpolation of the text from the "Молитва благословити царя и князя" (The Sermon on the blessed tsars and princes) in Sergei Posad, Trinity Lavra of St. Sergius, MS 304.1, fols. 159r–159v. The text of the sermon only minutely diverges from that of the chronicle.

64 Although not the exact phrasing, the terms reflect the Byzantine Καταξίωσον Κύριε found in the *Horologion* and, more generally, in Byzantine hymns, used in monastic rites. See Jeffrey Anderson and Stefano Parenti, *A Byzantine Monastic Office, A.D. 1105* (Washington, DC: Catholic University of America Press, 2016), pp. 177–78, 313.

65 For example, the sermon uses the term "поганы" (pagan) here, fol. 159v.

Духа ». И князь велики положилъ шапку на внука, и митрополитъ благословилъ внука.

И потомъ октения: « Помилуй насъ Боже » по обычю, молитва пречистей Богородици: « пресвятая Госпоже Дево Богородице. » И по молитве селъ митропилитъ да князь великий на своихъ местехъ, и возшедъ на амбонъ архидиаконъ и глагола велегласно многолетие великому князю Дмитрию. И священники въ олтари и дияки поютъ многолетие по обычаю.

И по « многолетии » митрополитъ, и архиепископъ, и епископы, весь съборъ, въставъ поклонишася и въздравиша обоихъ великихъ князей: « Божиею милостию радуйся здравствуй православный царю Иване, великий князь всея Руси на многа лета. » И великому князю Дмитрию митрополитъ рече: « Божиею милостию здравстуй господине и сыну мой князь великий Дмитрей Ивановичь всея Руси самодержцомъ на многа лета. »

И потомъ дети великого князя поклонишася и въздравиша великихъ князей обоихъ, и потомъ бояре и вси людие.

Поучение митрополиче

« Господине и сыну князь великий Дмитрей! Божиимъ изволениемъ дедъ твой князь великий пожаловалъ тебя и благословилъ княжествомъ; и ты, господине и сыну, имей страхъ Божий въ сердци. Люби правду и милость и судъ праведенъ, имей послушание къ своему государю и деду великому князю, и попечение имей отъ всего сердца о всемъ православномъ християнстве; а мы тебя, своего господина и сына, благословляемъ и Бога молимъ о вашемъ здравии. » По семъ князь великий рече: « внукъ Дмитрей! Пожаловалъ есми тебя и благословилъ великим княжествомъ; и ты имей страхъ въ сердци, люби правду и милость и судъ праведенъ., и имей попечение отъ всего сердца о всемъ православномъ християнстве. »

И митрополитъ свершилъ отпустъ молебну, и потомъ начаша литургию; и по съвершении литургии пошелъ князь великий Иванъ къ собе. А князь великий Дмитрей въ шапке и въ бармахъ исъ церкви изъ Пречистыя какъ идетъ изъ дверей, и ту его осыпалъ денгами златыми и сребряными трижды великого князя сынъ князь Юрий, а дети великого князя идутъ съ нимъ и бояре съ нимъ; такоже предъ Архангеломъ осыпалъ его трижды, и предъ Благовещениемъ трижды денгами златыми и сребряными.

Тоя же зимы, февраля, прииде Михайло Плещевъ изо Царягорода на Москву. [...]

Translation[66]

[*First Account*] During that same winter, on the fourth of February, which was a Sunday, Grand Prince Ivan [III] Vasilevich blessed and enthroned his grandson, Dmitrii Ivanovich, to rule over all of the lands of Vladimir and Moscow and over all of the lands of Rus. The investiture ceremony took place in the Church of the Assumption of the Most Pure Mother of God in Moscow. Following the blessing by the Metropolitan of all Rus, Simeon, and by the Archbishop of Rostov, Tikhon, and by the bishops Nifont of Suzdal, Basian of Tver, Protasius of Riazan, Abraham of Kolomna, Euthymius of Sarai, and by the entire sacred synod, he received the *barmy* of Monomakh and was crowned with the cap.[67] His uncle, Prince Iurii Ivanovich, showered the prince thrice with gold and silver, before entering the Church of the Assumption of the Most Pure Mother of God, then, before the Church of the Archangel Michael, and, finally, before the Church of the Annunciation.

[*Second Account*] This happened in 7006, the fourth of February, on a Sunday of the week of the Publican and the Pharisee.

On the Inauguration of the Grandson Over the Grand Principality

In the middle of the church they erected a large platform, upon which prelates usually stand, and they placed three seats there, for Grand Prince Ivan III, for his grandson, Dmitrii, and for the Metropolitan. Thus, when the time came, the Metropolitan, archbishop, bishops, archimandrites, abbots, as well as the entire congregation donned festal vestments. They ordered a lectern to be placed in the middle of the church, where they laid out the cap of Monomakh and the *barmy*. When the Grand Prince entered the church with his grandson, the Metropolitan and the entire congregation began singing prayers in honor of

---

66 The Nikonian Chronicle is one of few Rus/Muscovite chronicles to have been translated with notes. I undertook my own translation of this section with notes, which does not completely diverge from that of the Zenkovskys but reinterprets some of the terminology. For comparison, see *The Nikonian Chronicle*, ed. and trans. Serge Zenkovsky and Betty Jean Zenkovsky, 5 vols (Princeton: Kingston Press/Darwin Press, 1984–89), 5: 256–60.

67 The *barmy* is the equivalent of the Byzantine *loros*, as seen in paintings of Muscovite princes, such as the 1670 portrait of Tsar Aleksei Mikhailovich (Fig. 2.4). The crown, most likely of Mongol origin, is attributed to the 12th-century Prince of Kiev, Vladimir Monomakh, and may have been associated with the 11th-century Byzantine Emperor Constantine IX Monomachos. See Ostrowski, *Muscovy and the Mongols*, pp. 171–77, for a comprehensive discussion of this accoutrement in the Steppe context.

the Most Pure Mother of God and Holy Wonderworker Peter. And, following the singing of the "Dostoinno est," the "Trisviatoe," and the "Troparia," the Metropolitan and the Grand Prince entered and took their seats on the platform, while the grandson stood on the upper step without ascending to the platform.[68]

The Grand Prince Ivan III pronounced the following: "O father, the Metropolitan! By the will of God, from the time of our forefathers, the grand princes, our ancestors, to the present time: our fathers, the grand princes, have always rendered the Grand Principality to their first son. Thus, did I bless my first son, Ivan, to rule the Grand Principality together with me. By the grace of God, my son, Ivan, did not remain alive. But his own first son remained, Dmitrii, and now I bless him in my lifetime and for the time to come, to be Grand Prince of Vladimir, Moscow, and Novgorod. May you, Father, also bless this investiture over the Grand Principality."

Following the Grand Prince's words, the Metropolitan entreated the grandson to step up onto the platform, and once he had done so, he blessed him [the grandson] with the cross and bowed his head to him.

The Metropolitan put his hand on his head and said the following prayer so that all could hear: "Lord God, King of those who rule and Lord of those who lead: Thou, through the prophet Saul, chose Thy servant, David, and anointed him King of Thy people of Israel. O Holy one, now hear our prayer, the unworthy ones, and look out from Thy holy abode upon Thy faithful servant, Dmitrii, and by your blessing may he be raised to the rank of Tsar of Thy holy people. With the Most Pure blood of Thy only-begotten son give him strength and anoint him with the myrrh of joy. Endow him with divine power; place on his head the crown from the stone of honor; give him long life; place the sceptre of Tsardom in his right hand; enthrone him on the seat of justice; defend him with all of the weapons of the Holy Ghost; strengthen his arm; submit to him all of the barbarian peoples; inspire fear of Thee in his heart and make him merciful toward those who obey him; may he know the rules of Thy Church, so that he may render justice to the people according to Thy justice, and may he protect the sons of the poor and the weak. May he reign over Thy heavenly kingdom." All together the congregants exclaimed: "For Thine is the authority and the

---

68   "Dostoinno est'," the "It is meet" hymn ("Ἄξιόν ἐστιν), has been part of the Divine Liturgy, and its message is reflected in an icon of the Holy Virgin of the *Eleousa* or "merciful" type. "Trisviatoe" or *Trisagion*/Τρισάγιον (Thrice Holy) is a standard hymn of the Divine Liturgy: "Святы́й Бо́же, Святы́й Крепкий, Святы́й Безсмертный, помилуй нас." "Troparia" or *Troparion*/Τροπάριον is a repeated short hymn, here perhaps serving as a Dismissal hymn.

kingdom and power and the glory of the Father, the Son, and the Holy Ghost now and ever through ages and ages."

Having pronounced the prayer, the Metropolitan ordered two archimandrites to bring him the *barmy* from the altar, which he took and gave to the Grand Prince. He blessed the grandson with the cross, and the Grand Prince lay the *barmy* on his grandson.

And the Metropolitan [said], quietly: "God Almighty and King for ages and ages, this earthly man whom Thou has made Tsar has bowed his head to pray to Thee, Lord of all! Give him shelter, uphold his rule, may his deeds be pleasing to God. May righteousness and great peace shine on all of the days [of his reign], so that during his tranquil [reign] we may live our lives tranquilly and peacefully in piety and purity!" All together: "Thou art the King of the world and Savior of our souls." Followed by: "Amen."

The Metropolitan ordered two archimandrites to bring him the cap [of Monomakh], which he took and gave to the Grand Prince, and the Metropolitan blessed the grandson with the cross, saying, "In the name of the Father, the Son, and the Holy Ghost." And the Grand Prince placed the cap [of Monomakh] on his grandson's head, and the Metropolitan blessed him.

The litany followed: "Have mercy on us, o Lord!" And, as is the custom, the prayer to the Most Pure [the Holy Virgin] followed: "Most Pure, Our Lady, Virgin, Mother of God." Following the prayer, the Metropolitan and the Grand Prince sat down on their respective seats and the archdeacon, ascending the ambo, proclaimed loudly: "Long life to Grand Prince Dmitrii!" The prelates behind the altar also sang, "Long life!" as is the custom.

After the "Long life!" the Metropolitan, archbishop, bishops, and congregants stood, bowed, and congratulated both Grand Princes, [saying]: "By the grace of God, rejoice, and be well, Orthodox Tsar Ivan, Grand Prince of all Rus and many years." And to the Grand Prince Dmitrii, the Metropolitan said: "By the grace of God, be well, lord and my son, Grand Prince Dmitrii Ivanovich of all Rus, sovereign [with your grandfather] for many years!"

Then, the Grand Prince's children bowed and congratulated both Grand Princes, and then the boyars and all of the other people present did the same.

The Metropolitan's Sermon

"Our lord and son, Grand Prince Dmitrii! By the will of God, your grandfather, the Grand Prince, has favored you and blessed you with rule over the Grand Principality. And you, lord and son, keep the fear of God in your heart. Love truth and mercy and righteousness and justice. Show obedience to your lord and grandfather, the Grand Prince, and take care, with all of your heart, of all

Orthodox Christians. We bless and pray to God for your health, our sovereign and son." Then, the Grand Prince said: "Grandson Dmitrii! I have favored you and blessed you with dominion over the Grand Principality. Keep the fear of God in your heart; love truth and mercy and righteousness and justice, and care with all of your heart for all Orthodox Christians."

The Metropolitan read the final prayer before commencing the celebration of the liturgy. After the liturgy had been sung, the Grand Prince went home, and Grand Prince Dmitrii, still wearing the cap [of Monomakh] and the *barmy*, went out through the doors of the Church of the Most Pure Mother of God, and here he was showered three times with gold and silver coins by Prince Iurii, son of the Grand Prince. The children of the Grand Prince went with him [Dmitrii], along with the boyars, and they also showered him with gold and silver coins, three times, before the Church of the Archangel Michael and before the Church of the Annunciation.

That same winter, in February, Mikhailko Pleshchev arrived in Moscow from Constantinople.

Bibliography

Primary Sources

Herzen, Alexander Ivanovich. *Sobranie sochinenii v tridtsati tomakh*. Moscow: Akademiia nauk SSSR, 1954–66.

Hypatian Chronicle. *Polnoe sobranie russkikh letopisei*, vol. 2. Moscow: Izd. vostochnoi literatury, 1908/1962.

Ignatius of Smolensk. "The Journey of Ignatius of Smolensk." In *Russian Travelers to Constantinople in the Fourteenth and Fifteenth Centuries*, ed. and trans. George Majeska. 76–113. Washington, DC: Dumbarton Oaks Studies, 1984.

Laurentian Chronicle. *Polnoe sobranie russkikh letopisei*, vol. 1. Moscow: Izd. vostochnoi literatury, 1962/2001.

The Nikonian Chronicle, ed. and trans. Serge Zenkovsky and Betty Jean Zenkovsky, 5 vols. Princeton: Kingston Press/Darwin Press, 1984–89.

Patriarchal/Nikon Chronicle. *Polnoe sobranie russkikh letopisei*, vols 11–12. Moscow: Izd. vostochnoi literatury, 1901/2000.

Pokrovskii, Nikolai Nikolaevich, and Gail Lenhoff, eds. *Stepennaia kniga tsarskogo rodosloviia po drevneishim spiskam. Teksty i kommentarii v trekh tomakh*. Moscow: Iazyki slavianskikh kul'tur, 2007–12.

Russkii Khronograf. *Polnoe sobranie russkikh letopisei*, vol. 22, part 2. Moscow: Izd. Vostochnoi literatury, 1914/2005.

Voskressenskii Chronicle. *Polnoe sobranie russkikh letopisei*, vol. 8. Moscow: Izd. vostochnoi literatury, 1901/2001.

Secondary Sources

Alef, Gustav. *The Origins of Muscovite Autocracy: The Age of Ivan III*. Wiesbaden: Harrassowitz, 1986.

Anderson, Jeffrey, and Stephano Parenti. *A Byzantine Monastic Office, A.D. 1105*. Washington, DC: Catholic University of America Press, 2016.

Androshchuk, Fedir. "K istorii obriada intronizatsii drevnerusskikh kniazei ('sidenie na kurganakh')." In *Druzhnni starozhitnosti tsentral'no-skhidnoi Evropi VIII—X st. Materiali Mizhnarodnogo pol'ovogo arkheologichnogo seminaru*, 5–10. Chernihiv: Siverians'ka dumka, 2003.

Barsov, Elpidifor Vasilievich. *Drevnerusskie pamiatniki sviashchennogo venchaniia tsarei na tsarstvo*. Moscow: Imperial University Press, 1883.

Bazilevich, Konstantin Vasilievich. *Vneshniaia politika russkogo tsentralizovannogo gosudarstva: Vtoraia polovina XV veka*. Moscow: Moscow University Press, 1952.

Bogatyrev, Sergei. "Eshche raz o shapke Monomakha i kazne moskovskikh kniazei." *Studia Slavica et Balcanica Petropolitana* 2 (2011): 251–54.

Bogatyrev, Sergei. "Shapka Monomakha i shlem naslednika: Reprezentatsiia vlasti i dinasticheskaia politika pri Vasilii III i Ivane Groznom." *Studia Slavica et Balcanica Petropolitana* 1 (2011): 171–200.

Bogatyrev, Sergei. "Ivan IV (1533–84)." In *The Cambridge History of Russia*, ed. Maureen Perrie, 240–63. Cambridge, UK: Cambridge University Press, 2008.

Bogatyrev, Sergei. "Reinventing the Russian Monarchy in the 1550s: Ivan the Terrible, the Dynasty, and the Church." *Slavonic and East European Review* 85, no. 2 (2007): 271–93.

Boltunova, Ekaterina. "Imperial Throne Halls and Discourse of Power in the Topography of Early Modern Russia (Late 17th–18th Centuries)." In *Palaces from Augustus to the Age of Absolutism*, ed. Michael Featherstone, Jean-Michel Spieser, Gülru Tanman, and Ulrike Wulf-Rheidt, 341–53. Berlin: De Gruyter, 2015.

Bourdieu, Pierre. *La Distinction: Critique sociale du jugement*. Paris: Éditions de Minuit, 1979.

Bushkovitch, Paul. "Sofia Palaiologina in Life and Legend." *Canadian-American Slavic Studies* 52 (2018): 158–80.

Cannadine, David, and Simon Price, eds. *Rituals of Royalty Power and Ceremonial in Traditional Societies*. Cambridge, UK: Cambridge University Press, 1987.

Chichurov, Igor Sergeevich. *Politicheskaia ideologiia srednevekov'ia Vizantiia i Rus*. Moscow: History Institute SSSR, 1990.

Crummey, Robert Oliver. *The Formation of Muscovy*. London: Longman, 1987.

Dvornik, Francis. "Byzantine Political Ideas in Kievan Russia." *Dumbarton Oaks Papers* 9 (1956): 73–121.

Fine, John V.A. "The Muscovite Dynastic Crisis of 1497–1502." *Canadian Slavonic Papers/Revue canadienne des slavistes* 8 (1966): 198–215.

Flier, Michael. "Political Ideas and Ritual." In *The Cambridge History of Russia*, vol. 1, ed. Maureen Perrie, 387–408. Cambridge: Cambridge University Press, 2006.

Flier, Michael. "The Throne of Monomakh: Ivan the Terrible and the Architectonics of Destiny." In *Architectures of Russian Identity: 1500 to the Present*, ed. James Cracraft and Daniel Rowland, 21–33. Ithaca: Cornell University Press, 2003.

Franklin, Simon. "The Reception of Byzantine Culture by the Slavs." In *Byzantium—Rus—Russia: Studies in the Translation of Christian Culture* (Variorum Collected Studies Series 754), 383–97. Aldershot: Ashgate, 2002.

Frost, Robert. *The Oxford History of Poland-Lithuania*, vol. 1, *The Making of the Polish-Lithuanian Union, 1385–1569*. Oxford: Oxford University Press, 2015.

Gonneau, Pierre. *Ivan le Terrible ou le métier de tyran*. Paris: Tallandier, 2014.

Gorskii, Anton Anatolevich. "K voprosu o sostave Russkogo voiska na Kulikovom Pole." *Drevniaia Rus': Voprosy medievistiki* 6 (2001): 1–9.

Gorskii, Anton Anatolevich. *Moskva i Orda*. Moscow: Nauka, 2000.

Hajdu, Ada. "The Search for National Architectural Styles in Serbia, Romania, and Bulgaria from the Mid-nineteenth Century to World War I." In *Entangled Histories of the Balkans*, ed. Roumen Daskalov and Tchavdar Marinov, 394–440. Leiden: Brill, 2013.

Hobsbawn, Eric, and Terrence Ranger, eds. *The Invention of Tradition*. Cambridge: Cambridge University Press, 1983.

Iorga, Nicolae. *Byzance après Byzance: Continuation de l'histoire de la vie byzantine*. Bucharest: Institut d'études byzantines, 1971.

Ivanov, Sergey. "The Second Rome as Seen by the Third: Russian Debates on 'the Byzantine legacy.'" In *The Reception of Byzantium in European Culture since 1500*, ed. Przemsław Marciniak and Dion Smythe, 55–81. Abingdon: Ashgate, 2016.

Kalić, Jovanka. "Pretece Žice: Krunidbena mesta Srpskikh vladara." *Istorijski Časopis* 44 (1997): 77–87.

Kelly, Aileen. *The Discovery of Chance. The Life and Thought of Alexander Herzen*. Cambridge, MA: Harvard University Press, 2016.

Kivelson, Valerie. "Culture and Politics, or the Curious Absence of Muscovite State Building in Current American Historical Writing." *Cahiers du Monde russe* 46, no. 1–2 (2005): 19–28.

Kloss, Boris Mikhailovich. *Nikonovskii svod i russkie letopisi XVI–XVII vekov*. Moscow: Nauka, 1980.

Kollmann, Nancy Shields. *The Russian Empire 1450–1801*. Oxford: Oxford University Press, 2017.

Kollmann, Nancy Shields. "The Principalities of Rus' in the Fourteenth Century." In *The New Cambridge Medieval History*, ed. Michael Jones, 764–94. Cambridge, UK: Cambridge University Press, 2000.

Korpela, Jukka. "Stefan von Perm': Heiliger Täufer im politischen Kontext." *Jahrbücher für Geschichte Osteruropas* 49 (2001): 481–99.

Loparev, Khrisanf Mefodievich. *O chine venchaniia russkikh tsarei*. St. Petersburg: V.S. Balasheva, 1887.

Lur'e, Iakov Solomonovich. "Genealogicheskaia schema leteopisei XI–XVI vv." *Akademiia Nauk SSSR, TODRL* 40 (1985): 190–205.

Lur'e, Iakov Solomonovich. "Iz istorii russkogo letopisaniia kontsa XV veka." *Akademiia Nauk SSSR, TODRL* 11 (1955): 156–86.

Madariaga, Isabel de. *Ivan the Terrible: First Tsar of Russia*. New Haven: Yale University Press, 2005.

Majeska, George. "The Moscow Coronation of 1498 Reconsidered." *Jahrbücher für Geschichte Osteuropas* 26, no. 3 (1978): 353–61.

Marjanović-Dušanić, Smilja, and Sima Ćirković. *Vladarske insignije i državna simbolika u Srbiji od XIII do XV veka*. Belgrade: Serbian Academy, 1994.

Martin, Janet. *Medieval Russia, 980–1584*. Cambridge, UK: Cambridge University Press, 1995.

Miller, David. "Once Again about the Dating and Provenance of the *Skazanie o Kniaz'iakh Vladimirskikh*." *Russian History/Histoire Russe* 25, no. 1–2 (1998): 65–77.

Mishkova, Diana. *Beyond Balkanism. The Scholarly Politics of Region Making*. New York: Routledge, 2018.

Nairn, Tom. *The Enchanted Glass. Britain and its Monarchy*. London: Verso, 1989.

Nelson, Janet. "Symbols in Context: Rulers' Inauguration Rituals in Byzantium and the West." In *Politics and Ritual in Early Medieval Europe*, 259–83. London: Bloomsbury Publishing, 1986.

Németh, András. *The Excerpta Constantiniana and the Byzantine Appropriation of the Past*. Cambridge, UK: Cambridge University Press, 2019.

Ostrogorsky, George. "Evoliutsiia vizantiiskogo obriada koronovaniia." In *Vizantiia iuzhnye Slaviane i Drevniaia Rus' zapadnaia Evropa: Iskusstvo i Kul'tura. Sbornik statei v chest' V.N. Lazareva*, ed. Vladimir N. Grashchenkov, Tatiana B. Kniazevskaia, et al., 32–43. Moscow: Nauka, 1973.

Ostrowski, Donald. *Muscovy and the Mongols*. Cambridge, UK: Cambridge University Press, 1998.

Ostrowski, Donald. "The Mongol Origins of Muscovite Political Institutions." *Slavic Review* 49, no. 4 (1990): 525–42.

Parppei, Kati. *The Battle of Kulikovo Refought: The First National Feat*. Leiden: Brill, 2017.

Pavlov, Andrei, and Maureen Perrie. *Ivan the Terrible*. London: Longman, 2003.

Plokhy, Serhii. *Lost Kingdom: The Quest for Empire and the Making of the Russian Nation.* New York: Hachette, 2017.

Poe, Marshall. "Moscow, the Third Rome: The Origins and Transformations of a 'Pivotal Moment.'" *Jahrbücher für Geschichte Osteuropas* 49 (2001): 412–29.

Reinert, Stephen. "Political Dimensions of Manuel II Palaiologos' 1392 Marriage and Coronation." In *Novum Millennium: Studies on Byzantine History and Culture Dedicated to Paul Speck*, ed. Claudia Sode and Sarlota Takacs, 291–302. Aldershot: Ashgate, 2001.

Ronchey, Silvia. "Orthodoxy on Sale: The Last Byzantine, and the Lost Crusade." In *Proceedings of the 21st International Congress of Byzantine Studies (London 21–26 August 2006)*, ed. Elizabeth Jeffreys, 313–42. Aldershot: Routledge, 2006.

Rowell, Stephen Christopher. *Lithuania Ascending: A Pagan Empire within East-Central Europe, 1295–1345.* Cambridge, UK: Cambridge University Press, 1994.

Rowland, Daniel. "Architecture, Image, and Ritual in the Throne Rooms of Muscovy, 1550–1650: A Preliminary Survey." In *Rude and Barbarous Kingdom Revisited: Essays in Russian History and Culture in Honor of Robert O. Crummey*, ed. Chester Dunning, Russell Martin, and Rowland, 53–71. Bloomington: Slavica Publishers, 2008.

Rowland, Daniel. "Moscow—The Third Rome or the New Israel?" *Russian Review* 55, no. 4 (1996): 591–614.

Savva, Vladimir. *Moskovskie tsari i viszantiiskie vasilevsy. k voprosu o vliianii Vizantii na obrazovanie idei tsarskoi vlasti Moskovskikh gosudarei.* Kharkov: M. Zilberberg, 1901.

Schreiner, Peter. "Hochzeit und Krönung Kaiser Manuels II. im Jahre 1392," *Byzantinische Zeitschrift* 60, no. 1 (1967): 70–85.

Solovjev, Aleksandar. "Pojam države u srednjovekovnoj Srbiji." In *Godišnjica Nikole Čupića* 42 (1933): 64–123.

Stefanovich, Piotr. "Kreshchenie Rusi v istoricheskhikh sochineniiakh XVI–XVII vv." In *Narrativy rusi kontsa XV–serediny XVIII vv.: V poiskakh svoei istorii*, ed. Andrei Doronin, 80–102. Moscow: Politicheskaia entsiklopediia, 2017.

Stefanovich, Piotr. "Legenda o prizvanii Variagov v istorografii XVI–XVII vv.: Ot srednevekovykh mifov k rannemodernym." In *Dreviaia Rus' posle Drevnei Rusi: Diskurs vostrochnoslavianskogo (ne)edinstva*, ed. Andrei Doronin, 326–44. Moscow: Politicheskaia entsiklopediia, 2017.

Tolochko, Oleksiy Petrovich. *Kniaz' v drevnei Rusi: Vlast', sobstvennost', ideologiia.* Kiev: Naukova dumka, 1992.

Valeeva-Suleimanova, Guzel' Fuadovna. "Shapka Monomakha—Imperskii simbol tatarskogo proiskhozhdeniia." In *Zolotoordynskaia tsivilizatsiia*, ed. Il'nur Midkhatovich Murzaleev, 22–29. Kazan: Institut istorii, 2008.

Vukovich, Alexandra. "Enthronement in Early Rus: Between Byzantium and Scandinavia." *Viking and Medieval Scandinavia* 14 (2018): 211–39.

Vukovich, Alexandra. "Le Prince et son épée dans le Rous' du Nord à la suite de l'exil byzantin de Vsévolod Iourevich." In *Byzance et ses voisins*, ed. Élisabeth Yota. Bern: Peter Lang, 2020, forthcoming.

Vukovich, Alexandra. "The Enthronement Rituals of the Princes of Vladimir-Suzdal in the 12th and 13th centuries." *FORUM University of Edinburgh Journal of Culture and the Arts* 17 (2013): 1–15.

Wortman, Richard. *Scenarios of Power: Myth and Ceremony in Russian Monarchy from Peter the Great to the Death of Nicholas I*, vol. 1. Princeton: Princeton University Press, 1995.

Zimin, Aleksandr Aleksandrovich. *Russkie letopisi i khronografy kontsa XV–XVI vv*. Moscow: MGIAI, 1960.

CHAPTER 3

Intellectual Relationships between the Byzantine and Serbian Elites during the Palaiologan Era

Elias Petrou

The Palaiologan Era can be described as an uncertain period for the Byzantine Empire. Although the Palaiologan Dynasty regained Constantinople in 1261 and ruled for almost two centuries, the state never managed to fully recover from the consequences of the Fourth Crusade and regain its former glory.[1] The rising Ottoman Empire from the east along with the various Balkan turbulences in the north and west forced Byzantium to seek help overseas from Italian cities and other European states.[2] At the same time, the Byzantine emperors, through alliances with various neighbors, attempted to secure their constantly shrinking borders. Serbia played a vital role in this Byzantine effort as a reliable ally, due to its geographical, political, and religious proximity. Therefore, many cases of cultural and intellectual exchange extended between the Byzantine and Serbian world during the period. Churches, monasteries, charitable institutions, and schools were founded in the Byzantine Empire, sponsored by the Serbian elite, and vice versa. The present essay examines two of these cases along with their consequences for both sides on the eve of the Ottoman conquest of the Balkans: the Xenon of the Kral in Constantinople (14th–15th century) and the personal library of George Cantacouzenos Palaiologos (1390–1459) in Smederevo in Serbia. These two case studies reveal the close cultural and scholar connection between Byzantium and Serbia during the Palaiologan period, which evolved into a reciprocal and mutual relationship. For the first time, Serbia was not only the receiver but a dynamic equal partner who enabled a "back-and-forth" avenue of intellectual exchange, having as starting point the beginning of the 13th century and echoing even after the fall of Constantinople in 1453.

---

1 Donald M. Nicol, *The Last Centuries of Byzantium 1261–1451* (London: Rupert Hart-Davis, 1972), pp. 18–21.
2 Nicol, *The Last Centuries*, especially pp. 267–72; see also Angeliki E. Laiou, *Constantinople and the Latins: The Foreign Policy of Andronicus II 1282–1328* (Cambridge, MA: Harvard University Press, 1972); and Nevra Necipoğlu, *Byzantium between the Ottomans and the Latins. Politics and Society in the Later Empire* (New York: Cambridge University Press, 2009).

The alliance between the Byzantine Empire and Serbia was established primarily through marriages. Well-educated Constantinopolitan noblewomen were married to local Serbian *archontes*, while Serbian princesses moved to the south and married Byzantine lords, even emperors.[3] As a result, a dynamic intellectual relationship formed between the Byzantine and Serbian high society, as reflected in philanthropy, and patronage of the arts and sciences. One of the first and most important alliances was between King Uroš II Milutin (1253–1321) and the Byzantine princess Simonis (1299–ca. 1345). Only two decades after the reestablishment of the Byzantine administration in its former capital by the founder of the Palaiologan dynasty, Michael VIII (1223–82), the new king of Serbia attacked the Thracian borders. He conquered the city of Skopje, which became his new capital, and he advanced deep inside the Byzantine territory as far as the city of Kavala. The plans for a Byzantine counterattack were postponed due to Michael VIII's death, and his successor Andronicos II decided to solve the problem through a marriage of the Serbian king with his sister, the empress-dowager of Trebizond, Eudocia Palaiologina (ca. 1265–1302). The empress's refusal to comply with her brother's plan led Andronicos to send his six-year-old daughter, Simonis, as bride to Uroš II instead.[4] The marriage took place in Thessalonica in 1299, and the young princess moved to the Serbian court. She returned to Constantinople several decades later, after her husband's death. However, Simonis left her mark in both courts. She appears to have been a highly educated person for her time and had a great number of valuable codices in her possession. As the paleographical evidences show, manuscripts such as Varlaam 151 and Vind. theol. gr. 138 mention her title as "Κράλαινα" (queen) in their notes, while well-known contemporary scribes such as the monk Theoctistos of the monastery of Hodegon in Constantinople were in close contact with her.[5]

---

3   Examples of these marriages will be presented further below.
4   For the incidents between the Serbian king and the Byzantine emperor, including the marriage of Simonis, see George Pachymérès, *Relations Historiques* (Corpus Fontium Historiae Byzantinae 24), ed. Albert Failler, vol. 4 (Paris: Institut français d'études byzantines, 1999), [§IX, 30–32] pp. 299.11–305.16. On Princess Simonis, see Alexander P. Kazhdan, et al., *The Oxford Dictionary of Byzantium*, vol. 3 (New York and Oxford: Oxford University Press, 1991), p. 1901; and Erich Trapp, Rainer Walther, et al., *Prosopographisches Lexikon der Palaiologenzeit*, 12 vols, hereafter abbreviated as PLP (Vienna: Österreichische Akademie der Wissenschaften, 1976–94), nr. 21398.
5   George A. Papademetriou, "'Η 'κράλαινα τῶν Τριβαλῶν' καὶ ὁ κωδικογράφος Θεόκτιστος (±1340)," *Μεσαιωνικά καὶ Νέα Ἑλληνικά* [Medieval and Modern Greek] 1 (1984): 420–51. For Theoctistos, see also PLP 7488; and Herbert Hunger and Otto Kresten, "Archaisierende Minuskel und Hodegonstil im 14. Jahrhundert," *Jahrbuch der Österreichischen Byzantinistik* 29 (1980), 187–236, here 188–92.

1 The Xenon of the Kral in Constantinople

In addition to the various donations to the city of Thessalonica and to Mount Athos, King Uroš II made monetary donations for the establishment of a multipurpose building complex in Constantinople called the Xenon of the Kral.[6] The exact date of the establishment of Xenon is unknown. However, a *post quem* date can be considered 1299, the year of his marriage to Simonis. An *ante quem* date is 1321, since three "chrysobulls" (decrees) of the emperors Andronicos II and Andronicos III Palaiologos (1297–1341) of that year mention the construction of the institution in the Byzantine capital by the highly respected King of Serbia.[7] The location is mentioned as close to the monastery of St. John Prodromos "en Petra," in the area of Blachernae.[8] An incident in the specific

---

6   See, among others, Stanislaus Hafner, *Serbisches Mittelalter: Altserbische Herrscherbiographien* (Graz: Styria, 1976), pp. 177–78; and Timothy S. Miller, *The Birth of the Hospital in the Byzantine Empire* (Baltimore: Johns Hopkins University Press, 1997), p. 195.

7   See *Actes de Chilandar*, vol. 1, *Actes grecs* (Archives de l'Athos 5), ed. Louis Petit and Boris Korablev, *Vizantiiski Vremenik*, addendum to vol. 17 (St. Petersburg, 1911; rep. Amsterdam: Adolf M. Hakkert, 1975), nr. 58, chrysobull of Andronicos II Palaiologos, February 1321, pp. 137–39, here 138.49–51: "ἐν τῇ αὐλῇ τοῦ ἀνεγερθέντος ξενῶνος παρὰ τοῦ περιποθήτου υἱοῦ καὶ γαμβροῦ τῆς βασιλείας μου τοῦ ὑψηλοτάτου κράλη Σερβίας ἐν τῇ θεοδοξάστῳ θεομεγαλύντῳ καὶ θεοφυλάκτῳ Κωνσταντινουπόλει" (In the courtyard of the constructed by my beloved son and son-in-law His Highness the King of Serbia inn, in the God's glorious, God's great, and God's protected Constantinople); nr. 60, chrysobull of Andronicos II Palaiologos, June 1321, pp. 141–43, here 142.32–34: "ἐν τῇ θεοδοξάστῳ θεομεγαλύντῳ καὶ θεοφυλάκτῳ Κωνσταντινουπόλει ἀνεγερθέντος ξενῶνος παρὰ τοῦ αὐτοῦ περιποθήτου υἱοῦ καὶ γαμβροῦ τῆς βασιλείας μου τοῦ ὑψηλοτάτου κράλη" (In God's glorious, God's great, and God's protected Constantinople constructed inn by my beloved son and son-in-law His Highness the King); and nr. 61, chrysobull of Andronicos III Palaiologos, June 1321, pp. 143–45, here p. 144.29–31: "ἐν τῇ θεοδοξάστῳ θεομεγαλύντῳ καὶ θεοφυλάκτῳ Κωνσταντινουπόλει ἀνεγερθέντος ξενῶνος παρὰ τοῦ αὐτοῦ περιποθήτου θείου τῆς βασιλείας μου τοῦ ὑψηλοτάτου κράλη" (In God's glorious, God's great, and God's protected Constantinople constructed inn by my beloved uncle His Highness the King).

8   The location is mentioned by the 15th-century Spanish traveler Ruy González de Clavijo, *Embassy to Tamerlane, 1403–1406*, trans. Guy Le Strange (London: Billing and Sons, 1928; rep. London and New York: Routledge Curzon, 2005), p. 30. In addition, a metrical colophon found in many codices of the monastery library (among them Vat. gr. 537 and Vat. gr. 564, both from the 12th century) mentions its location next to Aetius's cistern in the northwest part of the city: "ἡ βίβλος αὕτη τῆς μονῆς τοῦ Προδρόμου | τῆς κειμένης ἔγγιστα τῆς Ἀετίου | ἀρχαϊκὴ δὲ τῇ μονῇ κλῆσις Πέτρα" (The specific book [belongs] to the monastery of the Forerunner, which is located next to Aetius's cistern, and its ancient name was Rock/Petra). See Otto Volk, "Die byzantinischen Kloster-bibliotheken von Konstantinopel, Thessalonike und Kleinasien" (inaugural diss., Munich, 1954), p. 67; Eleni Cacoulide, "Η βιβλιοθήκη τῆς μονῆς Προδρόμου—Πέτρας στὴν Κωνσταντινούπολη" [The library of the monastery of the Forerunner-Rock in Constantinople], *Hellenica* 21 (1968): pp. 3–39, here p. 3; and Annaclara Cataldi Palau, "The Manuscript Production in the Monastery of Prodromos Petra (Twelfth–Fifteenth Centuries)," in *Studies*

area during the period can be connected with the possible time and place of the monastery's establishment. According to the historian George Pachymérès, on September 17, 1305, a great fire spread from the area of Opaine to the Gate of the Hunters, threatening to burn the monastery of St. John Prodromos itself.[9] It is possible that the construction of the Xenon was part of the reconstruction plan of the whole area.[10]

Following the example of other *xenones* in the Byzantine capital under the authority of various monasteries, the Xenon of the Kral was administratively attached to the above-mentioned monastery of St. John Prodromos "en Petra." In a document of the Hilandar Monastery dated August 1, 1322, and dealing with an economic dispute between the institution and the monastery, the representative of the Xenon was the Abbot Meletius of St. John Prodromos monastery.[11] At the same time, since the monastery was considered an imperial institution, the Xenon was also indirectly under the authority of the current Emperor.[12] In the chrysobulls of the two Andronici, the emperors point out that no one is allowed to intervene in the Xenon's administration, as they regulate its incomes from "τῶν προαστείων κτημάτων τε καὶ ζευγηλατείων" (the suburban fields and

---

in Greek Manuscripts (Testi, Studi, Strumenti 1) (Spoleto: Centro Italiano di studi sull'Alto Medioevo, 2008), pp. 197–208. The location of the Xenon close to the St. John Prodromos "en Petra" monastery is also mentioned by Archbishop Danilo II; see Hafner, *Serbisches Mittelalter* vol. 2, pp. 177–78; Raymond Janin, *Le Géographie ecclésiastique, première partie: Le Siège de Constantinople et le Patriarcat Œcuménique*, vol. 3: *Les Églises et les Monastères* (Paris: Centre National de la Recherche Scientifique, 1953), p. 572; Vassilios Kidonopoulos, *Bauten in Konstantinopel 1204–1328: Verfall und Zerstörung, Restaurierung, Umbau und Neubau von Profan- und Sakralbauten* (Mainzer Veröffentlichungen zur Byzantinistik 1) (Wiesbaden: Harrassowitz Verlag, 1994), pp. 219–20; Miller, *Hospital*, p. 195; Volk, "Die byzantinischen Kloster-bibliotheken," p. 65; and Demetrios K. Agoritsas, *Κωνσταντινούπολη: Η πόλη και η κοινωνία της στα πρώτα χρόνια των πρώτων Παλαιολόγων (1261–1328)* [Constantinople: The city and its society at the first years of the first Palaiologans (1261–1328)] (Thessalonica: Byzantine Research Center, 2016), p. 126.

9 Pachymérès, *Relations Historiques*, [§XIII, 10] pp. 637.30–639.5.

10 For this hypothesis, see Mirjana Živojinović, "L'hôpital du roi Milutin à Constantinople," *Zbornik radova Vizantološkog instituta* 16 (1975): pp. 105–17 (French summary); for further sources on the Xenon, see Urs Benno Birchler-Argyros, "Die Quellen zum Kral-Spital in Konstantinopel," *Gesnerus* 45 (1988): pp. 419–44.

11 *Actes de Chilandar*, nr. 82 (August 1, 1322), pp. 175–77, here p. 176.12–15.

12 The Spanish traveler Ruy González de Clavijo noted the imperial authority over the monastery during his visit to the capital. In his personal diary he added that he did not manage to see all the relics of the specific monastery, since only the Emperor Manuel II Palaiologos had the key to the sacristy, and on that day he was away hunting; see González de Clavijo, *Embassy*, pp. 30–31.

farms) and from the taxation of the village of Mamytzona.[13] It is not irrelevant that many decades later, during the period 1444–48, the appointment of the scholar John Argyropoulos as teacher at the institution was made through an imperial order.[14]

Very few physical descriptions of the Xenon survive. The chrysobull of Andronicos II Palaiologos of February 1321 mentions the existence of three cells along with a small church, which were reserved for the private use of the abbot of the Hilandar Monastery when he was in the capital.[15] In addition, a miniature of the scholar John Argyropoulos teaching at the Xenon of the Kral on folio 33v of the codex Oxon. Barocci gr. 87 depicts two constructions in the background, a small tower with an arched roof and narrow windows, along with a rectangular building with peaked roof.[16] Although the latter may be an addition of the artist, it is the only extant visual representation (Fig. 3.1).

---

13 *Actes de Chilandar*, nr. 58, February 1321, pp. 138–39, here p. 139.56–58: "καὶ οὐδὲν ἔχῃ ἄδειαν ἄλλος τις ἢ τῶν ἐρχομένων ἀπὸ τῆς Σερβίας ἢ ἕτερός τις τῶν ἁπάντων τῶν ὑποχειρίων καὶ ὑποτεταγμένων τῇ βασιλείᾳ πίπτειν εἰς αὐτά" (and none will have any jurisdiction on them either coming from Serbia or any other liegeman). For the incomes of the Xenon, see *Actes de Chilandar*, nr. 60, June 1321, pp. 141–43, here 142.28–30; nr. 61, June 1321, pp. 143–45, here 144.26–27; and nr. 82, August 1, 1322, pp. 175–77, here 175.7–9. See also Volk, "Die byzantinischen Kloster-bibliotheken," pp. 64–74; and Cacoulide, *Library*, p. 38. For the village of Mamytzona, see George Theocharides, "Μία ἐξαφανισθεῖσα μονὴ τῆς Θεσσαλονίκης: ἡ μονὴ τοῦ Προδρόμου," *Macedonica* 18 (1978): 1–26, here 14–15, n. 2.

14 See Spyridon P. Lampros, Ἀργυροπούλεια [Argyropouleia], Ἰωάνου Ἀργυροπούλου λόγοι, πραγματεῖαι, ἐπιστολαί, προσφωνήματα, ἀπαντήσεις καὶ ἐπιστολαὶ πρὸς αὐτὸν καὶ τὸν υἱὸν Ἰσαάκιον. Ἐπιστολαὶ καὶ Ἀποφάσεις περὶ αὐτῶν (Athens: Sakellariou, 1910), pp. 227–31: "Μιχαὴλ Ἀποστόλη τοῦ Βυζαντίου Προσφώνημα εἰς τὸν αὐτοῦ διδάσκαλον Ἰωάννην τὸν Ἀργυρόπουλον ὅτε ἤρξατο διδάσκων προτροπῇ βασιλέως ἐν τῷ τοῦ ξενῶνος καθολικῷ μουσείῳ" (The address of Michael Apostoles of Byzantium to his teacher John Argyropoulos when he [Argyropoulos] started teaching at the general school of the inn after Emperor's order). On the date of his appointment, see Elias Petrou, "Higher Education in Constantinople in the 15th Century" (PhD diss., University of Ioannina, 2017), chap. 2.

15 *Actes de Chilandar*, nr. 58, February 1321, pp. 137–39, here p. 138.46–49: "ἐπεὶ δὲ ἐτάχθη ἵνα ὁ κατὰ καιροὺς εὑρισκόμενος εἰς καθηγούμενον τῆς δηλωθείσης σεβασμίας μονῆς τοῦ Χελανταρίου ἔχῃ κελλία τρία, ἐν οἷς εὑρίσκεται ναός, ἀπὸ τῶν ὀσπητίων τῶν ὄντων ἐν τῇ αὐλῇ τοῦ ἀνεγερθέντος ξενῶνος" (It was ordered that when the current abbot of the above-mentioned monastery of Hilandar is in Constantinople, he should have three cells, in which there is a church, from the buildings of the courtyard of the constructed inn).

16 Henry Octavius Coxe, *Bodleian Library Quarto Catalogues* 1: *Greek Manuscripts*, (Oxford: Bodleian Library, 1969), pp. 151–52; Lampros, *Argyropouleia*, p. 23; see Spyridon P. Lampros, "Ἀντώνιος Πυρόπουλος," *Νέος Ἑλληνομνήμων* [New Hellenomnemon] 10 (1913): pp. 127–34; and Joannis Spatharakis, *The Portrait in Byzantine Illuminated Manuscripts* (Leiden: Brill, 1976), pp. 258–61.

FIGURE 3.1
John Argyropoulos teaching at the Xenon of the Kral, folio 33v, Oxon. Barocci 87, Bodleian Library
DIGITAL REPRODUCTION BY THE BODLEIAN LIBRARY; REPRODUCED WITH PERMISSION

From its founding, the Xenon hosted an inn for travelers, as its title suggests, and a hospital.[17] The biographer of the Serbian ruler Archbishop Danilo II (1270–1337) mentioned that Uroš II provided a great amount of money for medical equipment and a large endowment for the salaries of the physicians and nurses who worked there.[18] It seems that the hospital was still operational almost a century after its founding, and possibly until the fall of Constantinople in 1453. According to a note dated 1406 in the codex Vind. Med. gr. 1, Nathanael, a monk and physician at the Xenon, asked the scholar John Chortasmenos to rebind and restore the old codex at his expense (Fig. 3.2).[19] The title of Nathanael

---

17   The Xenon of the Kral was probably providing basic services, as did other *xenones* in the capital, such as the one at Panteleimonos monastery. The latter, according to the December 1342 chrysobull of the Emperor John V Palaiologos, was offering "τοῖς ἀπανταχοῦ χειμαζομένοις ὅρμον ἀποδείξας ἄκλυστον, ὡς μετ' ἐλπίδων ἀγαθῶν ὁρμεῖν ἐν αὐτῷ καὶ καταίρειν κλύδωνα καὶ ναυάγιον τὰ κατ' οἶκον ἀτεχνῶς νομίζοντ(ας) καὶ βραχὺ καιροῦ διατρίψαντας ἐνταῦθα αὖθις ἐρρωμένους ἐπανήκειν οἴκαδε (καὶ) σώους, μηδ' ἴχνος κομίζοντας δυσχερῶν" (safe harbor for everyone who is suffering great difficulties, so they can come there with good hopes and stay safe from seastorm and shipwreck simply acknowledging at home, and after staying for a brief time here they can return back home, without any trace of hardship accompanying them), *Actes de Lavra* (Archives de l'Athos 14), ed. Paul Lemerle et al., vols. 5, 8, 10–11 (Paris: P. Lethielleux, 1970–82), 3:23–25, here 23.54–58.
18   See Hafner, *Serbisches Mittelalter*, vol. 2, pp. 177–78; and Miller, *Hospital*, p. 195.
19   Herbert Hunger, *Katalog der griechischen Handschriften der Österreichischen Nationalbibliothek* (Museion N.F. 4, 3 parts in 4 vols) (Vienna: Prachner Verlag, 1961–92), part 2, p. 40; and Herbert Hunger, *Johannes Chortasmenos (ca. 1370–ca. 1436–37), Briefe, Gedichte und kleine Schriften* (Wiener Byzantinische Studien 7) (Vienna: Österreichische Akademie der Wissenschaften, 1969), p. 153: "Τὸ παρὸν βιβλίον τὸν Διοσκουρίδην παντάπασι παλαιωθέντα καὶ κινδυνεύοντα τελέως διαφθαρῆναι ἐστάχωσεν ὁ Χορτασμένος Ἰωάννης προτροπῇ καὶ ἐξόδῳ τοῦ τιμιωτάτου ἐν μοναχοῖς κυροῦ Ναθαναὴλ νοσοκόμου τηνικαῦτα τυγχάνοντος ἐν

BYZANTINE AND SERBIAN INTELLECTUAL RELATIONSHIPS 77

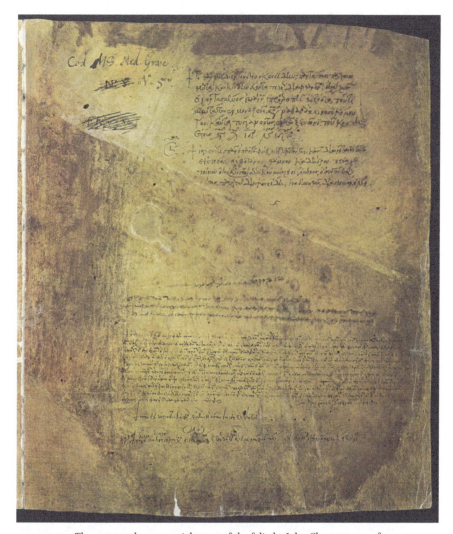

FIGURE 3.2 The note on the upper-right part of the folio by John Chortasmenos for the restoration of the codex, folio 1r, Vind. Med. gr. 1, Österreichische Nationalbibliothek (Austrian National Library)
DIGITAL REPRODUCTION BY THE AUSTRIAN NATIONAL LIBRARY; REPRODUCED WITH PERMISSION

along with the content of the manuscript implies the hospital's existence at the beginning of the 15th century. A few decades later, the miniature of the scholar John Argyropoulos in the codex Oxon. Barocci 87 and a note on folio

τῷ ξενῶνι τοῦ Κράλη ἔτους ‚ςλιδ' [1406] ἰν(δικτιῶν)ος ιδ'" (The present book of Dioscurides, which was in every way old and was in danger of total destruction, was rebound by

178v of the codex Marc. Class. v cod. 9 indicate not only the existence of the hospital in 1440s, but also the operation of a medical school on the premises. The inscription alongside the miniature reads (folio 33v):

> Argyropoulos is teaching the physician Antonius Pyropoulos
> and Marc Pyropoulos, along with the physician John Panaretos,
> and Angelos Demetrios and Agallona, Moschos's son, and the
> physician Vranan, (the son) of Protomastoros at the Xenon of the Kral.[20]

Moreover, the note in codex Marc. Class. v cod. 9 reveals:

> Diagram of Sir John Argyropoulos, philosopher and professor,
> when we were studying under him at the Xenon of the Kral
> the Galenos's art, me and sir Antonios Pyropoulos and Sir John
> Panaretos and Sir Manuel Pyropoulos, (son) of Jacob, and Sir
> Vranas, (son) of protomastoros, and Sir Maroules and Sir
> Manuel and Sir Andronicos Dioscurides, well-known as Eparchos.[21]

John Argyropoulos was already a great scholar in Constantinople before continuing his studies in Italy in 1440s, and he was later recalled by the Emperor

---

Chortasmenos John, with the advice and at the expense of the honorable monk Sir Nathanael, being a nurse at the Xenon of the Kral during the year 1406, indiction 14th).

20 Coxe, *Bodleian Library*, vol. 1, pp. 151–52: "ὁ Ἀργυρόπουλος καὶ διδάσκει Ἀντώνιον Πυρόπουλον ἰατρὸν καὶ Μαρκὸν (sic) Πυρόπουλον, ὁμοίως δὲ Πανάρετον Ἰωάννην ἰατρόν, καὶ Ἄγγελον Δημήτριον, καὶ Ἀγάλλωνα τὸν τοῦ Μόσχου, καὶ Βρανὰν τὸν τοῦ πρωτομάστορος ἰατρὸν ἐν τῷ τοῦ Κράλου ξενῶνι."

21 The specific epigram has been transcribed by three researchers with variations: Elpidio Mioni, *Bibliothecae Divi Marci Venetiarum: Codices Graeci Manuscripti*, 3 vols. (Rome: Istituto Poligrafico dello Stato, 1967–72), vol. 1.2, pp. 265–70; Brigitte Mondrain, "Jean Argyropoulos professeur à Constantinople et ses auditeurs médecins, d'Andronic Éparque à Démétrios Angelos," in *Πολυπλευρος Νουσ: Miscellanea für Peter Schreiner zu seinem 60. Geburtstag*, ed. Cordula Scholtz and Georgios Makris (Munich-Leipzig: K.G. Saur, 2000), pp. 223–50; and Véronique Boudon-Millot, "Un nouveau témoin pour l'histoire du texte de l'Ars medica de Galien: le Vlatadon 14," in *L'Ars medica (Tegni) de Galien: Lectures antiques et medievales*, ed. Nicoletta Palmieri (Saint-Etienne: Publications de l'Université de Saint-Étienne, 2008), pp. 11–29. I present all the transcriptions: "Διάγραμμα κυρίου (κυροῦ Mondrain) Ἰωάννου φιλοσόφου καὶ διδασκάλου τοῦ ἀργυροπούλου, ὁπότε ἐδιδασκόμεθα παρ' αὐτῷ (αὐτοῦ Mioni) ἐν τῷ ξενῶνι τοῦ κράλη (κράλου Mioni) τὸ περὶ τέχνης γαληνοῦ ἐγώ τε (περ Mioni) καὶ κύριος (αὐτὸς Mondrain) ἀντώνιος πυρόπουλος καὶ κύριος (αὐτὸς Mondrain) ἰωάννης ὁ πανάρετος καὶ κύριος (αὐτὸς Mondrain) μανουὴλ πυρόπουλος ὁ τοῦ ἰακώβου καὶ κύριος (αὐτὸς Mondrain) βρανὰς (βρανὰν Mioni) ὁ τοῦ πρωτομάστορος καὶ Μάρουλ(ες) κύριος κύριος (αὐτὸς Mondrain) μανουὴλ καὶ ἀνδρόνικος ὁ διοσκουρίδης (διοσκουρίευς Mioni· διοσκουριεὺς Mondrain) ὁ καὶ ἔπαρχος καλούμενος, μὴ ὢν δέ."

John VIII Palaiologos (1392–1448) himself to come back to the Byzantine capital and teach at the famous Xenon.[22] For this imperial appointment, the scholar Michael Apostoles sent a letter congratulating his former teacher, in which he implied that Argyropoulos was going to teach other courses besides medicine.[23] Keeping in mind the presence at the Xenon of the teacher John Chortasmenos, along with other scholars such as George Chrysococces, Leo Atrapes, and George Vaiophoros, we can assume that a school of general education was founded there decades before Argyropoulos arrived.[24]

At the same time, a scriptorium and a binding workshop were probably active on the same premises.[25] According to the notes in various manuscripts, we can assume that due to the close relationship of the monastery of St. John Prodromos "en Petra" and the Xenon of the Kral, the two institutions were sharing a library, which in fact was quite rich. New manuscripts were prepared from older codices stored there, not only with theological and ecclesiastical but also with secular content. Scribes, such as the monk Neophytos Prodromenos in the second half of the 14th century, and *skeuofylax* Stephanos, George Chrysococces, Leo Atrapes, and George Vaiophoros in the 15th century, copied many works there.[26] In addition, the intellectual interest of the Italian

---

22 Lampros, *Argyropouleia*, p. 19. On May 16 or 28, 1444, John Argyropoulos was examined at the University of Padua by Stephanus de Doctoribus, Sigismundus de Polcastris, Antonius de Roxellis, and Bartholomew (jr) de Sancta Sophia.

23 The reference to the classical rhetor Demosthenes along with Homer and Plato by Michael Apostoles to his teacher implies their possible presence in the Xenon's teaching curriculum; see Lampros, *Argyropouleia*, pp. 227–31.

24 On the presence of the last three scholar-scribes at the Xenon, see further below.

25 On the possible existence of a binding workshop, see Chortasmenos's note in cod. Vind. Med. gr. 1, cited above in n. 16, pp. 5–6.

26 On Neophytos Prodromenos, see *PLP* 19254; and Ernst Gamillscheg and Dieter Harlfinger, *Repertorium der griechischen Kopisten 800–1600* (hereafter abbreviated *RGK*), 3 vols (Vienna: Österreichische Akademie der Wissenschaften, 1981–1997), 2:411, and 3:481. See also Ivan Dujčev, ed., "Prouchvanija vurchu bulgarskoto srednovekovie. XVIII. Bulgarski dumi vuv vizantijski stichove ot XIV vek.," *Sbornik na Bulgarskata akademija na naukite i iskustvata* 41, no. 1 (1945), 130–50, here pp. 132 and 138; and Volk, "Die byzantinischen Kloster-bibliotheken," pp. 75–76. Neophytos prepared three medical works, an indication of his possible connection with the inn and hospital of the Xenon; see Aristotle P. Kouzes, "Τὸ περὶ τῶν ἐν ὀδοῦσι παθῶν' ἔργον Νεοφύτου τοῦ Προδρομηνοῦ," *Epetiris Etaireias Byzantinon Spoudon* 7 (1930): pp. 349–57; and Hermann-Alexander Diels, *Die Handschriften der Antiken Ärzte*, vol. 2 (Leipzig: Zentral-Antiquariat der Deutschen Demokratischen Republik, 1970), p. 68. On Stephanos, see Marie Vogel and Victor Gardthausen, *Die griechischen Schreiber des Mittelalters und der Renaissance* (Zentralblatt für Bibliothekwesen, supplement 33 (Leipzig: Harrassowitz, 1909), p. 404; *PLP* 26779; and *RGK* 1:366, 2:503, and 3:584. On George Chrysococces and the confusion about his name, see *PLP* 19254 and 31142; and *RGK* 3:126. On Leo Atrapes, see *PLP* 91400; and *RGK*

humanists of the early 15th century in Greek (and therefore Byzantine) education gave a new boost to the Xenon of the Kral. Various Italian scholars, including Guarino da Verona and Francesco Filelfo, among others, were searching in the Byzantine capital for distinguished mentors to teach them and for valuable codices for their personal collections.[27] They could find all of this on the premises of the Xenon.

The Xenon of the Kral was probably destroyed with the fall of Constantinople in 1453.[28] In fact, according to the historian Ducas (ca. 1400–ca. 1462), the monasteries of Chora and St. John Prodromos "en Petra" were the first sacked by the Ottoman armies when they entered the city.[29] Some one hundred years later the traveler Pierre Gilles mentioned in his journals that he found only ruins at the specific area, with any indication of the existence of the Xenon forever lost.[30] Any suggestion of its fate after the fall and its exact location in modern Istanbul is purely hypothetical.

The marriage of King Uroš II to Simonis was only the first of many to follow among the Serbian and the Byzantine elites. Stefan Uroš III Dečanski (1276–1331), Uroš II's son from a previous marriage, moved to Constantinople before marrying Maria Palaiologina, a granddaughter of Michael VIII Palaiologos.[31] Their son, Symeon Uroš Palaiologos (ca. 1326–70) took as wife a distant member of the imperial family, Thomais Comnena Angelina Orsini (ca. 1330–post

---

2:328 and 3:383. On George Vaiophoros see RGK 1:55, 2:74, and 3:90. See also Annaclara Cataldi Palau, "I colleghi di Giorgio Baiophoros: Stefano di Medea, Giorgio Crisococca, Leon Atrapes," in *Studies in Greek Manuscripts* (Testi, Studi, Strumenti 1) (Spoleto: Centro Italiano di studi sull'Alto Medioevo, 2008), pp. 303–44; Cataldi Palau, "The Manuscript Production"; and Ernst Gamillscheg, "Zur handschriftlichen Überlieferung byzantinischer Schulbücher," *Jahrbuch der Österreichischen Byzantinistik* 26 (1977): 211–30.

27 For Italian humanists in Constantinople in the 15th century, see Annaclara Cataldi Palau, "Learning Greek in Fifteenth-century Constantinople," in *Studies in Greek Manuscripts* (Testi, Studi, Strumenti 1) (Spoleto: Centro Italiano di studi sull'Alto Medioevo, 2008), pp. 219–34; and Petrou, "Higher Education," chap 3.

28 See Lampros, *Argyropouleia*, p. 24; translation: The Xenon was destroyed during the sack of Constantinople by the Turks, and most of the scholars escaped to Italy.

29 Ducas, *Ducae Michaelis Ducae Nepotis Historia Byzantina* (Corpus Scriptorium Historiae Byzantinae), ed. Immanuel Bekker (Bonn: Impensis Ed. Weberi, 1834), p. 288.1–4: "Οἱ δὲ τῆς αὐλῆς τοῦ τυράννου ἀζάπηδες, οἱ καὶ γενίτζαροι κέκληνται, οἱ μὲν ἐν τῷ παλατίῳ κατέδραμον, οἱ δὲ πρὸς τὴν Μεγάλου Προδρόμου μονὴν τὴν ἐπικεκλημένην Πέτραν καὶ ἐν τῇ μονῇ τῆς Χώρας" (The soldiers of the tyrant, called janissaries, some of them rushed to the palace, others to the monastery of the Great Forerunner called the Rock and to the monastery of Chora).

30 Pierre Gilles, *De topographia Constantinopoleos et de illius antiquitatibus*, 4:4 (Lyon: Gulielmus Rovillius, 1561), p. 198

31 On Stefan Uroš III, see PLP 21181; on Maria Palaiologina, PLP 21391.

1359).[32] However, more important was the marriage of Helena Dragaš (1372–1450), the great-granddaughter of Stefan Uroš III, to the Byzantine Emperor Manuel II Palaiologos (1350–1425) on February 10, 1392.[33] Helena Dragaš was the daughter of the Serbian magnate Constantine Dejanović Dragaš who died at the Battle of Rovine on May 17, 1395, and who was commemorated with great honors by his son-in-law at the monastery of St. John Prodromos "en Petra" in Constantinople.[34] Following the previous examples, Manuel and Helena's granddaughter, Helena Palaiologina (1431–73), married the Despot of Serbia, Lazar Branković Cantacouzenos (ca. 1421–58), son of the Serbian despot Đurađ Branković (George Vulcos) and Irene Cantacouzene (ca. 1400–57).[35] As her name indicates, Lazar's mother was one more case of marriage between the Byzantine and Serbian elites, as she was great-granddaughter of the former Emperor John VI Cantacouzenos.[36] In fact, Irene's family played a vital role in the second case of intellectual relationship between Byzantium and Serbia, to which we now turn.

2 The Library of George Cantacouzenos Palaiologos

Irene Cantacouzene, granddaughter of Matthew Cantacouzenos (son of the Emperor John VI Cantacouzenos), moved from Thessaloniki to Serbia to marry

---

32   On Symeon Uroš Palaiologos, see *PLP* 21185; on Thomais Comnena Angelina Orsini, *PLP* 7759.

33   On the Empress Helena Palaiologina Dragaš, see *PLP* 21366; for Emperor Manuel II Palaiologos, *PLP* 21513.

34   On Constantine Dejanović Dragaš, see *PLP* 5746. According to an imperial document dated October 1395, Emperor Manuel II and his wife Helena Palaiologina gave the monastery a great endowment so that "it will commemorate to the God three times per week for the soul of the illustrious lord of Serbia, Constantine, father of our holy lady" (my translation); see Franciscus Miklosich and Iosephus Müller, *Acta et diplomata graeca medii aevi*, vol. 2 (Vienna: Carolus Gerold, 1860–90), pp. 260–63, here p. 260.8–13.

35   On Helena Palaiologina, see *PLP* 21364; on Lazar Branković Cantacouzenos, *PLP* 14354; on Đurađ Branković, *PLP* 3076; and on Irene Cantacouzene, *PLP* 5970. On the Cantacouzenos family tree, see Donald M. Nicol, *The Byzantine Family of Kantakouzenos (Cantacuzenus) ca. 1100–1460: A Genealogical and Prosopographical Study* (Dumbarton Oaks Studies 11) (Washington, DC: Dumbarton Oaks Center for Byzantine Studies, 1968); and Donald M. Nicol, "The Byzantine Family of Kantakouzenos: Some Addenda and Corrigenda," *Dumbarton Oaks Papers* 27 (1973): 309–15.

36   There are many more cases of marriages between the Byzantine and Serbian elite, such as those of Iagaris's daughters and that of the aunt of the scholar George Amiroutzes; see *Historia Politica et Patriarchica Constantinopoleos: Epirotica* (Corpus Scriptorium Historiae Byzantinae), ed. Immanuel Bekker (Bonn: Impensis Ed. Weberi, 1849), pp. 96.20–97.6; and *Ecthesis Chronica and Chronicon Athenarum*, ed. Spyridon P. Lampros (London: Methuen, 1902), p. 26.17–20. I present only these few cases, due to the scope of the current essay.

George, the son of the Serbian ruler Vuk Branković (1345–97), on December 26, 1414. She was his second or third wife.[37] It seems that she did not make a positive impression on the Serbian people, since sources describe her as "the accursed Irene—Jerina proklita."[38] A possible reason for this negative description could have been the heavy taxes and the forced labor she demanded for the construction of the great fortress of Smederevo around 1430; in fact, one of the towers of the castle was named after her, Jerinina Kula (Fig. 3.3). However, it seems that Irene established a secure environment for Byzantine refugees, including many scholars, who were searching for a better future to the north and west of Constantinople. Among them were two of her brothers, Thomas Cantacouzenos Palaiologos, who was in the service of his brother-in-law from 1433 and onwards, and George Cantacouzenos Palaiologos, a great scholar of his time.[39] George was raised and educated in Constantinople before moving to Mystra under the service of Despot Constantine XI Palaiologos (1405–53).[40] According to John Chortasmenos's epistolography, the young George was taught by him—probably at the Xenon of the Kral.[41] After a certain time, he moved to the Peloponnese and more specifically to the Kalavryta region, taking with him all his Constantinopolitan manuscripts. On April 27, 1436, he was visited by the famous traveler Cyriacus of Ancona, who described his extensive and costly personal library of codices.[42] In fact, Cyriacus mentioned in

---

37   On his previous marriage(s), see Ioannes A. Papadrianos, "Τίνες οἱ δεσμοὶ συγγενείας τοῦ Γεωργίου Βράνκοβιτζ πρὸς τον οἶκον τῶν Παλαιολόγων," *Epetiris Etaireias Byzantinon Spoudon* 33 (1964): 140–42. See also Nicol, *The Family of Kantakouzenos (Cantacuzenus)*, p. 169, n. 21.

38   Nicol, *The Family of Kantakouzenos (Cantacuzenus)*, pp. 184–88.

39   On Thomas, see PLP 10968; on George, PLP 10959. See also Nicol, *The Family of Kantakouzenos (Cantacuzenus)*, p. 176, n. 3. A funeral oration dedicated to George can be found in the cod. Cair. gr. 35; see Hunger, *Chortasmenos*, p. 108; and Lampros, *Νέος Ελληνομνήμων* [New Hellenomnemon] 10 (1913): 219. However, Criton Chrysochoides suggests that the specific oration was composed for a different George Cantakouzenos; see Chrysochoides, "Ἀνέκδοτη μονῳδία στὸν 'οἰκεῖον' τοῦ αὐτοκράτορα Γεώργιο Καντακουζηνὸ (15ος αἰ.)," *Βυζαντινά Σύμμεικτα* 5 (1983): 361–72.

40   In a letter to Constantine Palaiologos dated 1431, George appeared as his representative in a trade agreement with the Venetians in Ragusa/Dubrovnik; for the edition of the letter, see Spyridon P. Lampros, *Παλαιολόγεια καὶ Πελοποννησιακά* [Palaiologeia kai Peloponnisiaka] 4 (Athens, 1926), pp. 29–30.

41   In letters nrs. 36 and 38 to George's father Theodoros Cantacouzenos, Chortasmenos mentions the progress of his son; see Hunger, *Chortasmenos*, pp. 101–8, 186.

42   See Edward W. Bodnar, *Cyriacus of Ancona and Athens* (Collection Latomus 43) (Brussels-Berchem: Latomus, 1960), p. 42: "per niveos Saturnei montis, et difficiles calles Calabrutam adveni, ubi Georgium Catacuzinon, virum hac aetate graecis litteris eruditum, ac librorum Graecorum omnigenum copiosissimum, qui mihi Herodotum historicum, ac alios plerosque suos optimos, et antiquos libros accomodavit." See also Nicol, *The Family of Kantakouzenos (Cantacuzenus)*, p. 178.

FIGURE 3.3 The fortifications of Smederevo along with the Jerinina Kula (Tower of Irene) next to the main gate, Smederevo, Serbia
PHOTOGRAPH BY DRAGAN BOSNIC; REPRODUCED WITH PERMISSION

his notes the existence of a very important manuscript of Herodotus's works, which unfortunately has not yet been identified. However, two other manuscripts can be identified by their colophons as parts of George's library. The codex Vat. Ottob. gr. 67, with works of Arrianus, Diodorus Siculus, Nicephorus Gregoras, and Ptolemaeus, and verses to Theodora Palaiologina and Cardinal Bessarion, was completed around 1435–36 by the scribe Peter of Bua for (in my translation): "the venerable and very venerable scholar, kind, and pleasant cousin of the great and holy Emperor (John VIII Palaiologos), Sir George Palaiologos Cantacouzenos."[43] A shorter note by the owner can be found on folio 55r of the codex Vat. gr. 1301 of the 15th century, containing Procopius's account of the Gothic Wars: to paraphrase, "Procopius Caesar about the Gothic Wars, which took place under Belisarius with the command of the Great

---

43 "†ἐγεγών ... τὸ παρὸν πυκτίδιον, διὰ συνδρομῆς τοῦ σεβαστοῦ καὶ πανσεβαστοῦ λογιωτάτου, ἀγανόφρων [sic] καὶ γλαφυροτάτου, περιποθήτου ἐξαδέλφου τοῦ κραταιοῦ καὶ ἁγίου ἡμῶν αὐθέντου καὶ βασιλέως. ἡμετέρου δὲ αὐθέντου καὶ εὐεργέτου κυρ. Γεωργίου Παλαιολόγου τοῦ Καντακουζηνοῦ· καὶ πόνημα ἐμοῦ Πέτρου τοῦ Μπούα ἐπὶ ἔτους ˓ς Λ μδ'. ἰνδ. ιδ'"; Ernest Feron and Fabiano Battaglini, *Codices Manuscripti Graeci Ottoboniani Bibliothecae Vaticanae* (Rome: Typographeo Vaticano, 1893), pp. 43–44, fol. 92v.

Justinian. Lord Jesus Christ, have mercy on me the sinner. The present book (belongs) to George Cantacouzenos."[44]

After the restoration of George Branković and Irene Cantacouzene in Smederevo by Murad II in 1444 and probably after the proclamation of Constantine XI Palaiologos Dragases as emperor in Mystra (January 6, 1449), George Palaiologos Cantacouzenos moved to Smederevo to be near his sister. Once again, his personal collection of manuscripts moved with him, now to Serbia, transforming Smederevo into a small center of Byzantine scholarship. It is not irrelevant that new codices were added to his library during his stay there. The codex of Copenhagen Det Kongelige Bibliothek, GkS 6,2 has on the folio 232r the note (my translation): "The present book was in the possession of Luke Notaras and before him of Calothetus. Now it belongs to George Cantacouzenos, and it came into his possession in Smederevo after the fall of his homeland (1453)" (Fig. 3.4).[45] In addition, the codex Vat. Pal. gr. 278 has on folio 174v the note: "The present book belongs to the glorious supreme commander George Cantacouzenos, who acquired it in Smederevo on May 31, 1454: + Demetrios Lascaris Notarius."[46] In both cases the scribe of the notes was Demetrios Lascaris Leontares.

Demetrios was a Byzantine émigré who fled Constantinople after the fall of 1453, finding refuge with George Cantacouzenos Palaiologos before continuing to the Italian royal courts of the West.[47] His personal notes on the margins of various folios of the codices Laur. Plut. 55,47 and Voss. Gr. F. 42 reveal the tragic odyssey of his life.[48] He was the grandson of Demetrios Lascares Leontares, the *oikeios* of the Emperor Manuel II Palaiologos, and a member of a large family—eleven siblings, seven of whom died at a very young age. His mother

---

44 Procopius, *Procopii Caesariensis Opera omnia*, ed. Jacobus Haury, vol. 1 (Leipzig: Teubner, 1962), pp. 48–49, here paraphrasing from p. 49.

45 Bjarne Schartau, *codices Graeci Haunienses* (Danish Humanist Texts and Studies 9) (Copenhagen: Museum Tusculanum Press, 1994), pp. 51–54. The codex is made of parchment and contains Old Testament fragments.

46 Henry M. Stevenson, *Codices Manuscripti Palatini graeci Bibliothecae Vaticanae* (Rome: Typographeo Vaticano, 1885), pp. 153–54.

47 See *PLP* 14677; Jonathan Harris, "Demetrius Leontaris: Constantinople to Otranto," *Patristic and Byzantine Review* 18–19 (2000): 27–40; and Rudolf S. Stefec, *"Die Handschriften der Sophistenviten Philostrats," Römische historische Mitteilungen* 56 (2014): 137–206.

48 For Demetrios's personal notes in the two codices, see Angelo-Maria Bandini, *Catalogus codicum manuscriptorum Bibliothecae Mediceae Laurentianae*, vol. 2–3 (Florence, 1764–70; rep. Leipzig: Zentral-Antiquariat der Deutschen Demokratischen Republik, 1961), pp. 218–38; and Karel Adriaan de Meÿier, *Codices Vossiani Graeci et Miscellanei* (Codices Manuscripti 6) (Leiden: Bibliotheca Universitatis Leidensis, 1955), pp. 46–48.

BYZANTINE AND SERBIAN INTELLECTUAL RELATIONSHIPS 85

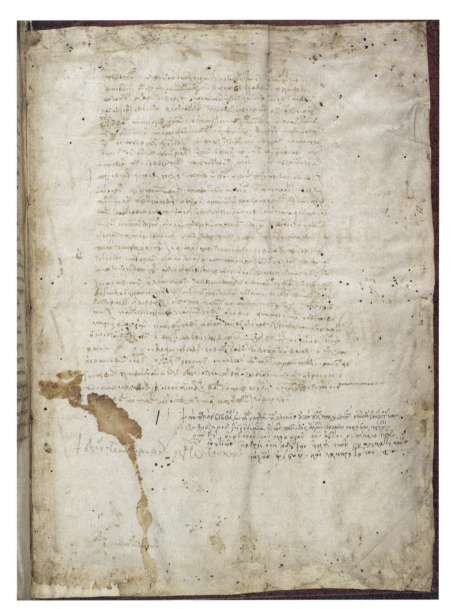

FIGURE 3.4 The note on the lower-right part of the folio by Demetrios Lascaris Leontares for George Palaiologos Cantacouzenos, folio 232r, GKS 6 folio, the Royal Danish Library
DIGITAL REPRODUCTION BY THE ROYAL DANISH LIBRARY; REPRODUCED WITH PERMISSION

died on January 16, 1450, and was buried next to his grandfather under the bell tower and close to the entrance of the monastery of St. John Prodromos "en Petra."[49] Demetrios was married to Efrosini Palaiologina Leontarina, who died on March 30, 1455, and left him with four children, one boy and three girls. Although a document dated December 26, 1454, mentioned him along with other members of the Byzantine elite visiting the Sultan Mehmed II, he appeared in Smederevo a few years later.[50] Demetrios's relationship to George Cantacouzenos is still unknown and can only be hypothesized. Indeed, it is possible they are related through Demetrios's wife, since her last name was Palaiologina. Also, their common intellectual background played a significant role. George Cantacouzenos was taught by the scholar John Chortasmenos, while Demetrios Lascaris Leontares had in his possession various codices of the famous scholar.[51] In addition, his family bond with the monastery of St. John Prodromos may imply a connection with the Xenon of the Kral. In any case, it seems that George Cantacouzenos Palaiologos through his scholarship and personal collection of manuscripts influenced the intellectual circles of Smederevo during the fourth and fifth decades of the 15th century. Old manuscripts were "saved" there from the destruction of 1453, while new ones were copied by scholars who sought a better future in Serbia.

3   Conclusion

In conclusion, Byzantium and Serbia maintained a very close cultural and intellectual relationship during the Palaiologan period, which was primarily facilitated through noble marriages between the two elites. The construction of the Xenon of the Kral in Constantinople at the beginning of the 14th century along with the relocation of the library of George Cantacouzenos Palaiologos to the Serbian court of George Vuk Branković in Smederevo—and the possible existence of a Greek scriptorium—during the first half of the 15th century are illustrative examples. However, more important is the fact of the establishment of a mutual and equal relationship between the two states for the first time. Byzantium became the recipient rather than just a purveyor of cultural goods, and Serbia made a significant impact on the Byzantine intellectual scene.

---

49   The inscription of the Leontaris family grave was copied in cod. Athen. Nat. Libr. 1075 and published by Ioannes Sakellion, "Ἐπιγραφαὶ Χριστιανικαὶ Ἐπιτύμβιοι," Ἐφημερὶς Ἀρχαιολογικὴ, vol. 1 (1886), pp. 238–39.
50   See Miklosich and Müller, *Acta et diplomata*, 2:290.
51   On Demetrios Lascaris Leontares's codices, see Petrou, "Higher Education," chap. 6.

Although several answers were offered here, more questions arise about this relationship. Since the Xenon of the Kral was, probably, a result of Simonis' relocation and influence over the Serbian court, what were the consequences of this event in the Byzantine court? What other intellectual exchange cases took place between the two states during the last two centuries of the Byzantine Empire? Are there any other evidences of this dynamic "two-way" intellectual relationship before the 13th century? Future research is needed to uncover additional aspects of the common intellectual history along with the reasons for their close relationship, especially during the period before the Palaiologan dynasty and the recapture of Constantinople in 1261.

Acknowledgements

I owe special thanks to the staff of the Bodleian Library; the Austrian National Library; the Royal Danish Library—especially Erik Petersen, senior researcher in Western manuscripts; the Museum of Smederevo Fortress—especially Miroslav P. Lazić, senior curator historian; and the Public Enterprise Smederevo Fortress company—especially Ana Mikić, for providing the pictures and digital reproductions of the manuscripts, along with the publications rights.

Unless otherwise noted, all translations and paraphrases from the Greek are mine.

Bibliography

Primary Sources

Actes de Chilandar (Archives de l'Athos 5), ed. Louis Petit and Boris Korablev. St. Petersburg, 1911; rep. Amsterdam: Adolf M. Hakkert, 1975.

Actes de Lavra (Archives de l'Athos), ed. Paul Lemerle et al., vols. 5, 8, and 10–11. Paris: P. Lethielleux, 1970–82.

Bandini, Angelo-Maria. *Catalogus codicum manuscriptorum Bibliothecae Mediceae Laurentianae*, 3 vols. Florence, 1764–70; rep. Leipzig: *Zentral-Antiquariat der Deutschen Demokratischen Republik*, 1961.

Bodnar, Edward W. *Cyriacus of Ancona and Athens* (Collection Latomus 43). Brussels-Berchem: Latomus, 1960.

Chrysochoides, Criton, ed. "Ἀνέκδοτη μονῳδία στὸν 'οἰκεῖον' τοῦ αὐτοκράτορα Γεώργιο Καντακουζηνὸ (15ος αἰ.)." *Βυζαντινὰ Σύμμεικτα* 5 (1983): 361–72.

Coxe, Henry Octavius. *Bodleian Library Quarto Catalogues 1: Greek Manuscripts*. Oxford: Bodleian Library, 1969.

de Meyïer, Karel Adriaan. *Codices Vossiani Graeci et Miscellanei* (Codices Manuscripti 6). Leiden: Bibliotheca Universitatis Leidensis, 1955.

Ducas. *Ducae Michaelis Ducae Nepotis Historia Byzantina* (Corpus Scriptorium Historiae Byzantinae), ed. Immanuel Bekker. Bonn: Impensis Ed. Weberi, 1834.

Dujčev, Ivan, ed. "Prouchvanija vurchu bulgarskoto srednovekovie. XVIII. Bulgarski dumi vuv vizantijski stichove ot XIV vek." *Sbornik na Bulgarskata akademija na naukite i iskustvata* 41, no. 1 (1945): 130–50.

Ecthesis Chronica and Chronicon Athenarum, ed. Spyridon P. Lampros. London: Methuen, 1902.

Feron, Ernest, and Fabiano Battaglini. *Codices Manuscripti Graeci Ottoboniani Bibliothecae Vaticanae*. Rome: Typographeo Vaticano, 1893.

Gilles, Pierre. *De topographia Constantinopoleos et de illius antiquitatibus* 4. Lyon: Gulielmus Rovillius, 1561.

González de Clavijo, Ruy. *Embassy to Tamerlane, 1403–1406*, trans. Guy Le Strange. London: Billing and Sons, 1928; rep. London—New York: Routledge Curzon, 2005.

Hafner, Stanislaus. *Serbisches Mittelalter: Altserbische Herrscherbiographien*. Graz: Styria, 1976.

Historia Politica et Patriarchica Constantinopoleos: Epirotica (Corpus Scriptorium Historiae Byzantinae), ed. Immanuel Bekker. Bonn: Impensis Ed. Weberi, 1849.

Hunger, Herbert. *Johannes Chortasmenos (ca. 1370–ca. 1436–37): Briefe, Gedichte und kleine Schriften* (Wiener Byzantinische Studien 7). Vienna: Österreichische Akademie der Wissenschaften, 1969.

Hunger, Herbert. *Katalog der griechischen Handschriften der Österreichischen Nationalbibliothek* (Museion, N.F. 4, 3 parts in 4 vols). Vienna: Prachner Verlag, 1961–92.

Kouzes, Aristotle P. "Τὸ περὶ τῶν ἐν ὁδοῦσι παθῶν᾽ ἔργον Νεοφύτου τοῦ Προδρομηνοῦ." *Epetiris Etaireias Buzantinon Spoudon* 7 (1930): 349–57.

Lampros, Spyridon P. Ἀργυροπούλεια [*Argyropouleia*], Ἰωάνου Ἀργυροπούλου λόγοι, πραγματεῖαι, ἐπιστολαί, προσφωνήματα, ἀπαντήσεις καὶ ἐπιστολαὶ πρὸς αὐτὸν καὶ τὸν υἱὸν Ἰσαάκιον. Ἐπιστολαὶ καὶ Ἀποφάσεις περὶ αὐτῶν. Athens: Sakellariou, 1910.

Lampros, Spyridon P. Παλαιολόγεια καὶ Πελοποννησιακὰ [Palaiologeia kai Peloponnisiaka], 4 vols. Athens, 1912–26.

Miklosich, Franciscus, and Iosephus Müller. *Acta et diplomata graeca medii aevi*, 4 vols. Vienna: Carolus Gerold, 1860–90.

Mioni, Elpidio. *Bibliothecae Divi Marci Venetiarum: Codices Graeci Manuscripti*, 3 vols. Rome: Istituto Poligrafico dello Stato, 1967–72.

Pachymérès, George. *Georges Pachymérès Relations Historiques* (Corpus Fontium Historiae Byzantinae 24), ed. Albert Failler, vol. 4. Paris: Institut français d'études byzantines, 1999.

Procopius. *Procopii Caesariensis Opera omnia*, ed. Jacobus Haury, vol. 1. Leipzig: Teubner, 1962.

Sakellion, Ioannes. "Ἐπιγραφαὶ Χριστιανικαὶ Ἐπιτύμβιοι," Ἐφημερίς Ἀρχαιολογική, 3 vols. (1886), 1: 238–39.

Schartau, Bjarne. *Codices Graeci Haunienses* (Danish Humanist Texts and Studies 9). Copenhagen: Museum Tusculanum Press, 1994.

Stevenson, Henry M. *Codices Manuscripti Palatini graeci Bibliothecae Vaticanae*. Rome: Typographeo Vaticano, 1885.

Secondary Literature

Agoritsas, Demetrios K. *Κωνσταντινούπολη. Η πόλη και η κοινωνία της στα πρώτα χρόνια των πρώτων Παλαιολόγων (1261–1328)*. Thessalonica: Byzantine Research Center, 2016.

Birchler-Argyros, Urs Benno. "Die Quellen zum Kral-Spital in Konstantinopel." *Gesnerus* 45 (1988): 419–44.

Boudon-Millot, Véronique. "Un nouveau témoin pour l'histoire du texte de l'Ars medica de Galien: le Vlatadon 14." In *L'Ars medica (Tegni) de Galien: Lectures antiques et médiévales*, ed. Nicoletta Palmieri, 11–29. Saint-Etienne: Publications de l'Université de Saint-Étienne, 2008.

Cacoulide, Eleni. "Η βιβλιοθήκη τῆς μονῆς Προδρόμου—Πέτρας στὴν Κωνσταντινούπολη." *Hellenica* 21 (1968): 3–39.

Cataldi Palau, Annaclara. *Studies in Greek Manuscripts* (Testi, Studi, Strumenti, 2 vols). Spoleto: Centro Italiano di studi sull'Alto Medioevo, 2008.

Diels, Hermann-Alexander. *Die Handschriften der Antiken Ärzte*. Leipzig: Zentral-Antiquariat der Deutschen Demokratischen Republik, 1970.

Gamillscheg, Ernst, and Dieter Harlfinger. *Repertorium der griechischen Kopisten 800–1600*, 3 vols. Vienna: Österreichische Akademie der Wissenschaften, 1981–97.

Gamillscheg, Ernst. "Zur handschriftlichen Überlieferung byzantinischer Schulbücher." *Jahrbuch der Österreichischen Byzantinistik* 26 (1977): 211–30.

Harris, Jonathan. "Demetrius Leontaris: Constantinople to Otranto." *Patristic and Byzantine Review* 18–19 (2000): 27–40.

Hunger, Herbert, and Otto Kresten. "Archaisierende Minuskel und Hodegonstil im 14. Jahrhundert." *Jahrbuch der Österreichischen Byzantinistik* 29 (1980): 187–236.

Janin, Raymond. *Le Géographie ecclésiastique, première partie: Le Siège de Constantinople et le Patriarcat Œcuménique*, vol. 3: *Les Églises et les Monastères*. Paris: Centre National de la Recherche Scientifique, 1953.

Kazhdan, Alexander P., et al. *The Oxford Dictionary of Byzantium*, 3 vols. New York and Oxford: Oxford University Press, 1991.

Kidonopoulos, Vassilios. *Bauten in Konstantinopel 1204–1328: Verfall und Zerstörung, Restaurierung, Umbau und Neubau von Profan- und Sakralbauten* (Mainzer Veröffentlichungen zur Byzantinistik 1). Wiesbaden: Harrassowitz Verlag, 1994.

Laiou, Angeliki E. *Constantinople and the Latins: The Foreign Policy of Andronicus II 1282–1328*. Cambridge, MA: Harvard University Press, 1972.

Lampros, Spyridon P. "Ἀντώνιος Πυρόπουλος." *Νέος Ἑλληνομνήμων* [New Hellenomnemon] 10 (1913): 127–34.

Miller, Timothy S. *The Birth of the Hospital in the Byzantine Empire*. Baltimore: Johns Hopkins University Press, 1997.

Mondrain, Brigitte. "Jean Argyropoulos professeur à Constantinople et ses auditeurs médecins, d'Andronic Éparque à Démétrios Angelos." In *Πολυπλευρος Νουσ: Miscellanea für Peter Schreiner zu seinem 60. Geburtstag*, ed. Cordula Scholtz and Georgios Makris, 223–50. Munich-Leipzig: K.G. Saur, 2000.

Necipoğlu, Nevra. *Byzantium between the Ottomans and the Latins. Politics and Society in the Later Empire*. New York: Cambridge University Press, 2009.

Nicol, Donald M. *The Byzantine Family of Kantakouzenos (Cantacuzenus) ca. 1100–1460: A Genealogical and Prosopographical study (Dumbarton Oaks Studies 11)*. Washington: Dumbarton Oaks Center for Byzantine Studies, 1968.

Nicol, Donald M. "The Byzantine Family of Kantakouzenos: Some Addenda and Corrigenda." *Dumbarton Oaks Papers* 27 (1973): 309–15.

Nicol, Donald M. *The Last Centuries of Byzantium 1261–1453*. London: Rupert Hart-Davis, 1972.

Papademetriou, George A. "Ἡ "κράλαινα τῶν Τριβαλῶν" καὶ ὁ κωδικογράφος Θεόκτιστος (± 1340)." *Μεσαιωνικά καὶ Νέα Ἑλληνικά* [Medieval and Modern Greek] 1 (1984): 420–51.

Papadrianos, Ioannes A. "Τίνες οἱ δεσμοὶ συγγενείας τοῦ Γεωργίου Βράνκοβιτζ πρὸς τὸν οἶκον τῶν Παλαιολόγων." *Epetiris Etaireias Byzantinon Spoudon* 33 (1964): 140–42.

Petrou, Elias. "Higher Education in Constantinople in the 15th Century." PhD diss., University of Ioannina, 2017.

Spatharakis, Joannis. *The Portrait in Byzantine Illuminated Manuscripts*. Leiden: Brill, 1976.

Stefec, Rudolf S. "*Die Handschriften der Sophistenviten Philostrats.*" *Römische historische Mitteilungen* 56 (2014): 137–206.

Theocharides, George. "Μία ἐξαφανισθεῖσα μονὴ τῆς Θεσσαλονίκης: ἡ μονὴ τοῦ Προδρόμου." *Macedonica* 18 (1978): 1–26.

Trapp, Erich, Rainer Walther, et al. *Prosopographisches Lexikon der Palaiologenzeit*, 12 vols. Vienna: Österreichische Akademie der Wissenschaften, 1976–94.

Vogel, Marie, and Victor Gardthausen. *Die griechischen Schreiber des Mittelalters und der Renaissance* (Zentralblatt für Bibliothekwesen, supplement 33). Leipzig: Otto Harrassowitz, 1909.

Volk, Otto. "Die byzantinischen Kloster-bibliotheken von Konstantinopel, Thessalonike und Kleinasien." Inaugural diss., Ludwig Maximillian University of Munich, 1954.

Živojinović, Mirjana. "L'hôpital du roi Milutin à Constantinople." *Zbornik radova Vizantološkog instituta* 16 (1975): 105–17 (French summary).

CHAPTER 4

An Unexpected Image of Diplomacy in a Vatican Panel

Marija Mihajlovic-Shipley

In 1941 Pimen Sofronov, a painter and restorer of Russian icons, was commissioned to repair an icon kept in the Treasury of St. Peter in the Vatican.[1] The icon was believed to have been painted by St. Methodius and to represent Constantine the Great being blessed by Pope Sylvester, flanked by two monks, beneath the busts of St. Peter and St. Paul.[2] During the restoration process, underneath the beard of Constantine, the face of a pious woman appeared, joined by two richly clad figures, hidden under the layers of monastic black color. That same year, after the restoration was completed, two researchers put forward their hypothesis on the identities of the figures in the lower register. Guido Anichini argued that the icon was from the 12th century and that the figures of the two richly dressed males could be brothers: Prince Stefan Nemanja (1166–1196) and Miroslav (1162–1190).[3] Wolfgang Fritz Volbach, however, claimed that the woman was Queen Jelena of Anjou (1236–1314), and that the lavishly adorned figures on her left and right were her sons, King Dragutin (King of Serbia, r. 1276–82; King of Mačva, r. 1282–1316) and King Milutin (r. 1282–1321).[4] Volbach's identification, based on historical record, has been widely accepted as correct. The panel of St. Peter and St. Paul, as it is known today, was probably commissioned by Queen Jelena and was presumably given as a gift to Pope Nicholas IV (r. 1288–92). It appears that, soon after it had been deposited in the Vatican Treasury, and prior to Sofronov's restoration, the icon took on a new appearance and different identity. By 1535, the identity of Queen Jelena's

---

1   "Nel 1941 un restauro razionale permise di meglio identificare un'icona che si era ritenuto risalisse al tempo di Constantino e poi ai santi Cirillo e Metodio. Rosa D'Amico, "Vatikanska ikona Jelene Anžujske i legendarna 'ikona cara Konstantina': ikonografski i politički aspekti srpske svetinje u Rimu," *Međunarodni Naučni Skup, Symposium, Niš i Vizantija* 10 (2011), 320.
2   See Mirjana Tatić-Djurić, "Ikona Apostola Petra i Pavla u Vatikanu," *Zograf: Časopis za Srednjovekovnu Umetnost* 2 (1967): 12.
3   Guido Anichini, "Di un antico quadro dei SS Pietro e Paolo nella Basilica Vaticana," *Rivista di archeologia cristiana* 17, no. 1–2 (1941): 141–49.
4   Wolfgang Fritz Volbach, "Die Ikone der Apostelfürsten in St. Peter in Rom," *Orientalia Christiana Perodica* 7, no. 3–4 (1941): 480–97.

icon had been replaced by another, based on a legend. After the sack of Rome in 1527, Leonardo da Pistoia, restoring the damaged icon, made alterations in which Jelena and her sons changed their identities.[5] Gradually, the belief that it was the Miraculous Icon of Emperor Constantine took over. Already in 1339, it was mentioned in the Vatican Inventory under this name. There is further evidence of this. In his description of the City of Rome in 1452, Nikolaus Muffel of Nuremberg states that "beneath the altar of Basilica of St. Peter lies the icon of Sts. Peter and Paul that St. Sylvester has given to Constantine."[6] This belief was maintained until Sofronov's restoration reestablished the panel's primary appearance and meaning.

1 The Panel and the Tradition of Giving

Dated to the end of the 13th century, the large panel, measuring 19–1/4 × 2–3/4 inches (49 × 7 cm) and now preserved in the Vatican Treasury, was painted on poplar wood in egg tempera on a gold background (Fig. 4.1).[7] The composition of the image is divided into two separate registers by a horizontal red line. The upper part, which occupies three-quarters of the whole panel, depicts Christ within a semi-circle, blessing the busts of St. Peter and St. Paul, who are denoted by the Cyrillic inscriptions above their heads. They are dressed in the chiton and the himation; Peter is holding a scroll and Paul a book of his epistles. As the commissioner of the work, Queen Jelena was probably aware of the contemporary religious politics in the region, especially from the Italian side of the Adriatic coast, where the idea of apostolic unity closely corresponded with the idea of the unification of two churches promoted by popes in the 13th century. The cult of the spiritual unity of the two apostles was established in the late 4th century, when Pope Damasus consistently promoted them as emblems of unity within the church.[8] The belief in the joint foundation of the Church of Rome by Sts. Peter and Paul was consciously developed by the bishops of Rome

---

5 See D'Amico, "Vatikanska ikona Jelene Anžujske," p. 320.

6 Nikolaus Muffel, *Descrizione della città di Roma nel 1452: Delle indulgenze e dei luoghi sacri di Roma (Der ablas und die heligen stet zu Rom)*, ed. Gerhard Wiedmann (Bologna: Patron, 1999); D'Amico, "Vatikanska ikona Jelene Anžujske." p. 218.

7 See Cecily J. Hilsdale, *Byzantine Art and Diplomacy in an Age of Decline* (Cambridge, UK: Cambridge University Press, 2014), p. 287. On the dimensions, see Tatić-Djurić, "Ikona Apostola Petra i Pavla u Vatikanu," p. 11.

8 See Gitte Lønstrup Dal Santo, "Concordia Apostolorum—Concordia Augustorum: Building a Corporate Image for the Theodosian Dynasty," in *East and West in the Roman Empire of the Fourth Century: An End to Unity?* ed. Roald Dijkstra, Sanne van Poppel, and Daniëlle Slootjes (Leiden: Brill, 2015), p. 102.

AN UNEXPECTED IMAGE OF DIPLOMACY 93

FIGURE 4.1 Exact copy of panel of St. Peter and St. Paul, second half of 13th century, egg tempera on wood, 29–1/8 × 19–1/4 in. (74 × 49 cm) from the Vatican Treasury. The copy was commissioned by the National Museum in Belgrade and was made by Zdenka Živkovic in 1967.
PHOTOGRAPH PROVIDED BY NATIONAL MUSEUM OF BELGRADE

during the second half of the 4th century as a justification for juridicial authority within the church as a whole. It was used as a weapon in the propaganda war waged against heresy, and against the claims of the East to an equal, if not superior, authority.[9] In the 13th century, this imagery was rekindled in the politics of the popes who promulgated the idea of the Union of the Church during the negotiations prior to the Council of Lyons in 1274. Ecclesiastical union continued to be promoted through the images of Sts. Peter and Paul during the pontificate of Nicholas IV (r. 1288–92).[10] This can be clearly observed in the apse of Santa Maria Maggiore in Rome, where the figure of Pope Nicholas is kneeling in front of the two apostles.

The lower register shows a woman in the center, being blessed by a Western bishop, contained within a semi-circular archway and flanked by two figures. She is demurely clad, with no royal insignia except for the red cape, and on her head she wears a black maphorion. Two male figures on either side are both dressed as Byzantine emperors wearing red sakkoi, maniakia, loroi, and stema crowns, with their hands raised in supplication. The lower figures are approximately 6 inches (16 cm) in height. The panel bears the marks of nails around the figures. Although the figures surrounding the queen are more or less clear, and the scholarship is fairly certain about their identities, the figure of the bishop still languishes in scholarly limbo. This essay will focus on the figures in the lower register, their mutual relationship and, in particular, the identity and the role of the Latin bishop. The recurring motif of this icon is duality. Visually, it is divided into two horizontal registers, representing two apostles, two sons, two iconographies, and two natures of rule, and it carries a plethora of double meanings. The object represents the visual communication between two officials; it carries within it vocabulary necessary for the two juxtaposed worlds to institute conversation and articulate contemporary problems. It was a visual means of establishing alliances and conveying messages.

This paper sheds light on the relationship between Serbia and Byzantium, and on the interactions between Catholic and Orthodox visual narratives. The object under consideration reflects intercultural dialogue in a realm situated on the border between East and West. When put in a rich historical context, the distinction between East and West at that specific time was blurred and

---

9   See Janet M. Huskinson, *Concordia Apostolorum: Christian Propaganda at Rome in the Fourth and Fifth Centuries; A Study in Early Christian Iconography and Iconology* (Oxford: British Archaeological Reports, 1982), p. 87.

10 For more on the upper register of the Vatican panel, see Marija Mihajlovic-Shipley, "Concordia Apostolorum—Concordia Regum and the Question of the True Portraits," chap. in "Queen Jelena between Two Worlds: The Icon of St. Peter and St. Paul" (MA thesis, Courtauld Institute of Art, 2017).

rather vague, which suited the complexity of local politics. Also, the lack of strict iconographies resulted in flexibility in the application of pictorial motifs, and this was consequently addressed, as shown in this essay, through the diplomatic correspondence that openly played with the ambiguity of the accessible visual vocabulary.

The icon was first documented in the inventory of the Vatican Treasury in 1295, a year after Pope Boniface VIII's inauguration.[11] The item was listed as: "Unam tabulam guarnitam de laminis argenti in qua sunt imagines apostolorum Petri et Pauli" (one panel adorned with silver plate, with images of apostles Peter and Paul).[12] The panel is also mentioned in 1304, among objects that belonged to the private treasury of Pope Boniface VIII, later to be inherited by his successors.[13] This date span could correspond with Volbach's hypothesis that the three figures in the lower register of the panel were, indeed, Queen Jelena, who coruled the kingdom of Serbia, with her sons, Dragutin and Milutin.[14] King Uroš I, Queen Jelena's husband, was deposed by his son Dragutin in 1276 and died in 1277. Rosa D'Amico suggests that the object was sent as a gift to Pope Boniface's predecessor Nicholas IV (r. 1288–92), with whom Queen Jelena had close correspondence.[15]

Diplomatic gifts from the East sent to the popes were usually politically instigated, as in the case of the embroidered silk of St. Lawrence that Michael VIII Palaiologos gave to Pope Gregory X.[16] The panel, with imagery evoking the idea of the unification of two churches from the Second Council of Lyons in 1274,

---

11   See D'Amico, "Vatikanska ikona Jelene Anžujske," p. 307.
12   Émile Molinier, "Inventaire du trésor du Saint-Siège sous Boniface VIII (1295) (Suite)," *Bibliothèque de l'École des Chartes* 45, no. 1 (1884): item 718, p. 53, trans. Mihajlovic-Shipley, "Queen Jelena between Two Worlds." The Inventory is also available online: https://www.persee.fr/doc/bec_0373-6237_1888_num_49_1_447531, as of December 10, 2019.
13   See D'Amico, "Vatikanska ikona Jelene Anžujske," p. 317.
14   For literature about King Milutin see Leonidas Mavromatis, *La Fondation de l'Empire Serbe: Le Kralj Milutin* (Thessaloniki: Kentron Vyzantinon Ereunon, 1978); Branislav Todić, *Srpsko Slikarstvo u Doba Kralja Milutina* (Beograd: Draganic, 1998). For King Dragutin see the collection of essays: Dinko Davidov ed., *Naučni Skup: Kralj Dragutin u Istoriji i Umetnosti*. Račanski Zbornik. Vol. 3 (Bajina Bašta: Fondacija Račanska baština, 1998); Dragan Vojvodić, *Zidno Slikarstvo Crkve Svetog Ahilija u Arilju* (Beograd: Stubovi Kulture, 2005). For Queen Jelena, see the collection of papers titled: Katarina Mitrović ed., *Jelena—Kraljica, Monahinja, Svetiteljka. Tematski Zbornik Radova Posvećenih Kraljici Jeleni* (Manastir Gradac: Ministarstvo Kulture i Informisanja, 2015). Gojko Subotić, "Kraljica Jelena Anžujska: ktitor crkvenih spomenika u Primorju," *Separat iz Istorijskog Glasnika* 1–2 (1958): 131–48.
15   D'Amico, "Vatikanska ikona Jelene Anžujske," p. 307.
16   See Hilsdale, *Byzantine Art and Diplomacy in an Age of Decline*, p. 46.

was first noted in the Vatican Inventory in 1295, as was Queen Jelena's panel.[17] The silk included an image of Pope Gregory leading the Byzantine Emperor to St. Peter.[18] The panel of Queen Jelena does not openly indicate the political agenda of the commissioner or the recipient of the object, but it does underline aspirations and agendas that reverberated on both sides of the Adriatic at the time. Unlike the silk of Michael VIII, Jelena's gift, by the inclusion of a Catholic bishop and not the pope, shows a subtler, indirect choice of visual communication, attesting to the queen's diplomatic awareness of the convoluted and problematic politics of her sons within the complex alliances in the Adriatic region. The sensitive political message conveyed via the panel could reflect the fragile and knotty relations between the papal chair and the Serbian Kingdom during the second half of the 13th century.

The liaisons between late medieval Italy and Serbia were strategically very important for the Nemanjić dynasty (1166–1371), especially with Venice and Rome, considering that without the papal and venetian influence King Stefan would not gain the royal crown.[19] The first information about Prince Nemanja's donations to churches in Rome and Bari is recorded in the Vita (1216) written by his son, Stefan the First-Crowned, the first king of Serbia.[20] By inviting papal envoys to the church council in Bar, in 1199, Nemanja's son Vukan further reinforced good relationships with the Sees of Rome.[21] The good will culminated with Stefan Nemanja's son receiving a royal crown from the hands of an official of Pope Honorius III in 1217. Subsequently, archbishop Sava sent a richly adorned censer to be hung above the tomb of St. Peter.[22] These diplomatic

---

17 Molinier, "Inventaire du Trésor du Saint-Siège," item 811, p. 18; and Hilsdale, *Byzantine Art and Diplomacy in an Age of Decline*, p. 46.
18 See Antony Eastmond, *The Glory of Byzantium and Early Christendom* (London and New York: Phaidon Press, 2013), pp. 250–51.
19 Specifically, for the relationship between Venice and Nemanjić kings see: Momčilo Spremić, *Srbija i Venecija (VI–XVI Vek)* (Beograd: Službeni Glasnik, 2016); Ruža Ćuk, *Srbija i Venecija u XIII i XIV Veku* (Prosveta, 1986); Katarina Mitrović, "Pismo Kralja Stefana Uroša III Mletačkom Duždu Frančesku Dandolu," *Stari Srpski Arhiv* 15 (n.d.): 9–18.
20 See Boško Bojović, *L'idéologie monarchique dans les hagio-biographies dynastiques du moyen âge serbe* (Rome: Pontificio Istituto Orientale, 1995), pp. 248 and 278; and Ljiljana Juhas Georgievska, Tomislav Jovanović, eds., *Стефан Првовенчани, Сабрана Дела* (Belgrade: Srpska Knjiga, 1999), p. 42.
21 See Bojan Miljković, "Nemanjići i Sveti Nikola u Bariju," *Zbornik Radova Vizantoloskog Instituta* 44 (2007): 277.
22 The highly embellished censer is mentioned only in the pages of the manuscript "The Life of Saint Sava" written by Domentijan, today in St. Petersburg. The copy of the manuscript in St. Petersburg differs in some details from the published manuscript found in Austrian National Library: Domentijan, *Život Svetoga Simeuna i Svetoga Save*, ed. Đura Daničić (Belgrade: Društvo Srpske Slovesnosti, 1865). The original text found in St. Petersburg

actions are recorded in Sava's Vita, written in 1250 by Domentijan, at the request of King Uroš I.[23] Following in this tradition, Queen Jelena contributed significantly to the image of the Nemanjić family as great patrons and donors. The hagiographer Danilo II, Queen Jelena's contemporary, dedicated a significant part of the Queen's Vita to her activities as a benefactor.[24] Danilo II writes that she donated numerous objects of immense value to churches, including gold and silver liturgical vessels, embellished with pearls and jewels; precious books; and liturgical vestments[25] A number of these are recorded, among them a cross made of wood from the Holy Cross encrusted with precious stones and exhibiting an inscription with the name of Queen Jelena.[26] The queen gave this cross to Sopoćani Monastery. It was last noted in Austria but has been considered lost since the 17th century.[27] The icon that Jelena gave to the church of St. Nicholas in Bari suffered the same fate. However, from the only surviving description of the Bari icon, we learn that the panel from the Vatican Treasury reveals many similarities.

2   The Icon in Bari and the Vatican Panel

The icon donated by Queen Jelena and her sons, Dragutin and Milutin, to the church of St. Nicholas in Bari, which possessed the relics of this saint, represented St. Nicholas. Although the icon no longer exists, its description is documented by Padre Antonio Beatillo in his 1620 text *Historia della Vita*.[28] According to the description by Beatillo, the icon's height was less than 40

---

was published in 1873: Vatroslav Jagić, "Kritički Dodatci Tekstu Života Svetoga Simeuna i Svetoga Save: [Opisi i Izvodi iz Nekoliko Južnoslovinskih Rukopisa]," *Starine* 5 (1873): 15–16.

23   Svetlana Tomin, ed., *Stara Srpska Knjizevnost* (Sremski Karlovci—Novi Sad: Izdavacka Knjizarnica Zorana Stojanovića, 2001), p. 95; and Ljiljana Juhas Georgievska, ed. "Житије Светог Саве," in *Стефан Првовенчани, Доментијан, Теодосије, Житије Светога Симеона* (Novi Sad: Matica Srpska Publishing Center, 2012), pp. 69–189.

24   Arhiepiskop Danilo II, *Životi Kraljeva i Arhiepiskopa Srpskih*, Kolo 38 (Srpska Književna Zadruga 257) (Belgrade: Srpska Književna Zadruga, 1935), pp. 43–76.

25   Tomin, ed., *Stara Srpska Književnost*, p. 213.

26   See Danica Popović, *Riznica Spasenja, Kult Relikvija i Srpskih Svetih u Srednjevekovnoj Srbiji* (Belgrade—Novi Sad: SANU, Balkanološki Institut, 2018), pp. 115–33.

27   Ibid.; and Leontje Pavlović, *Kultovi lica kod Srba i Makedonaca* (Smederevo: Narodni Muzej Smederevo, 1965), pp. 87–88.

28   Padre Antonio da Bari Beatillo, *Historia della vita, miracoli, traslatione e gloria dell'illustrissimo Confessore di Christo, San Nicolò il Magno, arcivescovo di Mira, patrono e protettore della città di Bari* (Naples and Palermo: Nella Stamperia di Pietro Coppola, 1642), p. 653.

inches (one meter) and its width more than 20 inches (a half meter). It was also divided into two horizontal registers but, instead of St. Peter and St. Paul, as shown in the Vatican panel, it depicted only a bust of St. Nicholas. In the lower area, Queen Jelena was shown flanked by her sons, King Dragutin and King Milutin, marked by inscriptions in Latin. Dragutin on the left was named REX STEPHANUS FILIUS UROSII REGIS SERVIE (King Stefan son of Uroš the ruler of Serbia) and Milutin on the right identified as "REX UROSIVS FILIUS UROSII REGIS SERVIE" (King Uroš (II) son of Uroš (I) the ruler of Serbia). An inscription placed by the figure of Queen Jelena stated: "MEMENTO DOMINE FAMULE TUE HELENE DEI GRATIA REGINE SERVIE UXORIS MAGNI REGIS UROSII MATRIS UROSII ET STEPHANI SUPRASCRIPTORUM REGUM HANC YCONAM AD HONOREM SANCTI NICOLAI ORDINAVIT" (Oh, Lord, remember Thy servant in the Grace of God Jelena the Queen of Serbia wife of the great King Uroš (I) and mother of Uroš (II) and Stefan, the above signed rulers, who commissioned this icon in honor of St. Nicholas).[29] To emphasize the devotional purpose of the Bari icon, the inscription articulated that Queen Jelena was giving this "YCONAM" in honor of St. Nicholas. In the *Lexicon Latinitatis Medii Aevi Iugoslaviae*, the noun "ycona," the equivalent of "icona," translates as Imago Sancta, or Saintly Image.[30] The figure of St. Nicholas, in this specific context, has the intercessory function of protecting and acting in the name of the beneficiary. He appears as a personal mediator whom the queen and her sons supplicate for help. The icon thus carries the notion of a spiritual plea, embodied in the figure of St. Nicholas: a subject suited for the contemplative and liturgical purpose of the Bari shrine.

Did the Vatican panel bear an inscription similar to that of the icon in Bari, and, if it did, could it therefore be an icon? In the Vatican inventory of 1295, the object is listed under the section entitled "Icone de Ebore" (Icons of Ivory), yet it is also described as "una tabula".[31] This adds to the confusion, as not only is it identified as a panel rather than an ivory, it is also not described as an icon, unlike all of the other items in the section.[32] Jelena's panel, therefore, even in 1295, was difficult to define. The division into two registers, of which the upper and more dominant one contains the images of Christ and two apostles,

---

29 Beatillo, *Historia della vita, miracoli, traslatione e gloria*, p. 653. Translation revised and verified by Marko Đurđević in 2017, at the request of the author.
30 Marko Kostrenčić, ed., *Lexicon Latinitatis Medii Aevi Iugoslaviae*, vol. 1, L–Z, trans. Veljko Gortan and Zlatko Herkov (Zagreb: Editio Instituti historici Academiae scientiarum et artium Slavorum meridionalium, 1973).
31 Trans. Mihajlovic-Shipley, "Queen Jelena between Two Worlds." "Una tabula" in Molinier, "Inventaire du trésor du Saint-Siège," item 718, p. 53.
32 Ibid., p. 53.

suggests that it is an icon. The lower register, however, depicts contemporary political figures, which could suggest that it is also a diplomatic panel. The object, therefore, could contain both devotional and political meaning. Jelena's icon, sent to Bari in the 17th century, according to Beatillo, was kept in the crypt and placed to the right-hand side of the relics of the saint above the wooden chest, unlike the Vatican panel that was held in the Pope's private Treasury.[33] It is possible to differentiate between an icon or relic sent to a church, to be used in worship, liturgy, or procession, and another type of panel, still an object of devotion, but sent as a politically motivated gift to a dignitary of another country. The latter perhaps carries distinct diplomatic messages. The difference could also be in its purpose. Latin inscriptions on the Bari icon were probably used in prayer during liturgies of dedication and protection of the family members. The panel, probably lavishly decorated, may have been of special significance for Pope Nicholas IV. The icon of St. Nicholas in Bari could offer some clues to its decorative features.

One of the similarities between the icon of Bari and the Vatican panel is in the possibility of the former having a silver revetment.[34] Padre Beatillo in his *Historia* compares the icon of St. Nicholas in Bari to the icon of a king that he has previously described. Beatillo comments that it was covered with a silver revetment with enamels. He then continues, claiming that it was similar to Jelena's icon: "le cose è similissimo al quadro grande del Re, fuorché nelle imagini che gli stanno ginocchioni all'intorno" (in everything else the picture [icon] is very similar to the other one of the King except for the figures kneeling around the saint).[35] Therefore, it can be argued that the icon of St. Nicholas in Bari could also have had a revetment. The silver cover on the Vatican panel is mentioned as "guarnitam laminis argenti" (adorned with silver plate) in the inventory of the Papal Treasury in 1295.[36] The word "guarnitam" is not referenced in the Oxford Latin Dictionary. However, the *Grande dizionario della lingua italiana* suggests that the word "guarnire", the Italian participle of which is "guarnita" means to burnish or plate.[37] The marks of the nails that would

---

33 Beatillo, *Historia della vita, miracoli, traslatione e gloria*, p. 635.
34 For more details see: Miljković, "Nemanjići i Sveti Nikola u Bariju," with additional explanations and bibliography.
35 Ibid., pp. 652–53, trans. Mihajlovic-Shipley, "Queen Jelena between Two Worlds."
36 Volbach, "Die Ikone der Apostelfürsten in St. Peter in Rom," pp. 480–97; Miljković, "Nemanjići i Sveti Nikola u Bariju," p. 278; and Molinier, "Inventaire du trésor du Saint-Siège," p. 53, trans. Mihajlovic-Shipley, "Queen Jelena between Two Worlds."
37 Salvatore Battaglia, ed., *Grande dizionario della lingua italiana* 7 (Grav—Ing) (Turin: Unione Tipografico – Editrice Torinese, 1971). In the *Lexicon Latinitatis Medii Aevi Iugoslaviae*, the word "guarnimenta" is plural of a noun "guarnimento," which means to equip or to ornament; it is also marked as Italian word.

have held the revetment can still be observed on the Vatican panel. Thus, the similarities between the Vatican and Bari icons could indicate that both were produced by the same artist or in the same workshop. This could explain the minimal inscriptions on the Vatican icon of St. Peter and St. Paul, suggesting that additional inscriptions could have been included on the revetment. The fact that only two Cyrillic inscriptions remain above the apostles' heads might also suggest the existence of the silver cover on certain portions of the image.[38] Another possible question is whether the silver revetment, removed from the icon, held any inscription and, if so, whether it was in Latin or Cyrillic. Keeping in mind the duality of this panel, it can be suggested that the revetment may have had a Latin inscription. However, there exist no known documents to confirm what secrets the missing revetment held, or how extensively it decorated the object, thus leaving the question open for discussion. An alternative explanation for the removal of the silver revetment, other than vandalism or theft, could be that when the icon was "rebranded" by Leonardo da Pistoia in 1527, any inscriptions that revealed the true identities of the four smaller figures at the bottom of the icon needed to be removed. However, the Bari icon, as well as the marks of revetment, confirm that the queen's gift to the pope was certainly precious and expensive, an offer of good will and support on behalf of the queen. The language of political discourse was enriched with the subtle incorporation of the Latin bishop.

3 The Figure of the Latin Bishop

A Western bishop with the nimbus, holding a book and the episcopal staff (crozier), is blessing Queen Jelena. The bishop is dressed in a green tunic and red chasuble, with pearls grouped in threes as a repetitive ornament, and a miter on his head. The extant visual evidence from the second half of the 13th century Kingdom of Serbia throws no light on the identity of the Latin bishop figure. However, the visual examples from the opposite side of Adriatic coast can offer some explanation. It is important to note that there were strong economic and political ties between the South of Italy and Jelena's domain.[39] The multiculturalism of the coastal trading towns and the ceaseless cultural exchange was reflected in the heartland of the Serbian Kingdom. The inclusion of the Latin-type religious figure is a confirmation of the active diplomatic,

---

38 See Miljković, "Nemanjići i Sveti Nikola u Bariju," p. 278.
39 See Miroslav Popović, "Kraljica Jelena i Katolička Crkva" (MA thesis, Filosofski Fakultet Univerziteta u Beogradu, 2007), p. 75.

cultural, and economic relations between two opposed religious and political authorities of the East and the West, filtering equally throughout the kingdom.

The coexistence of multiple ethnicities in the Adriatic region and the influence of Southern Italian culture in the Kingdom of Serbia can be observed through two icons now kept in St. Catherine's Monastery in Sinai. One is from the second half of the 12th century and shares stylistic similarities with the Vatican panel, in the treatment of the figure of St. Paul. The other is a panel of a 13th-century triptych that supports the hypothesis, posited by Hans Belting, that the unidentified figure in the Vatican panel is, in fact, St. Nicholas.[40] Both Sinai icons are rendered in established Western church iconography. The first in question, dated to the second half of the 12th century, is the icon of St. Paul, Jacob the Elder, Stephen, Lawrence, Martin of Tours, and Leonard of Limoges. Kurt Weitzmann connects this icon to an artist from the South of Italy.[41] The striking similarity between Jelena's panel and this Sinai icon is evident, not only in its iconography of St. Paul, but also in the artistic treatment of the figures (Fig. 4.2). This includes the style of apostle's dress, the identical design of the book that he is holding, the linear treatment, and the distinctive artistic manner in which the figure is painted. The same treatment of a figure of St. Paul and the book that he is holding can also be found on the fresco painted in 1296 of St. Peter and St. Paul in St. Achillius church in Arilje, which was King Dragutin's endowment church (Fig. 4.3). The treatment of the figure of St. Paul in the upper register of the queen's panel can only attest to the Southern Italian influence. Considering the iconographic similarities with Jelena's panel, the fresco could be interpreted as a commission done by an artist from the South of Italy, perhaps Apulia. By adopting a recognizable Italian style, Jelena may have wished to promote the Serbian Kingdom as a multicultural state, with strong Italian connections and affinities, or to have the icon appeal stylistically to its intended audience. However, if with this specific style the queen wanted to reinforce the ties between Italy and Serbia, the incorporation of the Latin bishop cemented her purpose.

The second panel held in St. Catherine's Monastery in Sinai is the icon depicting St. Nicholas from the second part of the 13th century, which Weitzmann suggests could also be attributed to a Southern Italian painter, possibly from Apulia (Fig. 4.4).[42] This icon may cast a light on the identity of the figure of

---

40 Hans Belting, *Likeness and Presence: A History of the Image before the Era of Art* (Chicago and London: University of Chicago Press, 1994), p. 337.
41 Kurt Weitzmann, "The Icons of the Period of the Crusades," in *The Icon*, ed. Kurt Weitzmann (London: Bracken Books, 1982), p. 206.
42 Ibid., p. 202.

FIGURE 4.2
Detail of icon of St. Paul, Jacob the Elder, Stephen, Lawrence, Martin of Tours, and Leonard of Limoges, second half of the 12th century, egg tempera on wood, 13–1/8 × 9–3/8 in. (33.3 × 23.7 cm)
REPRODUCED WITH PERMISSION OF SAINT CATHERINE'S MONASTERY, SINAI, EGYPT; PHOTOGRAPH PROVIDED BY MICHIGAN-PRINCETON-ALEXANDRIA EXPEDITIONS TO MOUNT SINAI

Latin bishop in the Vatican panel. On the Sinai icon, St. Nicholas is adorned as a Western bishop with a crozier and miter. However, an artist of the Eastern tradition would almost certainly have painted the bishop without a headdress or a staff. The cult of St. Nicholas of Myra became increasingly popular in Italy after the translation of the relics in 1087 to Bari.[43] Gradually, the iconography of the Eastern episcope evolved into a recognizably Latin type, with

---

43   See Edward G. Clare, *St. Nicholas: His Legends and Iconography* (Florence: Leo S. Olschki Editore, 1985), p. 54.

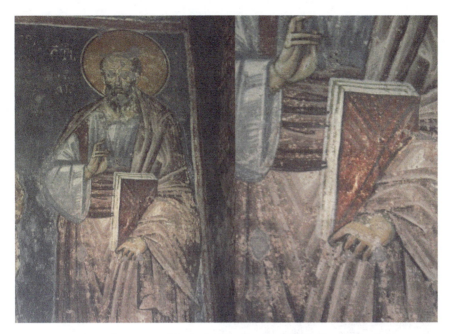

FIGURE 4.3 Fresco of St. Peter and St. Paul in the Church of St. Achillius, Arilje, 1296
PHOTOGRAPH BY MARIJA MIHAJLOVIC-SHIPLEY

St. Nicholas of Myra becoming St. Nicholas of Bari. It is, therefore, possible to distinguish between the Eastern and Western iconographical treatments of St. Nicholas. The hypothesis suggested by some researchers, that the bishop figure in the Vatican panel is in fact pontifex maximus and not St. Nicholas, is a problematic one.[44] When taking into account the visual evidence in the apse mosaic of the Basilica of Santa Maria Maggiore executed under the patronage of Pope Nicholas IV and the influential Colonna family, it is evident that the official attire of the pope does not match the iconographical vestments of St. Nicholas of Bari in both the Sinai and Vatican versions (Fig. 4.5).[45] The mosaic clearly distinguishes between the representative ceremonial adornment of the pope at that time and the attire of the Latin bishop on Queen Jelena's panel. By examining this piece of evidence, it should be clear that the bishop figure on the Vatican panel is not a pope. However, this clarification does not confirm

---

44   See Miljković, "Nemanjići i Sveti Nikola u Bariju," p. 278.
45   See Julian Gardner, "Pope Nicholas IV and the Decoration of Santa Maria Maggiore," *Zeitschrift für Kunstgeschichte* 36 (1973): 1–2.

FIGURE 4.4
Panel of triptych depicting St. Nicholas, second half of 13th century, egg tempera on wood, h. 22–3/4 in. (57.8 cm)
REPRODUCED WITH PERMISSION OF SAINT CATHERINE'S MONASTERY, SINAI, EGYPT; PHOTOGRAPH PROVIDED BY PRINCETON UNIVERSITY, MICHIGAN-PRINCETON-ALEXANDRIA EXPEDITIONS TO MOUNT SINAI

that the queen, by choosing St. Nicholas of Bari, was not openly stating her affinities with Nicholas IV.[46]

In the Basilica of Santa Maria in Aracoeli in Rome, prominent Colonna family members were depicted standing by St. Nicholas of Bari. Julian Gardner suggests that, in depicting St. Nicholas of Bari, the Colonna family visualized

---

46 See Anna Christidou, "Unknown Byzantine Art in the Balkan Area: Art, Power and Patronage in Twelfth to Fourteenth Century Churches in Albania" (PhD diss., Courtauld Institute of Art, 2010), p. 401, fig. 49.

FIGURE 4.5 Jacopo Torriti, detail of apse mosaic showing Pope Nicholas IV with St. Peter and St. Paul, 1290–95. Santa Maria Maggiore, Rome
REPRODUCED WITH PERMISSION OF THE CONWAY LIBRARY, THE COURTAULD INSTITUTE OF ART, DISTRIBUTED UNDER A CC BY-NC 4.0 LICENSE

its link with Pope Nicholas IV.[47] The saint, as a symbol of holiness and divine power, could also have been employed to mediate between individuals within high political communities.[48] Saints as political symbols helped to convey messages of royal legitimacy, as can be seen on the enamel from 1132, now kept

---

47   Julian Gardner, *The Roman Crucible: The Artistic Patronage of the Papacy 1198–1304* (Munich: Hirmer Verlag, 2013), p. 255.
48   See John M. Theilmann, "Political Canonization and Political Symbolism in Medieval England," *Journal of British Studies* 29, no. 3 (1990): 242.

in Bari, depicting St. Nicholas crowning Roger II. In the case of the Colonna family members, by recruiting St. Nicholas, a potent symbol of moral authority, they emphasized their political connections with the papal tiara, thus, turning a sacred symbol into a political one. Therefore, it could be argued, as in the example of the Colonna family, Queen Jelena, through the figure of St. Nicholas of Bari, wished to express her affinity with the politics of Nicholas IV. The extant letter exchange from 1288 to 1292 between the two could attest to the carefully nurtured diplomatic relationship in the region, with St. Nicholas as a diplomatic and symbolic point of tangency.[49]

The depiction of St. Nicholas of Bari was not only limited to the Apennine Peninsula. The image was disseminated on the opposite side of the Adriatic, to the coastal areas of the Balkans. It represented a part of an ecclesiastical propaganda for the supremacy of the Church of Rome in the region. In her thesis on the 12th- to 14th-century churches in Albania, Anna Christidou broadly discusses the intertwined influences of the Latin and Eastern iconographies. She specifically addresses the Savior Church in Rubik (northwest Albania) as an example of coexistence and a mixed social milieu that practiced traditions of both East and West.[50] Originally decorated in the Byzantine style in 1166, during its restoration in 1272 by the Franciscans the church had a Latin iconographic program, introduced to suit the then-Western ecclesiastical agenda.[51] Now severely damaged, but still identifiable, the figure of St. Nicholas clad in the Latin episcopal vestments and insignia can be seen in the apse in the lower register. This particular visual vocabulary was endorsed and spread as a vehicle for the dissemination of Latin propaganda, promoting the idea of the unification of the two churches.[52] Therefore, St. Nicholas was a potent tool in expressing the authority of the papal tiara, used as a pictorial religious slogan representing the politics of the Church of Rome.

However, the choice of St. Nicholas in Jelena's panel could suggest another, more subtle and intimate tone, disclosing the queen's personal relationships with her family. To the rich collection of meanings attributed to this powerful saintly figure, another, more feminine, quality could be added. In her essay on the Vita icon, Nancy Ševčenko adds another example of St. Nicholas painted in the Western style as a bishop.[53] This is a Pisan icon of the late 13th century,

---

49 Ernest Langlois, *Les Registres de Nicholas IV: Recueil des bulles de ce pape, publiées ou analysées d'après les manuscrits originaux des archives du Vatican*. vol. 1 (Paris: Bibliothèque des Écoles françaises d'Athènes et de Rome, 1905), Letters No. 599–600, 6707, 6708, 6709.
50 Christidou, "Unknown Byzantine Art in the Balkan Area," p. 43.
51 Ibid, p. 131.
52 Ibid.
53 Nancy Ševčenko, "The Vita Icon and the Painter as Hagiographer," *Dumbarton Oaks Papers* 53 (1999): 153; see also Paroma Chatterjee, *The Living Icon in Byzantium and Italy: The Vita*

devoted to St. Nicholas, in the church of San Verano in Peccioli, Italy. Notably, Ševčenko attributes this icon to a female commissioner. The icon includes family scenes from the life of St. Nicholas, each involving in some way the birth and protection of children.[54] It could be argued that the figure of St. Nicholas was used not only to propagate the idea of the supremacy of the Pope, but also to help address the specific female role of the donor and her relationship with children. Queen Jelena, then, would through St. Nicholas emphasize her position as a mother, flanked by her two sons, regardless of their frequently opposed political ambitions. By establishing the maternal identity, Queen Jelena is underlining the bond and the blood lineage combined within her children— one of an Eastern and the other of a Western quality. St. Nicholas was important for the Nemanjić dynasty into which Jelena had married. Through this specific saint, the queen was channeling an essential connection between her natal and her adopted marital heritages.

The cult of St. Nicholas was relevant for the Nemanjić dynasty and was rooted in its very beginnings. The popularity of the cult of St. Nicholas in this period in Serbia is evident on the basis of the extant sacral monuments. According to the *Studenica Typikon*, the first church that Stefan Nemanja built near Kuršumlija was dedicated to St. Nicholas.[55] Also, the very first church in the Studenica monastery complex, probably built by members of the Nemanjić family, was dedicated to St. Nicholas.[56] In the *katholikon* of Studenica, an elongated icon (7–1/2 × 2 feet, or 228 × 60 cm) of St. Nicholas is placed at the north side of the altar-screen, near the passage into the diaconicon dedicated to the saint.[57] Morača Monastery had a separate small church dedicated to the saint, built by Nemanja's grandson Prince Stefan, while Sopoćani had a chapel

---

Image, Eleventh to Thirteenth Centuries (New York: Cambridge University Press, 2014), pp. 86–103.

54 Ševčenko, "The Vita Icon," p. 153; and Chatterjee, *The Living Icon in Byzantium and Italy*, pp. 86–103.

55 See Alice Isabella Sullivan, "Architectural Pluralism at the Edges: The Visual Eclecticism of Medieval Monastic Churches in Eastern Europe," in "Marginalia: Architectures of Uncertain Margins," special issue, *Studii de Istoria și Teoria Arhitecturii / Studies in History and Theory of Architecture* 4 (2016): 135–51; Slobodan Ćurčić, *Architecture in the Balkans: From Diocletian to Suleyman the Magnificent, c. 300–1550* (New Haven: Yale University Press, 2010), pp. 492–93; and Aleksandar Deroko, *Monumentalna i Dekorativna Arhitektura u Srednjevekovnoj Srbiji* (Belgrade: Naučna Knjiga, 1962), p. 50.

56 See Sullivan, "Architectural Pluralism at the Edges," 136; Ćurčić, *Architecture in the Balkans*, p. 493; and Deroko, *Monumentalna i Dekorativna Arhitektura u Srednjevekovnoj Srbiji*, pp. 67–68.

57 See Gordana Babić, "O Živopisanom Ukrasu Oltarskih Pregrada," *Zbornik za Likovne Umetnosti Matice Srpske* 11 (1975): 21, drawing 3.

dedicated to this saintly cult.[58] On the southeast corner of the Gradac monastery, the endowment of Queen Jelena herself, are the remains of the small church dedicated to St. Nicholas. Inside, among preserved paintings on the western wall, is a monumental fresco of the saint. Olivera Kandić suggests that when the builders and craftsmen left, after the completion of the Gradac church, Queen Jelena used it as a private chapel.[59] The church was probably erected during the construction of Queen Jelena's endowment monastery, for the monks and builders to have a place of worship.[60] Finally, according to Danilo II, Queen Jelena took her monastic vows in the Church of St. Nicholas in Skadar.[61] Taking into account strong Nemanjić attachments to St. Nicholas, he acquired an important dynastical association, which was adopted by Queen Jelena. Thus, using this particular saint, Jelena not only underpinned her alliance with the pope, but also underlined the importance of this specific cult to the Nemanjić family and her adopted identity. The duality of the cult probably served the political agenda of the queen and also aided her assimilation into the Nemanjić dynasty and Serbian culture. With the figure of St. Nicholas, Queen Jelena managed to integrate both her Latin upbringing, heritage, and alliance and the blood legacy of the Nemanjić dynasty attached to the legitimacy, identity, and politics of her sons.

4   The Queen and Her Two Sons

The duality of the Vatican panel is amplified with the depiction of Queen Jelena herself. On the panel of St. Peter and St. Paul, she is shown bent and dressed in dark garments, her hands open, while St. Nicholas is blessing her. She is not dressed as a nun, and no insignia are to be seen, except for the red cloak. The crimson red mantle is of the same color used for depicting the sakkoi, loroi, maniakia, and stemma of her two sons. This possibly described her as a secular

---

58   On the Morača church, see Deroko, *Monumentalna i Dekorativna Arhitektura u Srednjevekovnoj Srbiji*, p. 70. On Sopoćani, see Branislav Živković, *Spomenici Srpskog Slikarstva Srednjeg Veka 3—Sopoćani, Crtezi Fresaka* (Belgrade: Republicki Zavod za Zastitu Kulture, 1984), p. 35.

59   Branislav Cvetković and Gordana Gavrić, "Kraljica Jelena i franjevci," in *Jelena: Kraljica, Monahinja, Svetiteljka* (Tematski Zbornik Radova Posvećen Kraljici Jeleni), ed. Katarina Mitrović (Manastir Gradac: Ministarstvo Kulture i informisanja, 2015), p. 131.

60   See Olivera Kandić, *Manastir Gradac* (Belgrade: Ministarstvo Kulture Republike Srbije, 2008), p. 43.

61   Tomin, ed. *Stara Srpska Knjizevnost*, p. 221; see also Subotić, "Kraljica Jelena Anžujska: ktitor crkvenih spomenika u Primorju," 144.

FIGURE 4.6 Queen Jelena depicted with Stefan the First-Crowned and King Uroš I as monks, 1296, fresco. Church of St. Achillius, Arilje
PHOTOGRAPH BY MARIJA MIHAJLOVIC-SHIPLEY

person yet, at the same time, a nun. The duality of this representation is certainly a reflection of the times, when the boundaries between politics and church were blurred. The fresco of Queen Jelena in the Church of St. Achillius in Arilje, an endowment church of Jelena's son Dragutin, painted in 1296, draws similarities with her image in the Vatican panel (Fig. 4.6).[62] In this fresco, a group of three royals are shown: Stefan the-First-Crowned (St. Simeon) is followed by his son, Uroš I, and finally by Jelena. She is depicted last and is presumably of less importance than the other two. However, the inscription states: Іелена

---

62 Dragan Vojvodić has dedicated an extensive study to the church: Vojvodić, *Zidno Slikarstvo Crkve Svetog Ahilija u Arilju* (Belgrade: Stubovi Kulture, 2005).

Краліца Вьсе Србскіе земле (Jelena the Queen of all Serbian lands); it emphasizes her regal significance and the contemporary power she held.[63] In the fresco, all three figures wear dark red cloaks, and Jelena has a dark head-scarf, which probably identifies her as a nun; however, the inscription, which identifies her as a queen, blurs this hypothesis. The fresco of Jelena in Dragutin's church corresponds with her depiction on the Vatican panel, with one alteration on the icon: the bright red cape on top of her dark garments. With the inscription stating her full title, the fresco image in Arilje raises the possibility that at the time (ca. 1296), she lived a dual existence as both a ruler and a devout and pious nun. In both examples, a living ruler is painted alongside Christ and saints. Jelena is not presented as one of the saints of the Nemanjić house, but her presence does underline many pertinent points: the divinity of her rule, the direct connection between her and the saints of the royal house, and that her rule on earth is guided every day by a community of saints, angels, and Christ Himself. The Church is one in Heaven and on Earth and it has one head—Christ.[64] The duality of the queen's rule is depicted in the panel of St. Peter and St. Paul, where the red cape as a royal insignia describes her secular rule, and the dark attire underneath the spiritual one. She is also sharing the same space with St. Nicholas. Examples of royals depicted both as secular and as monks can be found in Gelat'i Monastery (1290), where King Davit' v Narin had himself depicted twice in his burial chapel, as a youthful ruler and an older monk.[65] The same can be seen later in the second half of the 14th century in the manuscript now kept in the Bibliothèque Nationale in Paris, in which John VI Kantakouzenos is represented as both an emperor and a monk.[66] This imagery may underpin the nature of the rule that embodied the duality of the earthly and heavenly spheres, where the ruler was present in both. It seems that the portraits of living people (in this case, royals) were not painted on icons simply because they were commissioners and endowers, but also to emphasize the connection between the saints and living people. In that way, the community of angels, saints, and people was united in Christ.

---

63 Trans. Marija Mihajlovic-Shipley, "Queen Jelena between Two Worlds."
64 See Paul, in Rom. 12:5; and I Cor. 12:27. See also Janko Radovanović, "Jedinstvo nebeske i zemaljske crkve u srpskom slikarstvu srednjeg veka ili Likovi živih ljudi na freskama i ikonama srednjeg veka," *Zbornik za Likovne Umetnosti Matice Srpske* 20 (1984): 62.
65 See Antony Eastmond, "Art and Frontiers between Byzantium and the Caucasus," in *Byzantium: Faith and Power (1261–1557): Perspectives on Late Byzantine Art and Culture*, ed. Sarah T. Brooks (New York: Metropolitan Museum of Art, 2006), p. 157.
66 A digital copy of the manuscript is on the Bibliothèque Nationale website: http://gallica.bnf.fr/ark:/12148/btv1b10721737k.r=grec%201242?rk=21459;2, as of December 10, 2019.

The lower register of the Vatican panel and the duality of the two iconographies reflect both the internal and external politics of Jelena's two sons and their relationships with Pope Nicholas IV. Before Nicholas IV received his papal tiara in February 1288, as Girolamo d'Ascoli, a prominent representative of the Franciscan order, he had undertaken a diplomatic mission to both the Dalmatian coast, "Sclavonia," and to Constantinople, in order, it seems, to lay the foundations for possible union between the two churches (in Lyons 1272) and in order to organize a new crusade.[67] After his inauguration in 1288, and under his new title of Pope Nicholas IV, he attempted to strengthen further the close relationships between Dalmatia and the Balkans.[68] The four years of his papacy were marked by the politics of the unification of the two churches, with an emphasis on addressing liturgical and iconographical differences between the two traditions, something that Queen Jelena conceivably wanted to endorse by commissioning the panel.

Four months after his investiture (July 23, 1288), Nicholas IV notified King Milutin that he had sent two Franciscan envoys, Marin and Cyprian, with instructions to deliver letters of identical content to him and his brother Dragutin.[69] The letters contained a plea that the two kings should bring back their peoples to the true faith and accept the supremacy of the pope. In August of the same year (August 8, 1288), the pope sent another letter, which expressed his gratitude for Jelena's commitment and praised her true faith.[70] In the letter to Queen Jelena, she is addressed as "Carissime in Christo filiae Elenae ... lumini catholice fidei," with "apostolic blessing."[71] Nicholas IV is addressing the queen the same way he is addressing her Catholic female contemporaries of the same status in Europe (e.g., Carissime in Christo filie Margerite, regine Sicilie illustri).[72] Conversely, the two kings are addressed as non-Latin rulers according to church protocol, "Viro magnifico Urosio, illustri regi Sclavorum," as opposed to "Carissimo in Christo filio," as Nicholas IV addressed the Catholic kings. These letters to Kings Dragutin and Milutin did not include the apostolic

---

67 See D'Amico, "Vatikanska ikona Jelene Anžujske," p. 308.
68 Ibid., p. 308.
69 Ernest Langlois, *Les Registres de Nicholas IV: Recueil des bulles de ce pape, publiées ou analysées d'après les manuscrits originaux des archives du Vatican*, vol. 1 (Paris: Bibliothèque des Écoles françaises d'Athènes et de Rome, 1905), no. 599, p. 118.
70 "Hanc itaque fidem vigere in tua progenie cupientes, magnificos viros Stephanum et Urosium, illustres reges Sclavorum, natos tua, per nostras literas hortandos duximus, et monendos, ut pie considerantes, quod una est fides, extra quam nulus omnino salvatur, et sine qua deo impossibile est placer, ad ipsius veniant fidei unitatem." Popović, "Kraljica Jelena i Katolička Crkva," p. 84.
71 Langlois, *Les Registres de Nicholas IV*, no. 600, p. 118.
72 Ibid., no. 1301, p. 265.

blessing. In the panel, the arch separating Jelena from her sons may be suggestive of these political and diplomatic realities.

Another oddity of the lower register is the representation of the two kings, Dragutin and Milutin, identically dressed. The two are signified as equal in power by their attire and insignia. The identical dress of the two kings could date the icon to immediately after the Council of Deževo in 1282, where Dragutin yielded the supreme rule to his brother Milutin after he fell from a horse and became a permanent invalid.[73] At that time, a physical disability was usually considered an obstacle to performing royal duties, reflecting the milieu of Christian and political thought that a fall from a horse and its physical consequences were a sign from God that the ruler was no longer adequate to govern.[74] It was mutually agreed between the brothers that Milutin would rule the Serbian Kingdom, composed of several states, until his death, after which Dragutin's son would inherit the throne. Dragutin continued to rule the north, in the area called Mačva, with Belgrade and the northeast of Bosnia given to him by his father-in-law, while Milutin took the south.[75] Queen Jelena already ruled the coastal area of Zeta, Trebinje, and the area around the River Ibar, given to her by her son Dragutin after he overthrew his father King Uroš I.[76] The two brothers, identically dressed as corulers, can be seen in the funerary chapel built by Dragutin in the church Tracts of St. George (1283–85) near Novi Pazar, and again, ten years later, in King Dragutin's endowment: the Church of St. Achillius (1296) near Arilje (Fig. 4.7). The relationship between the two brothers was turbulent and always either on the edge of a conflict or in conflict. Even Danilo II writes in his Vita of Queen Jelena that keeping the peace between the brothers was the principal concern of their mother.[77] With the support of his mother, Dragutin, who had Hungarian ties through his Catholic wife, inclined toward the papal influence and to alliances with Charles of Anjou, whereas Milutin favoured Byzantium. However, the unity of the broth-

---

73 See Ivan Đurić, "Deževski Sabor u Delu Danila II," in *Arhiepiskop Danilo II I njegovo doba: Medjunarodni naučni skup povodom 650 godina od smrti*, conf. publication, ed. Vojislav J. Djurić (Belgrade: Serbian Academy of Sciences and Arts, 1991), pp. 169–70; and Danica Popović, "Kult Kralja Dragutina: Monaha Teoktista," *Zbornik Radova Vizantoloskog Instituta* 38 (1999–2000): 312.

74 See Stanislaus Hafner, *Studien zur altserbischen dynastischen Historiographie* (Munich: Oldenbourg, 1964), pp. 121–23.

75 See Smilja Marjanović-Dusanić, *Vladarska Ideologija Nemanjića* (Belgrade: Srpska Knjizevna Zadruga, Clio, 1997), p. 123; and Popović, "Kraljica Jelena i Katolička Crkva," p. 49.

76 Ibid., pp. 50–51.

77 Svetlana Tomin, ed., *Stara Srpska Knjizevnost* (Sremski Karlovci—Novi Sad: Izdavacka Knjizarnica Zorana Stojanovića, 2001), p. 214.

FIGURE 4.7 The brothers King Milutin and King Dragutin depicted in identical attire, 1283–85, fresco. Dragutin's Chapel in the church Tracts of St. George, Novi Pazar
PHOTOGRAPH BY MARIJA MIHAJLOVIC-SHIPLEY

ers was essential for the stability and development of the Serbian Kingdom. Consequently, it could be argued that the Vatican panel underlines the need of the mother to unify her sons under the banner of the papal tiara. By juxtaposing the iconography of the Latin bishop with the Eastern imperial attire of Dragutin and Milutin, the intention of the commissioner may have been to unify the tradition and legacy of her marital family with her own Western natal heritage. However, with contrasting visual signifiers of West and East in the lower register, Queen Jelena at its center, blessed by a bishop clad in Catholic vestments, is balancing both worlds. Whatever inner conflicts there must have been between mother and her sons, this panel formulates a bond that is capable of restraining that rivalry in order to facilitate a political gain and also demonstrate a spiritual unity.

5   Conclusion

The complexity of the queen Jelena's panel reflected the complicated late 13th-century political issues in the region. With the identification of the bishop figure, we can now tie loose ends around the fluidity of the representation of

St. Nicholas, both in East and West. The panel corresponds with the ongoing contemporary dialogue between East and West at the time of the still existing idea about the unification of the two churches. Through this analysis, we learn that Queen Jelena deeply understood the position of her dominion, placed between two strong influences and carefully constructed the imagery that manifested her political aspirations as well as her personal concerns. The position of Queen Jelena on the Vatican panel, paired with St. Nicholas, both separated and contained within an arch, reflects a myriad of possible explanations. The arch offers a parallel with the figure of Christ at the very top center of the panel, instigating a visual dialogue between these two "central sections"—one earthly and the other heavenly. While the top register deals with the spiritual aspect of this panel, the lower is addressing more diplomatic and personal issues of the queen. The lower register suggests the specific relationship between the mother and the sons, between Eastern and Western iconography and the opposing political agendas of the two sides of the Adriatic. The mutual relationship between the figures is reflected in its dualistic iconography and carefully planned composition and style. The inclusion of St. Nicholas resonates with multiple issues, as the saint offered fertile ground for planting alliances, defining political agendas, and even communicating personal gender narratives. The glue that holds all of these meanings together is the queen paired with the Latin bishop. Queen Jelena, on this panel, could represent an axis, from which the political powers of her two sons are suspended. That axis is reinforced with the authority of a Latin bishop, underpinning the queen's personal political alliance. Queen Jelena recognized the full implications of being in a position of power, and this panel, like a chess board, depicts a knowledge of how the image should be constructed for a diplomatic game.

Bibliography

Amman, Albert Maria. "Die Ikone der Apostelfürsten in St. Peter in Rom." *Orientalia Christiana Perodica* 8, no. 3–4 (1942): 457–68.

Anichini, Guido. "Di un antico quadro dei SS Pietro e Paolo nella Basilica Vaticana." *Rivista di archeologia Cristiana* 17, no. 1–2 (1941): 141–49.

Babić, Gordana. "O Živopisanom Ukrasu Oltarskih Pregrada." *Zbornik za Likovne Umetnosti Matice Srpske* 11 (1975): 1–41.

Babić, Gordana, and Chatzidakis, Manolis. "The Icons of the Balkan Peninsula and the Greek Islands." In *The Icon*, ed. Kurt Weitzmann, 129–201. London: Bracken Books, 1982.

Battaglia, Salvatore, ed. *Grande dizionario della lingua italiana* 7 (Grav-Ing). Turin: Unione Tipografico – Editrice Torinese, 1971.

Beatillo, Padre Antonio da Bari. *Historia della vita, miracoli, traslatione e gloria dell'illustrissimo confessore di Christo, San Nicolò il Magno, arcivescovo di Mira, patrono e protettore della città di Bari*. Naples and Palermo: Nella Stamperia di Pietro Coppola, 1642.

Belting, Hans. *Likeness and Presence: A History of the Image before the Era of Art*. Chicago and London: University of Chicago Press, 1994.

Bojović, Boško. *L'idéologie monarchique dans les hagio-biographies dynastiques du moyen âge serbe*. Rome: Pontificio Istituto Orientale, 1995.

Chatterjee, Paroma. *The Living Icon in Byzantium and Italy: The Vita Image, Eleventh to Thirteenth Centuries*. New York: Cambridge University Press, 2014.

Christidou, Anna. "Unknown Byzantine Art in the Balkan Area: Art, Power and Patronage in Twelfth to Fourteenth Century Churches in Albania." PhD diss., Courtauld Institute of Art, 2010.

Clare, Edward G. *St. Nicolas His Legends and Iconography*. Florence: Leo S. Olschki Editore, 1985.

Ćuk, Ruža. *Srbija i Venecija u XIII i XIV Veku*. Belgrade: Prosveta, 1986.

Ćurčić, Slobodan. *Architecture in the Balkans: From Diocletian to Suleyman the Magnificent, c. 300–1550*. New Haven: Yale University Press, 2010.

Cvetković, Branislav, and Gordana Gavrić. "Kraljica Jelena i Franjevci." In *Jelena: Kraljica, Monahinja, Svetiteljka* (Tematski Zbornik Radova Posvećen Kraljici Jeleni) ed. Katarina Mitrović, 119–39. Manastir Gradac: Ministarstvo Kulture i informisanja, 2015.

D'Amico, Rosa. "Vatikanska ikona Jelene Anžujske i legendarna 'ikona cara Konstantina': ikonografski i politički aspekti srpske svetinje u Rimu." *Medjunarodni Naučni Skup, Symposium, Niš i Vizantija* 10 (2011): 305–21.

Danilo II. *Životi Kraljeva i Arhiepiskopa Srpskih*. Kolo 38. Belgrade: Srpska Knjizevna Zadruga, 1935.

Davidov, Dinko, ed. *Naučni Skup: Kralj Dragutin u Istoriji i Umetnosti*. Račanski Zbornik. Vol. 3. Bajina Bašta: Fondacija Račanska baština, 1998.

Deroko, Aleksandar. *Monumentalna i Dekorativna Arhitektura u Srednjevekovnoj Srbiji*. Belgrade: Naučna Knjiga, 1962.

Domentijan. *Život Svetoga Simeuna i Svetoga Save*, ed. Đura Daničić. Belgrade: Društvo Srpske Slovesnosti, 1865.

Đurić, Ivan. "Deževski Sabor u Delu Danila II." In *Arhiepiskop Danilo II I njegovo doba: Medjunarodni naučni skup povodom 650 godina od smrti*, conf. publication, ed. Vojislav J. Djurić, 169–94. Belgrade: Serbian Academy of Sciences and Arts, 1991.

Eastmond, Antony. "Art and Frontiers between Byzantium and the Caucasus." In *Byzantium: Faith and Power (1261–1557): Perspectives on Late Byzantine Art and Culture*, ed. Sarah T. Brooks. New York: Metropolitan Museum of Art, 2006.

Eastmond, Antony. *The Glory of Byzantium and Early Christendom*. London and New York: Phaidon Press, 2013.

Gardner, Julian. "Pope Nicholas IV and the Decoration of Santa Maria Maggiore." *Zeitschrift für Kunstgeschichte* 36 (1973): 1–50.

Gardner, Julian. *The Roman Crucible: The Artistic Patronage of the Papacy 1198–1304*. Munich: Hirmer Verlag, 2013.

Hafner, Stanislaus. *Studien zur altserbischen dynastischen Historiographie*. Munich: Oldenbourg, 1964.

Hilsdale, Cecily J. *Byzantine Art and Diplomacy in an Age of Decline*. Cambridge, UK: Cambridge University Press, 2014.

Huskinson, Janet M. *Concordia Apostolorum: Christian Propaganda at Rome in the Fourth and Fifth Centuries; A Study in Early Christian Iconography and Iconology*. Oxford: British Archaeological Reports, 1982.

Jagić, Vatroslav. "Kritički Dodatci Tekstu Života Svetoga Simeuna i Svetoga Save: [Opisi i Izvodi Iz Nekoliko Južnoslovinskih Rukopisa]." *Starine* 5 (1873): 8–21.

Juhas Georgievska, Ljiljana, and Tomislav Jovanović, eds. *Стефан Првовенчани, Сабрана Дела*. Belgrade: Srpska Knjiga, 1999.

Juhas Georgievska, Ljiljana, ed. "Житије Светог Саве." In *Стефан Првовенчани, Доментијан, Теодосије, Житије Светога Симеона* 69–189. Novi Sad: Matica Srpska Publishing Center, 2012.

Kandić, Olivera. *Manastir Gradac*. Belgrade: Ministarstvo Kulture Republike Srbije, 2008.

Kostrenčić, Marko, ed. *Lexicon Latinitatis Medii Aevi Iugoslaviae*, vol. 1, L–Z. Trans. Veljko Gortan and Zlatko Herkov. Zaagreb: Editio Instituti historici Academiae scientiarum et artium Slavorum meridionalium, 1973.

Langlois, Ernest. *Les Registres de Nicholas IV: Recueil des bulles de de pape, publiées ou analysées d'après les manuscrits originaux des archives du Vatican*. vol. 1. Paris: Bibliothèque des Écoles françaises d'Athènes et de Rome, 1905.

Lønstrup Dal Santo, Gitte. "Concordia Apostolorum—Concordia Augustorum. Building a Corporate Image for the Theodosian Dynasty." In *East and West in the Roman Empire of the Fourth Century: An End to Unity?*. ed. Roald Dijkstra, Sanne van Poppel, and Daniëlle Slootjes. Leiden, Netherlands: Brill, 2015, 99–120.

Marjanović-Dušanić, Smilja. *Vladarska Ideologija Nemanjića*. Belgrade: Srpska Književna Zadruga, Clio, 1997.

Mavromatis, Leonidas. *La Fondation de l'Empire Serbe: Le Kralj Milutin*. Thessaloniki: Kentron Vyzantinon Ereunon, 1978.

Mihajlovic-Shipley, Marija. "Queen Jelena between Two Worlds: The Icon of St. Peter and St. Paul." MA thesis, Courtauld Institute of Art, 2017.

Miljković, Bojan. "Nemanjići i Sveti Nikola u Bariju." *Zbornik Radova Vizantoloskog Instituta* 44 (2007): 275–95.

Mitrović, Katarina, ed. *Jelena—Kraljica, Monahinja, Svetiteljka. Tematski Zbornik Radova Posvećenih Kraljici Jeleni*. Manastir Gradac: Ministarstvo Kulture I Informisanja, 2015.

Mitrović, Katarina. "Pismo Kralja Stefana Uroša III Mletačkom Duždu Frančesku Dandolu." *Stari Srpski Arhiv* 15 (n.d.): 9–18.

Molinier, Émile. "Inventaire du trésor du Saint-Siège sous Boniface VIII (1295) (Suite)." *Bibliothèque de l'École des Chartes* 45, no. 1 (1884): 31–57.

Muffel, Nikolaus. *Descrizione della città di Roma nel 1452: Delle indulgenze e dei luoghi sacri di Roma (Der ablas und die heligen stet zu Rom)*, ed. Gerhard Wiedmann. Bologna: Patron, 1999.

Pavlović, Leontije. *Kultovi lica kod Srba I Makedonaca*. Smederevo: Narodni Muzej Smederevo, 1965.

Pietri, Charles. "Concordia Apostolorum et Renovatio Urbis (Culte des Martyrs et Propagande Pontificale)." *Mélanges d'archéologie et d'histoire* 73, no. 1 (1961): 275–322.

Popović, Danica. "Kult Kralja Dragutina: Monaha Teoktista." *Zbornik Radova Vizantoloskog Instituta* 38 (1999–2000): 311–25.

Popović, Danica. *Riznica Spasenja, Kult Relikvija i Srpskih Svetih u Srednjevekovnoj Srbiji*. Belgrade—Novi Sad: SANU, Balkanološki Institut, 2018.

Popović, Miroslav. "Kraljica Jelena i Katolička Crkva." MA thesis, Faculty of Philosophy, University of Belgrade, 2007.

Radovanović, Janko. "Jedinstvo nebeske i zemaljske crkve u srpskom slikarstvu srednjeg veka ili Likovi živih ljudi na freskama i ikonama srednjeg veka." *Zbornik za Likovne Umetnosti Matice Srpske* 20 (1984): 47–66.

Ševčenko, Nancy. "The Vita Icon and the Painter as Hagiographer." *Dumbarton Oaks Papers* 53 (1999): 149–65.

Spremić, Momčilo. *Srbija i Venecija (VI–XVI Vek)*. Belgrade: Službeni Glasnik, 2016.

Subotić, Gojko. "Kraljica Jelena Anžujska: ktitor crkvenih spomenika u Primorju." *Separat iz Istorijskog Glasnika* 1–2 (1958): 131–48.

Sullivan, Alice Isabella. "Architectural Pluralism at the Edges: The Visual Eclecticism of Medieval Monastic Churches in Eastern Europe." In "Marginalia: Architectures of Uncertain Margins," special issue, *Studii de Istoria și Teoria Arhitecturii / Studies in History and Theory of Architecture* 4 (2016): 135–51.

Tatić-Djurić, Mirjana. *Poznate Ikone od XII–XVIII Veka*. Jugoslovenska Revija, 1984.

Tatić-Djurić, Mirjana. "Ikona Apostola Petra i Pavla u Vatikanu." *Zograf: Časopis za Srednjovekovnu Umetnost* 2 (1967): 11–16.

Theilmann, John M. "Political Canonization and Political Symbolism in Medieval England." *Journal of British Studies* 29, no. 3 (1990): 241–66.

Todić, Branislav. *Srpsko Slikarstvo u Vreme Kralja Milutina*. Belgrade: Draganic, 1998.

Tomić-De Muro, Vukosava. "Srpske Ikone u Crkvi Sv. Nikole u Bariju, Italija." *Zbornik za Likovne Umetnosti Matice Srpske* 2 (1966): 107–24.

Tomin, Svetlana, ed. *Stara Srpska Knjizevnost*. Sremski Karlovci—Novi Sad: Izdavacka Knjizarnica Zorana Stojanovića, 2001.

Vojvodić, Dragan. *Zidno Slikarstvo Crkve Svetog Ahilija u Arilju*. Belgrade: Stubovi Kulture, 2005.

Volbach, Wolfgang Fritz. "Die Ikone der Apostelfürsten in St. Peter in Rom." *Orientalia Christiana Perodica* 7, no. 3–4 (1941): 480–97.

Weitzmann, Kurt. "The Icons of the Period of the Crusades." In *The Icon*, ed. Kurt Weitzmann, 201–37. London: Bracken Books, 1982.

Živković, Branislav. *Spomenici Srpskog Slikarstva Srednjeg Veka 3—Sopoćani, Crtezi Fresaka*. Belgrade: Republički Zavod za Zaštitu Kulture, 1984.

CHAPTER 5

Byzantine Heritage and Serbian Ruling Ideology in Early 14th-Century Monumental Painting

Maria Alessia Rossi

At the end of the 13th century, the Serbian Kingdom emerged onto the political landscape of the eastern Mediterranean, initially as an enemy of the Byzantine Empire and later, from 1299 onwards, as one of its main allies. The 1299 marriage of the Serbian King Milutin (r. 1282–1321) with Simonis, the daughter of the Byzantine Emperor Andronicos II (r. 1282–1328), sanctioned a change in Serbian policies and opened the door to the so-called byzantinization of Serbia.[1] Although scholars have acknowledged this shared history, few have attempted to investigate it comparatively.[2] The case study of Christ's miracles in monumental painting is especially fitting, as this cycle proliferated

---

1 See Slobodan Ćurčić, *Gračanica: King Milutin's Church and Its Place in Late Byzantine Architecture* (University Park: Pennsylvania State University Press, 1979), p. 6; and John V.A. Fine, *The Late Medieval Balkans: A Critical Survey from the Late Twelfth Century to the Ottoman Conquest* (Ann Arbor: University of Michigan Press, 1987), pp. 222–23. On the marriage, see Donald M. Nicol, *The Last Centuries of Byzantium (1261–1453)* (Cambridge, UK: Cambridge University Press, 1993), p. 12; Angeliki E. Laiou, *Constantinople and the Latins: The Foreign Policy of Andronicus II, 1282–1328* (Cambridge, MA: Harvard University Press, 1972), pp. 95–100; and Antony Eastmond, "Diplomatic Gifts: Women and Art as Imperial Commodities in the Thirteenth Century," in *Liquid and Multiple: Individuals and Identities in the Thirteenth-Century Aegean*, ed. Guillaume Saint-Guillain and Dionysios Stathakopoulos (Paris: Association des amis du centre d'histoire et civilisation de Byzance, 2012), pp. 105–33.

2 For further bibliography, see Dragan Vojvodić and Danica Popović, eds. *Sacral Art of the Serbian Lands in the Middle Age* (Belgrade: Službeni Glasnik, 2016). For a historical overview of Milutin's reign and the early Palaiologan period in Serbia, see Leonidas Mavromatis, "La Serbie de Milutin entre Byzance et l'Occident," *Byzantion* 43 (1973): 120–50; Leonidas Mavromatis, *La Fondation de l'Empire Serbe: Le Kralj Milutin* (Thessaloniki: Kentron Vyzantinon Ereunon, 1978); Fine, *The Late Medieval Balkans*; Vlada Stanković, *Kralj Milutin: (1282–1321)* [King Milutin: 1282–1321] (Belgrade: Freska, 2012); and Mabi Angar and Claudia Sode eds., *Serbia and Byzantium: Proceedings of the International Conference Held on 15 December 2008 at the University of Cologne* (Frankfurt-am-Main and New York: PL Academic Research, 2013). For Andronicos II's reign, see Georges Pachymérès, *Relations Historiques*, ed. and trans. Albert Failler and Vitalien Laurent (Paris: Belles Lettres, 1984–99), vols 3 and 4; and Nikephoros Gregoras, *Byzantina Historia*, ed. and trans. Ludovici Schopeni (Bonn: Impensis Ed. Weberi, 1829–55). Modern accounts are Laiou, *Constantinople and the Latins*; and Nicol, *The Last Centuries*, pp. 93–166.

© KONINKLIJKE BRILL NV, LEIDEN, 2020 | DOI:10.1163/9789004421370_007

simultaneously in the Byzantine and Serbian cultural contexts.[3] This essay examines how such imagery was transformed and deployed in the Serbian territories, challenging the way scholars think about the artistic production of the period. Rather than labeling these monumental depictions as "byzantinizing" or as an expression of a Serbian identity, I argue that they should be treated as products of the fluid, multicultural, and multifaceted relationship between these neighboring territories.

Christ's miracles are rarely found in monumental depictions before the 13th century.[4] Between the 1290s and 1330s, however, this iconography abruptly proliferates in the Byzantine Empire and the Serbian Kingdom.[5] Among the churches that house these scenes, I will focus on the church of St. George at Staro Nagoričino (1315–17), the *katholikon* of the monastery of Gračanica

---

3   For the most recent scholarship on miracles and healings (with further bibliography), see Michael Goodich, *Miracles and Wonders: The Development of the Concept of Miracle, 1150–1350* (Aldershot: Ashgate, 2007); Matthew M. Mesley and Louise E. Wilson, eds., *Contextualizing Miracles in the Christian West, 1100–1500: New Historical Approaches* (Oxford: Society for the Study of Medieval Languages and Literature, 2014); Irina Metzler, *Disability in Medieval Europe: Thinking about Physical Impairment during the High Middle Ages, c. 1100–1400* (London and New York: Routledge, 2006); Joshua Eyler, ed., *Disability in the Middle Ages: Reconsiderations and Reverberations* (Farnham, Surrey: Ashgate, 2010); and John T. Chirban, *Holistic Healing in Byzantium* (Brookline, MA: Holy Cross Orthodox Press, 2010).

4   On Christ's miracle cycle, see Gabriel Millet, *Recherches sur l'iconographie de l'évangile aux XIVe, XVe et XVIe siècles: D'après les monuments de Mistra, de la Macédoine et du Mont-Athos* (Paris: Editions E. de Boccard, 1916); Paul A. Underwood, "Some Problems in Programs and Iconography of Ministry Cycles," in *The Kariye Djami*, ed. Underwood, vol. 4 (Princeton, NJ: Princeton University Press, 1975), pp. 243–302; Thalia Gouma-Peterson, "Christ as Ministrant and the Priest as Ministrant of Christ in a Palaeologan Program of 1303," *Dumbarton Oaks Papers* 32 (1978): 197–216; Silvia Pasi, "Il ciclo del ministero di Cristo nei mosaici della Kariye Djami: Considerazione su alcune scene," in *L'Arte di Bisanzio e l'Italia al Tempo dei Paleologi 1261–1453*, ed. Antonio Iacobini and Mauro della Valle (Rome: Nuova Argos, 1999), pp. 183–94; Rossitza Schroeder, "Healing the Body, Saving the Soul: Viewing Christ's Healing Ministry in Byzantium," in *Holistic Healing in Byzantium*, pp. 253–75; Maria Alessia Rossi, "The Miracle Cycle between Constantinople, Thessaloniki, and Mistra," in *From Constantinople to the Frontier: The City and the Cities*, ed. Nicholas Matheou, Theofili Kampianaki, and Lorenzo Bondioli (Leiden: Brill, 2016), pp. 226–42; and Maria Alessia Rossi, "Reconsidering the Early Palaiologan Period: Anti-Latin Propaganda, Miracle Accounts, and Monumental Art," in *Late Byzantium Reconsidered: The Arts of the Palaiologan Period in the Mediterranean*, ed. Andrea Mattiello and Rossi (New York: Routledge, 2019), pp. 71–84. For examples of images of Christ's miracles before the end of the 13th century, see Svetlana Tomeković, "Maladie et guérison dans la peinture murale byzantine du XIIe siècle," in *Maladie et société à Byzance*, ed. Évelyne Patlagean (Spoleto: Centro italiano di Studi sull'Alto Medioevo, 1993), pp. 103–18.

5   See Maria Alessia Rossi, "Christ's Miracles in Monumental Art in Byzantium and Serbia (1280–1330)" (PhD diss., Courtauld Institute of Art, 2017).

(1320–21), and the church of St Nikita near Čučer (ca. 1321), all located within the early 14th-century boundaries of the Serbian Kingdom and ascribed to the patronage of King Milutin.[6]

The church of St. George at Staro Nagoričino (hereafter Staro Nagoričino) was rebuilt by King Milutin in 1312–13 on the remains of an 11th-century church, as attested by an inscription carved on the west portal.[7] The frescoes are dated between 1315 and 1317 and were painted by Michael Astrapas in the days of the *hegoumenos* (abbot) Venjamin.[8] On the north wall of the narthex there is a depiction of Milutin with a model of the church, alongside Queen Simonis (b. 1293/4).[9] The founding charter of the church of Gračanica is preserved on the west wall of the southern lateral chapel and states that the building was built "from the foundations, and painted and decorated inside and outside" by King Milutin, and completed by 1321.[10] Slobodan Ćurčić has argued that this was probably "begun in 1311, and no later than early 1312" and finished by 1321.[11] The king's portrait, together with that of his wife, Simonis, is preserved on the arch connecting the *naos* and the narthex. Finally, the church of St. Nikita near

---

[6] More than forty churches have been assigned to Milutin's patronage; see Ćurčić, *Gračanica: King Milutin's Church*, p. 7; and Desanka Milosević, *Gračanica Monastery* (Belgrade: Institute for the Protection of Cultural Monuments of the Socialist Republic of Serbia, 1989), p. 5.

[7] For Staro Nagoričino, see Georges M. Bošković, "Deux Églises de Milutin: Staro Nagoričino et Gračanica" in *L'Art byzantin chez les Slaves: Les Balkans* (Paris: P. Geuthner, 1930), pp. 195–212; Branislav Todić, *Serbian Medieval Painting: The Age of King Milutin* (Belgrade: Draganić, 1999), pp. 320–25; Pera J. Popović and Vladimir R. Petković, *Staro Nagoričino, Psača, Kalenić* (Belgrade: Državna Štamparija Kraljevine Jugoslavije, 1933), pp. 1–50; and Branislav Todić, *Staro Nagoričino* (Belgrade: Republički zavod za zaštitu spomenika kultur, 1993).

[8] See Todić, *Serbian Medieval Painting*, p. 320.

[9] Recent scholarship has unanimously agreed on the association between the construction of the church and the triumph over the Turks in Asia Minor, which the Serbian army had attained in those years. See Todić, *Serbian Medieval Painting*, p. 325 (with further bibliography).

[10] Ćurčić, *Gračanica*, p. 13. The remains of the 13th-century structure were apparently razed to the foundations before the construction of the new church; that is probably why it is specified as "built from the foundations." Archbishop Danilo II (b. ca. 1270) writes that the church was dedicated to the Annunciation. Later sources instead indicate it was dedicated to the Dormition of the Virgin. The latter is the current dedication. See Ćurčić, *Gračanica*, p. 15. For Gračanica, see also Branislav Živković, *Грачаница* [Gračanica] (Belgrade: Republički zavod za zaštitu spomenika culture, 1989); Milosević, *Gračanica Monastery*; Todić, *Serbian Medieval Painting*, pp. 330–337; and Branislav Todić, *Грачаница: сликарство* [Gračanica: Paintings] (Belgrade: Prosveta, 1988), pp. 377–93.

[11] Ćurčić, *Gračanica*, p. 138.

Čučer was restored by King Milutin and was donated in 1308 as a *metohija* to the *pyrgos* of Chilandari.[12] Very different dating hypotheses have been suggested for this building. The fact that Milutin's portrait, common in other churches, is missing, led scholars to date the completion of the frescoes after 1321, the year of Milutin's death.[13] From this brief overview, it is clear that these three buildings are linked historically and geographically. They also share the same patron, most probably the same artist, and as will be discussed below, the same imagery pertaining to the cycle of Christ's miracles.

One of the most puzzling aspects of Christ's miracle cycle is that, notwithstanding its popularity by the early 14th century, it never achieved a canonical selection, grouping, or arrangement within the interior space of churches. In theory, this cycle could include any episode from the beginning of Christ's ministry to the Passion, excluding the Dodekaorton and with a majority of miracle episodes.[14] Other narrative themes, such as mid-Pentecost, Christ among the Doctors, Christ Reading in the Synagogue, and the Purging of the Temple, are also included. These episodes are chosen to confirm, establish, and stress Christ's powers. Even if not miracles per se, they are clearly selected as prefigurations and signifiers for the miraculous nature of the cycle. Although there was no canonical development of this cycle, some consistencies in its treatment in monumental depictions can be observed.[15] It is against these consistencies that I discuss the differences between the miracle cycles in the Byzantine and Serbian territories. I will first examine the layout of these scenes, and then move on to a consideration of their grouping and iconography.

---

12   On the church, see Todić, *Serbian Medieval Painting*, pp. 343–46. See also Miograd Marković, Свети Никита код Скопља: Задужбина краља Милутина [Saint Niketas near Skopje: A Foundation of King Milutin] (Belgrade: Sluzbeni glasnik, 2015). The paintings have been attributed to Michael Astrapas, thanks to his signature on the shield of St. Theodore Teron. The church was partially repainted in 1484, and recently, in 1967–68, restored and cleaned. See Ivan Bentchev, "The Restoration of the Wall-Paintings in the Church of St. Nikita at Čučer/Macedonia in 1483–1484," in *8th Triennial Meeting: Preprints / ICOM Committee for Conservation, Sydney, Australia, 6–11 September 1987* (Los Angeles: Getty Conservation Institute, 1987), pp. 533–37.

13   For the several dating hypotheses, see Todić, *Serbian Medieval Painting*, p. 343. Scholars have come to the conclusion that by the time Milutin donated the church as a *metohija* to Mount Athos, only the construction works were completed, while the dating of the frescoes should be postponed to 1320–21. See Todić, *Serbian Medieval Painting*, p. 346.

14   Amounting to more than 60 episodes. Among these, no more than 30 ever appear in early Palaiologan monumental decorations.

15   See Rossi, "Christ's Miracles in Monumental Art."

1 Christ's Miracles in Space

Starting with the setting: in Byzantine churches, miracles do not generally follow a chronological layout and are rarely found in the *naos*.[16] Instead, the episodes are grouped on the basis of liturgical, narrative, or didactic devices, and are usually depicted in the side aisles or in the narthex.[17] Key Byzantine examples include the monastery of Chora in Istanbul (1316–20), where the miracle cycle is found in the inner and outer narthex, and the *katholikon* of the monastery of Protaton on Mount Athos (end of the 13th century), where the miracle scenes appear in the southwest chapel, the northwest chapel, and the *diakonikon*.[18]

Interestingly, this is not as common in Serbian churches, where the miracle cycle is regularly in the *naos*, as in Gračanica, St. Nikita, and Staro Nagoričino. In

---

16 This lack of order in the arrangement of the miracles of Christ is remarkable when compared with the instructions specified by the *Hermeneia*, in the chapter concerning "How Churches Are Painted with Scenes." See Paul Hetherington, *The "Painter's Manual" of Dionysius of Fourna* (London: Sagittarius Press, 1974), pp. 86ff. This guide partly follows the "classical" middle Byzantine division in zones, except for the fact that there are four registers in the *naos*, rather than two. The first comprises the Dodekaorton; the second, Christ's miracle cycle; the third, the parables; and the fourth is filled with standing figures of saints.

17 Images of Christ's miracles in the early Palaiologan period can be found in the lateral aisles in the Metropolis (1282–1315) in Mystra, and in the northwest and southwest bays in the church of the Perivleptos in Ohrid (1294–95); in the narthex in the *katholikon* of the Virgin Hodegetria of the Brontochion monastery (1312–22) in Mystra; in the church of Omorphokklesia near Kastoria (last decade of the 13th century to the first years of the 14th century); and in the monastery of Chora in Istanbul (1316–20). In the *katholikon* of the monastery of Protaton (end of the 13th century) on Mount Athos, miracle episodes are depicted in the southwest and northwest chapels and the *diakonikon*. The only instances where Christ's miracles are presented in the *naos* are St. Catherine's Monastery in Sinai (1315–20), and the *parekklesion* of St. Euthymios (1303) in Thessaloniki.

18 For Christ's miracles, see Underwood, "Some Problems." For the monastery of Chora, with further bibliography, see Holger A. Klein, Robert G. Ousterhout, and Brigitte Pitarakis, eds., *Kariye Camii Reconsidered* (Istanbul: İstanbul Araştırmaları Enstitüsü, 2011); for an art history overview see Robert Ousterhout, *The Art of the Kariye Camii* (London: Scala Publishers, in association with Archaeology and Art Publications, 2002). On Protaton, see Paul M. Mylonas, "Το Πρωτάτο των Καρυών και ο ζωγράφος Μανουήλ Πανσέληνος" [The Katholikon of Protaton and its painter Manuel Panselinos], *Nea Estia* 1089 (1972): 1657–62; Branislav Todić, "Protaton et la peinture serbe des premières décennies du XIVᵉ siècle," in *L'Art de Thessalonique et des Pays Balkaniques et les courants spirituels au XIVᵉ siècle*, (Belgrade: Srpska akademija nauka i umetnosti, 1987), pp. 21–31. On the architecture of Protaton, see Paul M. Mylonas, "Les Étapes successives de construction du Protaton au Mont Athos," *Cahiers Archéologiques* 28 (1979): 143–60.

the latter, for the first time, this cycle extends from the *naos* to the sanctuary—the episodes are mostly damaged but still visible in the topmost register. In Gračanica and St. Nikita, by contrast, the miracles are found in the middle register, clearly visible and identifiable by the viewer. Thus, in Serbian churches, miracles are not restricted to side chapels or liminal spaces, as often happens in Byzantine churches, but play a prominent role in the *naos*. The question is, why does their setting change consistently in Serbian churches?

The architecture of the churches themselves may offer an initial explanation. Scholarship has unanimously agreed that the majority of the churches built by Milutin, with the exception of his mausoleum, St. Stephan at Banjska (1313–16), reference Byzantine models.[19] Yet the exaggerated verticality of Staro Nagoričino and Gračanica are unusual when compared to contemporary Byzantine churches, such as the monasteries of Chora and Protaton. The number of registers in the wall painting at Staro Nagoričino is revealing (Fig. 5.1). Byzantine churches have annexes, chapels, and narthexes, developing horizontally rather than vertically.[20] Thus, it seems as if the Serbian churches built by Milutin, while taking into account Byzantine prototypes, reveal a different outcome. The exaggerated proportions meant the buildings developed vertically, and therefore more cycles could be employed in the decorative program.[21] Suzy Dufrenne argues that "on assiste à une superposition de cycles divers qui s'adaptent sans doute à l'accentuation des proportions verticales de l'architecture, mais qui respectent un ordre hiérarchique: les espaces supérieurs restent consacrés au cycles des fêtes, les cycles secondaires de la vie du Christ occupent les zones plus basses des edifices."[22] And this is the case in St. Nikita, where the miracle cycle is on the second register from the bottom.

---

19 For Banjska, see Todić, *Serbian Medieval Painting*, pp. 338–39; for the reasons Banjska was built in the traditional Romanesque manner, see Ćurčić, *Gračanica*, p. 9, and chapter 5 with further bibliography. For the architectural relationship between the churches commissioned by Milutin and the Byzantine prototypes, see Ćurčić, *Gračanica*, chapter 4. For the Raška style, see Bratislav Pantelić, *The Architecture of Dečani and the Role of Archbishop Danilo II* (Wiesbaden: Reichert, 2002), pp. 4–9.

20 See Gordana Babić, *Les Chapelles annexes des églises byzantines: Fonction liturgique et programmes iconographiques* (Paris: Klincksieck, 1969); and Slobodan Ćurčić, "Architectural Significance of Subsidiary Chapels in Middle Byzantine Churches," *Journal of the Society of Architectural Historians* 36, no. 2 (1977): 94–110.

21 See Slobodan Ćurčić, *Architecture in the Balkans: From Diocletian to Süleyman the Magnificent* (New Haven: Yale University Press, 2010), pp. 664–66.

22 "There is a superimposition of different cycles that are adapting, no doubt, to the accentuated verticality of architecture while respecting the hierarchical order of monumental painting: the highest registers dedicated to the feast cycle; and the lower areas of the monument to the secondary cycles of the life of Christ." Suzy Dufrenne, "Problèmes iconographiques dans la peinture monumentale du début du XIVe siècle," in *L'Art*

HERITAGE AND IDEOLOGY IN 14TH-CENTURY MONUMENTAL PAINTING 125

FIGURE 5.1 Church of St. George at Staro Nagoričino, 1316–17, interior view toward west, with frescos by Michael Astrapas
PHOTOGRAPH BY MARIA ALESSIA ROSSI

Nonetheless, the greater space available in the *naos* does not explain why the miracles are depicted there and not elsewhere. I believe the answer lies in the new and different function of the narthex and the side chapels in the Serbian churches.[23] The introduction into the Serbian Church of the *Typikon* of Sabas, translated from the Greek by Archbishop Nikodim (1317–24), prescribes that many different services should be performed in the narthex.[24] The new roles played by these liminal spaces are echoed in their new decorative programs. Gordana Babić notices, for instance, that in Milutin's churches the narthex displays innovative iconographies, such as the prefigurations of the Virgin, the Tree of Jesse, and the Menologion.[25] The miracle cycle was not part of this new arrangement. Furthermore, I believe that one of the main concerns when decorating these churches was to create a narrative that would be easy for the viewer to follow—to some extent, a chronological or liturgical unfolding of the events of the life of Christ. This suggests the miracles were laid out in the *naos* in order to become part of the broader Gospel narrative and its reenactment in church rituals.

2 Miracles and Liturgy

A second discrepancy between the Serbian and Byzantine approaches to the miracle cycle regards the grouping of certain episodes within the cycle. For instance, the episodes of the Healing of the Paralytic at Bethesda, Christ and the Samaritan Woman, and the Healing of the Man Born Blind, are frequently grouped together in Byzantine churches, because they share a complex and

---

byzantin au début du XIVe siècle: Symposium de Gračanica 1973 (Belgrade, 1978), pp. 29–38, 36. See also Dufrenne, "L'Enrichissement du programme iconographique dans les églises byzantines du XIIème siècle," in *L'Art byzantin du XIIIe siècle: Symposium de Sopoćani 1965* (Belgrade, 1967), pp. 35–46.

23 See Slobodan Ćurčić, "The Twin-Domed Narthex in Paleologan Architecture," *Zbornik Radova Vizantološkog Instituta* 13 (1971): 333–44.

24 On Archbishop Nikodim, see Paul Pavlović, *The History of the Serbian Orthodox Church* (Toronto: Serbian Heritage Books, 1989), pp. 72–3. For the *Typikon*, see Job Getcha, *The Typikon Decoded: An Explanation of Byzantine Liturgical Practice* (Yonkers, NY: St. Vladimir's Seminary Press, 2012).

25 Gordana Babić, "Le Programme iconographique des peintures murales décorant les narthex des églises fondées par le roi Milutin," in *L'Art byzantin au début du XIVe Siècle*, pp. 105–26; see also Babić, "Chapelles latérales des églises serbes du XIIIème siècle et leur décor peint," in *L'Art byzantin du XIIIe siècle: Symposium de Sopoćani 1965* (Belgrade, 1967), pp. 179–88.

multilayered symbolism.[26] From the earliest Christian centuries, they were interpreted in terms of baptismal water, in view of the key role played by it in the healings.[27] Through it Jesus performs healings, both physical and spiritual; it is a life-giving instrument. In the monastery of Chora healings are represented in three of the four pendentives of the sixth bay of the outer narthex.[28] This can be explained only on the grounds that the miracles of the three pendentives would clearly stand together as a group. A similar arrangement can be seen in the Protaton monastery, where these three episodes are separately depicted in the southwest chapel. The Samaritan Woman is located on the east wall in direct dialogue with the Healings of the Man Born Blind and the Paralytic on the opposite wall.[29]

Yet in the Serbian churches, a different arrangement becomes the norm. In Staro Nagoričino, the Man Born Blind is on the south wall of the sanctuary, followed by the Paralytic. In the same register, on the eastern arch of the southern *naos*, is the Samaritan Woman, followed by the episode of the Calling of Zacchaeus on the south wall (Fig. 5.2). They are elements of a continuous narrative. In Gračanica, the Samaritan Woman is on the south wall of the *naos*, followed, on the west wall and on the same register, by the Man Born Blind, Christ Calling Zacchaeus, and the Healing of the Paralytic. In St. Nikita, the arrangement of the fixed episodes is more complex: the Samaritan Woman is on the north wall; on the south wall of the northwest pier is the Man Born Blind;

---

26 The episode of Christ and the Samaritan Woman has not been at the center of any general iconographic studies. Worth mentioning is Barbara Baert, "The Image Beyond Water: Christ and the Samaritan Woman in Sant'Angelo in Formis (1072–1087)," *Arte Cristiana* 823 (2004): 237–45. For the Healing of the Paralytic at Bethesda, see Barbara Baert, "The Pool of Bethsaida: The Cultural History of a Holy Place in Jerusalem," *Viator* 36 (2005): 1–22; and Maria Kazamia-Tsernou, "The Healing of the Paralytic in the Paleochristian and Byzantine Iconography" (PhD diss., Aristotle University of Thessaloniki, 1992). For the Healing of the Man Born Blind, see Pieter Singelenberg, "The Iconography of the Etschmiadzin Diptych and the Healing of the Blind Man at Siloe," *Art Bulletin* 40 (1958): 105–12; Barbara Baert, "The Healing of the Blind Man at Siloam, Jerusalem: A Contribution to the Relationship between Holy Places and the Visual Arts in the Middle Ages" (Part 1), *Arte Cristiana* 838 (2007): 49–60; and Barbara Baert, "The Healing of the Blind Man at Siloam, Jerusalem: A Contribution to the Relationship between Holy Places and the Visual Arts in the Middle Age" (Part 2), *Arte Cristiana* 839 (2007): 121–30.

27 See Craig R. Koester, *Symbolism in the Fourth Gospel: Meaning, Mystery, Community* (Minneapolis: Fortress Press, 1995), pp. 54–63; and Larry Paul Jones, *The Symbol of Water in the Gospel of John* (Sheffield: Sheffield Academic Press, 1997).

28 The fourth pendentive contains only some foliate ornament. See Paul A. Underwood, ed., *The Kariye Djami*, vol. 2 (Princeton, NJ: Princeton University Press, 1966), pp. 258–59.

29 For a discussion of the decorative program of the southwest chapel and its meaning, see Vojislav J. Djurić, "Les Conceptions hagioritiques dans la peinture du Protaton," *Recueil de Chilandar* 8 (1991): 37–82; and Rossi, "Christ's Miracles in Monumental Art," pp. 168–70.

FIGURE 5.2 Michael Astrapas, Christ calling Zacchaeus, 1316–17, fresco.
Church of St. George at Staro Nagoričino, *naos*, west wall
PHOTOGRAPH BY MARIA ALESSIA ROSSI

the Healing of the Paralytic is on the east wall of the southwest pier, opposite the Samaritan Woman; and on the south wall is Christ Calling Zacchaeus. In this instance, the episodes are not on the same wall or in the same register, yet they are not isolated; they create a dialogue across the space of the church, from one wall to the other. By moving within the church, the viewer experiences all four of the scenes together.

Why was the Calling of Zacchaeus, a very rare narrative, added to the established triad? In Luke, Zacchaeus was the chief tax collector of Jericho.[30] When Christ passed through Jericho, the crowd was so big and Zacchaeus's stature so short that he decided to climb a tree in order to see Christ. But it was Christ who saw Zacchaeus and told him to "come down immediately. I must stay at

---

30   Luke 19:1–10.

your house today."[31] The episode, as represented in all three churches, centers on the encounter between Christ and the tax collector (Figs. 5.3 and 5.4). The latter is represented as a small man standing on top of a sycamore-fig tree while Christ blesses him. The meaning of this narrative focuses on Zacchaeus's response to Christ: "Look, Lord! Here and now I give half of my possessions to the poor, and if I have cheated anybody out of anything, I will pay back four times the amount."[32] In this case, charity, almsgiving, and distribution to the poor are the means for salvation highlighted in the visual program. In other words, the Calling of Zacchaeus does not seem to have much in common with the other three episodes. While it could be read as a conversion miracle, it does stand in striking contrast to the physical healings of the paralytic and the blind man. Furthermore, it is a scene derived from a reading from Luke, while the other three are taken from John.[33] But most important, it bears no connection with water and its multiple layers of symbolism. Nevertheless, in Serbian churches, these four scenes are repeatedly grouped together.

I believe that the proliferation of this episode in the Serbian territory can be linked to the liturgical importance assumed by this scene in the Slavic liturgy, which would also explain the link with the three miraculous healings.[34] All have a common liturgical function: they are Sunday lections. The Paralytic, the Samaritan Woman, and the Man Born Blind are celebrated respectively on the fourth, fifth, and sixth Sundays after Easter, while the fifth Sunday before the beginning of Great Lent is dedicated, in the Slavic tradition, to Christ calling Zacchaeus.[35] In the Byzantine liturgical tradition, by contrast, the preparatory period starts with the Sunday of the Publican and Pharisee, not with the episode of the Calling of Zacchaeus.[36] The latter falls on the thirty-first

---

31   Luke 19:5. The inscription in Staro Nagoričino is in good condition and I believe it refers exactly to Christ's invitation to Zacchaeus to come down from the tree.
32   Luke 19:8.
33   The Samaritan Woman (John 4:4–26); the Paralytic (John 5:1–18); the Man Born Blind (John 9:1–34).
34   To my knowledge, among the Byzantine churches of the early Palaiologan period, this episode only appears in the Chora monastery and in the Perivleptos in Ohrid, while it can be found in all Serbian churches, including Staro Nagoričino, Gračanica, St. Nikita, Chilandari, and in the following decades also in the monastery of Dečani.
35   In the Pentekostarion and the Lectionaries, the fourth Sunday is entitled the Sunday of the Paralytic, the fifth is the Sunday of the Samaritan Woman, and the sixth is the Sunday of the Man Born Blind. On Zacchaeus, see Gabriel Bertonière, *The Sundays of Lent in the Triodion: The Sundays without a Commemoration* (Rome: Pontificio Istituto Orientale, 1997).
36   See Getcha, *The Typikon Decoded*, pp. 141–61.

FIGURE 5.3 Christ calling Zacchaeus, 1320–21, fresco. Monastery of Gračanica, *naos*, west wall
PHOTOGRAPH PROVIDED BY BLAGO FUND, USA/SERBIA,
WWW.SRPSKOBLAGO.ORG

FIGURE 5.4 Attributed to Michael Astrapas, Christ calling Zacchaeus, ca. 1321, fresco. Church of St. Nikita, near Čučer, *naos*, south wall
PHOTOGRAPH BY MARIA ALESSIA ROSSI

Sunday after Pentecost and so never "officially" becomes one of the preparatory Sundays in the Triodion book itself, unlike the order in the Serbian liturgy.[37]

In addition to the liturgical role played by this episode, it is worth taking briefly into account the meanings the visualization of this narrative might have carried. The appearance of a repentant chief tax collector who decides to donate half of his fortune to the poor does seem quite a meaningful choice.[38] The benefits that charity and almsgiving can have on an individual are made clear by Christ's answer to Zacchaeus: "Today salvation has come to this house."[39] To the lay viewer, especially the wealthy one, this is an exhortation. To the monastic community, it is evidence of Christ's miraculous powers. But to the richest man in the kingdom, who had already spent half of his fortune building churches and hospitals, and donating countless artifacts to monasteries, it is irrevocable proof of (his) salvation. In fact, King Milutin's strongest ally was not the Byzantine Empire, but the Church. When the Serbian Orthodox Church was proclaimed autocephalous in 1219, the reorganization of the ecclesiastic network was prioritized, adding new eparchies to the already existing ones and expanding others, in order for the secular administration of the state and the ecclesiastical leadership of the church to cooperate as closely as possible.[40] The new territories conquered and ratified by the 1299 peace treaty were important additions to the system and included both lands formerly under the jurisdiction of the Archbishopric of Ohrid and new ones, such as the "Diocese of Lipanj, Machva, Konchul, Branichevo, Belgrade, and Skopje."[41] The locations of Milutin's endowments appear to be strategically chosen within these new areas, suggesting his gifts should be seen not just as expressions of piety, but also as a way to create a network of churches and monasteries under his control. With this in mind, the meeting between Christ and Zacchaeus embodies and visually represents the partnership between Milutin and the Serbian Orthodox Church.

---

37   Bertonière, *The Sundays of Lent*, p. 32, explains: "The case of the 'Sunday of Zacchaeus' seems to witness to an extension of the process to still one more Sunday, although this process was never 'canonized' and thus never achieved full status as one of the preparatory Sundays in the Triodion book itself."

38   I would like to thank Prof. Robert Nelson for pointing this out to me in the discussion following my paper at the 2018 Byzantine Studies Conference.

39   Luke 19:9.

40   See Pavlović, *The History of the Serbian Orthodox Church*, p. 67. For the list of eparchies, see Dušan Kasić, "Serbian Archbishops and Patriarchs," *Serbian Orthodox Church: Its Past and Present* 1, no. 1 (1965): 10–15.

41   Pavlović, *The History of the Serbian Orthodox Church*, p. 71.

3   The Iconography of the Marriage at Cana

Alongside layout and grouping, differences in the way the miracle cycle was treated can be detected also in the iconography of specific episodes. A good example is the scene of the Marriage at Cana. This is Christ's first miracle and defines the beginning of his ministry.[42] A wedding feast takes place in the town of Cana in Galilee, to which Christ and his mother are invited. When the wine runs out, Christ performs a miracle, turning water into wine. By the end of the 13th century, the Marriage at Cana is represented as a continuous narrative, merging the episode of the transformation of the water into wine with the feast (Fig. 5.5). In Byzantine churches, usually there are several fixed characters including Christ sitting at the table together with the Virgin, the newlyweds, and the governor of the feast. The latter is portrayed as a man holding up a glass. In Serbian churches, in contrast, there is a great variation in the number of other figures seated at the table and of the servants attending, ranging from

FIGURE 5.5   Marriage at Cana, 1320–21, fresco. Monastery of Gračanica, *naos*, west wall
PHOTOGRAPH PROVIDED BY BLAGO FUND, USA/SERBIA,
WWW.SRPSKOBLAGO.ORG

---

42   John 2:1–12.

FIGURE 5.6 Marriage at Cana, detail of the two newlyweds, 1320–21, fresco. Monastery of Gračanica, *naos*, west wall
PHOTOGRAPH PROVIDED BY BLAGO FUND, USA/SERBIA, WWW.SRPSKOBLAGO.ORG

one to fourteen, as in St. Nikita. They are portrayed in lively conversation with one another and participating in the feast.

A particularly revealing instance is that of the Marriage at Cana in the monastery of Kalenić (mid-15th century).[43] Draginja Simić-Lazar has argued that the depiction, where the groom is represented holding a knife against the bride's hand, is linked to the Slavic ritual of the wedding ceremony, where the two newlyweds mix their blood and drink it.[44] She suggests that this ritual was transposed in the iconographic cycle of Kalenić. Is it possible to explain the depiction of the animated wedding feast and all the guests in the Serbian churches in a similar way? Could the liturgical aspect of the wedding ceremony have been transposed as well as the more informal one?

In both Gračanica and St. Nikita, the attendees at Cana are represented wearing conventional long garments, with long sleeves, trimmed with gold borders. This style of clothing, as Maria Parani discusses, was used to distinguish

---

43 For further bibliography, see Ivan Stevović, *The Monastery of Kalenić* (Belgrade: Institute for the Protection of Cultural Monuments of the Republic of Serbia, 2007).

44 Draginja Simić-Lazar, *Kalenić et la dernière période de la peinture byzantine* (Skopje: Matica Makedonska, 1995), p. 121.

FIGURE 5.7   Portrait of Simonis, 1302–21, fresco. Monastery of Gračanica, *naos*, west wall
PHOTOGRAPH PROVIDED BY BLAGO FUND, USA/SERBIA, WWW.SRPSKOBLAGO.ORG

members of the upper class from the poor, who were represented in short garments and often had their arms bare.[45] Similarly, the depiction of the two

---

45   Maria Parani, *Reconstructing the Reality of Images: Byzantine Material Culture and Religious Iconography (11th–15th Centuries)* (Leiden, Boston: Brill, 2002), p. 93.

newlyweds also deserves further attention. In Gračanica, the married couple is easily identifiable at the top left corner of the table (Fig. 5.6). The depiction of the bride is strikingly similar to the portrait of the Byzantine princess and Serbian queen Simonis in the same church (Fig. 5.7). As mentioned, the Serbian King Milutin married the Byzantine Emperor's daughter Simonis in 1299. At the time of the wedding, Simonis was five or six years old, while Milutin was about 40.[46] Furthermore, Milutin had already been married (at least) three times. The union was thus opposed, unsuccessfully, not just because Simonis was too young, but also because it would have violated Church canons that prohibit fourth marriages. In the wall paintings in Gračanica, none of these factors comes into play. What we are left with is two female figures portrayed with similar regalia: the earrings and the size and the decoration of the crown. Why was the bride in the Marriage at Cana represented as the living queen? Could the feast scene reflect the Serbian court rather than that of a universal banquet? If one were to interpret the Marriage at Cana as the visual staging of Milutin's own marriage, the visual pairing of the two would offer a not-so-subtle effort to legitimize it by associating it with the biblical event—one in which Christ himself participates, thus sanctioning its sacredness. Similarly, it would speak to Milutin's marriage into the Byzantine imperial family. The monastery was Milutin's foundation, after all. And it is not unreasonable to suppose he might have wanted to display his status, as well as his ties with the Byzantine Empire through Simonis, in the decorative program. This interpretation is further enhanced by Milutin's monograms, displayed just below the scene.

4   Conclusion

This essay is not an attempt to list all the differences between the treatments of the miracle cycle in Byzantine and Serbian churches, but to shed light on a few of them in order to prove that the use of the miracle cycle in the Serbian territories is not just an empty repetition of Byzantine models, and to discuss why new solutions for the grouping and iconography of these episodes might have been chosen. The fact that Christ's miracles are displayed in the *naos*, frequently in the middle register, suggests that they were meant to be visible and easily recognizable and understood. The cycle's expansion into the sanctuary

---

46   See Nicol, *The Last Centuries*, p. 120; Laiou, *Constantinople and the Latins*, pp. 93–100; and Pachymérès, *Relations Historiques*, vol. 2, pp. 247–53, Elisabeth Malamut, "Les Reines de Milutin," *Byzantinische Zeitschrift* 93 (2000): 490–507.

in Staro Nagoričino proves the need for a reinterpretation of the sacred space. I have also emphasized how miracles were laden with liturgical and theological meanings, playing an important role in church decoration. The interpretation of the iconography of the Marriage at Cana in Kalenić suggests that images of miracles become performative; they embody the rituals and liturgical developments. The introduction of the episode of Christ and Zacchaeus stresses the independence of the Slavic calendar and liturgy from Byzantine practices.

Through the examination of the Marriage at Cana in Gračanica and the Calling of Zacchaeus, it appears to me that a twofold interpretation of the treatment of the miracle cycle emerges in the Serbian churches: the choice of this iconography implies the desire to prove a shared Byzantine heritage, while at the same time, the innovations and alterations stress a need for independence and the development of a new visual vocabulary. Milutin openly embraced Byzantine culture and stressed his ties with Andronicos II, as seen in the transformation of the Marriage at Cana into the staging of Milutin's own wedding. The layout, grouping, and iconography of the miracle cycle seem also to reflect the Serbian Kingdom's own political and religious ideology. Christ's miracles become a vehicle to empower the Serbian Orthodox Church by proving its connection to the See of the Ecumenical Patriarchate and Constantinople and at the same time show its independence, by means of the Slavic liturgy. The traditional grouping of the triad of the Healing of the Paralytic at Bethesda, Christ and the Samaritan Woman, and the Healing of the Man Born Blind is valued, yet the episode of Christ Meeting Zacchaeus is added, showcasing the different liturgical calendar of the Serbian Orthodox Church. The latter episode is also telling of Milutin's ruling ideology, based on the close collaboration of secular authorities and ecclesiastical hierarchy. Zacchaeus's salvation is possible due to his double role as administrator and benefactor of the church. Milutin's kingdom flourished as the outcome of the cooperation between the ruling class and the religious authorities, and one can expect Christ to say, as with Zacchaeus, "Today salvation has come to this house."[47]

Acknowledgements

This essay is based on material presented at the 43th Annual Byzantine Studies Conference in San Antonio, Texas, in October 2018. The session, titled "North of Byzantium: Art and Architecture at the Crossroads of the Latin, Greek, and Slavic Cultural Spheres, c. 1300–c. 1500 (II)," was generously sponsored

---

47   Luke 19:9.

by the Mary Jaharis Center for Byzantine Art and Culture. I am grateful to all speakers and audience members for their comments, and to Meseret Oldjira, Marija Mihajlovic-Shipley, Alice Isabella Sullivan, and the anonymous reviewer for their thoughtful suggestions on the text. I am indebted to Prof. Antony Eastmond for his valuable guidance on a previous draft of the essay. The Index of Medieval Art at Princeton University generously provided me with financial assistance.

Bibliography

Primary Sources

Gregoras, Nikephoros. *Byzantina Historia*, ed. and trans. Ludovici Schopeni. Bonn: Impensis Ed. Weberi, 1829–55.

Pachymérès, Georges. *Relations Historiques*, ed. and trans. Albert Failler and Vitalien Laurent. Paris: Belles Lettres, 1984–99.

Secondary Sources

Angar, Mabi, and Claudia Sode, eds. *Serbia and Byzantium: Proceedings of the International Conference Held on 15 December 2008 at the University of Cologne*. Frankfurt-am-Main and New York: PL Academic Research, 2013.

Babić, Gordana. "Chapelles latérales des églises serbes du XIIIème siècle et leur décor peint" in *L'Art byzantin du XIIIe siècle: Symposium de Sopoćani 1965*, 179–88. Belgrade: Faculté de philosophie, Département de l'histoire de l'art, 1967.

Babić, Gordana. *Les Chapelles Annexes des églises byzantines: Fonction liturgique et programmes iconographiques*. Paris: Klincksieck, 1969.

Babić, Gordana. "Le Programme iconographique des peintures murales décorant les narthex des églises fondées par le roi Milutin." In *L'Art byzantin au début du XIVe siècle, Symposium de Gračanica 1973*, 105–26. Belgrade: Faculté de philosophie, Département de l'histoire de l'art, 1978.

Baert, Barbara. "The Image Beyond Water: Christ and the Samaritan Woman in Sant'Angelo in Formis (1072–1087)." *Arte Cristiana* 823 (2004): 237–45.

Baert, Barbara. "The Pool of Bethsaida: The Cultural History of a Holy Place in Jerusalem." *Viator* 36 (2005): 1–22.

Baert, Barbara. "The Healing of the Blind Man at Siloam, Jerusalem: A Contribution to the Relationship between Holy Places and the Visual Arts in the Middle Ages" (Part 1). *Arte Cristiana* 838 (2007): 49–60.

Baert, Barbara. "The Healing of the Blind Man at Siloam, Jerusalem: A Contribution to the Relationship between Holy Places and the Visual Arts in the Middle Ages" (Part 2). *Arte Cristiana* 839 (2007): 121–30.

Bentchev, Ivan. "The Restoration of the Wall-Paintings in the Church of St. Nikita at Čučer/Macedonia in 1483–1484." In *8th Triennial Meeting: Preprints / ICOM Committee for Conservation, Sydney, Australia, 6–11 September 1987*, 533–37. Los Angeles: Getty Conservation Institute, 1987.

Bertonière, Gabriel. *The Sundays of Lent in the Triodion: The Sundays without a Commemoration*. Rome: Pontificio Istituto Orientale, 1997.

Bošković, Georges M. "Deux Églises de Milutin: Staro Nagoričino et Gračanica." In *L'Art byzantin chez les Slaves: Les Balkans*, 195–212. Paris: P. Geuthner, 1930.

Ćurčić, Slobodan. *Gračanica: King Milutin's Church and Its Place in Late Byzantine Architecture*. University Park: Pennsylvania State University Press, 1979.

Ćurčić, Slobodan. "Architectural Significance of Subsidiary Chapels in Middle Byzantine Churches." *Journal of the Society of Architectural Historians* 36, no. 2 (1977): 94–110.

Ćurčić, Slobodan. *Architecture in the Balkans: From Diocletian to Süleyman the Magnificent*. New Haven: Yale University Press, 2010.

Ćurčić, Slobodan. "The Twin-Domed Narthex in Paleologan Architecture." *Zbornik Radova Vizantološkog Instituta* 13 (1971): 333–44.

Djurić, Vojislav J. "Les Conceptions hagioritiques dans la peinture du Protaton." *Recueil de Chilandar* 8 (1991): 37–82.

Dufrenne, Suzy. "L'Enrichissement du programme iconographique dans les églises byzantines du XIIème siècle." In *L'Art byzantin du XIIIe siècle: Symposium de Sopoćani 1965*, 35–46. Belgrade: Faculté de philosophie, Département de l'histoire de l'art, 1967.

Dufrenne, Suzy. "Problèmes iconographiques dans la peinture monumentale du début du XIVe siècle." In *L'Art byzantin au début du XIVe siècle: Symposium de Gračanica 1973*, 29–38. Belgrade: Faculté de philosophie, Département de l'histoire de l'art, 1978.

Eastmond, Antony. "Diplomatic Gifts: Women and Art as Imperial Commodities in the Thirteenth Century." In *Liquid and Multiple: Individuals and Identities in the Thirteenth-Century Aegean*, ed. Guillaume Saint-Guillain and Dionysios Stathakopoulos, 105–33. Paris: Association des amis du centre d'histoire et civilisation de Byzance, 2012.

Eyler, Joshua, ed. *Disability in the Middle Ages: Reconsiderations and Reverberations*. Farnham, Surrey: Ashgate, 2010.

Fine, John V.A. *The Late Medieval Balkans: A Critical Survey from the Late Twelfth Century to the Ottoman Conquest*. Ann Arbor: University of Michigan Press, 1987.

Getcha, Job. *The Typikon Decoded: An Explanation of Byzantine Liturgical Practice*. Yonkers, NY: St. Vladimir's Seminary Press, 2012.

Goodich, Michael. *Miracles and Wonders: The Development of the Concept of Miracle, 1150–1350*. Aldershot: Ashgate, 2007.

Gouma-Peterson, Thalia. "Christ as Ministrant and the Priest as Ministrant of Christ in a Palaeologan Program of 1303." *Dumbarton Oaks Papers* 32 (1978): 197–216.

Hetherington, Paul. *The "Painter's Manual" of Dionysius of Fourna*. London: Sagittarius Press, 1974.

Hilsdale, Cecily. *Byzantine Art and Diplomacy in an Age of Decline*. New York: Cambridge University Press, 2014.

Jones, Larry Paul. *The Symbol of Water in the Gospel of John*. Sheffield: Sheffield Academic Press, 1997.

Kasić, Dušan. "Serbian Archbishops and Patriarchs." *Serbian Orthodox Church: Its Past and Present* 1, no. 1 (1965): 10–15.

Kazamia-Tsernou, Maria. "The Healing of the Paralytic in the Paleochristian and Byzantine Iconography." PhD diss., Aristotle University of Thessaloniki, 1992.

Klein, Holger A., Robert G. Ousterhout, and Brigitte Pitarakis, eds. *Kariye Camii Reconsidered*. Istanbul: İstanbul Araştırmaları Enstitüsü, 2011.

Koester, Craig R. *Symbolism in the Fourth Gospel: Meaning, Mystery, Community*. Minneapolis: Fortress Press, 1995.

Laiou, Angeliki E. *Constantinople and the Latins: The Foreign Policy of Andronicus II, 1282–1328*. Cambridge, MA: Harvard University Press, 1972.

Malamut, Elisabeth. "Les Reines de Milutin." *Byzantinische Zeitschrift* 93 (2000): 490–507.

Marković, Miograd. *Свети Никита код Скопља: Задужбина краља Милутина* [Saint Niketas near Skopje: A Foundation of King Milutin]. Belgrade: Sluzbeni glasnik, 2015.

Mavromatis, Leonidas. "La Serbie de Milutin entre Byzance et l'Occident." *Byzantion* 43 (1973): 120–50.

Mavromatis, Leonidas. *La Fondation de l'Empire Serbe: Le Kralj Milutin*. Thessaloniki: Kentron Vyzantinon Ereunon, 1978.

Mesley, Matthew M., and Louise E. Wilson, eds. *Contextualizing Miracles in the Christian West, 1100–1500: New Historical Approaches*. Oxford: Society for the Study of Medieval Languages and Literature, 2014.

Metzler, Irina. *Disability in Medieval Europe: Thinking about Physical Impairment during the High Middle Ages, c. 1100–1400*. London and New York: Routledge, 2006.

Millet, Gabriel. *Recherches sur l'iconographie de l'évangile aux XIVe, XVe et XVIe siècles: D'après les monuments de Mistra, de la Macédoine et du Mont-Athos*. Paris: Editions E. de Boccard, 1916.

Milosević, Desanka. *Gračanica Monastery*. Belgrade: Institute for the Protection of Cultural Monuments of the Socialist Republic of Serbia, 1989.

Mylonas, Paul M. "Το Πρωτάτο των Καρυών και ο ζωγράφος Μανουήλ Πανσέληνος" [The Katholikon of Protaton and its painter Manuel Panselinos]. *Nea Estia* 1089 (1972): 1657–62.

Mylonas, Paul M. "Les Étapes successives de construction du Protaton au Mont Athos." *Cahiers Archéologiques* 28 (1979): 143–60.

Nelson, Robert, S. "Taxation with Representation: Visual Narrative and the Political Field of the Kariye Camii." *Art History* 22 (1999): 56–82.

Nelson, Robert, S. "Heavenly Allies at the Chora." *Gesta* 43 (2004): 31–40.

Nicol, Donald M. *The Last Centuries of Byzantium (1261–1453)*. Cambridge, UK: Cambridge University Press, 1993.

Ousterhout, Robert. *The Art of the Kariye Camii*. London: Scala Publishers, in association with Archaeology and Art Publications, 2002.

Pantelić, Bratislav. *The Architecture of Dečani and the Role of Archibishop Danilo II*. Wiesbaden: Reichert, 2002.

Parani, Maria G. *Reconstructing the Reality of Images: Byzantine Material Culture and Religious Iconography (11th–15th Centuries)*. Leiden, Boston: Brill, 2002.

Pasi, Silvia. "Il ciclo del ministero di Cristo nei mosaici della Kariye Djami: Considerazione su alcune scene." In *L'Arte di Bisanzio e l'Italia al Tempo dei Paleologi 1261–1453*, ed. Antonio Iacobini and Mauro della Valle, 183–94. Rome: Nuova Argos, 1999.

Pavlović, Paul. *The History of the Serbian Orthodox Church*. Toronto: Serbian Heritage Books, 1989.

Popović, Pera J., and Vladimir R. Petković. *Staro Nagoričino, Psača, Kalenić*. Belgrade: Državna Štamparija Kraljevine Jugoslavije, 1933.

Rossi, Maria Alessia. "Christ's Miracles in Monumental Art in Byzantium and Serbia (1280–1330)." PhD diss., Courtauld Institute of Art, 2017.

Rossi, Maria Alessia. "The Miracle Cycle between Constantinople, Thessaloniki, and Mistra." In *From Constantinople to the Frontier: The City and the Cities*, ed. Nicholas Matheou, Theofili Kampianaki, and Lorenzo Bondioli, 226–42. Leiden: Brill, 2016.

Rossi, Maria Alessia. "Reconsidering the Early Palaiologan Period: Anti-Latin Propaganda, Miracle Accounts, and Monumental Art." In *Late Byzantium Reconsidered: The Arts of the Palaiologan Period in the Mediterranean*, ed. Andrea Mattiello and Rossi, 71–84. New York: Routledge, 2019.

Schroeder, Rossitza. "Healing the Body, Saving the Soul: Viewing Christ's Healing Ministry in Byzantium." In *Holistic Healing in Byzantium*, ed. John T. Chirban, 253–75. Brookline, MA: Holy Cross Orthodox Press, 2010.

Simić-Lazar, Draginja. *Kalenić et la dernière période de la peinture byzantine*. Skopje: Matica Makedonska, 1995.

Singelenberg, Pieter. "The Iconography of the Etschmiadzin Diptych and the Healing of the Blind Man at Siloe." *Art Bulletin* 40 (1958): 105–12.

Stanković, Vlada. *Kralj Milutin: (1282–1321)* [King Milutin: 1282–1321]. Belgrade: Freska, 2012.

Stevović, Ivan. *The Monastery of Kalenić*. Belgrade: Institute for the Protection of Cultural Monuments of the Republic of Serbia, 2007.

Todić, Branislav. "Protaton et la peinture serbe des premières decennies du XIVe siècle." In *L'Art de Thessalonique et des Pays Balkaniques et les courants spirituels au XIVe siècle*, 21–31. Belgrade: Srpska akademija nauka i umetnosti, 1987.

Todić, Branislav. *Грачаница: сликарство* [Gračanica: Paintings]. Belgrade: Prosveta, 1988.

Todić, Branislav. *Staro Nagoričino*. Belgrade: Republički zavod za zaštitu spomenika kultur, 1993.

Todić, Branislav. *Serbian Medieval Painting: The Age of King Milutin*. Belgrade: Draganić, 1999.

Tomeković, Svetlana. "Maladie et guérison dans la peinture murale byzantine du XIIe siècle." In *Maladie et société à Byzance*, ed. Évelyne Patlagean, 103–18. Spoleto: Centro italiano di Studi sull'Alto Medioevo, 1993.

Underwood, Paul A. *The Kariye Djami*, 3 vols. New York: Pantheon Books, 1966–75.

Underwood, Paul A. "Some Problems in Programs and Iconography of Ministry Cycles." In *The Kariye Djami*, ed. Underwood, vol. 4, 243–302. Princeton, NJ: Princeton University Press, 1975.

Vojvodić, Dragan, and Danica Popović, eds. *Sacral Art of the Serbian Lands in the Middle Age*. Belgrade: Službeni Glasnik, 2016.

Živković, Branislav. *Грачаница* [Gračanica]. Belgrade: Republički zavod za zaštitu spomenika culture, 1989.

CHAPTER 6

Dečani between the Adriatic Littoral and Byzantium

Ida Sinkević

The Church of Christ Pantokrator, the *katholikon* of the Monastery of Dečani in Kosovo (hereafter referred to as Dečani) is one of the largest, most impressive, and best-preserved Serbian royal foundations.[1] Built between 1327 and 1335, the church was begun by the Serbian King Stefan Uroš III, also known as Dečanski (r. 1322–31), and completed by his son, Stefan Dušan (r. king 1331–46, tsar until 1355). Dečani displays the most comprehensive and largest extant ensemble of monumental paintings from medieval Serbia and is therefore exceptionally important to scholars (Fig. 6.1). Completed by 1347/48, the fresco decoration reveals hundreds of images and scenes distributed in twenty cycles that include Great Feasts, and Christ's miracles, parables, and sufferings, as well as numerous scenes from the Akathist, Calendar, and Genesis cycles.[2] Dečani is also distinguished for the remarkably preserved 14th-century furnishings that include a large bronze *choros* (candle holder) suspended from the dome, two original stone iconostases, and both a wooden and a marble throne.[3] The superb marble floor that includes a large rosette design under the dome is also attributed to the initial building campaign.[4]

---

1 Dečani is located in the region of Metohija of the disputed territory of Kosovo. Kosovo unilaterally declared independence from Serbia in 2008, but international recognition of Kosovo has been mixed, and the international community continues to be divided on the issue. The Republic of Serbia views Kosovo (which it often refers to as Kosovo and Metohija) as a part of its territory, but it does not have de facto rule in the province, which is protected by a United Nations peacekeeping force (UNMIK).
2 For a comprehensive treatment of the monument with bibliography, see Branislav Todić and Milka Čanak-Medić, *The Dečani Monastery*, trans. Randall A. Major (Belgrade: Serbian Official Gazette, 2013; first published in Serbian in Belgrade: Museum of Priština [displaced] and Mnemosyne—Center for the Protection of Natural and Cultural Heritage in Kosovo and Metohija, 2005); Bratislav Pantelić, *The Architecture of Dečani and the Role of Archbishop Danilo II* (Wiesbaden: Ludwig Reichert, 2002); Vojislav J. Djurić, ed., *Dečani i vizantijska umetnost sredinom XIV veka: Medjunarodni naučni skup povodom 650 godina manastira Dečana*, conf. publication (Belgrade: Serbian Academy of Sciences and Arts, 1989); and V.R. Petković and Djurdje Bošković, *Manastir Dečani*, 2 vols (Belgrade: Academia Regalis Serbica, 1941).
3 The original iconostases have been preserved in the *naos* and in the chapel of St. Demetrios. On the furnishings, see Čanak-Medić in *The Dečani Monastery*, 224–41.
4 Ibid.

FIGURE 6.1   Interior of the Church of Christ Pantokrator, Dečani Monastery, mid-14th century, east view
PHOTOGRAPH BY PLATONEUM PUBLISHING

Due to its overwhelming artistic, architectural, and historical importance, Dečani has received significant scholarly attention, especially in Serbia.[5] However, one of the most distinguished features of this church, a rather complex combination of Western, mostly Romanesque and Gothic, and Byzantine

---

5   See note 1.

FIGURE 6.2   Church of Christ Pantokrator, Dečani Monastery, 1327–35, southwest view
PHOTOGRAPH BY PLATONEUM PUBLISHING

characteristics of its architecture and sculpture, requires further scrutiny.[6] Generally, the church is described as displaying a Byzantine interior dressed in the garb of the Western exterior (Figs. 6.1 and 6.2). On a closer inspection, however, the combination of Byzantine- and Western-inspired stylistic and structural features is solidly present throughout the church, both in its interior and exterior. It is the purpose of this essay to discuss the origin, meaning, and significance of this distinctive, eclectic interpretation of styles at Dečani and to explore its implications for our understanding of local style. Built at the crossroads of the Slavic, Latin, and Greek cultural spheres, Dečani reveals a new visual idiom, its architecture and sculpture simultaneously absorbing and transforming different artistic traditions.[7] Thus, the visual eclecticism at

---

6   The terms "Western" and "Latin" refer to political, religious, and artistic tendencies attributed to Western European countries under the influence of the Roman Catholic Church. "Romanesque" and "Gothic" refer to artistic and architectural styles that originated in Western Europe and were most commonly employed in Catholic churches. The terms "Eastern" and "Byzantine" designate historical, religious, and artistic trends of the Byzantine Empire and the lands under the orbit of its influence; they followed the practices of the Eastern Orthodox Church.

7   The fresco cycles at Dečani, while predominantly Byzantine in their overall appeal, also reveal the impact of the cross-cultural exchange between the Greek, Latin, and Slavic cultural spheres in the region. However, considering the immense size and complexity of these

Dečani is examined both as a reflection of the cross-cultural exchange of the ethnically and religiously diverse population in the region, and as a manifestation of the political aspirations of its royal patrons.

The church is a royal mausoleum containing the relics of Stefan Dečanski. Both the monumental marble sarcophagus and a specially decorated reliquary shrine with the remains of the king have been preserved.[8] The royal patronage is also honored by portraits throughout the church: father and son, Stefan Dečanski and Stefan Dušan, are shown above the main portal extending their hands toward Christ Pantokrator and holding scrolls; they are portrayed holding the model of the church near the royal tomb on the south wall of the southwest bay; both are shown again in the Nemanjić family tree in the narthex; and finally Dečanski alone is represented by the altar, near the above-mentioned shrine that contains his remains.[9]

The combined influences of both the Latin West and the Byzantine East are already apparent in the circumstances surrounding the building of the church. The history of the monument is documented in both contemporary 14th-century and later literary sources. The original Monastic Charter, issued by King Stefan Dečanski, has been preserved and reveals information about the founders of the monastery, conditions of its construction, and its landholdings.[10] The history of the monument and its patronage are also recorded by the royal biographer, the Archbishop Danilo II (1324–37) in *The Lives*

---

murals, the examination of painted decoration goes beyond the scope of the current essay and requires a separate study.

8   A smaller marble sarcophagus, located next to the king's, most likely belongs to his second wife, Maria Palaiologina, whom he married in 1324. See Petković and Bošković, *Manastir Dečani*, vol. 1, p. 104.

9   The bibliography on royal portraits in Dečani is vast and includes Svetozar Radojčić, *Portreti srpskih vladara u srednjem veku* (Skopje: Skopje Muzej Južne Srbije u Skopju, 1934), pp. 41–42. 46, and 51–59; Branislav Todić, "O nekim preslikanim portretima u Dečanima," *Zbornik Narodnog muzeja* 11, no. 2 (Belgrade, 1982): 55–67; Ivan Djordjević, "Predstava Stefana Dečanskog uz oltarsku pregradu u Dečanima," *Saopštenja republičkog zavoda za zaštitu spomenika culture SR Srbije* 15 (Belgrade, 1983): 35–42; Gordana Babić, "Les portraits de Dečani représentant ensemble Dečanski et Dušan," in *Dečani i vizantijska umetnost*, pp. 273–86; Dušan Korać, "Kanonizacija Stefana Dečanskog i promene na vladarskim portretima u Dečanima," in *Dečani i vizantijska umetnost*, pp. 287–93; and Dragan Vojvodić, "Portreti vladara, crkvenih dostojanstvenika i plemića u naosu i priprati," in *Zidno slikarstvo manastira Dečana: Gradja i Studije*, ed. Vojislav J. Djurić (Belgrade: Serbian Academy of Sciences and Arts, 1995), pp. 288–92.

10 For the text, commentary, and earlier bibliography, see Milica Grković, *Prva Hrisovulja Manastira Dečani* (The First Charter of the Dečani Monastery), trans. Randall A. Major (Belgrade: Mnemosyne—Center for Protection of Natural and Cultural heritage of Kosovo and Metohija; Serbian Orthodox Monastery, Visoki Dečani; Museum of Priština (displaced); and Archive of Serbia, 2004).

of Serbian Kings and Archbishops.[11] Additional sources include the Bulgarian writer and cleric Gregory Tsamblak (1365–1420), who documented the events surrounding the monastery in later times.[12] These sources reveal that, in designing the church, Stefan Dečanski and his son relied on the wisdom and knowledge of Archbishop Danilo II, who was also the spiritual and diplomatic advisor of Dečanski's father, King Milutin (r. 1282–1321).[13] As a devout Orthodox Christian, Archbishop Danilo also served as the *hegumenos* (superior of a monastery) and later as an ascetic monk in Hilandar Monastery, the heart of Serbian Orthodoxy on Mount Athos. While the depth of Archbishop Danilo's Orthodox faith is unquestionable, his aesthetic excursus into Western culture is clearly manifested in the many Romanesque and Gothic features of the ecclesiastical and secular buildings he commissioned.[14] Testifying to his personal taste, the preponderance of Gothic architectural elements is evident, for example, in the palace that the Archbishop intended for his own private use in the Maglič Castle, the best-preserved fortification of medieval Serbia.[15] Thus, in its design Dečani may have also—at least in some part—responded to the aesthetic preferences of the archbishop and perhaps the patron himself.

The Romanesque and Gothic stylistic and structural elements could be also attributed to the input of the master builder of Dečani whose name has been preserved in the inscription above the south entrance to the narthex. Written in Church Slavonic, the dedication reads:

> Fra Vita, a Friar Minor, master builder from Kotor, the royal city, built this church of the Holy Pantokrator for the lord King Stefan Uroš III and his son, the majestic and very great and very glorious lord King Stefan

---

[11] Arhiepiskop Danilo, *Životi kraljeva i arhiepiskopa srpskih*, trans. Lazar Mirković (Belgrade: Srpska književna zadruga, 1935). For an edition in Church Slavonic, see Arhiepiskop Danilo, *Životi kraljeva i arhiepiskopa srpskih*, ed. Djuro Daničić (Zagreb, 1866; rep. London: Variorum, 1972).

[12] Gregory Tsamblak was also a metropolitan of Kiev (r. 1413–20). See Grigorije Camblak, "Žitije Stefana Dečanskog," in *Književni rad u Srbiji*, trans. Lazar Mirković (Belgrade: Prosveta, 1989), pp. 63–80; earlier editions of the text appear on 131–35 and 166–68.

[13] For the role of Archbishop Danilo and bibliography, see Pantelić, *The Architecture of Dečani*. See also Vojislav J. Djurić, ed., *Arhiepiskop Danilo II I njegovo doba: Medjunarodni naučni skup povodom 650 godina od smrti*, conf. publication (Belgrade: Serbian Academy of Sciences and Arts, 1991).

[14] See, for example, the Romanesque-Gothic stone window frames in the Church of the Holy Apostles in the Patriarchate of Peć that was intended to house Danilo's tomb; Slobodan Ćurčić, *Architecture in the Balkans: From Diocletian to Suleyman the Magnificent* (New Haven: Yale University Press, 2010), p. 668.

[15] See Marko Popović, *Zamak: Maglič Castle* (Belgrade: Archaeological Institute, 2012), esp. pp. 118–41 and 198–99; and Ćurčić, *Architecture in the Balkans*, pp. 625–26.

(Dušan). It was built in eight years. And the church was fully completed in the year 6843 [1334/35].[16]

The inscription reveals that the master builder, Fra Vita, was a Franciscan friar from the city of Kotor, located on the southern portion of the Adriatic coast in what is now Montenegro. It also gives a significant, yet seldom recognized prominence to the master builder. Little is known about Fra Vita, but he must have been a very important builder, since he took the liberty to place his name, his profession, and even his city before mentioning the royal patronage of the building and revealing the identity of not one but two kings who commissioned him.[17] Thus, while the precise role of Fra Vita remains ambiguous, the wording of the inscription suggests that the significance of his contribution was not limited only to his skills as a stonemason.[18]

1   The Architecture

Dečani resembles a basilica composed of a three-aisled narthex, a five-aisled nave crowned with a dome, and a deep altar space (Figs. 6.2 and 6.3). The basilican plan is also upheld in the superstructure, since the bays of the nave and the aisles are spanned with cross vaults reinforced by both semicircular and pointed ribs, thus revealing the builder's familiarity with Gothic structural principles.[19] However, the basilica type accommodates the centralized space of the interior, which was articulated to house the needs of the Orthodox liturgy. Essentially, the space of the *naos* is enlarged and connected with the short side aisles that assume the function of subsidiary chapels: one dedicated to St. Demetrios extending on the north, and another dedicated to St. Nicholas facing south. While the painted decoration clearly delineates these different

---

16   For the original text in Church Slavonic and earlier bibliography, see Branislav Todić, "The Construction of the Church and Monastery," in *The Dečani Monastery*, pp. 22–23.

17   Although Fra Vita is the subject of a separate book—Risto Kovijanić, *Vito Kotoranin, neimar Dečana* (Belgrade: Nolit, 1962)—and is mentioned in every major text on Dečani, information about him has been limited to this inscription. For another opinion about the importance of Fra Vita and relevant bibliography, see Pantelić, *The Architecture of Dečani*, 13–34.

18   Considering that the master builder was commissioned either by the king or by his adviser, Archbishop Danilo, or both, we should assume that he followed their orders. His exact role is unknown. For a discussion about the possible role of the master builder and relevant bibliography, see Robert Ousterhout, *Master Builders of Byzantium* (Princeton, NJ: Princeton University, 1999), pp. 55–57.

19   See Čanak-Medić, "The Architecture of the Katholikon," in *The Dečani Monastery*, p. 186.

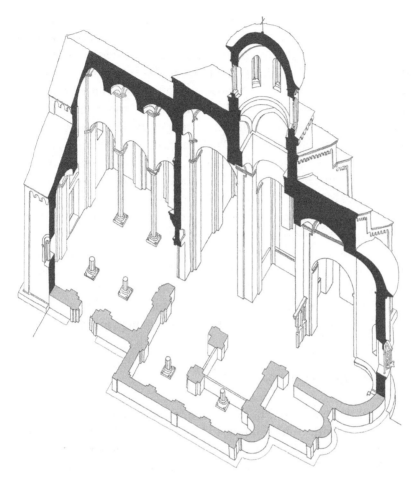

FIGURE 6.3 Axonometric view of the Church of Christ Pantokrator Dečani Monastery
FROM SLOBODAN ĆURČIĆ, *ARCHITECTURE IN THE BALKANS*, P. 661, FIG. 773

spatial units, the walls have been replaced by tall parapets, thus removing the barrier and enhancing the sense of open central space in the upper zones and under the dome, as was common in Byzantine churches (Fig. 6.3).[20]

The architecture of Dečani has been commonly attributed to the style of the so-called Raška (Rascia) School, defined at the beginning of the 20th century by the French scholar Gabriel Millet.[21] The style is characterized in churches built during the 12th and 13th centuries in the Rascia region, as well

20 See Ćurčić, *Architecture in the Balkans*, pp. 660–61.
21 Gabriel Millet, *L'ancien art serbe* (Paris: De Boccard, 1919).

as several later, mostly royal, monuments. Although scholars have debated whether Dečani belongs to an earlier or an advanced version of this type, with some even negating the existence of the Raška School type as such, Dečani's basic structure—a domed basilica with marble-faced facades and Romanesque sculptural decoration—compares to earlier Serbian monuments of the Rascia region.[22] The Western appeal of this school is inherent in the geographic position of the medieval Serbian state, since it included significant areas under the influence of the Latin church, such as Diokletia (Zeta, today Montenegro) and parts of Zahumlia (Herzegovina and southern Dalmatia). While predominant in 12th-century Serbia, by the time of King Stefan Dečanski, as well as his father Milutin and son Dušan, Western features in monuments became a matter of choice, an exception rather than the rule. In the 14th century, the Serbian lands were populated by many important examples of Byzantine-influenced architecture, such as the Church of the Annunciation (later Dormition) at Gračanica Monastery, the Church of the Virgin of Ljeviška in Prizren, and the Church of St. George in Staro Nagoričino.[23] Moreover, the Eastern Orthodox faith defined both the Serbian Church and the Serbian state. Thus, the hybrid features of Dečani were both intentional and potent in their messages.

2 The Interior Decoration

The sculptural decoration of both the interior and exterior of the church also combines Byzantine and Western stylistic, iconographic, and programmatic traditions. As is well known, most sculpture in the interior of Byzantine churches is limited to the iconostasis and tombs. At Dečani, the sculptural

---

22 For a discussion of this problem and relevant literature, see Pantelić, *The Architecture of Dečani*, esp. pp. 1–13 and 88–98; Milka Čanak-Medić and Djurdje Bošković, *Arhitektura Nemanjinog doba*, vol. 1, *Crkve u Toplici i dolinama Ibra i Morave* (Belgrade: Republički Zavod za Zaštitu Spomenika Kulture SR Srbije, 1986); and Vojislav Korać, "Rad jedne skupine majstora u Raškoj u XII veku," *Glas Srpske Akademije Nauka i Umetnosti* 334, no. 4 (1983): 23–38. See also Ćurčić, *Architecture in the Balkans*, pp. 660–61.

23 See Slobodan Ćurčić, *Gračanica: King Milutin's Church and Its Place in Late Byzantine Architecture* (University Park: Pennsylvania State University Press, 1979); Slobodan Nenadović, *Bogorodica Ljeviška: Njen postanak i njeno mesto u arhitekturi Milutinovog vremena* (Belgrade: Narodna Knjiga, 1963); and Branislav Todić, *Staro Nagoričino* (Belgrade: Beograd Republički zavod za zaštitu spomenika kulture, 1993). See also Ivan Stevović, "Byzantium and Romanesque-Gothic Conceptions in Serbian Architecture and Sculpture in the 14th Century (till 1371)," in *Sacral Art of the Serbian Lands in the Middle Ages*, ed. Dragan Vojvodić and Danica Popović, Byzantine Heritage and Serbian Art, vol. 2 of 3 (Belgrade: Serbian National Committee of Byzantine Studies, 2016), pp. 317–30.

FIGURE 6.4 Sculpture from the portal between the narthex and the *naos*,
approx. date 1327–35, Church of Christ Pantokrator, Dečani Monastery
PHOTOGRAPH BY PLATONEUM PUBLISHING

decoration extends to other areas, such as portals, windows, and columns. In the interior of the church, four big statues of griffins and lions flank the portal that leads from the narthex into the *naos* (Fig. 6.4).

Lions form the base of the columns and are shown with open mouths carrying human heads between their paws; two consoles on the capitals of the columns display griffins, one with open wings and a rabbit in his paws (left) and the other with a lion who has a ram's head between his paws (right). The capitals of the narthex and the nave are also carved in the Western tradition. Those in the *naos* display acanthus leaves, while those in the narthex exhibit figures of the four evangelists and various fantastic animals. Such ensembles of sculptural decoration are not commonly displayed in Byzantium and attest to emulation of Western stylistic and iconographic models.[24]

---

24   For the most elaborate description and discussion of the sculpture at Dečani, see Djurdje Bošković, "Plastična dekoracija," in Petković and Bošković, *Manastir Dečani*, vol. 1, pp. 62–98. For the most recent study of the entire sculptural ensemble with excellent illustrations and earlier bibliography, see Čanak-Medić, "The Sculpture of the Katholikon, in *The Dečani Monastery*, pp. 278–321; see also Jovanka Maksimović, *Srpska srednjovekovna skulptura* (Novi Sad: Matica srpska, 1971), pp. 100–6.

Another not so commonly discussed but important Western feature is seen in the placement and the form of the sarcophagi.[25] The large sarcophagus of King Stefan Dečanski and a smaller one, apparently intended for his second wife, Maria Palaiologina, are both freestanding and detached from the surrounding walls.[26] While their location in the southwestern bay of the church recalls the position of other royal tombs of the 13th-century members of the Nemanjić family, at Dečani we witness the first surviving example in medieval Serbia of freestanding sarcophagi.[27] Freestanding sepulchral monuments, known since early Christian times, became popular again in Western Europe during the Romanesque era of the 11th through 12th centuries. As with the sculptural decorations, the tombs in Dečani also exhibit clear Western tendencies within the sacred space of the Orthodox church.[28] The freestanding structure of the tombs enhanced the aura of the sacred space and the importance of the royal family. Like the royal portraits, they added potency and power to the individual ruler, which was very important for the royal ideology promoted by the members of the Serbian ruling family.[29] The sarcophagi served as prominent markers of remembrance and commemoration in the sacred space of the church.

It is also interesting that, for the first time in the history of Serbian royal mausolea, the tombs and tombstones of local noblemen were also located within the sacred space of the church.[30] Prior to Dečani, it was the practice to bury them outside, in the courtyard (*porta*) of the monastery. In Dečani, the northeast bay of the narthex displays both painted decoration and a sarcophagus dedicated to the distinguished aristocratic family, assuming the

---

25   For the most substantial discussion about Serbian royal tombs, see Danica Popović, "Srednjevekovni nadgrobni spomenici u Dečanima" (with English summary), in *Dečani i vizantijska umetnost*, pp. 225–38; and Popović, *Srpski vladarski grob u srednjem veku* (Belgrade: Filozofski fakultet, 1992).

26   It was initially believed that the smaller sarcophagus belonged to the sister of Dečanski, Jelena, who later became the Bulgarian queen; subsequent scholarship maintained that it was intended for the Queen Maria Palaiologina, whom Dečanski married in 1324. See Popović, *Srpski vladarski grob*, pp. 104–5.

27   Ibid.

28   This new westernizing style of sepulchral monuments is further developed in the mausoleum of the cofounder of Dečani, the son of Stefan Dečanski, who was King and Tsar Stefan Dušan. In the Church of the Holy Archangels, the now mostly destroyed sarcophagus of Dušan was topped by a horizontal figure of the deceased above which hovered a ciborium, a practice very common in Western funerary monuments and rarely practiced in Byzantium. See Popović, *Srpski vladarski grob*, pp. 114–20.

29   See ibid; and Smilja Marjanović-Dušanić, *Sveti kralj: Kult Stefana Dečanskog* (Belgrade: Clio, 2007), especially pp. 17–85.

30   See Popović, "Srednjevekovni nadgrobni spomenici u Dečanima," pp. 232–35.

appearance of a family chapel. While atypical of Serbian royal mausolea and the Byzantine context in general, such chapels were prominently situated in Western European churches.[31] It is therefore likely that they were introduced to Dečani via Adriatic routes and Italy. All of these elements of the interior are wrapped in the design adjusted to the Orthodox rite and, along with predominantly Byzantine painted decoration, project an eclectic image strongly rooted in Byzantine tradition yet receptive to the influence of the Western world.

3   The Exterior Decoration

The exterior of Dečani offers the appearance of a Western church (Fig. 6.2). In addition to its elongated, basilican form, the church facades are plated in marble and primarily decorated with Romanesque sculpture. Alternating horizontal bands of pale-yellow onychites marble, quarried about 19 miles (30 km) away from the monastery, and the deep magenta Bistrica marble found at the site adorn the tall and spacious structure.[32] The beauty of the building is also enhanced by sculptural decoration concentrated on portals, windows, and the consoles that accentuate the corbel-tables framing all levels of the roof. As is typical in Romanesque churches, these consoles display human heads, centaurs, and other mythical creatures, as well as a variety of floral ornaments.

According to scholars, the 12th-century Church of the Virgin at Studenica Monastery, built by the founder of the Nemanjić dynasty, Stefan Nemanja (r. 1183–96), provided a source for this hybrid structural and decorative style.[33] A combination of Byzantine and Western features similar to those at Dečani

---

31   Ibid.
32   See Bošković, "Plastična dekoracija," in *Manastir Dečani*, vol. 1, pp. 30–31.
33   The bibliography on Studenica and its impact on later Serbian art and architecture is extensive. For the most recent study and bibliography, see Miloš Živković, "Studenica: The Funerary Church of the Dynastic Founder—the Cornerstone of Church and State Independence," in *Sacral Art of the Serbian Lands in the Middle Ages*, pp. 193–212; Čanak-Medić and Bošković, *Arhitektura Nemanjinog doba*, vol. 1, pp. 78–140; and Vojislav Korać, ed., *Studenica i vizantijska umetnost oko 1200. godine: Medjunarodni skup povodom 800 godina, manastira Studenice i stogodišnjice SANU* (Belgrade: Serbian Academy of Sciences and Arts, 1988). See also Jelena Erdeljan, "Studenica: All Things Constantinopolitan," in *ΣYMEIKA: Collection of Papers Dedicated to the 40th Anniversary of the Institute of Art History, Faculty of Philosophy, University of Belgrade*, ed. Ivan Stevović (Belgrade: Institut za Istoriju Umetnosti, 2012), pp. 93–102. Erdeljan's views were recently challenged in Danica Popović, "Srpski vladarski i arhiepiskopski grob u srednjem veku: nova saznanja i tumačenja," in *Kraljevstvo i arhiepiskopija u srpskim i pomorskim zemljama Nemanjića: Tematski zbornik u čast 800 godina proglašenja kraljevstva i autokefalne arhiepiskopije svih srpskih i pomorskih zemalja*, ed. Ljubomir Maksimović and Srdjan Pirivatrić

is also seen, or, according to literary evidence was also intended, in later royal mausolea, such as those of the Church of St. Stefan in Banjska (1313–15), built by King Milutin (r. 1282–1321), and the church of the Holy Archangels (1343–47), commissioned by the son of Stefan Dečanski, King and Tsar Dušan (r. 1331–55).[34] As a pledge of loyalty to the long-established tradition, the members of the Nemanjić dynasty that ruled Serbia from ca. 1166 to 1371 claimed to have built their royal mausolea in imitation of Studenica—the first royal mausoleum that, according to medieval standards, may have served as the "prototype." While differing in their overall appearances and structures, Dečani and Studenica share several important features: both have polychrome marble facades; both display corbel-tables with sculpted consoles; both have figural sculpture on the portals; and in both churches reliefs of the three-light windows on the east facade include vine leaves with zoomorphic and floral designs and a quatrefoil design flanked by a basilisk and a dragon.[35] Dečani is, however, larger and structurally more complex, and its sculptural ensemble presents many questions that require further scholarly scrutiny. That is particularly true of questions relating to the stylistic and iconographic origins of figural sculptures represented on the tympana of the exterior portals, which remained unanswered.[36] Aesthetically, this combination of intertwined Romanesque and Gothic styles relates to monuments of the south Adriatic coast and Italy. Perhaps most relevant as points of transmission are churches found in the towns of Kotor and Dubrovnik and their major monuments, such as the Cathedral of St. Tryphun in Kotor and the sculpture of the Benedictine cloister and now destroyed 13th-century Cathedral of St. Mary in Dubrovnik.[37]

(Belgrade: Serbian Academy of Sciences and Arts, 2019), pp. 358–63. I am grateful to the author for sharing the unpublished version of this article.

34 For the most recent discussion and bibliography, see Ivan Stevović, "Byzantine and Romanesque-Gothic Conceptions in Serbian Architecture," pp. 317–30.

35 For Studenica, see Živković, "Studenica," p. 198, fig. 155; for Dečani, see Čanak-Medić, "The Sculpture of the Katholikon," in *The Dečani Monastery*, p. 319, fig. 251.

36 For a discussion on the sculpture of the portals of Dečani, see Ivanka Nikolajević, "Portali u Dečanima" (with French résumé), in *Dečani i vizantijska umetnost*, pp. 185–92; Janko Maglovski, "Dečanska skulptura—program i smisao" (with English summary), in *Dečani i vizantijska umetnost*, pp. 193–224; Bošković, "Plasticna dekoracija," pp. 62–98; Čanak-Medić, "The Sculpture of the Katholikon," in *The Dečani Monastery*, pp. 278–321; and Maksimović, *Srpska srednjovekovna skulptura*, pp. 100–6.

37 For a recent study, see Zorica Čubrović, "Kotorski svetac i skulptura Dečana," *Zograf* 40 (2016): 95–116. See also Jovanka Maksimović, *Kotorski ciborij iz XIV veka i kamena plastika susednih oblasti* (Belgrade: Izdavačka ustanova Naučno Delo, 1961); Cvito Fisković, "Dečani i arhitektura istočnojadranske obale u XIV vijeku," in *Dečani i vizantijska umetnost*, pp. 169–84; Cvito Fisković, "Dibrovački i primorski graditelji XIII–XVI stoljeća u

FIGURE 6.5　The Ascension of Christ, approx. date 1327–35, Church of Christ Pantokrator, Dečani Monastery, west portal
PHOTOGRAPH BY PLATONEUM PUBLISHING

The west entrance of Dečani displays the enthroned Christ flanked by two angels in the tympanum carved in high relief (Fig. 6.5). The armrests of the throne are elaborate and supported by two lions; a pedestal supports Christ's feet and displays trefoil arches with pointed central cusps. Christ is blessing with his right hand and holding a closed book with three seals in his left. Christ's blessing gesture, with thumb, second, and third fingers extended and the other two fingers folded, is customary in the Latin ritual.[38] In fact, the whole scene reveals not only a Western style, as has been discussed by scholars, but also an iconography derived from Western models.

Moreover, representations of Christ surrounded by two angels are frequently seen in the main tympana of Romanesque and Gothic facades. Similar renditions reduced to only the main participants are seen, for example, on the tympanum of the late 11th- to 12th-century priory church in Anzy-le-Duc in Burgundy, France, and in the mosaic of the Basilica of S. Frediano in Lucca,

---

Srbiji, Bosni i Hercegovini," *Peristil* 5 (1962): 36–44; and Vojislav Korać, *Graditeljska škola Pomorja* (Belgrade: Serbian Academy of Sciences and Arts, 1965).

38　As discussed by Bošković, "Plasticna dekoracija," 62.

Italy (1128).[39] Since Early Christian times, such representations, based on the Scriptures, were interpreted as a combination of the Ascension and the Last Judgment.[40]

Dečani was dedicated to the feast of the Ascension of Christ, and the appearance of an image of the Ascension on the tympanum of the main door is by no means surprising. However, the representation at Dečani also has many elements of the Last Judgment: the throne, the book with seals, and the rendition of angels. While the angel to the right of Christ is clasping his hands in prayer, the angel to the left has a puffy cheek, as if blowing; the position of his hand indicates that he may have once held a now-lost trumpet. Although reduced to the main participants, the rendition can be associated with the Second Coming, as the trumpeting angel is mentioned in both Revelation 4:2–5:10 and in Matthew 24:31, who says that in order to announce that day [the day of the second coming of Christ], "he will send his angels with a loud trumpet blast."[41]

Above the west portal is the three-light window displaying, in its tympanum, the relief of St. George saving the princess from a dragon. The representation of St. George is by no means surprising, as he was the patron saint of the Nemanjić dynasty. Moreover, according to literary sources, Dečanski himself prayed to the warrior saint before the battle of Velbužd, in which he fought and defeated the Bulgarians in 1330.[42] Thus, the belief in salvation through faith, implied in the image of St. George and the dragon, was especially meaningful to the patron of the church.

The tympanum of the south portal depicts the Baptism of Christ (Fig. 6.6) and is also reduced to the main protagonists: Christ and St. John the Baptist, who holds Christ's arm with his left hand and pours holy water with the right. Iconographic and stylistic parallels for this rendition of the Baptism are also

---

39 See Yves Christe, *Les Grands Portails romans: Études sur l'iconologie des théophanies romanes* (Geneva: Librairie Droz, 1969), pl. 8, figs. 1 and 2.

40 "And while they looked steadfastly toward heaven as he went up, behold, two men stood by them in white apparel" (Acts 1:10–11); the passage indicates that at the Last Judgment, Christ would appear in the same manner as seen in the Ascension. See Bošković, "Plasticna dekoracija," pp. 62–98; and Čanak-Medić, "The Sculpture of the Katholikon," pp. 278–321.

41 The figure of Christ in the Ascension was also seen as glorifying the ruler, and a number of Serbian rulers dedicated churches to this event, for example, Stefan the First-Crowned's dedication of Žiča, and the dedication of Mileševa by his son, Vladislav. Considering that the *katholikon* at Dečani was dedicated to the feast of the Ascension of the Pantokrator and that it is also a funerary monument, the sculptural ensemble appears a logical, albeit not a very Byzantine choice. See Čanak-Medić, "The Sculpture of the Katholikon," pp. 301–2 (with earlier bibliography); and Nikolajević, "Portali u Dečanima," p. 185.

42 See Čanak-Medić, "The Sculpture of the Katholikon," 302, n30.

FIGURE 6.6 Baptism of Christ, approx. date 1327–35, Church of Christ Pantokrator, Dečani Monastery, south portal
PHOTOGRAPH BY PLATONEUM PUBLISHING

found in Western art, particularly in Italy—the gesture of St. John resembling a similar rendition seen in Benedetto Antelami's reliefs in the Baptistery of Parma (last quarter of the 12th century).[43] The representation of water in Dečani is, however, peculiar, and I have not been able to find a parallel for the sepulchral connotations of what appears to be a rectangular, coffin-shaped baptistry with wavy lines suggestive of the river. Like the combination of the Ascension and the Last Judgment, the visual inclusion of the tomb in the scene of the Baptism also conflates Theophany with the Passion, and thus emphasizes the memorial and funerary function of the church.

It is important to note that the south door leads into a section of the narthex where the actual baptismal font stands and rites related to baptism were performed. The section also displays the Nemanjić family tree, thus relating the Baptism to the themes of imperial ideology.[44] Interestingly enough, the scene above the south door also displays the Baptism, but in fresco and following

---

43 See Dorothy F. Glass, "The Sculpture of the Baptistery of Parma: Context and Meaning," *Mitteilungen des Kunsthistorischen Institutes in Florenz* 57, no. 3 (2015): 261, fig. 6.

44 See Zaga Gavrilović, "Kingship and Baptism in the Iconography of Dečani and Lesnovo," in *Dečani i vizantijska umetnost*, pp. 297–306.

traditional Byzantine iconography.[45] Immediately underneath the Baptism is the representation of the Crucifixion, drawing a close parallel between the Baptism and the death of Christ implied in the exterior sculpture. Thus, the close connection between the two faces of the church, exterior and interior, featuring bilingual, Byzantine, and Romanesque appearances, is underscored and reveals how different stylistic models were developed to accentuate visually the baptismal function of the space.

The tympanum of the north portal displays a flowering cross on the stepped base, a theme seen in earlier Serbian sculpture that most likely also originated in the Romanesque art of the Adriatic region (Fig. 6.7).[46] The abbreviated inscription in Church Slavonic is placed next to the upper arm of the cross and reads "Jesus Christ the King of Glory."[47] The flowering cross was interpreted as the Tree of Life and a symbol of the Resurrection. Its placement above the door that was apparently used for funerary ceremonies, more specifically for the ceremonial bringing of the remains of the deceased monks into the church, recalls the funerary function of that section of the narthex.[48]

The location and decoration of the portals of Dečani provide another example of the multiplicity of ways in which Orthodox East and Latin West synergistically interacted in Dečani. Despite significant scholarly efforts to emphasize the adherence of the sculpture of Dečani's portals solely to Orthodox theology, neither the aesthetic appeal of this sculpture nor its iconography fully supports that claim. For example, it is apparent that the themes of the Ascension combined with the Last Judgment, the Baptism, and the Tree of Life would resonate both with the Orthodox and the Latin rites—especially so, since there are examples of such programs on Romanesque and Gothic portals.[49] Moreover, stylistically the sculpture of Dečani's portals belongs to an early Romanesque idiom, and it adheres to Western aesthetic and iconographic models. In contrast to their decoration, the Byzantine origin of these portals is evident in their location, since the actual position of the portals is

---

45 Ibid.
46 We see it, for example, already in the 13th century on the sarcophagus of Archbishop Ioanikius in Sopoćani. See Maksimović, *Srpska srednjevekovna skulptura*, p. 102; and Popović, *Srpski vladarski grob*, pp. 61–66.
47 For the inscription in Church Slavonic, see Čanak-Medić, *The Dečani Monastery*, p. 284.
48 See Nikolajević, "Portali u Dečanima," pp. 186–87; Čanak-Medić, "The Sculpture of the Katholikon," in *The Dečani Monastery*, p. 303; and Maksimović, *Srpska srednjovekovna skulptura*, p. 103.
49 Such programs are found, for example, in churches of 12th- and 13th-century Italy, such as the Church of Santa Maria della Pieve in Arezzo, as discussed in Nikolajević, "Portali u Dečanima," pp. 189–91.

FIGURE 6.7 The Tree of Life, approx. date 1327–35, Church of Christ Pantokrator, Dečani Monastery, north portal
PHOTOGRAPH BY PLATONEUM PUBLISHING

predicated on the Orthodox liturgy and its demands for structuring sacred space. In Romanesque and Gothic churches, the portals leading into the narthex are generally located on the west facade. In Dečani, the three entrances are placed on the west, north, and south sides of the narthex, as is typical in Byzantine churches. The location of the portals reveals the functional aspects of the interior spaces by delineating the sections where the baptismal and funerary rites were performed.[50]

---

50 See Nebojša Stanković, "Art at the Treshold of the Heavens: The Narthex and Adjacent Spaces in Middle Byzantine Churches of Mount Athos (10th–11th Centuries); Architecture, Function, and Meaning" (PhD diss., Princeton University, 2017); Vasileios Marinis, *Architecture and Ritual in the Churches of Constantinople: Ninth–Fifteenth Centuries* (Cambridge, UK: Cambridge University Press, 2014), pp. 64–77; and Ida Sinkević, "Prolegomena for a Study of Royal Entrances in Byzantine Churches: The Case of Marko's Monastery," in *Approaches to Byzantine Architecture and Its Decoration: Studies in Honor of Slobodan Ćurčić*, ed. Mark J. Johnson, Robert Ousterhout, and Amy Papalexandrou (Burlington, VT: Ashgate, 2012), pp. 121–43.

4 Dečani in Context

The presence of different traditions at Dečani reveals both the personal desires of the founders and the complexity of the sociopolitical and religious situation in Serbia at the time. Throughout its history, Serbian lands included territories under the influence of both the Roman Catholic and the Orthodox Byzantine church. The official selection of Orthodoxy as the religion of the Serbian state came with the establishment of the Hilandar Monastery on Mount Athos in 1198; the Serbian church acquired autocephalous status in 1219.[51] However, most Serbian rulers fostered close ties with the Latin courts as well. It will suffice to say that the first Serbian King, Stefan Nemanjić, received the crown from Pope Honorius II (r. 1216–27) in 1217 and became Stefan Prvovenčani (the First Crowned).[52] Moreover, dynastic marriages with aristocratic and royal families from both Byzantium and the West had been a strategic part of the Serbian political agenda. Stefan Dečanski was no exception to this practice.

Following the death of his wife, the Bulgarian princess Theodora, in 1322, Dečanski asked for the hand of Blanche, the daughter of Philip I of Taranto (1278–1332), who was a son of Charles II of Anjou, King of Naples, and Maria of Hungary, daughter of King Stephen V of Hungary.[53] His potential father-in-law—the despot of Epirus, King of Albania, Prince of Achaea and Taranto, and Lord of Durazzo—was also the titular Latin Emperor of Constantinople, who apparently informed the Pope that the Serbian king, along with his clergy and all people in the kingdom of Serbia, wished to join the Catholic church.[54] Negotiations, however, did not work out, and Dečanski married a Byzantine aristocrat, Maria Palaiologina, in 1324.[55]

Stefan Dečanski's interest in acquiring a Western bride was inspired by his need to secure support in becoming the ruler of Serbia. Dečanski's accession to the throne was complicated. First, according to sources, he was a child of

---

51 For the most recent study and earlier bibliography, see Bojan Krsmanović and Ljubomir Maksimović, "Byzantium in Serbia: Serbian Authenticity and Byzantine Influence," in *Sacral Art of the Serbian Lands in the Middle Ages*, pp. 48–50.

52 Stefan Nemanjić's decision was undoubtedly influenced by the Latin conquest of Constantinople in 1204. See ibid., p. 50; and Dragan Vojvodić, "On the Boundary among Worlds and Cultures: The Essence and Spaces of Serbian Medieval Art," in *Sacral Art of the Serbian Lands in the Middle Ages*, pp. 13–40.

53 For more on Philip of Taranto, see Deno Geanakoplos, "Byzantium and the Crusades, 1354–1453," in *A History of the Crusades*, ed. Harry W. Hazard, vol. 3, *The Fourteenth and Fifteenth Centuries* (Madison: University of Wisconsin, 2005), pp. 27–68.

54 For an interesting discussion, see Miodrag Al Purković, *Avinjonske pape i srpske zemlje* (Požarevac, 1934; rep. Gornji Milanovac: Lio, 2002), pp. 23–28.

55 See Marjanović-Dušanić, *Sveti Kralj*, p. 265.

King Milutin and a commoner, a situation which would preclude his legitimate inheritance of the throne.[56] Moreover, although he somehow overcame that obstacle and was slated to inherit the throne, he was accused of plotting to unseat his father. Thus, after Milutin's orders, Dečanski was blinded and sent into exile to the Pantokrator monastery in Constantinople.[57] Following the death of his father, Dečanski claimed that he had miraculously regained his sight and, with the help of noblemen, he ascended to the throne. Subsequently, he faced competition from his siblings and other hopeful relatives and had to use all available resources to prove his legitimacy as a ruler.

Byzantine influence was predominant in all cultural spheres in Serbia at the time. Stefan Dečanski, however, as previously discussed, modeled his mausoleum after the royal mausolea of his dynastic predecessors, the founder of the Serbian dynasty, Stefan Nemanja, and his father, King Milutin. In essence, the basilican form, the glow of the marble facades, and the fusion of Byzantine and Romanesque features provided potent images of Serbian dynastic power. In the design of Dečani, Dečanski, who reigned as Stefan Uroš III, incorporated himself into the Nemanjić lineage and presented a symbol of the grandeur of his own world that was rooted in the Byzantine tradition and yet wide open to the Latin domain. Essentially, he created a building that by virtue of its design, materials, and decoration confirmed his legitimacy as a member of the Serbian ruling dynasty.

The Western appeal of the church may have also responded to the requirements of the Catholic population that resided in the region. Moreover, it is well known that Serbia witnessed economic expansion and prosperity in the 14th century that initiated an influx of new settlers in the area. Numerous merchants and tradesmen commonly traveled from the coastal region inland, seeking work and customers. The economic growth has often been attributed to a growing number of mines, a few located in the vicinity of Dečani, which brought foreign mine workers from various Western territories. Even mercenaries, hired by the king for his military pursuits, may have resided in the region in between the battles.[58]

It is with the recipients in mind that we should consider the eloquent, bilingual aspects of Dečani. In a region that had such a long history of combined, complex, and constant fusion of influences, did it really matter whether the

---

[56] In 1308, King Milutin appointed Stefan Dečanski a ruler of the region of Zeta—a post that usually announced the future successor of the throne. For a discussion and bibliography, see ibid., p. 231.
[57] Ibid., pp. 240–69.
[58] See Sima Ćirković, "Srbija uoči carstva," in *Dečani i vizantijska umetnost*, pp. 3–13.

rendition of the Baptism followed the Western or the Orthodox iconography? Accustomed to the widespread political and religious aspirations of their rulers, the faithful, I believe, may not have cared or even noticed. Such a complex and intertwined organism of Western and Byzantine elements created messages that resonated with the faithful regardless of their aesthetic and iconographic preferences. It seems that this fusion of cultural and historical circumstances, specific for the region, created a unique visual language, a type of *koine*, or common language, as global and multicultural as the people by whom and for whom it was made.

In sum, in creating the fusion of Eastern and Western styles at Dečani, Stefan Dečanski reaffirmed his belonging to the Nemanjić dynastic tradition and thereby confirmed his royal lineage and legitimacy. Along with his son Dušan, his advisor Danilo II, and his master builder Fra Vita, he also highlighted the aspirations of the Serbian court to open the playing field to both Byzantine and Western worlds. In their church, they thus gave rise to a local Serbian style and created an icon of the political, religious, and even military power of the medieval Serbian state.

Acknowledgments

I would like to thank my friend and colleague, Diane Cole Ahl, Arthur J. '55 & Barbara S. Rothkopf Professor Emerita of Art History, for her invaluable comments and editing remarks on many drafts of this essay. I also extend my thanks to Professor Dragan Vojvodić of the University of Belgrade and to Dušan Vujičić of Platoneum Publishing for their generous help with photography.

Bibliography

Primary Sources

Arhiepiskop Danilo. *Životi kraljeva i arhiepiskopa srpskih*, trans. Lazar Mirković. Belgrade: Srpska književna zadruga, 1935.

Camblak, Grigorije. "Žitije Stefana Dečanskog." In *Književni rad u Srbiji*, trans. Lazar Mirković. Belgrade: Prosveta, 1989.

Prva Hrisovulja Manastira Dečani (The First Charter of the Dečani Monastery), ed. Milica Grković, trans. Randall A. Major. Belgrade: Mnemosyne—Center for Protection of Natural and Cultural heritage of Kosovo and Metohija; Serbian orthodox Monastery, Visoki Dečani; Museum of Priština (displaced); and the Archive of Serbia, 2004.

Secondary Sources

Babić, Gordana. "Les portraits de Dečani représentant ensemble Dečanski et Dušan." In *Dečani i vizantijska umetnost sredinom XIV veka: Medjunarodni naučni skup povodom 650 godina manastira Dečana*, ed. Vojislav J. Djurić. Conf. publication, 273–86. Belgrade: Serbian Academy of Sciences and Arts, 1989.

Čanak Medić, Milka, and Djurdje Bošković. *Architektura Nemanjinog doba, vol. 1, Crkve u Toplici i dolinama Ibra i Morave*. Belgrade: Republički Zavod za Zaštitu Spomenika Kulture SR Srbije, 1986.

Christe, Yves. *Les Grands Portails Romans: Études sur l'iconologie des théophanies romanes*. Geneva: Librairie Droz, 1969.

Ćirković, Sima. "Srbija uoči carstva." In *Dečani i vizantijska umetnost sredinom XIV veka: Medjunarodni naučni skup povodom 650 godina manastira Dečana*, ed. Vojislav J. Djurić. Conf. publication, 3–13. Belgrade: Serbian Academy of Sciences and Arts, 1989.

Čubrović, Zorica. "Kotorski svetac i skulptura Dečana." *Zograf* 40 (2016): 95–116.

Ćurčić, Slobodan. *Architecture in the Balkans: From Diocletian to Suleyman the Magnificent*. New Haven: Yale University Press, 2010.

Ćurčić, Slobodan. *Gračanica: King Milutin's Church and Its Place in Late Byzantine Architecture*. University Park: Pennsylvania State University Press, 1979.

Djordjević, Ivan. "Predstava Stefana Dečanskog uz oltarsku pregradu u Dečanima." *Saopštenja republičkog zavoda za zaštitu spomenika culture SR Srbije* 15 (Belgrade, 1983): 35–42.

Djurić, Vojislav J., ed. *Arhiepiskop Danilo II I njegovo doba: Medjunarodni naučni skup povodom 650 godina od smrti*. Conf. publication. Belgrade, Serbian Academy of Sciences and Arts, 1991.

Djurić, Vojislav J., ed. *Zidno slikarstvo manastira Dečana: Gradja i Studije*. Belgrade: Serbian Academy of Sciences and Arts, 1995.

Djurić, Vojislav J., ed. *Dečani i vizantijska umetnost sredinom XIV veka: Medjunarodni naučni skup povodom 650 godina manastira Dečana*. Conf. publication. Belgrade: Serbian Academy of Sciences and Arts, 1989.

Erdeljan, Jelena. "Studenica: All Things Constantinopolitan." In *ΣΥΜΜΕΙΚΤΑ: Collection of Papers Dedicated to the 40th Anniversary of the Institute of Art History, Faculty of Philosophy, University of Belgrade*, ed. Ivan Stevović, 93–102. Belgrade: Institut za Istoriju Umetnosti, 2012.

Fisković, Cvito. "Dečani i arhitektura istočnojadranske obale u XIV vijeku." In *Dečani i vizantijska umetnost sredinom XIV veka: Medjunarodni naučni skup povodom 650 godina manastira Dečana*, ed. Vojislav J. Djurić. Conf. publication, 169–84. Belgrade: Serbian Academy of Sciences and Arts, 1989.

Fisković, Cvito. "Dubrovački i primorski graditelji XIII–XVI stoljeća u Srbiji, Bosni i Hercegovini." *Peristil* 5 (1962): 36–44.

Geanakoplos, Deno. "Byzantium and the Crusades, 1354–1453." In *A History of the Crusades*, ed. Harry W. Hazard, vol. 3, *The Fourteenth and Fifteenth Centuries*, 27–68. Madison: University of Wisconsin, 2005.

Glass, Dorothy F. "The Sculpture of the Baptistery of Parma: Context and Meaning." *Mitteilungen des Kunsthistorischen Institutes in Florenz* 57, no. 3 (2015): 255–91.

Korać, Dušan. "Kanonizacija Stefana Dečanskog i promene na vladarskim portretima u Dečanima." In *Dečani i vizantijska umetnost sredinom XIV veka: Medjunarodni naučni skup povodom 650 godina manastira Dečana*, ed. Vojislav J. Djurić. Conf. publication, 287–93. Belgrade: Serbian Academy of Sciences and Arts, 1989.

Korać, Vojislav. *Graditeljska škola Pomorja*. Belgrade: Serbian Academy of Sciences and Arts, 1965.

Korać, Vojislav. "Rad jedne skupine majstora u Raškoj u XII veku." *Glas Srpske Akademije Nauka i Umetnosti* 334, no. 4 (1983): 23–38.

Korać, Vojislav, ed. *Studenica i vizantijska umetnost oko 1200. godine: Medjunarodni skup povodom 800 godina, manastira Studenice i stogodišnjice SANU*. Belgrade: Serbian Academy of Sciences and Arts, 1988.

Kovijanić, Risto. *Vito Kotoranin, neimar Dečana*. Belgrade: Nolit, 1962.

Krsmanović, Bojana, and Ljubomir Maksimović. "Byzantium in Serbia: Serbian Authenticity and Byzantine Influence." In *Sacral Art of the Serbian Lands in the Middle Ages*, ed. Dragan Vojvodić and Danica Popović. Byzantine Heritage and Serbian Art, vol. 2 of 3, 41–55. Belgrade: Serbian Academy of Sciences and Arts, 2016.

Maglovski, Janko. "Dečanska skulptura—program i smisao" (with English summary). In *Dečani i vizantijska umetnost sredinom XIV veka: Medjunarodni naučni skup povodom 650 godina manastira Dečana*, ed. Vojislav J. Djurić. Conf. publication, 193–224. Belgrade: Serbian Academy of Sciences and Arts, 1989.

Maksimović, Jovanka. *Kotorski ciborij iz XIV veka i kamena plastika susednih oblasti*. Belgrade: Izdavačka ustanova Naučno Delo, 1961.

Maksimović, Jovanka. *Srpska srednjovekovna skulptura*. Novi Sad: Matica srpska, 1971.

Marinis, Vasileios. *Architecture and Ritual in the Churches of Constantinople: Ninth—Fifteenth Centuries*. Cambridge, UK: Cambridge University Press, 2014.

Marjanović-Dušanić, Smilja. *Sveti kralj: Kult Stefana Dečanskog*. Belgrade: Clio, 2007.

Millet, Gabriel. *L'ancien art serbe*. Paris: De Boccard, 1919.

Nenadović, Slobodan. *Bogorodica Ljeviška: Njen postanak i njeno mesto u arhitekturi Milutinovog vremena*. Belgrade: Narodna Knjiga, 1963.

Nikolajević, Ivanka. "Portali u Dečanima" (with French résumé). In *Dečani i vizantijska umetnost sredinom XIV veka: Medjunarodni naučni skup povodom 650 godina manastira Dečana*, ed. Vojislav J. Djurić. Conf. publication, 185–92. Belgrade: Serbian Academy of Sciences and Arts, 1989.

Ousterhout, Robert. *Master Builders of Byzantium*. Princeton, NJ: Princeton University, 1999.

Pantelić, Bratislav. *The Architecture of Dečani and the Role of Archbishop Danilo II*. Wiesbaden: Ludwig Reichert, 2002.

Petković, V.R., and Djurdje Bošković. *Manastir Dečani*, 2 vols. Belgrade: Academia Regalis Serbica, 1941.

Popović, Danica. *Srpski vladarski grob u srednjem veku* (with English summary). Belgrade: Filozofski fakultet, 1992.

Popović, Danica. "Srpski vladarski i arhiepiskopski grob u srednjem veku: Nova saznanja i tumačenja." In *Kraljevstvo i arhiepiskopija: Tematski zbornik u čast 800 godina proglašenja kraljevstva i autokefalne arhiepiskopije svih srpskih i pomorskih zemalja*, ed. Ljubomir Maksimović and Srdjan Pirivatrić, 355–82. Belgrade, Serbian Academy of Sciences and Arts, 2019.

Popović, Danica. "Srednjevekovni nadgrobni spomenici u Dečanima." In *Dečani i vizantijska umetnost sredinom XIV veka: Medjunarodni naučni skup povodom 650 godina manastira Dečana*, ed. Vojislav J. Djurić. Conf. publication, 225–38. Belgrade: Serbian Academy of Sciences and Arts, 1989.

Popović, Marko. *Zamak: Maglič Castle*. Belgrade: Archaeological Institute, 2012.

Purković, Miodrag Al. *Avinjonske pape i srpske zemlje*. Požarevac, 1934; rep. Gornji Milanovac: Lio, 2002.

Radojčić, Svetozar. *Portreti srpskih vladara u srednjem veku*. Skopje: Skopje Muzej Južne Srbije u Skoplju, 1934.

Sinkević, Ida. "Prolegomena for a Study of Royal Entrances in Byzantine Churches: The Case of Marko's Monastery." In *Approaches to Byzantine Architecture and Its Decoration. Studies in Honor of Slobodan Ćurčić*, ed. Mark J. Johnson, Robert Ousterhout, and Amy Papalexandrou, 121–43. Burlington VT: Ashgate, 2012.

Stanković, Nebojša. "Art at the Treshold of the Heavens: The Narthex and Adjacent Spaces in Middle Byzantine Churches of Mount Athos (10th–11th Centuries); Architecture, Function and Meaning." PhD diss., Princeton University, 2017.

Stevović, Ivan. "Byzantium and Romanesque-Gothic Conceptions in Serbian Architecture and Sculpture in the 14th Century (till 1371)." In *Sacral Art of the Serbian Lands in the Middle Ages*, ed. Dragan Vojvodić and Danica Popović. Byzantine Heritage and Serbian Art, vol. 2 of 3, 317–30. Belgrade: Serbian National Committee of Byzantine Studies, 2016.

Todić, Branislav. "O nekim preslikanim portretima u Dečanima." *Zbornik Narodnog muzeja* 11, no. 2 (Belgrade, 1982): 55–67.

Todić, Branislav. *Staro Nagoričino*. Belgrade: Beograd Republički zavod za zaštitu spomenika kulture, 1993.

Todić, Branislav, and Milka Čanak Medić. *The Dečani Monastery*. Belgrade: Serbian Official Gazette, 2013; first published in Serbian in Belgrade: Museum of Priština [displaced] and Mnemosyne—Center for the Protection of Natural and Cultural Heritage in Kosovo and Metohija, 2005.

Vojvodić, Dragan. "Portreti vladara, crkvenih dostojanstvenika i plemića u naosu i priprati." In *Zidno slikarstvo manastira Dečana: Gradja i Studije*, ed. Vojislav J. Djurić, 288–92. Belgrade: Serbian Academy of Sciences and Arts, 1995.

Vojvodić, Dragan, and Danica Popović, eds. *Sacral Art of the Serbian Lands in the Middle Ages*. Byzantine Heritage and Serbian Art, vol. 2 of 3. Belgrade: Serbian Academy of Sciences and Arts, 2016.

Živković, Miloš. "Studenica: The Funerary Church of the Dynastic Founder—The Cornerstone of Church and State Independence." In *Sacral Art of the Serbian Lands in the Middle Ages*, vol. 2, ed. Dragan Vojvodić and Danica Popović, 193–209. Belgrade: Serbian National Committee of Byzantine Studies; P.E. Službeni Glasnik: Institute for Byzantine Studies, and Serbian Academy of Sciences and Arts, 2016.

CHAPTER 7

Triconch Churches Sponsored by Serbian and Wallachian Nobility

Jelena Bogdanović

Architectural activities of remarkable quality continued to thrive north of Byzantium under the sponsorship of Serbian and Wallachian nobility long after the fall of Byzantium and occasionally even in territories under Ottoman rule.[1] As suggested by Slobodan Ćurčić, triconch domed churches, which have been enduring examples of Middle Byzantine architecture and especially of monastic architecture on Mount Athos, shaped notions of an Orthodox Christian identity shared by Serbs and Wallachians, as opposed to the Islamic architecture of the Ottoman Turks.[2] Interest in triconch domed churches in the Balkans started with the studies of the French archeologist and historian Gabriel Millet. Widely recognized as a pioneer of Byzantine studies, Millet proposed the idiosyncratic concept of stylistic "schools" that were located

---

1 Although architectural activities in Constantinople likely took place after the 1330s, nothing monumental was recorded. I summarize the major features of Late Byzantine architecture in Constantinople and relevant bibliography in Jelena Bogdanović, "Late Byzantine Religious Architecture in Constantinople / Υστεροβυζαντινή ναοδομία στην Κωνσταντινούπολη," in *Encyclopaedia of the Hellenic World, Constantinople* (2008), available at http://www2.egeonet.gr/Forms/fLemmaBodyExtended.aspx?lemmaid=10893&boithimata_State=&kefalaia_State=#chapter_1, accessed March 3, 2019. See also Slobodan Ćurčić, *Architecture in the Balkans from Diocletian to Süleyman the Magnificent (c. 300–1550)* (New Haven: Yale University Press, 2010), 528–45; and Slobodan Ćurčić, "Religious Settings of the Late Byzantine Sphere," in *Byzantium: Faith and Power (1261–1557)*, ed. Helen C. Evans (New York: Metropolitan Museum of Art, 2004), pp. 65–94, with references to Semavi Eyice, *Son Devir Bizans Mimârisi: Istanbul'da Palaiologos'lar Devri Antilari* (Istanbul: Üniversite Edebiyat Fakültesi, 1980).
2 Triconch (trefoil) churches have a centralized floor plan in the form of a trefoil, or three conches (apses) attached on three sides of the central core of the structure. On some of these churches in the Balkans, see, Ćurčić, *Architecture in the Balkans*, pp. 671–80, 787–98. See also the excellent and highly relevant contribution by Alice Isabella Sullivan, "The Athonite Patronage of Stephen III of Moldavia, 1457–1504," *Speculum* 94, no. 1 (2019): 1–46. Sullivan analyzes the royal patronage of Moldavian ruler Stephen III and convincingly demonstrates that the primary aspirations behind his generous support of Athonite monasteries were piety and a wish to act as a protector of Orthodox Christianity. The latter he modeled on the role of the Byzantine emperors, who similarly supported Mount Athos as a center of Orthodox spirituality and steadfast religious practices.

regionally in the nation-states of the Balkans originally in reference to painting and then, by extension, to religious architecture.[3] At the time of World War One, when nation-states in the Balkans were trying to promote and maintain their sovereignty, Millet opened up a discussion of national styles in art and architecture with a regional emphasis.[4] His pioneering work spurred development of national studies of historical architecture and arts in the Balkan states and remains critical as it documented numerous building sites in the wider region. A student of Millet's, the architect and architectural historian Aleksandar Deroko, has promoted the more neutral terminology of "architectural groups," rather than "national schools."[5] Because so few historical documents and texts survive to establish the historical context of medieval architecture in the Balkans, these buildings themselves retain important documentary and historical value.

In Serbia, Millet recognized three distinct architectural "schools" that were localized within discrete cultural and geographic regions and grouped by the national identity of their patrons: a) the so-called School of Raška was associated with architecture in the central region of the medieval kingdom of Serbia and was built under patronage of the Nemanjić dynasty predominantly during the 12th and 13th centuries; b) the so-called Serbo-Byzantine School was a general category for the emulation of art and architecture of Constantinople by Serbian rulers in the late 13th and 14th centuries in the wider territories of the Serbian medieval state, including along the Vardar River, in Macedonia, Epirus, and Thessaly; and c) the so-called Morava School was a unique national style of Serbian architecture in the Morava Valley built from approximately the 1370s until the Ottoman conquest of Serbia in 1459.[6] A typical

---

3 Gabriel Millet, *La Serbie glorieuse* (Paris: L'art ancien et moderne aux mondes, 1917); Gabriel Millet, *Recherches sur l'iconographie de l'évangile aux XIVe, XVe et XVIe siècles: D'après les monuments de Mistra, de la Macédoine et du Mont-Athos* (Paris: Fontemoing/E. de Boccard, succ., 1916); Gabriel Millet, *L'école grecque dans l'architecture byzantine* (Paris: Ernest Leroux, 1916); Gabriel Millet, *L'ancien art serbe: Les églises* (Paris: E. de Boccard, 1919).

4 The close relationship between nationalist and regionalist studies opens up numerous possibilities for further research, which go well beyond the focus and limits of this essay.

5 Deroko's assessment was based on firsthand studies of more than three hundred medieval structures in the Balkans. On the reasons for using such rather neutral but, architecturally speaking, more appropriate terminology related to various typological groups of medieval structures, I write in somewhat greater detail in Jelena Bogdanović, "Aleksandar Deroko's Work on Medieval Architecture and Its Relevance Today," in "Aleksandar Deroko," special issue, *Serbian Architectural Journal* 11, no. 1 (2019): 141–56.

6 See Millet, *L'ancien art serbe*, esp. chaps. 2 and 3. Millet formulated the "School of Raška," the "Serbo-Byzantine School," and the "Morava School" as three large groups of architectural monuments built in Serbia or under the Serbian domain. For the "Morava School" as a "national" type of architecture, see Millet, *L'ancien art serbe*, pp. 172, 198. On "schools" of medieval architecture as formulated by Millet and their relevance today, see especially Ćurčić,

example of the "Morava" church is the Church of St. Stephen, also known as Lazarica, in Kruševac, built under the patronage of Serbian Prince Stefan Lazar Hrebeljanović (r. 1370–89) (Fig. 7.1).[7] It may be summarized that in their architectural style, Morava churches are recognized by scholars as being triconch in plan and lavishly decorated in extensive mural cycles on the interior and carved stone sculptural decoration on the exterior. By promoting a typological definition and development of Morava churches, Millet traced their predominant geographical and chronological distributions and situated them as a final phase of Late Byzantine architecture. According to Millet, the "Morava school" was a kind of a national school created by Serbs and later spread beyond Serbian borders, first to Wallachia, the Romanian principality situated to the north of the Danube River.[8] He also proposed that the architectural

---

Architecture in the Balkans, pp. 8–10; Slobodan Ćurčić, "Architecture in Byzantium, Serbia and the Balkans through the Lenses of Modern Historiography," in *Serbia and Byzantium: Proceedings of the International Conference Held on 15 December 2008 at the University of Cologne* (Frankfurt am Main: Peter Lang/PL Academic Research, 2013), pp. 9–31; Dubravka Preradović, "Contribution de Gabriel Millet à l'étude de l'art Serbe" in *Z' Επιστημονικό Συνέδριο « Το Άγιον Όρος στα χρόνια της Απελευθέρωσης », Φόρος Τιμής στον Gabriel Millet* [Mount Athos during the years of liberation, Mount Athos Center 7th Scientific Conference, round table on Gabriel Millet] (Thessaloniki: Mount Athos Center, 2013), pp. 77–85; Dubravka Preradović, "Le premier voyage de Gabriel Millet en Serbie et ses résultats," in *Les Serbes à propos des Français—Les Français à propos des Serbes*, ed. J. Novaković and Lj. P. Ristić (Belgrade: University of Belgrade, 2014), pp. 187–205; Ivan Stevović, "Serbian Architecture of the Morava Period: A Local School or an Epilogue to the Leading Trends in Late Byzantine Architecture; A Study in Methodology," *Zbornik radova vizantološkog instituta* 43 (2006): 231–53; Dragan Vojvodić, and Danica Popović, eds., *Sacral Art of the Serbian Lands in the Middle Ages*, Byzantine Heritage and Serbian Art, vol. 2 of 3 (Belgrade: Serbian Academy of Sciences and Arts, 2016); Dubravka Preradović, ed., *Gabrijel Mije i istraživanja stare srpske arhitekture* [Gabriel Millet et l'étude de l'architecture médiévale serbe] (Belgrade: Srpska akademija nauka i umetnosti, 2019); Dubravka Preradović, "Gabrijel Mije: Terenska istraživanja srpskih spomenika i njihovi rezultati [Gabriel Millet: Ses études de terrain sur les monuments serbes et leurs résultats]," in *Gabrijel Mije i istraživanja stare srpske arhitekture*, pp. 25–36; Jelena Jovanović and Olga Špehar, "L'ancien art serbe: Les églises i definisanje škola u staroj srpskoj arhitekturi [L'ancien art serbe: Les églises and the definition of schools in old Serbian architecture]," in *Gabrijel Mije i istraživanja stare srpske arhitekture*, pp. 65–71; Olga Špehar, "Modaliteti recepcije L'ancien art serbe: Les églises u domaćoj istoriografiji [L'ancien art serbe: Les églises et les modalités de sa réception dans l'historiographie locale]," in *Gabrijel Mije i istraživanja stare srpske arhitekture*, pp. 75–80; and Ivan Stevović, "L'ancien art serbe: Les églises jedan vek kasnije [L'ancien art serbe: Les églises, un siècle plus tard]," in *Gabrijel Mije i istraživanja stare srpske arhitekture*, pp. 81–84.

7   See Vladislav Ristić, *Lazarica i Kruševački grad* (Belgrade: Republički zavod za zaštitu spomenika kulture, 1989); and Ćurčić, *Architecture in the Balkans*, pp. 671–74.

8   "Ainsi, les Serbes, aux derniers jours de l'indépendance, font oeuvre personnelle, créent un type national, qu'ils répandent hors de leur frontière, d'abord, chez leurs alliés, en Valachie." Millet, *L'ancien art serbe*, p. 198, note.

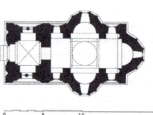

FIGURE 7.1 A typical example of the triconch Morava churches: Church of the Holy Protomartyr Stephen (Lazarica), Serbia, ca. 1375–78, sponsored by Prince Lazar Hrebeljanović of Serbia (r. 1373–89), exterior view and floor plan
PHOTOGRAPH COURTESY IVAN KRSTIĆ; DRAWING BY JELENA BOGDANOVIĆ

development of triconch churches originated on Mount Athos and reached the Morava Valley in the north as well as the territories of Serbia, via Skopje, the capital of the Serbian medieval state.[9] Ćurčić further clarified the important role of the Serbian monastery of Hilandar (ca. 1300–11), on Mount Athos, as a model and inspiration for the formation of the sumptuous architecture built under Serbian rulers and nobility in the Morava Valley.[10] Like the *katholikon* (main church) of Hilandar, the major Morava churches have a fully articulated triconch design, impressive scale, and rich architectural articulation.

9   Millet, *L'ancien art serbe*, pp. 152–53. Vladislav Ristić, *Moravska arhitektura* (Kruševac: Narodni muzej, 1996), pp. 64–65, 81–88, 107–8, 144–57, considers the Skopian churches Matka, Kučevište, Matejič, and Markov Manastir when discussing the origins of architectural features of Morava architecture.
10 Ćurčić, *Architecture in the Balkans*, pp. 671–82, with further references.

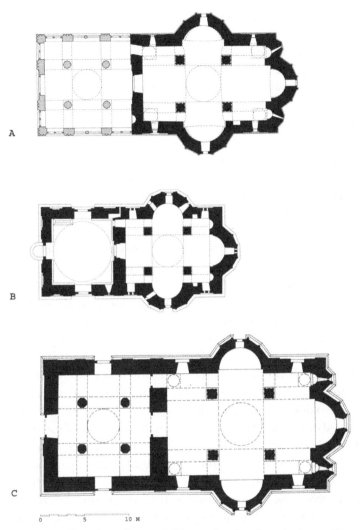

FIGURE 7.2 Floor plans of monastic Morava churches: Ravanica (1375–78), Ljubostinja (ca. 1389), and Resava (Manasija, 1407–18), Serbia
DRAWINGS BY JELENA BOGDANOVIĆ

These characteristics are particularly observable in case of monastic foundations built under Serbian rulers, such as the *katholika* of Ravanica (1375–78), Ljubostinja (ca. 1389), and Manasija (also known as Resava, 1407–18), which were founded, respectively, by Prince Lazar Hrebeljanović, his wife Princess Milica Hrebeljanović (née Nemanjić), and their son, the Serbian Prince and Despot, Stefan Lazarević (Fig. 7.2).

1 Architecture in the Skopje Region

In my research on churches in the region of Skopje, a major cultural and political hub in the wider region of northern Balkans, I examined structures built after the 1330s, at a time when other important architectural activities in Constantinople had virtually ceased.[11] The remarkable continuation of vibrant architectural undertakings in the area of Skopje was supported by Serbian rulers and aristocracy. Going beyond the ethnic, gender, and social identities of their patrons, which indeed point to shared cultural values as a group, these architectural projects are contextualized by relating them to the major artistic and civic centers in the wider region. This analysis revealed that the various architects and building workshops were familiar with Western European, Byzantine, and local traditions and engaged in the process of achieving specific design and building solutions. The multiple lines of development of Morava architecture were traced along the already recognized major south-north axis of Mount Athos—Morava Valley and also along the east-west axis of Constantinople, via Thessaloniki to the east, and the Adriatic Littoral, via Prizren to the west. Evidence that manifold, simultaneous architectural processes resulted in the recognizable architecture of the Skopje region has brought into question the narrative about medieval architecture in the Balkans as a direct offspring of Byzantine architecture. Furthermore, distinctive architectural features of post-1330s Skopian churches are identified, namely an additive and modular design combined with the gradual clustering of architectural volumes based on distinct proportional systems; the structural use of pyramidal, "triumphal arch" tectonics; the use of stone-and-brick construction; geometric articulation of the facades through the use of pilasters, stone string courses, and niches on the exterior; and rather moderate use of architectural sculpture. These elements have made it possible to point out the wider chronological and geographical spread of triconch churches and the role of various building workshops in the physical articulation of architectural concepts.

The investigation of churches built in the region of Skopje after the 1330s challenges the idea of a clearly defined "Morava school" as unique to a single nation or region. Additionally, it confirms the suggestion that triconch Byzantine-rite churches were typologically and architecturally developed

---

11   Jelena Bogdanović, "Regional Developments in Late Byzantine Architecture and the Question of 'Building Schools': An Overlooked Case of the Fourteenth-Century Churches from the Region of Skopje," *Byzantinoslavica* 69, no. 1–2 (2011): 219–66.

from the Middle Byzantine cross-in-square structures.[12] I agree with Stavros Mamaloukos, who convincingly placed the fully formulated triconch church plan in Constantinople, or in the cultural area of its influence, before this architectural plan was applied on Mount Athos and spread further throughout the Balkans and north of Byzantium.[13] As also analyzed in a larger study about Byzantine church design, the triconch typology emanated from the essentially diagrammatic but highly generative nine-square design and was enriched by the modular and hierarchical use of the four-columned domed canopy that serves as a spatial and symbolic core of Byzantine-rite churches.[14]

This analysis can be narrowed down by focusing on the generative design of the triconch churches. They could have derived from fully articulated cross-in-square churches by adding lateral conches along the southern and northern exterior walls either on Mount Athos, as initially proposed by Paulos Mylonas, or in Constantinople and its area of influence, as demonstrated by Stavros Mamaloukos.[15] Their design should also be related to churches built after the 1330s in the Skopian region, starting from the large-scale, five-domed cross-in-square edifices, such as the church of Matejič (ca. 1350), to those of the so-called atrophied versions that have been reduced to a single-domed core, as in the case of the churches at Šiševo (ca. 1334), Matka (before 1371), Devič (probably after the 1350s), and Modrište (probably after the 1350s).[16] The latter group is closely related to the compressed version of the triconch church of St. Andrew in Treska (ca. 1389), which Millet considered an example of the "Morava school" due to its triconch plan—although contextual and architec-

---

12   See Paulos Mylonas, "Η Αρχιτεκτονική του Αγίου 'Ορους" "[The architecture of Mount Athos]," *Nea Hestia* 74 (1963): 189–207; Paulos Mylonas, "Two Middle Byzantine Churches on Athos," *Actes du XVe Congrès international d'études byzantines*, II (Athens, 1976), pp. 545–74; Paulos Mylonas, "Le plan initial du catholicon de la Grande Lavra," *Cahiers archéologiques* 32 (1984): 89–112; Anastasios Tantsis, "The So-called 'Athonite' Type of Church and Two Shrines of the Theotokos in Constantinople," *Zograf* 34 (2010): 3–11; and Stavros Mamaloukos, "A Contribution to the Study of the 'Athonite' Church Type of Byzantine Architecture," *Zograf* 35 (2011): 39–50.

13   Mamaloukos, "A Contribution to the Study of the 'Athonite' Church," pp. 39–50.

14   Jelena Bogdanović, *The Framing of Sacred Space: The Canopy and the Byzantine Church* (New York: Oxford University Press, 2017), pp. 251–67.

15   See note 12 above. Mylonas also proposed that the conches of the triconch-church plan developed to meet the needs of monastic antiphonal psalmody, whereby two choirs perform while occupying the southern and northern conches. Later sources attest to this practice, which continues on Mount Athos in the present day. The conches of some other contemporaneous and earlier churches have also been used for relics, tombs, and shrines. Thus, the specific functions of the triconch churches and their individual elements, including conches as the most obvious, remain open to further investigation.

16   Bogdanović, "Regional Developments," pp. 219–66.

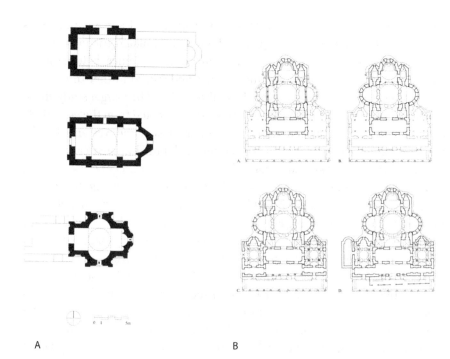

FIGURE 7.3 Development of triconch churches from cross-in-square Middle Byzantine type: a) in the region of Skopje by showcasing the churches at Šiševo, Matka and Andreaš (after Ćurčić and Bogdanović), b) on Mt. Athos based on the Great Lavra Monastery
DRAWINGS BY JELENA BOGDANOVIĆ
AFTER MYLONAS, DRAWING BY PAULOS MYLONAS

tural analyses reaffirm its stronger association with cross-in-square Skopian churches (Fig. 7.3).[17]

The architectural design of triconch churches was open to various stylistic interpretations and solutions resulting from the sophisticated understanding and implementation of architectural principles on the part of architects and various building workshops. It is my reasoning that medieval architects and builders fluidly exchanged their architectural ideas and practices beyond state and national divides and strict chronological thresholds determined by sociopolitical events, two convenient but imprecise demarcations which we still too often use in our studies of medieval architecture. Moreover, the questions I am raising related to nationalist approaches and cultural identities coupled with

17 Ibid; and Ćurčić, *Architecture in the Balkans*, pp. 637–44, esp. 639. On the church of St. Andrew in Treska as an example of the "Morava School" structure, see Millet, *L'ancien art serbe*, p. 133.

questions related to the methodologies employed in architectural studies may be used to enrich discussions about the creative processes and networks of architectural production. This approach, whereby the focus shifts from a sociopolitical framework to material culture, could extend to the study of other medieval artworks and artifacts, including a variety of portable church objects as well as monumental and smaller-scale images found in medieval structures.

2   Serbian and Wallachian Architectural Connections

Following Millet's studies, and in particular his thesis that Morava churches represented the final phase of Late Byzantine architecture, scholars of architecture in the Balkans have maintained that triconch churches built in Wallachia—a principality including territories south of the Carpathian mountains and north of the Danube River that gained its independence ca. 1310— were direct offspring of the Morava style brought there by the Serbian monks.[18] Such linearly explained sociopolitical development of post-Byzantine architecture starts in the western Balkans, in medieval Serbia, first reaching neighboring Wallachia and then traveling further northeast to Moldavia. This latter included the territories that remained Christian for less than a decade longer than Constantinople, as Serbia fell to the Ottomans in 1459 and Wallachia became an Ottoman tributary state in 1462. Recently, Alice I. Sullivan has questioned this narrative.[19] She considers multiple lines of artistic and architectural developments and related ideologies hailing from the fluctuating territories of the medieval states of Bulgaria, Serbia, Hungary (more specifically related

---

18 See, for example, Georges Balş, "Influence du plan serbe sur le plan des églises roumaines," in *L'art byzantin chez les slaves: Les Balkans; Premier recueil dédié à la mémoire de Théodore Uspenskij*, vol. 1 (Paris: Librairie Orientaliste Paul Geuthner, 1930), pp. 277–94; Cyril Mango, *Byzantine Architecture* (New York: Harry N. Abrams, 1976), p. 192; Ćurčić, *Architecture in the Balkans*, p. 682. For an important historiographical overview of the scholarship on triconch churches in Serbia and Wallachia, see also Alice Isabella Sullivan, "The Painted Fortified Monastic Churches of Moldavia: Bastions of Orthodoxy in a Post-Byzantine World" (PhD diss., University of Michigan, 2017), pp. 106–7.

19 Alice Isabella Sullivan, "The Painted Fortified Monastic Churches of Moldavia," pp. 106–7; and eadem, "The Athonite Patronage of Stephen III of Moldavia," 1–46. See also Elisabeta Negrău, "Tipologiile arhitecturale ale ctitoriilor domneşti din Ţara Românească în secolele XIV–XVI [Architectural Types of Princes' Church Foundations in Wallachia in the 14th–16th Centuries]," *Analele Universităţii din Craiova, Seria Istorie* 16, no. 2 (Craiova, 2009): 95–114.

to the German and Hungarian traditions in Transylvania), and Byzantium.[20] Moreover, she provides a detailed chronological overview of the triconch churches in Wallachia and demonstrates that their construction was nearly concurrent with the construction of those in the Morava Valley starting in the 1370s. She also highlights how architecture in Moldavia relates to contemporaneous Byzantine trends in architecture.

My independent research on this topic additionally suggests that the architectural experimentations and plastic treatment of triconch churches built by Serbian and Wallachian nobility within and beyond the territories of their domains were the result of highly complex architectural processes. Simultaneously, the churches became architecturally recognizable, pervasive statements of cultural, religious, and familial identity, rather than national identity alone. In making this claim, I too question established narratives of the autonomous national development of the so-called "Morava-style" churches and their linear and exclusive influence on churches in Wallachia.

This essay does not aim to provide a comprehensive overview and study of all triconch churches associated with Serbian and Wallachian nobility. Rather, in the following sections, several triconch churches are analyzed to exemplify continuities in Byzantine material culture and triconch Byzantine-rite churches (Table 7.1). In the process, I point out how their legacy was transformed and reinterpreted in architecture north of Byzantium after the 1350s.

The aforementioned church at Lazarica dedicated to the Holy Protomartyr Stephen, possibly a court church of Prince Lazar Hrebeljanović of Serbia (r. 1373–89), and Prince Lazar Hrebeljanović's mausoleum at Ravanica dedicated to the Ascension of Christ were both built around 1375–78 and are considered the prototypes of the Morava architectural group. The Holy Trinity Church at Cozia Monastery (1387–91) in Wallachia, built by Voivode Mircea I of Wallachia (r. 1386–95 and 1397–1418), is considered the prototypical example of Wallachian architecture.[21] The Church of St. Nicholas in Lapušnja

---

20 The first documented triconch church in Wallachia is the *katholikon* of Vodița Monastery, built under the guidance of the monk Nikodemos/Nikodim around 1374. Shortly afterward, the Church of the Dormition of the Virgin at Tismana Monastery was consecrated on August 15, 1378. The Church of the Trinity at Cozia Monastery, consecrated on May 18, 1388, became a major example of the Wallachian triconch churches. See Sullivan, "The Painted Fortified Monastic Churches," p. 107, with references.

21 See, for example, Gamaliil Vaida, *The Monastery of Cozia: In the Past and Nowadays* (Călimănești-Vîlcea: Stăreția Mînăstirii Cozia, 1977); Mișu Davidescu, *Mănăstirea Cozia* (Bucharest: Editura Meridiane, 1968); and Heinrich L. Nickel, *Medieval Architecture in Eastern Europe* (New York: Holmes and Meier, 1983), pp. 83–120, esp. 84. The first acknowledged dynastic church of the Wallachian rulers is the cross-in-square Church of St. Nicholas at Curtea de Argeș (ca. 1340). Like Skopian churches, it may have been a precursor

TABLE 7.1　Comparative list of triconch churches sponsored by Serbian and Wallachian nobility

Date	Place	Dedication	Donor	Plan	Elevation view
1375–78	Kruševac, Serbia	The Holy First Martyr Stephen Lazarica	Prince Lazar Hrebeljanović of Serbia (r. 1373–89)		
1375–78	Ravanica Monastery, Serbia	Ascension of Christ	Prince Lazar Hrebeljanović of Serbia (r. 1373–89)		
c. 1387–91	Cozia Monastery, Wallachia	The Holy Trinity Church	Voivode Mircea I of Wallachia (r. 1386–95; 1397–1418)		
1500–10	Lapušnja Monastery, Serbia	St. Nicholas	Voivode Radu cel Mare (r. 1495–1508) Princess Katalina Crnojević of Zeta, *Joupan* Gergina, Prince Bogoje and his family		
~1500s? restored in 16th and 17th c.	Govora Monastery, Wallachia	Assumption of the Mother of God	Voivode Radu cel Mare ?; restored Voivodes Matei Basarab and Constantin Brâncoveanu		

TABLE 7.1 Comparative list of triconch churches sponsored by Serbian and Wallachian nobility (*cont.*)

Date	Place	Dedication	Donor	Plan	Elevation view
1356–72; remod. in 1540s	Great Meteoron Monastery, Kalabaka, Greece	Transfiguration of Christ	St. Athanasios and King and later monk Ioannis-Ioasaph Uroš Palaiologos (r. 1370–73, d. 1387/88) Remodeled		
1350s–60s establ. re-built c.1540	Koutloumousiou Monastery, Mount Athos, Greece	Transfiguration of Christ	Wallachian Voivodes Nicolae Alexandru (r. 1344–64) and Vladislav Vlaicu (r. 1364–77) around the 1350s–60s		

DRAWINGS BY JELENA BOGDANOVIĆ AND TIANLING (RUSTY) XU; PHOTOGRAPHS BY IVAN KRSTIĆ (LAZARICA), DEKANSKI (RAVANICA), ANDREI STROE (COZIA), JELENA BOGDANOVIĆ (LAPUŠNJA), RAZVAN SOKOL (GOVORA), JELENA BOGDANOVIĆ (GREAT METEORON), AND ADRIATICUS (KOUTLOUMOUSIOU).

Monastery (1500–10) in Serbia—built by Voivode Radu cel Mare (r. 1495–1508) and his wife, Princess Katalina Crnojević of Zeta, with the support of Joupan (or local count) Gergina and Prince Bogoje and his family—is a critical example of the perseverance of triconch churches built together by Serbian and Wallachian rulers often connected by family ties.[22] In this case, the church

to the later development of the triconch churches in Wallachia. This possibility points to the same paradigmatic development of royal foundations from the compressed—or so-called atrophied—cross-in-square design toward the compressed triconch design. See note 17 above.

22 See Branka Knežević, "Manastir Lapušnja," *Saopštenje* 18 (1986): 83–114; and Ćurčić, *Architecture in the Balkans*, pp. 788–89.

was built by a Wallachian ruler married to a Serbian princess. The church at Lapušnja is also an important case because Voivode Radu cel Mare sponsored the church in Serbian territory, which at the time of its construction was then under the Ottoman domain. It demonstrates the significant and diverse building activities shared by the Wallachians and Serbs in the broader area of the northern Balkans.

Another example of complex activities outside established narratives about architecture in the Balkans is the relatively understudied Church of the Assumption of the Mother of God at Govora Monastery in Wallachia, which was possibly originally built by Voivode Radu cel Mare and later restored under Wallachian Voivodes Matei Basarab and Constantin Brâncoveanu in the 16th and 17th centuries.[23] Two other examples showcase the prolonged tradition of building triconch churches in the much wider region of the Balkans from the 1350s until the 1540s. The first is the *katholikon* of the Great Meteoron Monastery (1356–72) in Greece, which was founded by St. Athanasios and the king and later monk Ioannis-Ioasaph Uroš Palaiologos (r. 1370–73, d. 1387/88) and remodeled in the 1540s when the territory was under Ottoman authority.[24] Another is the *katholikon* of the Koutloumousiou Monastery on Mount Athos, which was built during the Ottoman reign in 1540 after its initial establishment with support from Wallachian Voivodes Nicolae Alexandru (r. 1344–64) and Vladislav Vlaicu (r. 1364–77) around the 1350s–60s.[25]

---

23 See Radu Florescu, *Mănăstirea Govora* (Bucharest: Meridiane, 1965); and Gherasim Cristea, *Istoria mânăstirii Govora* (Râmnicu Vâlcea: Editura Sf. Episcopii a Râmnicului, 1995). The still-existing, though severely damaged, fresco of the ktitors (founders) at Lapušnja is closely related to the preserved ktitors fresco from the 16th-century Govora monastery.

24 See Konstantinos M. Vafeiadēs, *Holy Monastery of the Great Meteroron: History, Prospography and Spiritual Life of the Monastery on the Basis of the Written and Archeological Evidence (12th–20th Century)* (Meteora: Holy Monasteries of Meteora, 2019); *The Lives of the Monastery Builders of Meteora: Saint Athanasios of New Patras and Saint Ioasaph the Monk-King, Builders of the Great Meteoron Monastery, and Saints Nectarios and Theophanes of Ioannina, Builders of the Varlaam Monastery* (Buena Vista, CO: Holy Apostles Convent, 1991); and Theoteknē Metsikosta, *Meteora: History, Art, Monastic Presence* (Meteora: Holy Monasteries of Meteora, 1987). See also Slobodan Ćurčić, "The Role of Late Byzantine Thessalonike in Church Architecture in the Balkans," *Dumbarton Oaks Papers* 57 (2003): 65–84; Bogdanović, "Regional Developments," pp. 219–66; and Ćurčić, *Architecture in the Balkans*, pp. 790–91.

25 See Paulos Mylonas, "Le Catholicon de Kutlumus (Athos)," *Cahiers archéologiques* 42 (1994): 75–86. See also Ćurčić, *Architecture in the Balkans*, pp. 789–90; and Sullivan, "The Athonite Patronage of Stephen III of Moldavia," 1–46.

3 Implications of the Serbian and Wallachian Connections

My major findings touch upon issues of patronage, national identity, the training and practices of builders, and some typical and atypical features of triconch churches that may provide more nuanced understandings of their architecture. These sumptuous, memorable triconch structures reveal royal and aristocratic patronage that was occasionally strengthened by intermarriage between the Wallachians and Serbs and that was based on their shared identity of Orthodox Christianity, rather than national identity. The concept of national architectural schools is essentially a late 19th-century and early 20th-century convention.[26] While detailed typological analysis in a given region is undoubtedly important, it also localizes studies of architecture, leading to oversimplifications and overemphasis on the role of architecture as a mere tool for documenting and supporting the sociohistorical narrative. So often we miss an opportunity to study larger groups of dispersed buildings based on their shared architectural features across a wider geographical scope. The simple example of triconch churches on Mount Athos and the Great Meteoron Monastery in Greece reinforces the undeniable and long-lasting connections between Byzantine and Constantinopolitan architectural traditions and opens questions about the exclusivity and linearity of Serbian-Wallachian architectural developments after the 1350s (Fig. 7.4).

The training and practices of builders are occasionally revealed through textual sources, inscriptions, and patronage based on family connections between the Serbs and Wallachians. By extension, this evidence points to the possibility that patrons had access to the same building groups or those trained in a similar idiom. Following the initial research by Millet, both Cyril Mango and Ćurčić in their architectural studies demonstrated how the building of prototypical churches in the Morava and Wallachia regions—that is, Lazarica and Cozia, respectively—resulted from the historically attested activities of monks, who were predominantly responsible for the geographically widespread exchange of ideas and concepts about the buildings' design.[27] As a consideration of those involved in the church's design, the donors' inscription from the church at Lapušnja confirms not only the shared commitment

---

26   See also notes 6, 19, 21. The concept of the "national style" for Morava-style and Wallachian churches is continually used in major books on Byzantine architecture. See, for example, Mango, *Byzantine Architecture*, p. 192.

27   Gabriel Millet, "Cozia et les églises serbes de la Morava," in *Mélanges offerts à M. Nicolas Iorga par ses amis de France et des pays de langue française*, ed. Nicolae Iorga (Paris: J. Gamber, 1933), pp. 827–56; Mango, *Byzantine Architecture*, p. 119; and Ćurčić, *Architecture in the Balkans*, p. 682.

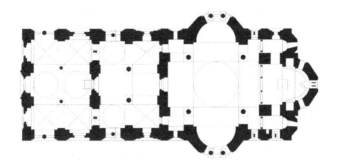

FIGURE 7.4 Serbian and Wallachian triconch churches in the territories of Byzantine Greece: a) Serbian Monastery Hilandar, Mt. Athos, Greece, established 1196–98, rebuilt ca. 1300–11; b) Wallachian Monastery Koutloumousiou, Mt. Athos, Greece, established 1350s–60s, rebuilt ca. 1540; c) Transfiguration of Christ, Great Meteoron Monastery, Kalabaka, Greece, 1356–72, established by St. Athanasios and king and later monk Ioannis-Ioasaph Uroš Palaiologos (r. 1370–73, d. 1387/8), remodeled in the 1540s
DRAWING BY JELENA BOGDANOVIĆ

of Wallachian and Serbian rulers but also of hieromonks—in this case, the monks Gelasios (ca. 1500) and Theodor (1510).[28]

The obvious architectural similarities in the construction of the churches at Lazarica and Cozia, including the idiosyncratic use of elegant, vertical colonettes for the exterior wall articulation of all three conches in both churches, indicate a high possibility that the churches were built by, if not the same building workshops, than certainly building workshops trained in the same idiom (Fig. 7.5). Similar use of half-engaged vertical colonettes in the exterior of the Constantinopolitan monastery of Christ Pantokrator (now Zeyrek camii), which was built during the Middle Byzantine period ca. 1118–34, was followed by other, opulent examples of Late Byzantine architecture, such as the late 13th-century and early 14th-century additions to the Chora, Pammakaristos, and Constantine Lips monasteries, and these highlight the Constantinopolitan imperial aesthetics.[29] This atypical but memorable architectural decoration shows that the inclusion of likewise-articulated, half-engaged vertical colonettes in the 14th-century foundations of Serbian and Wallachian rulers was not arbitrary, but instead a highly educated choice. The churches of Lazarica and Cozia are further related in their compact design—here pointing to a sophisticated articulation of monumentality understood not through size but rather by means of recognizable architectural aesthetics.

Architecturally, all churches analyzed in my research share the triconch typology, be it a fully developed or compact plan (see Table 7.1). At the same time, shared features point to a variety of plastic solutions for buildings with different functions and meanings. As such, they cannot easily fit categorical and straightforward typologies related to the function of a building, which is essentially a modernist method we still retroactively apply when studying medieval structures. The lens of material culture allows the structures themselves to yield historical insights about the people who built and used them through the presence of physical continuities and discontinuities. The majority of the monastic triconch churches, such as the well-known Athonite Hilandar, demonstrate that the triconch plan basically developed by adding lateral conches to the typical cross-in-square church with a fully established three-partite sanctuary commonly seen in Byzantine-rite churches.[30] The entire concept

---

28 See Knežević, "Manastir Lapušnja," pp. 83–114.
29 See Ćurčić, *Architecture in the Balkans*, pp. 361–64, 533–45.
30 Ibid, pp. 653–55. See also note 12.

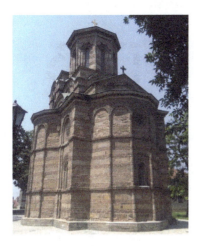
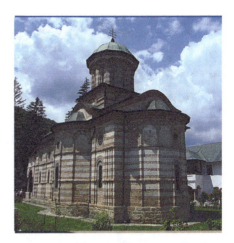
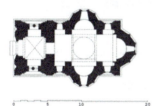

FIGURE 7.5 Comparative analysis of typical examples of triconch churches in Serbia and Wallachia, with exterior views and floor plans: a) Church of the Holy Protomartyr Stephen (Lazarica), Serbia, ca. 1375–78, sponsored by Prince Lazar Hrebeljanović of Serbia (r. 1373–89) b) Holy Trinity Church at Cozia Monastery, Wallachia, ca. 1387–91, built by Voivode Mircea I of Wallachia (r. 1386–95; 1397–1418)
PHOTOGRAPH COURTESY IVAN KRSTIĆ, DRAWING BY JELENA BOGDANOVIĆ
PHOTOGRAPH BY CRISTIAN CHIRIȚĂ, DRAWING BY TIANLING (RUSTY) XU

was later literally adopted in Ravanica, the church that exemplifies the Morava group (Fig. 7.6).[31]

Some other triconch churches, such as Lazarica, another prototypical example of a Morava church, are actually compact solutions without a developed tripartite sanctuary.[32] The design for Lazarica may be explained by its urban context and the high possibility that it essentially functioned as a

---

31 See Ćurčić, *Architecture in the Balkans*, pp. 674–75; and Branislav Vulović, *Ravanica: Njeno mesto i njena uloga u sakralnoj arhitekturi Pomoravlja* [Ravanica: Its place and role in sacred architecture of the Morava Valley] (Belgrade: Republički zavod za zaštitu spomenika culture, 1966).

32 See Ćurčić, *Architecture in the Balkans*, pp. 671–73; and Ristić, *Lazarica i Kruševački grad*, passim.

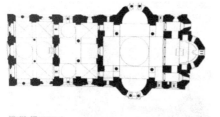 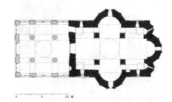

Hilandar, Mt Athos, ca. 1300-11   Ravanica, Serbia, ca. 1375-8

a) Monastic, "mausolea" triconch churches

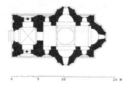 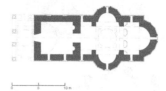

Lazarica, Serbia, ca. 1375-78   Cozia Monastery, Wallachia, c. 1387-91

b) Urban, "court-type" triconch churches

FIGURE 7.6   a) Monastic, "mausolea" triconch churches: Hilandar, Mt. Athos, ca. 1300–11, and Ravanica, Serbia, ca. 1375–78; b) urban, "court" triconch churches: Lazarica, Serbia ca. 1375–78, and Cozia, Wallachia, ca. 1387–89
DRAWINGS BY JELENA BOGDANOVIĆ AND TIANLING (RUSTY) XU

court church.[33] Furthermore, in its design and architectural articulation, Lazarica can be directly related to Cozia, a Wallachian example of a "court" type of church. Yet Cozia is also a royal mausoleum. It was larger than the Lazarica church, and its size approaches the Ravanica church in the Serbian context. The latter church was a mausoleum actually built within the monastery. Hence, with regard to the function of Cozia, the structure emerges as a hybrid of a court and a mausoleum church. Its urbanity is the result of being located not in a city but rather in a monastic setting of high density. Layered, multifunctional structures within the complex additionally reflect urban usage.

The compact exonarthex of the Cozia church with the central domical vault may be related architecturally and conceptually to the use of central domical vaults in dynastic monastic and funerary foundations. These appear in sizable Morava churches including the aforementioned Ravanica (1375–78), which was the royal mausoleum of Prince Lazar Hrebeljanović, and Ljubostinja

---

33   See Ćurčić, *Architecture in the Balkans*, p. 673.

(ca. 1389), which was built by Prince Lazar Hrebeljanović's wife, the Serbian Princess Milica Hrebeljanović (née Nemanjić), to be her monastic foundation and mausoleum.[34] A third example is Manasija (also known as Resava, 1407–18), which was founded by the son of Prince Lazar Hrebeljanović and Princess Milica Hrebeljanović, the Serbian Prince and Despot Stefan Lazarević, as his own major monastic foundation and mausoleum (Fig. 7.2).[35] This emblematic use of canopied, domical vaults in central narthex bays was often combined with impressive opus sectile work, as in the case of the still-preserved narthex of the Manasija church. Such a combination points to the distinctive, multilayered evocations of imperial, funerary, and religious canopied installations that could be further enriched by associated rites for the veneration of the Holy (True) Cross and liturgical Easter celebrations—as were practiced in numerous Byzantine-rite churches that were also imperial. These rites and ceremonies also took place in the ruler's foundations and, recurrently, in their mausolea.[36] While scholars have acknowledged imperial references for the veneration of the True Cross and its role in the building of a ruler's Christian

---

34   See Ljubica D. Popovich, "Portraits of Kneginja Milica," *Serbian Studies* 8, no. 1–2 (1994): 94–95; Zaga Gavrilović, "Women in Serbian Politics, Diplomacy and Art at the Beginning of Ottoman Rule", in *Byzantine Style, Religion, and Civilization: In Honour of Sir Steven Runciman*, ed. Elizabeth M. Jeffreys (New York: Cambridge University Press, 2006), pp. 75–78; Ćurčić, *Architecture in the Balkans*, pp. 678–81; and Srdjan Djurić, *Manastir Ljubostinja* (Belgrade: Republički zavod za zaštitu spomenika kulture, 1983).

35   See Ćurčić, *Architecture in the Balkans*, pp. 680–82; Vojislav J. Djurić, *Resava (Manasija)* (Belgrade: Jugoslavija, 1966); and Jadranka Prolović, *Resava (Manasija): Geschichte, Architektur und Malerei einer Stiftung des serbischen Despoten Stefan Lazarević* (Vienna: Verlag der Österreichischen Akademie der Wissenschaften, 2017).

36   On the architectural and spatial integration of canopied vaulted bays with smaller-scale, portable canopied installations during services, see Bogdanović, *The Framing of Sacred Space*, pp. 235–41. For the imperial connections with the veneration of the relic of the True Cross and extended ceremonies, albeit without detailed discussion of their architectural settings, see Holger A. Klein, "Sacred Relics and Imperial Ceremonies at the Great Palace of Constantinople," in *Visualisierungen von Herrschaft*, ed. Franz Alto Bauer, BYZAS 5 (2006): 79–99; Holger A. Klein, "Constantin, Helena, and the Cult of the True Cross in Constantinople," in *Byzance et les reliques du Christ*, ed. Jannic Durand and Bernard Flusin (Paris: Association des amis du Centre d'histoire et civilisation de Byzance: 2004), pp. 31–59; Jelena Bogdanović, "The Relational Spiritual Geopolitics of Constantinople, the Capital of the Byzantine Empire," in *Political Landscapes of Capital Cities*, ed. Jessica Christie, Bogdanović, and Eulogio Guzmán (Boulder: University Press of Colorado, 2016), pp. 97–153, esp. 117–18; and Jelena Erdeljan, "Trnovo: Principi i sredstva konstruisanja sakralne topografije srednjevekovne bugarske prestonice / Tŭrnovo: Principles and Means of Constructing the Sacral Topography of a Medieval Bulgarian Capital," *Zbornik Radova Vizantološkog Instituta* 47 (2010): 199–214.

identity, little is known about the architectural settings of such ceremonies.[37] The historical record remains predominantly silent about the possession and use of the relics of the True Cross in Serbia after the 14th century. The relics were last documented as guarded by Mara Branković (ca. 1416–87), a member of the last ruler's dynasty of medieval Serbia. Some references point to their division and dissemination as gifts to the Athonite Vatopedi monastery but also to Italy, Russia, and elsewhere.[38] Nevertheless, the reminiscent references to the ceremonial religious and imperial stations of the True Cross, including the central domical bay of the narthex of the ruler's foundations and mausolea, should not be underestimated.

In her work, Danica Popović details the use of the relics of the True Cross in medieval Serbia and additionally highlights the healing ceremony using water sanctified by the True Cross as documented in Serbian hagiographies.[39] Very little is recorded regarding the site of such ceremonies. The rite of the blessing of water by the cross was related to the domed architectural canopy, known as *phiale*, and points essentially to two major locations within the Byzantine-rite churches: in front or south of the western entrance to the church or incorporated within the domical bay of its narthex.[40] Especially telling in that regard

---

37   See, for example, Antony Eastmond, "Byzantine Identity and Relics of the True Cross in the Thirteenth Century," in *Eastern Christian Relics*, ed. Alexei Lidov (Moscow: Progress-Tradicija, 2003), pp. 204–61; and Alexei Lidov, "A Byzantine Jerusalem: The Imperial Pharos Chapel as the Holy Sepulchre," in *Jerusalem as Narrative Space*, ed. Annette Hoffmann and Gerhard Wolf (Leiden and Boston: Brill, 2012), pp. 63–104.

38   See Danica Popović, "Реликвије Часног крста у средњовековној Србији" "[Relikvije Časnog krsta u srednjovekovnoj Srbiji, The relics of the Holy Cross in medieval Serbia]," in *Konstantin Veliki u vizantijskoj i srpskoj tradiciji*, ed. Ljubomir Maksimović (Belgrade: Zavod za udžbenike, 2014), pp. 99–121, esp. 110; and Ida Sinkević, "Afterlife of the Rhodes Hand of St. John the Baptist," in *Byzantine Images and Their Afterlives: Essays in Honor of Annemarie Weyl Carr*, ed. Lynn Jones (Farnham: Ashgate, 2014), pp. 125–41.

39   Danica Popović, *Relikvije Časnog krsta*, pp. 99–121, esp. 107–8, with references to Domentijan, Живот Светога Саве и Живот Светога Симеона (Život Svetoga Save i Život Svetoga Simeona), ed. Radmila Marinković (Belgrade: Prosveta and Srpska književna zadruga, 1988), p. 142; and Teodosije, Житија (Žitija), ed. Dimitrije Bogdanović (Belgrade: Prosveta and Srpska književna zadruga, 1988), p. 202. Both sources record the healing ceremony using water sanctified by the True Cross. Moreover, Popović locates this practice in medieval Serbia within a wider network of healing practices and ceremonies using the remnants of the True Cross, as studied by Anatole Frolow, *La relique de la vraie croix: Recherches sur le développement d'un culte* (Paris: Institut français d'études byzantines, 1961), pp. 174, 195, 251, 334; and Holger A. Klein, *Byzanz, der Westen und das "wahre" Kreuz: Die Geschichte einer Reliquie und ihrer künstlerischen Fassung in Byzanz und im Abendland* (Wiesbaden: Reichert, 2004).

40   On *phiale*, see, for example, Bogdanović, *The Framing of Sacred Space*, pp. 241–43; and Bogdanović, "The Phiale as a Spatial Icon in the Byzantine Cultural Sphere," in *Holy*

is the triconch design of the Pătrăuți Church of the Holy Cross, the oldest surviving church of the Moldavian ruler Stephen III, also known as Stephen the Great, which was built in 1487.[41] The Pătrăuți *katholikon* is highly comparable in plan and size to representative monastic churches in the Morava Valley built by Serbian rulers, such as those of Naupara, built by Prince Lazar Hrebeljanović in the late 14th century, and Ljubostinja, built by his wife, Princess Milica Hrebeljanović (Figs. 7.1 and 7.2). Even if the *katholikon* at Pătrăuți is architecturally articulated as a mixture of traditionally recognized Byzantine- and Gothic-style elements, in my opinion, its floor plan belongs to the compact version of the triconch with a single, square bay of the narthex and a domical vault.[42] The domical vault may be related to its evocative imperial references and veneration of the Holy Cross in this eponymous church. Moreover, this monastery, one of the Moldavian foundations built during Stephen III's rule and one populated by nuns, initially was intended for healing and care of the wounded from the battles around Suceava.[43]

While noteworthy architectural elements shared by select churches may point to specific functions and rituals within, it is also possible for them to reveal some shared architectural practices and roles of the building workshops. The undeniable architectural and spatial resemblances between Lazarica and Cozia indicate potentially the same builder(s), who may have used similar and highly sophisticated, generative architectural designs for the two churches. The question of the use of architectural concepts by building workshops becomes even more complex when we consider the *katholikon* of the Koutloumousiou Monastery (see Table 7.1). The church demonstrates the renewal of building traditions on Mount Athos under Wallachian nobility in the

---

Water in the Hierotopy and Iconography of the Christian World, ed. Alexei Lidov (Moscow: Theoria, 2017), pp. 372–96, with further references.

41 See Gabriel Herea and Petru Palamar, *Pătrăuți 1487—Monument UNESCO* (Pătrăuți: Heruvim, 2015); Gabriel Herea, *Pelerinaj în spațiul sacru Bucovinean* (Cluj-Napoca: Patmos, 2010); and Gabriel Herea and Petru Palamar, *Pătrăuți* (Suceava: Asociația Prietenii Bucovinei, 2011).

42 See Herea and Palamar, *Pătrăuți 1487*, passim; and Nickel, *Medieval Architecture*, pp. 87–88. On Gothic and Byzantine references in Moldavian churches, see Dragoș Năstăsoiu, *Gothic Art in Romania* (Bucharest: NOI Media Print, 2011), pp. 30–49; Alice Isabella Sullivan, "Western-Byzantine 'Hybridity' in the Ecclesiastical Architecture of Northern Moldavia," *Romanian Medievalia: Thraco-Dacian and Byzantine Romanity of Eastern Europe and Asia Minor* 12–13 (New York: Romanian Institute of Orthodox Theology and Spirituality, 2015): 29–49; and Alice Isabella Sullivan, "Architectural Pluralism at the Edges: The Visual Eclecticism of Medieval Monastic Churches in Eastern Europe," in "Marginalia: Architectures of Uncertain Margins," special issue, *Studii de Istoria și Teoria Arhitecturii / Studies in History and Theory of Architecture* 4 (2016): 135–51, esp. 141, 146.

43 See Gabriel Herea, *Pătrăuți*, online at www.biserica.patrauti.ro, accessed April 22, 2019.

1540s. Its architecture demonstrates recognizable regional characteristics of Athonite architecture, which since Middle Byzantine times adhered to a developed triconch design. Simultaneously, and seen through the lens of Byzantine architecture, this church also strongly references architecture in other parts of Byzantine Greece, beyond Mount Athos. Among those referenced are the massive triconch churches within both urban and monastic contexts, such as the Church of Prophet Elias in Thessaloniki (ca. 1360s–70s) and the *katholika* of the monasteries of H. Demeterios at Mount Ossa (1543) and H. Dionysios at Mount Olympos (16th century).[44] Such a wide chronological and geographical span elucidates the perseverance of design principles and goes well beyond a simple explanation of building workshops based on master-and-apprentice practice or the unquestionable relationships between the architectural form and function of a given structure. In my opinion, this phenomenon points to more developed and sophisticated architectural training and practices.

In my research on medieval architecture, I distinguish the role of architects and their use of various design principles from the work of builders who were responsible for the actual construction at the building site and who may or may not have been aware of all the nuances of highly complex architectural concepts. The lack of textual evidence about the architectural training of medieval builders as well as the nonexistence of surviving architectural drawings in the wider Mediterranean region after the 7th century are usually taken as definitive proof that medieval architects were merely master builders who oversaw construction.[45] By embracing more recent methodologies stemming from the studies of material culture, the buildings themselves as material evidence challenge this proposition about the lack of architects and architectural practices. The profession of medieval architect, indeed, may have been significantly different from the one established during the Renaissance or early

---

44 See Ćurčić, *Architecture in the Balkans*, pp. 792–93, fig. 907.

45 Based on our inability to confirm systematic architectural education in the Mediterranean basin after the 7th century, Oleg Grabar, *The Mediation of Ornament* (Princeton: Princeton University Press, 1992), pp. 174–78, suggests the nonexistence of architectural drawings. Robert Ousterhout, *Master Builders of Byzantium*, 2nd ed. (Philadelphia: University of Pennsylvania Museum of Archaeology and Anthropology, 2008), p. 58, similarly embraces the opinion that architectural drawings were not used in Byzantium. I concur with Slobodan Nenadović, *Gradjevinska tehnika u srednjevekovnoj Srbiji* (Belgrade: Gradjevinska Knjiga, 2003), pp. 46–49, who, based on the architectural evidence itself, claims that preparatory models and schemes were used within the Byzantine realm. I discuss this topic also in Bogdanović, "Regional Developments," pp. 219–66.

modern periods.[46] Whether medieval architects and builders used some essential design tools that had been applied in architecture since antiquity, such as grid or proportional systems, and whether they communicated their designs by using plans, drawings, or models are hotly debated topics in Byzantine scholarship.[47] We may even speculate that donors and monks, who are often mentioned as creators of sacred architecture, communicated their ideas about architectural projects through more luxurious, three-dimensional tools, such as models.[48] Similarly, the role of a few surviving architectural drawings has

46 See, for example, Catherine Wilkinson, "The New Professionalism in the Renaissance," in *The Architect: Chapters in the History of the Profession*, ed. Spiro Kostof (New York: Oxford University Press, 1977), pp. 124–60.

47 Among the texts that address the opposing views about the architectural design processes and the role of architects and building workshops are Richard Krautheimer (with Slobodan Ćurčić), *Early Christian and Byzantine Architecture* (New Haven: Yale University Press, 1986), pp. 238–57; Ousterhout, *Master Builders of Byzantium*, pp. 58–127; Marina Mihaljević, "Change in Byzantine Architecture: Architects and Builders," in *Approaches to Byzantine Architecture and Its Decoration*, ed. Mark Johnson, Robert Ousterhout, and Amy Papalexandrou (Surrey: Ashgate, 2012), pp. 99–119; Bogdanović, "Regional Developments," pp. 219–66; Bogdanović, *The Framing of Sacred Space*, pp. 251–63, 299; Stavros Mamaloukos, "Από τον σχεδιασμό στην κατασκευή: Ζητήματα εφαρμογής στη βυζαντινή αρχιτεκτονική / From Design to Construction: Aspects of Implementation in Byzantine Architecture," *Δελτίον της Χριστιανικής Αρχαιολογικής Εταιρείας* 4, no. 39 (2018): 83–97; and Magdalena S. Dragović, Aleksandar A. Čučaković, Jelena Bogdanović, et al., "Geometric Proportional Schemas of Serbian Medieval Raška Churches Based on Štambuk's Proportional Canon," *Nexus Network Journal: Architecture and Mathematics* 21, no. 1 (2019): 33–58. On the role and meaning of architectural models and drawings in Byzantium, see, for example, Čedomila Marinković, *Слика подигнуте цркве: Представе архитектуре на ктиторским портретима у српској и византијској уметности* [The image of the built church: Representations of architecture in donors' portraits in Serbian and Byzantine art] (Belgrade: Bonart, 2007); Slobodan Ćurčić, Evangelia Hadjitryphonos, et al. *Architecture as Icon* (New Haven: Yale University Press, 2010); Evangelia Hadjitryphonos, "Presentations and Representations of Architecture in Byzantium: The Thought behind the Image," in *Architecture as Icon*, pp. 113–54; Maria Cristina Carile, "Buildings in Their Patrons' Hands? The Multiform Function of Small-Size Models between Byzantium and Transcaucasia," *Kunsttexte.de* 3 (2014): 1–14; and Dominik Stachowiak, "Church Models in the Byzantine Culture Circle and the Problem of Their Function," *Novae: Studies and Materials VI. Sacrum et Profanum*, ed. Elena Ju. Klenina (Poznan: Instytut Historii UAM, 2018), pp. 243–56.

48 The role of monks in spreading architectural building types and styles across vast geographies is well attested to, as when the monk Nikodemos from Mount Athos was mentioned as involved in the construction of the Cozia Monastery. See also note 20. On the proposition that neither the donors nor the artisans but, instead, specially trained individuals were fully aware of the cultural and theological references behind the design of sacred space, see Alexei Lidov, "The Creator of Sacred Space as a Phenomenon of Byzantine

not been adequately explained.[49] Architectural drawings have been used in Western Europe and potentially in the Byzantine periphery, on the borders with the West, since at least the 13th century.[50] The use by painters in the 1400s of preparatory working drawings to depict important iconographic scenes in monumental church painting, known as *anthivola*, has been confirmed not only through texts that record their existence in wills and selling deeds, but also by the few late-medieval *anthivola* that remain.[51] The existence of *anthivola* opens the possibility that similar schemes and preparatory drawings were used for architecture as well. Certain atypical but shared architectural features of the built structures analyzed in this essay reinforce the high possibility of the existence of architects and architectural designs, including how these related to building workshops. Architectural drawings and models could be circulated over a prolonged period. The triconch churches analyzed here were built over hundreds of years, from ca. 1350s until ca. 1550s. This expansive period includes multiple generations of builders, who would typically work for some 20 to 30 years in a given locale. The triconch churches were likewise built across far-flung territories. In this study of Serbian-Wallachian architectural domains, the concepts of triconch design were derived from various corners of the territories of the former Byzantine Empire, including its centers in Constantinople, Thessaloniki, and Mount Athos. They then expanded further north and to the territories of medieval Serbia and Wallachia. For example, the sanctuary of the Great Meteoron near Kalabaka, Greece, was remodeled in the 1540s from what was essentially an older, 14th-century cross-in-square church with a tripartite sanctuary and an original but atypical access point to the sanctuary only through the prothesis to the north (see Table 7.1).[52] Exactly the same solution for the tripartite sanctuary was adopted in the early 1500s for St. Nicholas Church at Lapušnja in a rural area of eastern Serbia. The entire solution of basing such a triconch structure on the cross-in-square design is in this case more closely related to the earlier and contemporaneous solutions of

---

Culture," in *L'artista a Bisanzio e nel mondo cristiano-orientale*, ed. Michele Bacci (Pisa: Edizioni della Normale, 2007), pp. 135–76. On the question of models, see note 47 above.

49 Again, see note 47 above.
50 See Nenadović, *Gradjevinska tehnika*, pp. 46–49.
51 See Maria Vassilaki, ed., *The Hand of Angelos: An Icon Painter in Venetian Crete* (Farnham, Surrey, UK, and Burlington, VT: Lund Humphries in association with the Benaki Museum, Athens, 2010); and Vassilaki, "From Constantinople to Candia: Icon Painting in Crete around 1400," in *The Hand of Angelos*, pp. 58–65. I thank Alice I. Sullivan for her suggestion to point to *anthivola* as an important counterpart of similar drawing tools used in architecture.
52 See note 24 above, and especially Ćurčić, *Architecture in the Balkans*, pp. 790–91.

Athonite monastic churches, rather than, strictly speaking, Morava churches, and especially not those of the urban, court type.

4   Conclusion

It is notable and telling that some of the churches discussed in this essay were built after the fall of Constantinople. In fact, the majority of these churches were built when Serbia and Wallachia were under the Ottoman domain. When one considers the current scholarly narrative through the lens of Constantinople that church architecture in the Balkans declined after the downturn of Byzantine architecture—especially in Islamic territories, which witnessed the rise of mosques and other Islamic religious structures—it might seem paradoxical or surprising that these churches are remarkably sizable and architecturally impressive. The churches share certain aesthetic qualities, such as the attenuated proportions, the "pyramidal" clustering of volumes, and the use of predominantly stone and stone-and-brick construction. Most also demonstrate highly sophisticated architectural articulation. Occasionally, exterior architectural elements and their uses—as in the case of the distinctive engaged vertical colonettes framing the conches—represent recognizable features of Constantinopolitan imperial architecture established in Middle Byzantine times. Therefore, such atypical, idiosyncratic features suggest a subtle eclecticism and their ultimate source in Byzantine material culture. Somewhat modest sculptural decoration following the definite economic and political decline of Serbia and Wallachia, indeed, points to fluctuating possibilities for the use of secondary architectural elements, like exterior architectural decoration, beyond the building envelope. In that regard, for example, Lapušnja has moderate architectural decoration and is much closer in its appearance to post-1330s Skopian churches rather than the more exuberant and chronologically and territorially closer Morava churches (Fig. 7.7).

The methodological question of establishing the cultural context of artistic and architectural traditions and the architectural considerations here expanded upon through several examples of triconch churches in Serbia and Wallachia may be also extended to the examination of the churches' interior and exterior decorations and to artistic accomplishments and churches in other geopolitical domains. By expanding beyond the territorial and chronological domain of triconch churches built by Serbian and Wallachian nobility ca. 1350s to the 1550s, the research definitely demonstrates that the state and national divides that have been used to define and explain the churches north of Byzantium are essentially modern and incorrect constructs. Indeed,

FIGURE 7.7 Church of St. Nicholas, Lapušnja Monastery, Serbia, 1500–10, sponsored and built by Voivode Radu cel Mare (r. 1495–1508), Princess Katalina Crnojević of Zeta, Joupan Gergina, Prince Bogoje and his family, Hieromonks Gelasios (ca. 1500), and Theodor (ca. 1510)
PHOTOGRAPH BY JELENA BOGDANOVIĆ

Serbian and Wallachian rulers and nobility were major sponsors of monumental structures, yet especially their joint projects reinforced a primary aim—to maintain their common Christianity above distinct ethnic identities. At a time when Mount Athos was the foremost center of Orthodox Christianity, its recognizable triconch churches—originally stemming from Middle Byzantine Constantinopolitan traditions—seemingly became the most desired and predominant architectural paradigm. It has already been revealed that monks, such as the Athonite monk Nikodemos, originally from Prilep, could have been responsible for enabling the transmission of architectural concepts for triconch churches that were widely dispersed in the Balkan regions and as far removed from one another as were Morava Valley and Wallachia.[53] That these monks—as representatives of the medieval intellectual elite—also shared

---

53   See notes 20 and 48 above.

architectural drawings or models is highly possible, based on the architectural solutions of the built structures themselves, although this is almost impossible to prove due to the lack of explicit historical texts. The design of triconch domed churches is highly complex, and the ability of architects to promote and modify these plans to achieve diverse spatial solutions across remote territories and over hundreds of years should not be underestimated either. This focus on architecture and concepts of architectural design as inseparable parts of material culture within wider networks of their production and reception, and well beyond national identity or territory, points to vibrant, continuous, and enriching processes within the developments of Byzantine and post-Byzantine architecture.

Acknowledgments

The material for this essay was originally presented at a conference panel organized by Alice Isabella Sullivan and Maria Alessia Rossi and sponsored by the Mary Jaharis Center for Byzantine Art and Culture. I am grateful to the organizers for inviting me to be part of this book, as well as for their suggestions and patience in the process of book production. Many thanks to the anonymous reviewer and editorial board for their time and comments. Additionally, I am thankful to Ida Sinkević for her help and scholarly communication while working on this essay. Tianling (Rusty) Xu helped with the architectural drawings. Ivan Krstić provided some of the photographs. Erika Zinsmeister and Joe Hannan copyedited the text. As always, my family members supported my work. The last time we all visited Lapušnja was in August 2005. Although it was in a ruinous state, we enjoyed the structure and its impressive setting. My late mother Selena would have been glad to see the published material and to greet the birth of her grandson Danilo Dragoslav, who was born at the time of this book's writing.

Bibliography

Primary Sources

Domentijan. *Живот Светога Саве и Живот Светога Симеона* (Život Svetoga Save i Život Svetoga Simeona), ed. Radmila Marinković. Belgrade: Prosveta and Srpska književna zadruga, 1988.

Teodosije. *Житија* (Žitija), ed. Dimitrije Bogdanović. Belgrade: Prosveta and Srpska književna zadruga, 1988.

Secondary Sources

Balş, Georges. "Influence du plan serbe sur le plan des églises roumaines." In *L'art byzantin chez les slaves: Les Balkans; Premier recueil dédié à la mémoire de Théodore Uspenskij*, vol. 1, 277–94. Paris: Librairie Orientaliste Paul Geuthner, 1930.

Bogdanović, Jelena. "Aleksandar Deroko's Work on Medieval Architecture and Its Relevance Today." In "Aleksandar Deroko," special issue, *Serbian Architectural Journal* 11, no. 1 (2019): 145–56.

Bogdanović, Jelena. "Late Byzantine Religious Architecture in Constantinople / Υστεροβυζαντινή ναοδομία στην Κωνσταντινούπολη." In *Encyclopaedia of the Hellenic World, Constantinople* (2008). Available at www2.egeonet.gr/Forms/fLemmaBodyExtended.aspx?lemmaid=10893&boithimata_State=&kefalaia_State=#chapter_1. Accessed March 3, 2019.

Bogdanović, Jelena. "Regional Developments in Late Byzantine Architecture and the Question of 'Building Schools': An Overlooked Case of the Fourteenth-Century Churches from the Region of Skopje." *Byzantinoslavica* 69, no. 1–2 (2011): 219–66.

Bogdanović, Jelena. "The Phiale as a Spatial Icon in the Byzantine Cultural Sphere." In *Holy Water in the Hierotopy and Iconography of the Christian World*, ed. Alexei Lidov, 372–96. Moscow: Theoria, 2017.

Bogdanović, Jelena. "The Relational Spiritual Geopolitics of Constantinople, the Capital of the Byzantine Empire." In *Political Landscapes of Capital Cities*, ed. Jessica Christie, Bogdanović, and Eulogio Guzmán, 97–153. Boulder: University Press of Colorado, 2016.

Bogdanović, Jelena. *The Framing of Sacred Space: The Canopy and the Byzantine Church*. New York: Oxford University Press, 2017.

Carile, Maria Cristina. "Buildings in Their Patrons' Hands? The Multiform Function of Small-Size Models between Byzantium and Transcaucasia." *Kunsttexte.de* 3 (2014): 1–14.

Cristea, Gherasim. *Istoria mânăstirii Govora*. Râmnicu Vâlcea: Editura Sf. Episcopii a Râmnicului, 1995.

Ćurčić, Slobodan, Evangelia Hadjitryphonos, et al. *Architecture as Icon*. New Haven: Yale University Press, 2010.

Ćurčić, Slobodan. "Architecture in Byzantium, Serbia and the Balkans through the Lenses of Modern Historiography." In *Serbia and Byzantium. Proceedings of the International Conference Held on 15 December 2008 at the University of Cologne* (Frankfurt am Main: Peter Lang/PL Academic Research, 2013), 9–31.

Ćurčić, Slobodan. "Religious Settings of the Late Byzantine Sphere." In *Byzantium: Faith and Power (1261–1557)*, ed. Helen C. Evans, 65–94. New York: Metropolitan Museum of Art, 2004.

Ćurčić, Slobodan. "The Role of Late Byzantine Thessalonike in Church Architecture in the Balkans." *Dumbarton Oaks Papers* 57 (2003): 65–84.

Ćurčić, Slobodan. *Architecture in the Balkans from Diocletian to Süleyman the Magnificent (c. 300–1550)*. New Haven: Yale University Press, 2010.
Davidescu, Mişu. *Mănăstirea Cozia*. Bucharest: Editura Meridiane, 1968.
Djurić, Srdjan. *Manastir Ljubostinja*. Belgrade: Republički zavod za zaštitu spomenika kulture, 1983.
Djurić, Vojislav J. *Resava (Manasija)*. Belgrade: Jugoslavija, 1966.
Dragović, Magdalena S., Aleksandar A. Čučaković, Jelena Bogdanović, et al. "Geometric Proportional Schemas of Serbian Medieval Raška Churches based on Štambuk's Proportional Canon." *Nexus Network Journal: Architecture and Mathematics* 21, no. 1 (2019): 33–58.
Eastmond, Anthony. "Byzantine Identity and Relics of the True Cross in the Thirteenth Century." In *Eastern Christian Relics*, ed. Alexei Lidov, 204–61. Moscow: Progress-Tradicija, 2003.
Erdeljan, Jelena. "Trnovo: Principi i sredstva konstruisanja sakralne topografije srednjevekovne bugarske prestonice / Tŭrnovo: Principles and Means of Constructing the Sacral Topography of a Medieval Bulgarian Capital." *Zbornik Radova Vizantološkog Instituta* 47 (2010): 199–214.
Eyice, Semavi. *Son Devir Bizans Mimârisi: Istanbul'da Palaiologos'lar Devri Antilari*. Istanbul: Üniversite Edebiyat Fakültesi, 1980.
Florescu, Radu. *Mănăstirea Govora*. Bucharest: Meridiane, 1965.
Frolow, Anatole. *La relique de la vraie croix: Recherches sur le développement d'un culte*. Paris: Institut français d'Etudes byzantines, 1961.
Gavrilović, Zaga. "Women in Serbian Politics, Diplomacy and Art at the Beginning of Ottoman Rule. In *Byzantine Style, Religion, and Civilization: In Honour of Sir Steven Runciman*, ed. Elizabeth M. Jeffreys, 75–78. New York: Cambridge University Press, 2006.
Grabar, Oleg. *The Mediation of Ornament*. Princeton: Princeton University Press, 1992.
Hadjitryphonos, Evangelia. "Presentations and Representations of Architecture in Byzantium: The Thought behind the Image." In *Architecture as Icon*, ed. Slobodan Ćurčić, Evangelia Hadjitryphonos, et al., 113–54. New Haven: Yale University Press, 2010.
Herea, Gabriel. *Pelerinaj în spaţiul sacru Bucovinean*. Cluj-Napoca: Patmos, 2010.
Herea, Gabriel. *Pătrăuţi*, online at www.biserica.patrauti.ro, accessed April 22, 2019.
Herea, Gabriel, and Petru Palamar. *Pătrăuţi*. Suceava: Asociaţia Prietenii Bucovinei, 2011.
Herea, Gabriel, and Petru Palamar. *Pătrăuţi 1487—Monument UNESCO*. Pătrăuţi: Heruvim, 2015.
Jovanović, Jelena, and Olga Špehar. "L'ancien art serbe: Les églises i definisanje škola u staroj srpskoj arhitekturi [L'ancien art serbe: Les églises and the definition of schools in old Serbian architecture]." In *Gabrijel Mije i istraživanja stare* srpske

arhitekture, ed. Dubravka Preradović, 65–71. Belgrade: Srpska akademija nauka i umetnosti, 2019.

Klein, Holger A. "Sacred Relics and Imperial Ceremonies at the Great Palace of Constantinople." *Visualisierungen von Herrschaft*, ed. Franz Alto Bauer. BYZAS 5 (2006): 79–99.

Klein, Holger A. "Constantin, Helena, and the Cult of the True Cross in Constantinople." In *Byzance et les reliques du Christ*, ed. Jannic Durand and Bernard Flusin, 31–59. Paris: Association des amis du Centre d'histoire et civilisation de Byzance: 2004.

Klein, Holger A. *Byzanz, der Westen und das "wahre" Kreuz: Die Geschichte einer Reliquie und ihrer künstlerischen Fassung in Byzanz und im Abendland*. Wiesbaden: Reichert, 2004.

Knežević, Branka. "Manastir Lapušnja." *Saopštenje* 18 (1986): 83–114.

Krautheimer, Richard, with Slobodan Ćurčić. *Early Christian and Byzantine Architecture*. New Haven: Yale University Press, 1986.

Lidov, Alexei. "A Byzantine Jerusalem: The Imperial Pharos Chapel as the Holy Sepulchre." In *Jerusalem as Narrative Space*, ed. Annette Hoffmann and Gerhard Wolf, 63–104. Leiden and Boston: Brill, 2012.

Lidov, Alexei. "The Creator of Sacred Space as a Phenomenon of Byzantine Culture." In *L'artista a Bisanzio e nel mondo cristiano-orientale*, ed. Michele Bacci, 135–76. Pisa: Edizioni della Normale, 2007.

Mamaloukos, Stavros. "Από τον σχεδιασμό στην κατασκευή: Ζητήματα εφαρμογής στη βυζαντινή αρχιτεκτονική / From Design to Construction: Aspects of Implementation in Byzantine Architecture." *Δελτίον της Χριστιανικής Αρχαιολογικής Εταιρείας* 4, no. 39 (2018): 83–97.

Mamaloukos, Stavros. "A Contribution to the Study of the 'Athonite' Church Type of Byzantine Architecture." *Zograf* 35 (2011): 39–50.

Mango, Cyril. *Byzantine Architecture*. New York: Harry N. Abrams, 1976.

Marinković, Čedomila. *Слика подигнуте цркве: Представе архитектуре на ктиторским портретима у српској и византијској уметности* [The image of the built church: Representations of architecture in donors' portraits in Serbian and Byzantine art.] Belgrade: Bonart, 2007.

Metsikosta, Theoteknē. *Meteora: History, Art, Monastic Presence*. Meteora: Holy Monasteries of Meteora, 1987.

Mihaljević, Marina. "Change in Byzantine Architecture: Architects and Builders." In *Approaches to Byzantine Architecture and Its Decoration*, ed. Mark Johnson, Robert Ousterhout, and Amy Papalexandrou, 99–119. Surrey: Ashgate, 2012.

Millet, Gabriel. *L'ancien art serbe: Les églises*. Paris: E. de Boccard, 1919.

Millet, Gabriel. *La Serbie glorieuse*. Paris: L'art ancien et moderne aux mondes, 1917.

Millet, Gabriel. *L'école grecque dans l'architecture byzantine*. Paris: Ernest Leroux, 1916.

Millet, Gabriel. *Recherches sur l'iconographie de l'évangile aux XIVᵉ, XVᵉ et XVIᵉ siècles: D'après les monuments de Mistra, de la Macédoine et du Mont-Athos*. Paris: Fontemoing/E. de Boccard, succ., 1916.

Millet, Gabriel. "Cozia et les églises serbes de la Morava." In *Mélanges offerts à M. Nicolas Iorga par ses amis de France et des pays de langue française*, ed. Nicolae Iorga, 827–56. Paris: J. Gamber, 1933.

Mylonas, Paulos. "Le Catholicon de Kutlumus (Athos)." *Cahiers archéologiques* 42 (1994): 75–86.

Mylonas, Paulos. "Le plan initial du catholicon de la Grande Lavra." *Cahiers archéologiques* 32 (1984): 89–112.

Mylonas, Paulos. "Two Middle Byzantine Churches on Athos." *Actes du XVᵉ Congrès international d'études byzantines*, II (Athens, 1976): 545–74.

Mylonas, Paulos. "Η Αρχιτεκτονική του Αγίου Όρους" [The architecture of Mount Athos]. *Nea Hestia* 74 (1963): 189–207.

Năstăsoiu, Dragoş. *Gothic Art in Romania*. Bucharest: NOI Media Print, 2011.

Negrău, Elisabeta. "Tipologiile arhitecturale ale ctitoriilor domneşti din Țara Românească în secolele XIV–XVI [Architectural Types of Princes' Church Foundations in Wallachia in the 14th–16th Centuries]." *Analele Universității din Craiova: Seria Istorie, Craiova* 16, no. 2 (2009): 95–114.

Nenadović, Slobodan. *Gradjevinska tehnika u srednjevekovnoj Srbiji*. Belgrade: Gradjevinska Knjiga, 2003.

Nickel, Heinrich L. *Medieval Architecture in Eastern Europe*. New York: Holmes and Meier, 1983.

Ousterhout, Robert. *Master Builders of Byzantium*, 2nd ed. Philadelphia: University of Pennsylvania Museum of Archaeology and Anthropology, 2008.

Popović, Danica. "Реликвије Часног крста у средњовековној Србији [Relikvije Časnog krsta u srednjovekovnoj Srbiji, The relics of the Holy Cross in medieval Serbia]." In *Konstantin Veliki u vizantijskoj i srpskoj tradiciji*, ed. Ljubomir Maksimović, 99–121. Belgrade: Zavod za udžbenike, 2014.

Popovich, Ljubica D. "Portraits of Kneginja Milica." *Serbian Studies* 8, no. 1–2 (1994): 94–95.

Preradović, Dubravka, ed. *Gabrijel Mije i istraživanja stare srpske arhitekture* [Gabriel Millet et l'étude de l'architecture médiévale serbe]. Belgrade: Srpska akademija nauka i umetnosti, 2019.

Preradović, Dubravka. "Gabrijel Mije: Terenska istraživanja srpskih spomenika i njihovi rezultati" [Gabriel Millet: Ses études de terrain sur les monuments serbes et leurs résultats]. In *Gabrijel Mije i istraživanja stare srpske arhitekture*, ed. Preradović, 25–36. Belgrade: Srpska akademija nauka i umetnosti, 2019.

Preradović, Dubravka. "Contribution de Gabriel Millet à l'étude de l'art Serbe." In *Z' Επιστημονικό Συνέδριο « Το Άγιον Όρος στα χρόνια της Απελευθέρωσης », Φορος Τιμης* στον Gabriel Millet [*Mount Athos during the ears of Liberation, Mount Athos Center 7th Scientific Conference, round table on Gabriel Millet*], 77–85. Thessaloniki: Mt. Athos Center, 2013.

Preradović, Dubravka. "Le premier voyage de Gabriel Millet en Serbie et ses résultats." In *Les Serbes à propos des Français—Les Français à propos des Serbes*, ed. J. Novaković and Lj. P. Ristić, 187–205. Belgrade: University of Belgrade, 2014.

Prolović, Jadranka. *Resava (Manasija): Geschichte, Architektur und Malerei einer Stifung des serbischen Despoten Stefan Lazarević*. Vienna: Verlag der Österreichischen Akademie der Wissenschaften, 2017.

Ristić, Vladislav. *Lazarica i Kruševački grad*. Belgrade: Republički zavod za zaštitu spomenika kulture, 1989.

Ristić, Vladislav. *Moravska arhitektura*. Kruševac: Narodni muzej, 1996.

Sinkević, Ida. "Afterlife of the Rhodes Hand of St. John the Baptist." In *Byzantine Images and Their Afterlives: Essays in Honor of Annemarie Weyl Carr*, ed. Lynn Jones, 125–41. Farnham: Ashgate, 2014.

Špehar, Olga. "Modaliteti recepcije L'ancien art serbe: Les églises u domaćoj istoriografiji [L'ancien art serbe: Les églises et les modalités de sa réception dans l'historiographie locale]. In *Gabrijel Mije i istraživanja stare srpske arhitekture*, ed. Dubravka Preradović, 75–80. Belgrade: Srpska akademija nauka i umetnosti, 2019.

Stachowiak, Dominik. "Church Models in the Byzantine Culture Circle and the Problem of Their Function." In *Novae: Studies and Materials VI. Sacrum et Profanum*, ed. Elena Ju. Klenina, 243–56. Poznan: Instytut Historii UAM, 2018.

Stevović, Ivan. "Serbian Architecture of the Morava Period: A Local School or an Epilogue to the Leading Trends in Late Byzantine Architecture; A Study in Methodology." *Zbornik radova vizantološkog instituta* 43 (2006): 231–53.

Stevović, Ivan. "L'ancien art serbe: Les églises jedan vek kasnije [L'ancien art serbe: Les églises, un siècle plus tard]." In *Gabrijel Mije i istraživanja stare srpske arhitekture*, ed. Dubravka Preradović, 81–84. Belgrade: Srpska akademija nauka i umetnosti, 2019.

Sullivan, Alice Isabella. "Western-Byzantine 'Hybridity' in the Ecclesiastical Architecture of Northern Moldavia." *Romanian Medievalia: Thraco-Dacian and Byzantine Romanity of Eastern Europe and Asia Minor* 12–13 (New York: Romanian Institute of Orthodox Theology and Spirituality, 2015): 29–49.

Sullivan, Alice Isabella. "Architectural Pluralism at the Edges: The Visual Eclecticism of Medieval Monastic Churches in Eastern Europe." In "Marginalia: Architectures of Uncertain Margins," special issue, *Studii de Istoria și Teoria Arhitecturii / Studies in History and Theory of Architecture* 4 (2016): 135–51.

Sullivan, Alice Isabella. "The Painted Fortified Monastic Churches of Moldavia: Bastions of Orthodoxy in a Post-Byzantine World." PhD diss., University of Michigan, 2017.

Sullivan, Alice Isabella. "The Athonite Patronage of Stephen III of Moldavia, 1457–1504." *Speculum* 94, no. 1 (2019): 1–46.

Tantsis, Anastasios. "The So-called 'Athonite' Type of Church and Two Shrines of the Theotokos in Constantinople." *Zograf* 34 (2010): 3–11.

The Lives of the Monastery Builders of Meteora: Saint Athanasios of New Patras and Saint Ioasaph the Monk-King, Builders of the Great Meteoron Monastery, and Saints Nectarios and Theophanes of Ioannina, Builders of the Varlaam Monastery. Buena Vista, CO: Holy Apostles Convent, 1991.

Vafeiadēs, Konstantinos M. *Holy Monastery of the Great Meteroron: History, Prospography and Spiritual Life of the Monastery on the Basis of the Written and Archeological Evidence (12th–20th Century).* Meteora: Holy Monasteries of Meteora, 2019.

Vaida, Gamaliil. *The Monastery of Cozia: In the Past and Nowadays*. Călimăneşti-Vîlcea: Stăreţia Mînăstirii Cozia, 1977.

Vassilaki, Maria. "From Constantinople to Candia: Icon Painting in Crete around 1400." In *The Hand of Angelos*, ed. Maria Vassilaki, 58–65. Farnham, Surrey, UK, and Burlington, VT: Lund Humphries in association with the Benaki Museum, Athens, 2010.

Vassilaki, Maria, ed., *The Hand of Angelos: An Icon Painter in Venetian Crete*. Farnham, Surrey, UK, and Burlington, VT: Lund Humphries in association with the Benaki Museum, Athens, 2010.

Vojvodić, Dragan, and Danica Popović, eds. *Sacral Art of the Serbian Lands in the Middle Ages*, Byzantine Heritage and Serbian Art, vol. 2 of 3. Belgrade: Serbian Academy of Sciences and Arts, 2016.

Vulović, Branislav. *Ravanica: Njeno mesto i njena uloga u sakralnoj arhitekturi Pomoravlja* [Ravanica: Its place and role in sacred architecture of the Morava Valley]. Belgrade: Republički zavod za zaštitu spomenika culture, 1966.

Wilkinson, Catherine. "The New Professionalism in the Renaissance." In *The Architect: Chapters in the History of the Profession*, ed. Spiro Kostof, 124–60. New York: Oxford University Press, 1977.

CHAPTER 8

Moldavian Art and Architecture between Byzantium and the West

Alice Isabella Sullivan

Some of the most striking architectural monuments of the post-Byzantine world stand along the eastern slopes of the Carpathian Mountains in modern Romania. The painted and fortified Orthodox monastic churches of the former principality of Moldavia are remarkable for their distinctive architectural features and brightly colored mural cycles that interpret models with roots in distinct visual traditions.[1] Given Moldavia's location at the point of intersection of diverse cultures, especially from the 14th century onward, the art and architecture of the principality came to exhibit an eclecticism with respect to artistic and architectural sources, with elements adapted from Western medieval and Byzantine artistic models alongside forms developed locally. This visual syncretism, most evident in the main monastic churches (or *katholika*) built initially under the patronage of Prince Stephen III "the Great" (r. 1457–1504) and then with support from his illegitimate son and heir, Prince Peter Rareş (r. 1527–38; 1541–46), contributed to the development of a local style that underwent further transformations in the centuries that followed.[2]

Both princes, Stephen and Peter, through their artistic patronage, self-consciously reflected upon the past glory of Byzantium and their contemporary situation, and with guidance from Church officials, contributed to projects that gradually transformed Moldavia's sacred landscape.[3] Their efforts in deploying especially Byzantine artistic and architectural models to shape

---

1   The medieval principality of Moldavia declared its independence in 1359 and extended within the borders of northeastern modern Romania and the Republic of Moldova.
2   See Alice Isabella Sullivan, "The Painted Fortified Monastic Churches of Moldavia: Bastions of Orthodoxy in a Post-Byzantine World" (PhD diss., University of Michigan, 2017). For a recent general overview, see Robert G. Ousterhout, *Eastern Medieval Architecture: The Building Traditions of Byzantium and Neighboring Lands* (Oxford: Oxford University Press, 2019), esp. pp. 667–76.
3   See Alice Isabella Sullivan, "The Athonite Patronage of Stephen III of Moldavia, 1457–1504," *Speculum* 94, no. 1 (2019): 41–44; and Jelena Bogdanović, "The Relational Spiritual Geopolitics of Constantinople, the Capital of the Byzantine Empire," in *Political Landscapes of Capital Cities*, ed. Jessica Joyce Christie, Bogdanović, and Eulogio Guzmán (Boulder: University Press of Colorado, 2016), pp. 97–153, esp. 112–14.

Moldavia's spiritual identity reveal the scope, significance, and global reception of Byzantium in a period after the empire's collapse and in a region that was never part of the empire but certainly under its spiritual power. The distinguishing architecture and iconographic features of the Moldavian *katholika*—for which the Church of the Annunciation at Moldovița Monastery serves as a key example in this study (Fig. 8.1)—express complex social and religious politics. Moreover, the spatial and visual forms of these edifices elucidate local processes of image translations, the transfer of artistic ideas, and particular dynamics of cultural contact in a region that developed at the crossroads of different traditions and that took on a central role in the continuation and refashioning of Byzantine models in the centuries after the fall of Constantinople in 1453.

1 Byzantium in Moldavia after 1453

During Prince Stephen III's long and prosperous reign—spanning almost half a century—Moldavia was consciously transformed into a bastion and buttress protector of the Christian faith. Between 1457 and 1487, Stephen engaged in an extensive project to fortify his principality at key sites, initially in anticipation of, and then in response to, the Ottoman incursions into his territory.[4] Between 1476 and 1479, Stephen strengthened the key fortresses in the north and west, and then the fortresses at Cetatea Albă and Chilia in the south, along the Black Sea coast.[5] The Ottoman historian and chronicler Tursun Beg (b. mid-1420s) described Chilia Fortress, for example, as "the lock [*kilit*] to Moldavia."[6] Once it was captured, he noted, the path to the principality and to other lands in

---

4 See Sullivan, "The Painted Fortified Monastic Churches of Moldavia," 58–64.
5 The fortress at Cetatea Albă was rebuilt and enlarged by Stephen in 1476. See *Repertoriul monumentelor și operelor de artă din timpul lui Ștefan cel Mare* (Bucharest: Editura Academiei, 1958), pp. 217–19 (with bibliography).

   Chilia Fortress was rebuilt entirely in just a few months. *The Anonymous Chronicle of Moldavia* (fol. 242r) states that on June 22, 1479, work started on the fortress at Chilia and was completed on July 16 of the same year; Petre P. Panaitescu and Ion Bogdan, *Cronicile slavo-române din sec. XV–XVI* (Bucharest: Editura Academiei, 1959), p. 10 (Church Slavonic), 18 (Romanian). The fourteenth entry in *The Moldo-German Chronicle*, fol. 294v, states: "On 22 July 6987 [1479], the prince [Stephen III] started building Chilia, and he finished it in the same summer with the help of 80 master masons and seventeen thousand additional helpers." Panaitescu and Bogdan, *Cronicile slavo-române din sec. XV–XVI*, p. 34 (Romanian). See also *Repertoriul*, pp. 219–20 (with bibliography).
6 Mihail Guboglu and Mustafa Mehmet, eds., *Cronici Turcești privind țările române*, vol. 1 (Bucharest: Editura Academiei, 1955), p. 77.

FIGURE 8.1 Church of the Annunciation, 1532–37, view from southeast, Moldoviţa Monastery, Moldavia, Romania
PHOTOGRAPH BY ALICE ISABELLA SULLIVAN

the West could finally be unlocked.[7] Under Stephen's leadership, the cleverly devised infrastructure of fortresses and fortified royal courts delineated the perimeter of the principality and ensured Moldavia's protection from all sides. The monasteries with their massive rectilinear fortification walls contributed to this defense project as well.

By the spring of 1487, Stephen's military initiatives and strategic planning allowed Moldavia to enter a period of relative political, military, and economic stability. This moment was marked by a peace agreement ratified between Moldavia and the Ottoman Porte that ensured the protection and freedom of Stephen's realm in exchange for the annual tribute payment.[8] It was also precisely at this time—after three decades of extensive civic and military building campaigns and numerous battles to ensure the safety of his domain—that Stephen turned his attention to the building of monasteries, churches, and chapels that gradually transformed the sacred landscape of Moldavia.[9] His heirs continued these efforts, and for much of the 16th century Moldavia's rulers and noblemen built numerous ecclesiastical sites throughout the principality.[10]

One of the first churches that Stephen built, at Pătrăuți Monastery, he dedicated to the Holy Cross. Begun on June 13, 1487, this edifice served as the main church of one of the few convents built by the Moldavian ruler. Its dedicatory inscription—written in Church Slavonic and set in a narrow register at the center of the west facade above the main entrance—makes this clear: "John Stephen voivode, prince of the land of Moldavia, son of Bogdan voivode, started building this edifice dedicated to the Holy Cross in the year 6995 [1487], in the month of June 13."[11] The church was consecrated on September 14, the Feast of the Holy Cross. On this same day in 1472, the Moldavian prince had

---

7   Ibid., 1:78: "The lock to that country [Moldavia] was Chilia, because once it was captured the roads opened to other countries as well. When the key piece opened the way for holy war, he [the Sultan] became the ruler of the world from here to there."
8   See Nicoară Beldiceanu, *La Moldavie ottomane à la fin du XV*^{e} *siècle et au début du XVI*^{e} *siècle* (Paris: Librairie Orientaliste Paul Geuthner, 1969), p. 244; Ștefan S. Gorovei, "Pacea moldo-otomană din 1486: Observații pe marginea unor texte," *Revista de Istorie* 35, no. 7 (1982): 807–21; rep. *Ștefan cel Mare și Sfânt, 1504–2004: Portret în istorie* (Putna: Sfânta Mănăstire Putna, 2003), pp. 496–515; and Guboglu and Mehmet, eds., *Cronici Turcești*, 1:137, 1:187.
9   See Sullivan, "The Athonite Patronage of Stephen III," 41–44.
10 See the "Catalog of Ecclesiastical Monuments," in Sullivan, "The Painted Fortified Monastic Churches of Moldavia," pp. 648–738; and Sullivan, "The Athonite Patronage of Stephen III," 41–44.
11 *Repertoriul*, p. 61 (Church Slavonic and Romanian). Unlike all other dedicatory inscriptions that are roughly square or rectangular in shape, the one at Pătrăuți is the only one presented in a long and narrow register and placed directly above the main entrance to the church.

married his second wife, Maria Asanina Palaiologina of Mangup (d. 1477)[12]—whose visage only survives on the richly embroidered cover designed for her grave in Putna Monastery in Moldavia, the monastic church built to serve as Stephen's princely mausoleum.[13] Clearly this day and the cult of the cross that it celebrates were important to Stephen.

The union between Stephen and Maria of Mangup set in motion an array of cultural, artistic, and ideological transformations for Moldavia and its ruler.[14] For one thing, following his union with this Byzantine princess, Stephen continued to assume the title of "tsar/emperor";[15] he also began establishing in his principality the civil and ecclesiastical laws outlined by the Greek monk Matthew Blastares in his *Syntagma Canonum*, written in Thessaloniki in the early 14th century and subsequently copied and circulated in the Byzantine-Slavic world.[16] Stephen also initiated a series of ongoing endowments to monasteries in his own domain but also to monastic communities on Mount Athos at a moment when the Bulgarian, Serbian, Muscovite, Georgian, and Wallachian rulers were reducing or ending altogether their Athonite patronage.[17] His efforts ensured his perpetual commemoration by the Athonite communities and, by extension, rendered Moldavia, as a polity, an heir to Byzantine Orthodoxy.[18] Moreover, Stephen's Athonite patronage and his marriage to Maria of Mangup certainly had collateral effects of contributing to the promotion of significant forms of Byzantine spirituality and artistic practices in Moldavia. For one thing, Moldavian workshops and scriptoria began producing manuscripts and liturgical embroideries rooted in predominantly

---

12 See Ştefan S. Gorovei and Maria Magdalena Székely, *Maria Asanina Paleologhina: O prinţesă bizantină pe tronul Moldovei* (Putna: Sfânta Mănăstire Putna, 2006).
13 Maria's tomb cover is now in the collection of Putna Monastery. On this object, see Ernst Diez, "Moldavian Portrait Textiles," *Art Bulletin* 10, no. 4 (1928): 377–85, esp. 377; *Repertoriul*, pp. 288–90, figs. 202, 203; Maria Magdalena Székely, "Mănăstirea Putna: Loc de memorie," *Studii şi Materiale de Istorie Medie* 22 (2004): 73–99; and Alice Isabella Sullivan, "Byzantine Artistic Traditions in Moldavian Church Embroideries," in *L'évolution de la broderie de tradition byzantine dans la Méditerranée et le monde slave (1200–1800)*, ed. Elena Papastavrou and Marielle Martiniani-Reber (Paris: Presses d'Inalco), forthcoming.
14 See Sullivan, "The Athonite Patronage of Stephen III," esp. 35–41.
15 Ibid., 36–40.
16 On Moldavian and Wallachian manuscripts of Blastares's code, see Victor Alexandrov, *The Syntagma of Matthew Blastares: The Destiny of a Byzantine Legal Code among the Orthodox Slavs and Romanians 14–17 Centuries* (Frankfurt am Main: Löwenklau Gesellschaft, 2012), esp. chapter 5, pp. 99–115.
17 See Sullivan, "The Athonite Patronage of Stephen III," esp. 9–31.
18 The Byzantine emperors had been notable patrons of Mount Athos, especially during the Palaiologan dynasty (1260–1453). See Graham Speake, *Mount Athos: Renewal in Paradise* (New Haven: Yale University Press, 2002).

Byzantine techniques, styles, and patterns.[19] This was the case in architecture and mural decorations as well, as evidenced in the ecclesiastical monuments that survive from the second half of the 15th century. The visual vocabulary of these buildings, however, included forms adopted from Gothic models as well, and was further transformed during the first half of the 16th century under the patronage of Peter Rareș, Stephen's son and heir.

2   The Layout and Architecture of the Moldavian *Katholika*

When Peter Rareș took the throne of the principality on January 20, 1527, he initially concerned himself with political and military matters, just as his father had done. However, the failed Ottoman siege of Vienna in 1529 gave new hope to Christian leaders and their subjects, the Moldavians included, that perhaps the Ottomans could, after all, be defeated and pushed back from Europe.[20] These newly kindled hopes and ambitions also carried various political, military, cultural, and artistic ramifications. Peter's artistic and architectural patronage ought to be considered in the context of these epochal events. It is precisely at this time that the distinctive architecture and the expansive interior and especially exterior mural cycles on the Moldavian churches further developed. Indeed, whereas Stephen built more than 47 ecclesiastical sites during his extensive reign, it was under Peter's patronage that architectural forms were consolidated in individual buildings, and 17 of the older churches and newly built ones received extensive murals both inside and outside. A case in point, and the focus of the remaining pages of this essay, is the Church of the Annunciation at Moldovița Monastery, erected and painted under Peter's patronage between 1532 and 1537 (Figs. 8.1–8.3).[21] With his building projects,

---

[19] See Alice Isabella Sullivan, "Byzantine Artistic Traditions in Moldavian Church Embroideries," forthcoming; and Sullivan, "Medieval Moldavian Tetraevangelia and their Afterlives: Preliminary Considerations," in *Fruits of Devotion: Essays in Honor of Predrag Matejic*, ed. M.A. Johnson and Sullivan, *Ohio Slavic Papers* 11 (Columbus, OH: Department of Slavic and East European Languages and Cultures, 2020), forthcoming.

[20] See Alice Isabella Sullivan, "Visions of Byzantium: *The Siege of Constantinople* in Sixteenth-Century Moldavia," *The Art Bulletin* 99, no. 4 (December 2017): 55–59.

[21] On this *katholikon* and its monastic complex, see especially, Gheorghe Balș, *Bisericile și mănăstirile moldovenești din veacul al XVI-lea* (Bucharest: Cultura Națională, 1928), pp. 31–39, 194, 201–7; Ștefan Balș and Corina Nicolescu, *Mănăstirea Moldovița* (Bucharest: Editura Academiei, 1958); Petru Comărnescu, *Îndreptar artistic al monumentelor din nordul Moldovei, arhitectura și fresca în sec. XV–XVI* (Suceava: Casa Regională a Credinței Populare Suceava, 1961), pp. 262–73; Corina Nicolescu, *Mănăstirea Moldovița* (Bucharest: Meridiane, 1965), trans. Elisa Madolciu into English as *Moldovița* (Bucharest: Sport-Turism, 1978); and *Mănăstirea Moldovița* (Iași: Editura Mitropoliei Moldovei și Sucevei, 1971).

FIGURE 8.2   Church of the Annunciation, 1532–37, view from southwest, Moldoviṭa Monastery, Moldavia, Romania
PHOTOGRAPH BY ALICE ISABELLA SULLIVAN

FIGURE 8.3   Church of the Annunciation, 1532–37, view from northwest, Moldoviṭa Monastery, Moldavia, Romania
PHOTOGRAPH BY ALICE ISABELLA SULLIVAN

Peter not only continued and enhanced his father's ecclesiastical foundations, but also left his own mark on Moldavia's sacred landscape.

At Moldoviţa Monastery, as elsewhere in Moldavia, the large central *katholikon* was built first, and the surrounding buildings were then erected (Fig. 8.4). These included the cells of the nuns, the living quarters of the abbess, the princely house (now a museum), the treasury, and the refectory (or dining hall), with other auxiliary rooms and cellars below. The semi-eremitic life carried out at this site, and others like it in Moldavia, places emphasis on silence, prayer, temperance, and humility. Thus, the church and the refectory, which is often the second largest building in the monasteries, serve as the main common meeting places for the monks and nuns and are thus the larger and more prominent buildings in the monastic complex. The remote location of these monastic communities, like the one at Moldoviţa, the need for defense in time of conflict, and the desire to set the monastic world apart from the rest explain, in part, the presence of the massive rectilinear fortification walls and towers that surround the monasteries.

In their layout, organization, and functions, the Moldavian monasteries emulate Byzantine, and in particular Athonite examples.[22] In the monasteries of Mount Athos—the Great Lavra being chief among them—the church is the central feature of the architectural compound; it is surrounded on four sides with a series of ancillary buildings that together form the space of a square or rectangle.[23] This rectilinear monastic layout differs markedly from the circular or polygonal organization of Orthodox monasteries in the Balkan Peninsula, an example being Studenica Monastery in Serbia, founded by Prince Stefan Nemanja (r. 1166–96) between 1190 and 1196.[24] This aspect, in conjunction with others, such as the triconch plan layout, suggests that there must have existed more direct points of contact between the Moldavian monastic communities and those of the Byzantine world, without regions of the Balkans—such as Serbia and Bulgaria, for example—serving as points of mediation of artistic

---

22 The Moldavian monasteries served as centers of cultural activity, sites of artistic production, and princely mausoleums, and also participated in political and economic matters related to the governing body. The monasteries, thus, met the spiritual needs of the monks or nuns, and the laity, and those of the state.

23 See Sotiris Voyatzis, "Evidence on the Building History of the Holy Monastery of the Great Lavra on Mount Athos: The Gateway in the Circuit Wall," *Deltion tes Christianikes Archaiologikes Hetaireias* 21, no. 4 (2000): 55–68.

24 See Miloš Živković, "Studenica: The Funerary Church of the Dynastic Founder—The Cornerstone of Church and State Independence," in *Sacral Art of the Serbian Lands in the Middle Ages*, vol. 2, ed. Dragan Vojvodić and Danica Popović (Belgrade: Serbian National Committee of Byzantine Studies, P.E. Službeni Glasnik: Institute for Byzantine Studies, and Serbian Academy of Sciences and Arts, 2016), pp. 193–209.

FIGURE 8.4 Moldovița Monastery, 1532–37, aerial view, Moldavia, Romania
IMAGE FROM TEREZA SINIGALIA AND OLIVIU BOLDURA, *MONUMENTE MEDIEVALE DIN BUCOVINA* [BUCHAREST: ACS, 2010], 171

and architectural forms between these distant cultural centers.[25] In fact, the monastic communities on Mount Athos offered this direct point of contact for regions of the Balkans and the Carpathians through traveling monks and artists, as well as the exchanges of gifts and ideas.

25   On the triconch plan, see Alice Isabella Sullivan, "Western-Byzantine 'Hybridity' in the Ecclesiastical Architecture of Northern Moldavia," *Romanian Medievalia: Thraco-Dacian and Byzantine Romanity of Eastern Europe and Asia Minor* 12/13 (New York: Romanian Institute of Orthodox Theology and Spirituality, 2015): 35–37. On artistic exchange in the larger region, see especially Gheorghe Balș, "Influence du plan serbe sur le plan des églises roumaines," in *L'art byzantin chez les slaves: Les Balkans; Premier recueil dédié à*

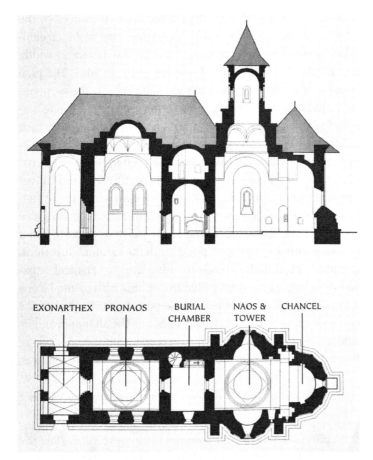

FIGURE 8.5   Elevation and layout, Church of the Annunciation, 1532–37, Moldoviţa Monastery, Moldavia, Romania
IMAGE FROM *BUCOVINA: A TRAVEL GUIDE TO ROMANIA'S REGION OF PAINTED MONASTERIES* [HELSINKI AND IAŞI: METANEIRA, 2006], 401

The layout of the *katholikon* at Moldoviţa is also distinctly Athonite in its general features, although of a local Moldavian character (Fig. 8.5).[26] The church,

la mémoire de Théodore Uspenskij (Paris: P. Geuthner, 1930), pp. 277–94; Tereza Sinigalia, "L'église de l'ascension du monastère du Neamţ et le problème de l'espace funéraire en Moldavie aux XVe–XVIe siècles," *Revue Roumaine d'Histoire de l'Art: Série Beaux-Arts* 25 (1998): 19–32; and Horia Teodoru, "Contribuţii la studiul originii şi evoluţiei planului triconc în Moldova," *Buletinul Comisiunii Monumentelor Istorice* 31, no. 1 (1970): 31–33.

26   Scholars have determined that the *katholikon* of the Great Lavra Monastery on the Holy Mountain (963) was the first Athonite building to adopt the triconch plan. The *katholikon*

characteristic of Moldavian monastic church architecture as it evolved by the initial decades of the 16th century, is built with local stone on a so-called elongated triconch plan. It measures 32.9 meters in length, 8.6 meters in width, and 18.2 meters in height under the *naos* dome (36 × 9 × 20 yds.). The plan of the church consists of an open barrel-vaulted exonarthex at the west end with three arched entrances on the north, south, and west sides. A single narrow entryway leads into the domed rectangular *pronaos* of the church, which has two large windows on each of the north and south walls. This space, in turn, leads through another small entryway into a small barrel-vaulted burial chamber (*gropniță*) with a single small window facing south.[27] This room gives access, through another small entrance, to the triconch *naos* where the liturgical ceremonies are celebrated. The *naos* comprises a central rectangular space with two lateral semicircular apses, extending to the north and south, and a cylindrical tower above with four windows pointing in the cardinal directions. Toward the east end of the church extends the altar area, or chancel, separated from the *naos* by a large carved and gilded iconostasis with painted icons in multiple registers. This wall of icons within the performance space of the Orthodox liturgy physically divides and visually conceals the altar area and its spiritual orchestration of the mysteries of the Eucharist from the *naos* where the faithful gather.[28] It becomes clear from the layout, architectural features,

---

was initially rectangular in shape and had three semicircular apses only toward the east end. In the late 10th century, however, the *naos* area received a north and south apse. According to one explanation, this was accomplished in order to facilitate the antiphonal singing of the two choirs of monks that assembled in these spaces during liturgical rituals. Pavlos Mylonas, "Le plan initial du catholicon de la Grande-Lavra au Mont Athos et la genèse du type du catholicon athonite," *Cahiers archéologiques* 32 (1984): 89–112. Mylonas's architectural drawings of the religious buildings on Mount Athos are accessible through the website of the Neohellenic Architecture Archives, Benaki Museum. Robert G. Ousterhout supported Mylonas's argument in his study *Master Builders of Byzantium* (Princeton, NJ: Princeton University Press, 1999; rep. Philadelphia: University of Pennsylvania Museum of Archaeology and Anthropology, 2008), esp. pp. 92–93. See also Mihaela Palade, "Aspects of Mount Athos' Contribution to the Maintenance of the Triconchial Plan in Romanian Sacred Architecture," in *The Romanian Principalities and the Holy Places along the Centuries: Papers of the Symposium held in Bucharest, 15–18 October 2006*, ed. Emanoil Băbuș, Ioan Moldoveanu, and Adrian Marinescu (Bucharest: Editura Sophia, 2007), pp. 145–56.

27 The term *gropniță* to denote the burial chamber is derived from the term for grave: гробъ in Church Slavonic; *groapă* in Romanian; *Grab* in German. The Church Slavonic version appears repeatedly in the dedicatory inscriptions sculpted on the gravestones. The burial chamber at Moldovița contains the grave of Bishop Ephrem of Rădăuți (d. 1626), who is regarded as a second founder of the monastery.

28 On the iconostasis, see Pavel Florensky, *Iconostasis* (1922), trans. Donald Sheehan and Olga Andrejev (Crestwood, NY: St. Vladimir's Seminary Press, 1996); Alexei Lidov, ed., *The*

and furnishing that the interior of the church at Moldoviţa, as elsewhere in Moldavia, comprises a longitudinal progression of spaces of different dimensions and serving diverse functions. For the faithful progressing through the church, these spaces grow progressively darker as one approaches the altar area.

One of the key local features of the Moldavian churches is the design of the dome supports—the so-called oblique arches—found at the transition from the rectilinear space of the *naos* or *pronaos* below to the circular drum of the dome above.[29] The *pronaos* displays more shallow domes, while a steeple-like dome rises over the *naos*, significantly increasing the height of this space. The support system of the domes consists of overlapping arches and pendentives, with the upper set at a 45-degree angle to the vertical. This design is specific to the Moldavian churches built beginning in the second half of the 15th century. It offers an intricate visual scheme at the point of transition to the dome above the *naos* or *pronaos*, and additional surfaces for painted decorations.

3 An Eclectic Visual Idiom

Although built on a plan suited for the needs of the Orthodox faith and its rituals, the church at Moldoviţa, as elsewhere in Moldavia, also displays markedly Gothic features.[30] For one thing, the mode of construction of the *katholikon*, using mainly quarried stone, emulates the building techniques

---

Iconostasis: Origins—Evolution—Symbolism (Moscow: Progress-Tradition, 2000); and Sharon Gerstel, ed., *Thresholds of the Sacred: Architectural, Art Historical, Liturgical, and Theological Perspectives on Religious Screen, East and West* (Washington, DC: Dumbarton Oaks Research Library and Collection and Harvard University Press, 2006). On the iconostasis at Moldoviţa, see Olimpia Mitric, "Nouveaux éléments concernant la datation des iconostases des monastères de Voroneţ et de Moldoviţa," *Revue Roumaine d'Histoire de l'Art, Série Beaux-Arts* 41–42, no. 10 (2005): 103–6; and Marina Ileana Sabados, "L'iconostase de Moldoviţa: Un repère dans l'évolution de l'iconostase moldave," *Series Byzantina* 6 (2008): 27–43.

29 On the Moldavian vaulting system and the so-called oblique arches, see Virgil Vătăşianu, "Bolţile moldoveneşti: Originea şi evoluţia lor istorică," *Anuarul Institutului de Istorie Naţională*, no. 5 (1928–30): 415–31; Tamara Nesterov, "Bolta moldovenească: Aport original al meşterilor moldoveni la tezaurul arhitectural universal," *Akademos* 30, no. 3 (2013): 110–19; and Ousterhout, *Eastern Medieval Architecture*, p. 673.

30 On the topic, see Gheorghe Balş, "Influence de l'art gothique sur l'architecture roumaine," *Bulletin de la section historique de l'Académie Roumaine* 15 (1929): 9–13; and Hermann Fabini, "Le chiese-castello della Transilvania ed i monasteri fortificati Ortodossi della Moldavia in Romania," *Castellum: Rivista dell'Istituto italiano dei castelli* 46 (2004): 7–22.

found in Western Gothic civic and religious structures.[31] The subdivisions of the roof, with steep slopes and large, smooth eaves following the undulating line of the apses, and the three-tier buttresses on the exterior find visual parallels in Gothic buildings, such as the Saxon churches from neighboring Transylvania and the Catholic churches in nearby Hungary.[32] Moreover, the door and window framings and the window tracery also derive from Gothic models. Variants of the *Spitzbogenportal* and the *Schulterbogenportal* appear at the thresholds, and the larger windows of the *pronaos* display two lancets with trefoil cusps supporting a quatrefoil oculus.[33] Although little information survives about the masons who worked on the *katholikon* at Moldovița or on the other Moldavian churches, certain stonecutters, we know, were trained in Transylvanian workshops that generally followed east-central European Gothic building practices and designs. One figure in particular, Ioan Zidarul (John the Mason) from Bistrița in Transylvania, was summoned to Peter's court to work on his ecclesiastical projects, especially the Church of St. Demetrios in Suceava, begun in 1534.[34] Architectural ideas would thus have circulated in

---

31   Moldavia's neighbor to the west, the region of Transylvania, had churches built in a similar fashion. Saxon colonies that settled throughout Transylvania at this time, in which churches were built following Gothic models, existed also in Moldavia, in the cities of Rădăuți, Baia, Chilia, and Siret, for example. See Vasile Drăguț, "Introducere. I. Arhitectura religioasă, pictură murală," in *Monumente istorice bisericești din Mitropolia Moldovei și Sucevei* (Iași: Editura Mitropoliei Moldovei și Sucevei, 1974), p. 10.

32   Although buttresses were used in Byzantine architecture as well—as evidence from select monuments including Hagia Sophia makes clear—the three-tier buttresses found on the Moldavian churches find more direct visual parallels in Gothic buildings. On the form of the Moldavian roofs, see Paraschiva-Victoria Batariuc, "Acoperișul bisericilor din Moldova: Secolele XV–XVI," *Ars Transilvaniae* 14/15 (2004–5): 35–50.

33   See Balș, "Influence de l'art gothique sur l'architecture roumaine," 10. The Graphic Collection of the Akademie der Bildenden Künste in Vienna preserves comparable examples. See Johann Josef Böker, *Architektur der Gotik: Bestandskatalog der weltgrößten Sammlung an gotischen Baurissen (Legat Franz Jäger) im Kupferstichkabinett der Akademie der bildenden Künste Wien* (Vienna: Verlag Anton Pustet, 2005). A few relevant examples include: 16.996—the elevation drawing of a portal frame with uninterrupted profiles and a tympanum, southern German, 1446 (307); 17.004 and 17.004v—drawings of tracery windows, ca. 1465, attributed to Laurenz Spenning (316); 17.01—the drawing of a four-part tracery with trilobes and quadrilobes connected, as executed (with slight variations) at Spišský Štvrtok, attributed to Laurenz Spenning, ca. 1456 (325); and 17.026—the elevation drawing of the porch of the former chapel of Saint Maria Magdalene, situated southwest of Saint Stephen's Cathedral in Vienna, ca. 1460 by Laurenz Spenning (337).

34   On the figure of Ioan Zidarul (John the Mason), see Alexandru Lăpedatu, "Ioan Zidarul lui Petru-Vodă Rareș," *Buletinul Comisiunii Monumentelor Istorice* 5 (1912): 83–86; Vasile Ilovan, "Casa 'Ioan Zidarul' din Bistrița," *File de Istorie* 3 (1974): 190–96; and Ana Maria Orășanu, "Une maison patricienne de Bistriza au XVIe siècle 'La maison de Ion Zidaru,'" *Revue Roumaine d'Histoire* 15, no. 1 (1976): 57–69.

medieval lodges of stone masons and architects, informing practices of building construction across Europe.[35]

Changing patterns of patronage that emerged in the new sociopolitical atmosphere of the post-1453 world could have also contributed to the distinctive character of the Moldavian monuments. Despite the lack of extensive archival documentation on the builders and artists who worked on these churches, and the nature of their patronage, a careful examination of the buildings themselves could yield insight into their builders and patrons alike, as well as the cultural contacts that extended in this region at this time. The lack of written sources should not preclude learning about these issues because, in fact, as the architectural historian Slobodan Ćurčić has argued in regard to Serbian architecture, which poses similar problems, there is always "documentary value of the physical evidence at hand."[36]

The eclecticism with respect to sources evident in the *katholikon* at Moldovița, and in general in the Moldavian monastic churches of the late 15th and early 16th centuries, is not a synthesis of artistic and architectural elements drawn from distinct church building traditions. Rather, these buildings display an adaptation and translation of select elements, such as the triconch layout, in order to fulfill certain needs. For instance, the desire of the patron to be buried within the church in a special burial chamber that precedes the *naos* ensured his perpetual remembrance by the faithful upon entering and leaving the church building. As such, the visual plurality of these monuments is neither a direct synthesis nor a form of hybridity, since a hybrid, in the most straightforward of definitions, implies two purities that are mingled, and this is not the case with these examples. In a more nuanced sense, a hybrid is "the sign of an attempt to reconcile forms of cultural exchange, with attendant aspects of both assimilation and resistance."[37] In this regard, the phenomenon of cultural contact and translation is a give and take, with elements and meanings accepted, rejected, and transformed dependent on the new context(s) and the motivation(s) of the patrons, the artists, and the larger communities.

---

35 For example, the architectural lodge of St. Stephen's Cathedral in Vienna, led by the architects Hanns Puchsbaum and Lorenz Spenning, served as the leading lodge for much of the 15th century. Spenning was among the professional architects present at the 1459 Regensburg Congress (Regensburger Bauhüttentagung) that was intended to regulate practices and rules governing building construction among all affiliated lodges.

36 Slobodan Ćurčić, "The Role of Late Byzantine Thessalonike in Church Architecture in the Balkans," *Dumbarton Oaks Papers* 57 (2003): 84.

37 Thomas DaCosta Kaufmann, *Court, Cloister, and City: The Art and Culture of Central Europe, 1450–1800* (Chicago: Chicago University Press, 1995), p. 114.

Although it is important to consider the distinctive facets of Moldavian monastic church architecture from this period and their affinities with earlier Byzantine and Gothic traditions, among others, the element of the local should not be forgotten.[38] Synthesis and translations between old and new, domestic and foreign, aristocratic and popular traditions all come into play in the development of what we may refer to as a Moldavian type of monastic architecture that prevailed in the century following the destruction of Constantinople—a type of monument that presents different kinds of responses to the crisis of 1453 and to the emergence of the Ottoman Empire as a dominant force in southeastern Europe, the eastern Mediterranean, and the western Black Sea regions in the decades that followed.[39]

4   The Murals of the Moldavian *Katholika*

Aside from the distinctive architecture of the Moldavian churches, the brightly colored mural cycles in multiple registers that cover their interior and exterior walls are, perhaps, some of their most striking visual features.[40] Executed by local and traveling artists, these image programs accomplished in the fresco technique display Christological, Mariological, and hagiographical stories interspersed with monumental images of historical and apocalyptic scenes, as

---

38   Corina Nicolescu discusses the element of the "local" in relation to the artistic production of Moldavia at the turn of the 16th century, during the last third of Stephen the Great's reign. Nicolescu, "Arta in epoca lui Ștefan cel Mare: Antecedentele și etapele de dezvoltare ale artei moldovenești din epoca lui Ștefan cel Mare," in *Cultura moldovenească în timpul lui Ștefan cel Mare*, ed. Mihai Berza (Bucharest: Editura Academiei, 1964), p. 362.

39   On aspects of how the visual vocabulary of the Moldavian material relates to that of Serbia and Bulgaria, see, for example, Alice Isabella Sullivan, "Architectural Pluralism at the Edges: The Visual Eclecticism of Medieval Monastic Churches in Eastern Europe," in "Marginalia: Architectures of Uncertain Margins," special issue, *Studii de Istoria și Teoria Arhitecturii / Studies in History and Theory of Architecture* 4 (2016): 135–51.

40   See Sullivan, "The Painted Fortified Monastic Churches of Moldavia," pp. 161–215. For the Moldavian murals, clay earth pigments (red and yellow ochre, terre verte), copper pigments (azurite blue, malachite green), charcoal black, and white (calcium carbonated from lime) were most common. Azurite blue, commonly used for backgrounds, proved to be most durable, especially on exterior surfaces. Although the color palettes are relatively limited, yellows dominate the mural cycles at Moldovița, reds at Humor, greens at Arbore, and blues at Voroneț.

well as full-length depictions of saintly figures and angels.[41] Some examples carry *tituli* and inscriptions in Greek, others in Church Slavonic.[42] Just like the architecture of the churches, the mural cycles follow by and large Byzantine stylistic and iconographic forms, but selected iconographies derive from Western medieval prototypes.[43] Moreover, the images were carefully conceived in relation to the architecture of the buildings and the various functions of their separate spaces. The *katholikon* at Moldoviţa demonstrates how this is so.

It is evident that the interior layout of the church at Moldoviţa is not easily discernible from the exterior of the edifice. Since the exonarthex, *pronaos*, and burial chamber serve as additions (so to speak) to the triconch liturgical space of the church, the faithful progressing through these spaces are mentally primed for their eventual passage into the *naos*.[44] The single, central entryways leading from one space to the next guide and control the physical progression through the building. This passage is further inflected visually. The extensive image cycles set in multiple registers on the interior walls of the *pronaos* and burial chamber display scenes from the *Menologium*—the texts describing the religious feasts and martyrdoms of Orthodox saints corresponding to each day of the year (Fig. 8.6). Each register shows saints celebrated in a particular month—thus the images wrap clockwise around the spaces of the *pronaos* and the burial chamber from top to bottom, visualizing a passage of earthly time on the inner walls of the church.[45] Although this iconography is common in Byzantine manuscripts and icons, in the Slavic-Orthodox cultural spheres it

---

41   See Gheorghe Balş, "Zugravi moldoveni," *Buletinul Comisiunii Monumentelor Istorice* 22 (1929): 141; and Eugen Stănescu, "Meşteri constructori pietrari şi zugravi din timpul lui Ştefan cel Mare," *Studii şi Cercetări de Istoria Artei* no. 1–2 (1955): 361–65.

42   The majority of the churches carry inscriptions and *tituli* in Church Slavonic, but the Church of the Holy Cross at Pătrăuţi Monastery (1487) is one example where the *tituli* in the fresco decorations are offered in Greek.

43   One example is the image of Agnus Dei that appears in both the interior and exterior murals. See Vlad Bedros, "The Lamb of God in Moldavian Mural Decoration," *Revue des Etudes Sud-Est Européennes* 49 (2011): 53–72.

44   Gabriel Herea, *Pelerinaj în spaţiul sacru Bucovinean* (Cluj-Napoca: Patmos, 2010), p. 15.

45   On the *Menologium* in the Moldavian cultural context, see Ecaterina Cincheza-Buculei, "Menologul de la Dobrovăţ (1529)," *Studii şi Cercetări de Istoria Artei, Seria Arte Plastice* 39 (1992): 7–32; Cincheza-Buculei, "Le programme iconographique des peintures murales de la chambre des tombeaux de l'église du monastère de Dobrovăţ," *Cahiers Balkaniques* 21 (1994): 21–58; Cincheza-Buculei, "Programul iconografic al gropniţelor Moldoveneşti," in *Arta Românească, Arta Europeană: Centenar Virgil Vătăşianu*, ed. Marius Porumb (Oradea: Editura Muzeului Ţării Crişurilor, 2002), pp. 85–93; and Cincheza-Buculei, "Tema Menologului din pictura Bisericii Mănăstirii Neamţ," in *Artă, istorie, cultură:*

FIGURE 8.6 Menologium, 1535–37, interior mural, *pronaos*, Church of the Annunciation, Moldoviţa Monastery, Moldavia, Romania
PHOTOGRAPH BY ALICE ISABELLA SULLIVAN

takes on monumental proportions beginning in the 13th century. The calendar of the Constantinopolitan Church finds visual manifestations on the interior walls of the Church of St. George in Staro Nagoričino (1317–18), and then at the Church of the Virgin at Gračanica Monastery (ca. 1321), with another early iteration in the interior of the Church of St. Nicholas Orphanos in Thessaloniki (ca. 1320)—all churches sponsored (or restored) by the Serbian King Stefan Milutin (r. 1282–1321).[46] But whereas in the Serbian milieu the *Menologium* was represented partially and allocated to the upper zones of the inner walls of the narthex of the church, in the Moldavian context this cycle was painted in full and covered the entire inner walls of the *pronaos* and burial chamber of the building.

Reflecting Byzantine traditions of church decoration, the interior of the *naos* received scenes from the life of Christ and the Virgin, representations of

---

Studii în onoarea lui Marius Porumb, ed. Ciprian Firea and Coriolan Horaţiu Opreanu (Cluj-Napoca: Nereamia Napocae, 2003), pp. 135–42.

46 See Branislav Todić, *Serbian Medieval Painting: The Age of King Milutin* (Belgrade: Draganić, 1999); and Vojvodić and Popović, eds., *Sacral Art of the Serbian Lands in the Middle Ages*, vol. 2, esp. pp. 213–315.

full-length figures of military saints, and a votive painting that often shows the patron presenting a model of the church to Christ enthroned via the intercessory role of the holy figure to whom the church is dedicated.[47] At Moldovița, the votive mural shows Peter Rareș and members of his immediate family alongside the Virgin Mary and Christ. Furthermore, the unusual height of these Orthodox-rite churches also allowed for larger wall surfaces and the inclusion of additional religious scenes, such as Christ's miracles, which appear in Byzantine and Serbian monumental mural cycles.[48] This suggests that the conception (and execution) of the Moldavian frescoes may have come about through both direct Byzantine models and others mediated through regions of the Balkans, such as Serbia, Bulgaria, and Macedonia, with which Moldavia established connections especially though the Orthodox Church.

The extant material evidence may thus help shed new light on the relations that extended between the Moldavian Church and the Metropolitanates in Ohrid and Peć, for example, for much of the 15th century and after the fall of Constantinople. One figure in particular, the Metropolitan Bishop of Moldavia and Stephen III's main advisor—Teoctist I (metropolitan of Moldavia 1453–77)—was ordained at Peć and fostered relations through the Church with

---

47   The scenes from Christ's life are described in Dionysius of Fourna's *Hermeneia* as "How the principal feasts and the other works and miracles of Christ are represented, according to the Holy Gospels." *The "'Painter's Manual'" of Dionysius of Fourna: An English Translation, with Commentary, of Cod. Gr. 708 in the Saltykov-Shchedrin State Public Library, Leningrad*, trans. Paul Hetherington (London: Sagittarius Press, 1974; rep. 1978, 1981, and 1989 by Oakwood Publications), pp. 32–40. See also "How the Feasts of the Mother of God Are Represented," ibid., pp. 50–52.

On votive portraits, see Matei Cazacu and Ana Dumitrescu, "Culte dynastique et images votives en Moldavie au XVe siècle," *Cahiers Balkaniques* 15 (1990): 13–102; Teodora Voinescu, "Portretele lui Ștefan cel Mare în arta epocii sale," in *Cultura moldovenească în timpul lui Ștefan cel Mare*, pp. 463–78; Tereza Sinigalia, "Ctitori și imagini votive în pictura murală din Moldova la sfârșitul secolului al XV-lea și în prima jumătate a secolului al XVI-lea: O ipoteză," in *Arta istoriei, Istoria Artei: Academicianul Răzvan Theodorescu la 65 de ani* (Bucharest: Editura Enciclopedică, 2004), pp. 59–65; and Elena Firea, "Concepție dinastică în tablourile votive ale lui Petru Rareș," *Ars Transsilvaniae* 14/15 (2004): 143–61. For a general discussion of Moldavian and Wallachian votive paintings and their functions, see Laura-Cristina Ștefănescu, "Gift-Giving, *Memoria*, and Art Patronage in the Principalities of Walachia and Moldavia: The Function and Meaning of Princely Votive Portraits (14th–17th Centuries)" (MA thesis, Utrecht University, 2010).

48   On the topic of Christ's miracles, see Maria Alessia Rossi, "Christ's Miracles in Monumental Art in Byzantium and Serbia (1280–1330)" (PhD diss., Courtauld Institute of Art, 2017); and Rossi, "The Miracle Cycle between Constantinople, Thessaloniki, and Mistra," in *From Constantinople to the Frontier: The City and The Cities*, ed. Nicholas Matheou, Theofili Kampianaki, and Lorenzo Bondioli (Leiden: Brill, 2016), pp. 226–42.

that region.[49] These interactions certainly helped facilitate the movement of people, such as artists, and artistic ideas between these distant regions. And we know, for example, that a certain artist, George from Trikala, Greece, came and painted at the Moldavian court and, upon his death in 1530, was honored with burial in a local church.[50] Although fragments of mural cycles survive on the exteriors of medieval Orthodox churches from the Byzantine and Slavic cultural spheres, the Moldavian corpus is the only extant example that interprets and amplifies this phenomenon in striking ways, revealing how Byzantine artistic traditions of church building and decoration were continued but also transformed in a new context after the events of 1453.[51]

In contrast to the predominantly narrative mode of representation characteristic of the majority of the interior and exterior paintings, the exterior of the *naos* shows images in a more iconic mode (Fig. 8.1). Here, around the triconch space, five registers display figures arranged in a hierarchical fashion, beginning with monks and hermits at the bottom, followed by martyrs, apostles, prophets, and angels. These figures are shown full-length and directing their attention toward the east, as if partaking in a procession around the building that culminates at the axis of the altar window where Eucharistic imagery abounds. At Moldovița, for example, this area displays the Eucharistic Christ in a chalice on the short buttress below the altar window, the Lamb of God above the window, and on top of that an image of the Virgin enthroned with the Christ Child. The kinds of exterior images found on the Moldavian churches would have welcomed a circumambulation of the monuments in the context of certain liturgical ceremonies, such as those that occurred (and still do today) during the Easter celebrations.[52]

---

49 See Sullivan, "The Athonite Patronage of Stephen III," esp. 31.
50 His tombstone is now in the National Museum of Art in Bucharest (MNAR 14 888/37). See André Grabar, "Les croisades de l'Europe orientale dans l'art," *Mélanges Charles Diehl* (Paris: Ernest Leroux, 1930), pp. 19–27, esp. p. 26; Florin Marinescu, "Pictori greci în țările române," *Istorie și cultură* 44, no. 2 (2009): 690–95, esp. 691–92; and Vlad Bedros, "Gheorghe din Trikkala," in *Allgemeines Künstlerlexikon: Die bildenden Künstler aller Zeiten und Völker* (AKL), vol. 52 (Leipzig and Munich: Saur, 2006), p. 498.
51 An example of a church with a fragmentary exterior mural cycle is the Church of St. Niketa near Skopje (1329; rest. 1480s). See Ivan Stevović, "Byzantine and Romanesque-Gothic Conceptions in Serbian Architecture and Sculpture in the 14th Century (till 1371)," in *Sacral Art of the Serbian Lands in the Middle Ages*, vol. 2, pp. 317–29, fig. 253. Another example is the Church of St. George at Kurbinovo (1191). See Slobodan Ćurčić, *Architecture in the Balkans from Diocletian to Süleyman the Magnificent* (New Haven: Yale University Press, 2010), p. 392.
52 See Sullivan, "Visions of Byzantium," 49–51, esp. fig. 25. The Russian monk and traveler Vasil Grigorovich-Barsky (1701–1747) recorded similar processions during his visit to the monastery of Hosios Loukas in 1745, for example. See Mikhaïl Iakouchev, *Vassili*

FIGURE 8.7   The Akathistos Hymn, the Siege of Constantinople, the Tree of Jesse, 1537, exterior mural, south wall, Church of the Annunciation, Moldovița Monastery, Moldavia, Romania
PHOTOGRAPH BY ALICE ISABELLA SULLIVAN

Among the scenes painted on the exterior of the Moldavian churches, Christological and Mariological iconographies take center stage. These image cycles were calibrated to enhance and give visual expression to the specific purpose of the part of the building on which they were painted, and some were even adapted to address princely and local needs and concerns. For example, the south wall of the burial chamber at Moldovița, as elsewhere, received a monumental scene of the Tree of Jesse (Fig. 8.7).[53] This image type traces the

---

   Grigorovich-Barski, Pérégrinations (1723–1747), trans. Myriam Odayski (Geneva: Les Syrtes, 2019).

53   On this image type, see Arthur Watson, *The Early Iconography of the Tree of Jesse* (London: Oxford University Press, 1934). See also Paul Henry, "L'arbre de Jessé dans les églises de Bukovine," in "Mélanges 1928," issue of *Extrait de la Bibliothèque de l'Institut Français de Hautes-Etudes en Roumanie* 2, (Bucharest: Cultura Națională, 1929): 1–31; Michael D. Taylor, "Three Local Motifs in Moldavian Trees of Jesse, with an Excursus on the Liturgical Basis of the Exterior Mural Programs," *Revue des Études Sud-Est Européennes* 12 (1974): 267–75; and Taylor, "A Historiated Tree of Jesse," *Dumbarton Oaks Papers* 34/35 (1980–81): 125–76.

genealogy of Christ, and in particular his human lineage, through Jesse, his son David, the kings of the Old Testament, and then finally through the Virgin Mary. The Moldavian renditions of this iconography also display narrative vignettes of prophetic moments from the Old Testament and full-length depictions of Greek philosophers, such as Plato and Aristotle, whose texts were read as containing allusions to the coming of Christ.[54] As such, the elaborate representations of the Tree of Jesse were both genealogical and prophetic in content, and were intended to highlight first and foremost the notion of lineage—that of Christ in the painted representation, and that of the prince (or patron) buried in the space extending beyond the painted exterior.[55]

Moreover, such monumental iconographic cycles were likely conceived using working drawings, also known as *anthivola*.[56] One of the largest known *anthivolon*, discovered in the archives of Dionysiou Monastery on Mount Athos, shows the vertical and horizontal arrangement of individual scenes that make up the Tree of Jesse image.[57] These kinds of drawings reveal some of the working methods of artists and attest to the collective process of art making in the later Byzantine period, as well as to the modes of transmission of ideas and forms among artists and successive generations of painters.

---

54 For a detailed consideration of the literary sources that explain the inclusion of the ancient Greek philosophers in the Moldavian murals, and the meanings of the texts they carry on their individual scrolls, see Constantin Ion Ciobanu, *Stihia Profeticului: Sursele literare ale imaginii "Asediului Constantinopolului" și ale "Profețiilor" înțelepților antichității din pictura murală medievală Moldavă* (Chișinău: Institutul Patrimoniului Cultural, Academia de Științe a Moldovei, 2007), pp. 125–309.

55 The Tree of Jesse also appears frequently in Athonite and Serbian monasteries. In the Serbian cultural context of the 14th century, for instance, this iconography was common in foundations that either served or were intended to serve as princely mausolea. Examples are found at the monasteries of Gračanica, Dečani, Peć, and Matejić, to name a few. At Dečani, the Tree of Jesse is found back to back, on the opposite side of the same wall, to the representation of the Nemanjid Dynastic Tree, drawing strong parallels among faith, royal lineage, and ideology.

56 For more on *anthivola* and the execution and functions of working drawings in Byzantium, see Laskarina Bouras, "Working Drawings of Painters in Greece after the Fall of Constantinople," in *From Byzantium to El Greco: Greek Frescoes and Icons*, ed. Myrtalē Acheimastou-Potamianou (Athens: Greek Ministry of Culture and Byzantine Museum of Athens, 1987), pp. 54–56, plates 72 and 73 on pp. 143, 144, 198–99, with Supplement to the Catalog; Andromachi-Maria Nanou Katselaki, *Anthivola—The Holy Cartoons from the Chioniades at the Cathedral of Saint Alexander Nevski in Sofia* (Sofia: National Art Gallery, 2011); and Maria Vassilaki, *Working Drawings of Icon Painters after the Fall of Constantinople: The Andreas Xyngopoulos Portfolio at the Benaki Museum* (Athens: Peak Publishing, 2015).

57 Tree of Jesse, 16th century, *anthivolon*, 28 × 9–1/4 in. (71 cm × 23.5 cm), Archives of Dionysiou Monastery, Mount Athos.

In addition to the Tree of Jesse, the exterior south wall of the church at Moldoviţa, as in other Moldavian churches, shows imagery drawn from the Akathistos Hymn (Fig. 8.7). As the oldest performed hymn dedicated to the Virgin Mary sung in the Eastern Orthodox Church, the Akathistos was often represented in twenty-four scenes that stand for its twenty-four stanzas.[58] Like the Hymn, the murals of the Akathistos celebrate the important events in the life of the Virgin, praising her role in the Incarnation, Redemption, and other mysteries. The Akathistos eventually evolved into a war hymn believed to bring divine protection to the Byzantine capital during moments of struggle, and, by extension, to the entire empire. During the later Palaiologan era, and in particular after the fall of the Byzantine Empire, the representations of the Akathistos acquired historical dimensions and came to incorporate scenes depicting the Siege of Constantinople that show the Byzantine capital saved through divine interventions.[59] The mural of the Siege at Moldoviţa references a number of historical moments, in particular the triumphant victories of the imperium during the sieges of 626 by the Avars and the Persians, 717/18 by the Arabs, and 860 by the Rus'. The inclusion of contemporary artillery presents an anachronism that brings the relevance of these earlier victories into the present. In light of the conquest of Constantinople in 1453 and the ongoing Ottoman threat in regions of the Balkans and the Carpathians, the image seems to hold out assurance that divine aid is forthcoming. Indeed, in drawing on older Byzantine sources, this powerful, multilayered story of divine aid in the fight against non-Christian enemies functioned as a pictorial commentary on the continuing Ottoman threat against Moldavia's independence, political stability, and religious identity. The scene was painted on the exterior of several Moldavian *katholika*, and situated above eye level and close to the main entrance to the church.[60] This location suggests that the image had a crucial message to convey to the faithful entering and leaving the church building.

---

58 Significant studies on the illustration of the Akathistos Hymn include: Irineu Crăciunaş, "Acatistul Maicii Domnului în pictura exterioară din Moldova," *Mitropolia Moldovei şi Sucevei* 48, no. 5–6 (1972): 297–340; Casian Crăciun, *Reprezentarea imnului Acatist în iconografia moldovă din secolul al XVI-lea* (Galaţi: Episcopia Dunării de Jos, 1999); Leena Mari Peltomaa, *The Image of the Virgin in the Akathistos Hymn* (Leiden: Brill, 2001); Ioannis Spatharakis, *The Pictorial Cycles of the* Akathistos Hymn *for the Virgin* (Leiden: Alexandros Press, 2005); and Constantin Ion Ciobanu, "L'iconographie de l'Hymne Acathiste dans les fresques de l'église St. Onuphre du monastère Lavrov et dans la peinture extérieure moldave au temps du premier règne de Petru Rareş," *Revue Roumaine d'Histoire de l'Art, Série Beaux-Arts* 47 (2010): 3–24.
59 Sullivan, "Visions of Byzantium," 31–68.
60 Ibid., n. 9.

Before the exonarthex of the church at Moldoviţa, the west facade displays scenes from Genesis interspersed, as revealed through the narrow arched openings of the exonarthex, with moments from the Last Judgment painted on the entire inner eastern wall of the space (Fig. 8.2).[61] On one level, the juxtaposition of scenes from Genesis and the Last Judgment would have prompted a scriptural awareness of what came at the beginning and what will be at the end of times. On another level, this visual dialogue conflated temporalities on a single visual plane, stressing existence in time and serving as an appropriate marker for the beginning of the path to salvation, through the church proper. As such, the open exonarthex, as evident at Moldoviţa and elsewhere, provided a space of transition between the natural world and the sacred space of the church that, in turn, was further charged visually and spatially.

Through the distinctive architecture, the particular choice and placement of the image cycles, their iconographies, and the conflation of temporalities within individual images and among groups of scenes, the Moldavian monastic churches of the early 16th century continually stimulated the faithful. As they progressed physically around the church and from the outside to the inside of the edifice, along a carefully structured and defined horizontal axis leading toward the altar, and spiritually along a vertical axis once within the *naos*, the faithful were encouraged to approach the chancel and stand under the great Pantokrator in the dome in the spiritual mindset appropriate for the celebrations of the Divine Liturgy (Fig. 8.8).[62] As evident at Moldoviţa and in all other Moldavian churches of the late-15th and early-16th centuries, the architecture, image cycles, and ritual performances were carefully conceived in dialogue in order to choreograph sacred space and the varied experiences of those present.

---

61   The *katholikon* at Moldoviţa preserves the most extensive rendition of the Genesis iconography. The rich iconography of the Last Judgment is difficult to appreciate in its entirety due to the narrow space of the exonarthex. The *katholikon* at Voroneţ lacks an exonarthex and displays the scene of the Last Judgment on its western facade. At this site, the composition and visual complexity of the scene can be appreciated in full.

    For general observations on the Last Judgment iconography in regions of the Carpathian Mountains, see John-Paul Himka, *Last Judgment Iconography in the Carpathians* (Toronto: Toronto University Press, 2009); and Gheorghiţa Daniela Giugea, "The Last Judgment as Represented in the Sistine Chapel by Michelangelo and in the Romanian Byzantine Voroneţ," *IJASOS—International E-Journal of Advances in Social Sciences* 3, no. 9 (December 2017): 1082–93.

62   For a brief consideration of the ritual dimensions of the Moldavian churches that certainly welcomed circumambulatory ceremonies, see Sullivan, "Visions of Byzantium," 49–51.

FIGURE 8.8 Pantokrator, 1535–37, interior mural, *naos*, Church of the Annunciation, Moldovița Monastery, Moldavia, Romania
PHOTOGRAPH BY ALICE ISABELLA SULLIVAN

5   Conclusion

The Romanian historian Gheorghe Balș characterized the Moldavian ecclesiastical monuments of the 15th and 16th centuries as "Byzantine churches built with Gothic hands and following principles that were in part Gothic."[63] Indeed, the layout of the churches and the nature of their interior spaces, dimly lit and with extensive image cycles in multiple registers entirely covering the walls, inside as well as outside, demonstrate affinities with Byzantine church building and decorating traditions. Other features of the buildings, such as the large three-tier buttresses set against the thick walls, the curvilinear tracery found in the upper sections of the windows, and the receding pointed arches of the door frames, for example, derive mainly from Gothic models predominant in church architecture in Western Europe. Various aspects of these religious monuments are of a local character as well, such as the elongated proportions

---

63   Gheorghe Balș, *Bisericile lui Ștefan cel Mare* (Bucharest: Cartea Românească, 1926), p. 14: "s-a putut caracteriza biserica moldovenească ca fiind un plan bizantin executat cu mâini gotice și după principii în parte gotice."

of the triconch plan, the supports of the dome, and the translation of certain iconographic cycles—which developed in efforts to fulfill particular needs of the patron and of the community at large. In this guise, the Moldavian churches present a special synthesis of Eastern- and Western-inspired aesthetic and symbolic conventions adapted for a local context. The Church of the Annunciation at Moldoviţa Monastery, built under the patronage of Prince Peter Rareş during the third decade of the 16th century, serves as a particularly apt example that reveals the key contemporary architectural and iconographic developments in Moldavian *katholika*, which were later further transformed and elaborated under princely patronage. The church also displays the best-preserved cycle of images, both inside and outside.

The extensive mural decorations of the Moldavian churches—perhaps some of their most striking visual features—offer a refashioning of especially Byzantine artistic models. Certainly not of a provincial or secondary character, and certainly not unique, the mural cycles of these buildings are an exceptional example of the cultural continuity and local interpretations of a tradition of church building and decoration with roots in the Byzantine cultural sphere and readapted throughout regions of the Mediterranean, the Balkans, and the Carpathians from at least the 12th century onward—as a common claim of inheritance from Byzantium.[64] The cool and relatively dry climate of the Carpathians and the remote location of the Moldavian churches may explain the extraordinary preservation of their exterior frescoes.

Because of Moldavia's strong Orthodox roots, Byzantium initially contributed to the definition of the region's new and expansive sacred landscape made up of numerous churches, chapels, and monasteries. Byzantium also helped the region and its rulers claim legitimacy with a strong Christian past at a moment when the Christian world was increasingly coming under threat from the Ottoman Empire. Indeed, Byzantium offered the dominant visual, religious, and ideological models, especially in the decades after the fall of Constantinople in 1453. But the art and architecture of Moldavia—like that of 12th-century Sicily and 12th- to 14th-century Serbia and Bulgaria, for example—took form as a result of the region's networked position relative to other cultures as well.[65] The Moldavian artistic production of the late-15th and

---

64 For example, churches from the regions of Northern Macedonia, dated to the 14th century, display similar mural cycles on their exterior walls, although not in a good state of preservation.

65 On Sicily, see William Tronzo, *The Cultures of His Kingdom: Roger II and the Cappella Palatina in Palermo* (Princeton, NJ: Princeton University Press, 1997). On Serbia and Bulgaria in the later period, see Elena N. Boeck, *Imagining the Byzantine Past: The Perception of History in the Illustrated Manuscripts of Skylitzes and Manasses* (Cambridge,

early-16th centuries is indebted to both Byzantine and Gothic building and decorating traditions, transformed in a local context. In the post-1453 world, however, the afterlife of Byzantium's spiritual power and glorious past was dominant, and it found new and powerful visual iterations in Moldavia as the region became a bastion of orthodoxy and assumed a strong position at the borders of Europe and of Christendom.

Acknowledgements

A preliminary version of this essay was presented at the 44th Annual Byzantine Studies Conference (2018, San Antonio, Texas) in the session titled "North of Byzantium: Art and Architecture at the Crossroads of the Latin, Greek, and Slavic Cultural Spheres, c.1300–c.1500 (I)." The Mary Jaharis Center for Byzantine Art and Culture generously sponsored the event. I thank the audience members for their thoughtful comments and questions, as well as for the stimulating discussion. I am also grateful to Maria Alessia Rossi, Jelena Bogdanović, and the anonymous reviewer for carefully reading and commenting on earlier versions of this study, and to Joe Hannan for copyediting the manuscript. Finally, I thank the Archbishopric of Suceava and Rădăuți in Romania and the nuns at Moldovița Monastery for granting me permissions to photograph and study the church and its monastic compound.

Unless otherwise noted, all translations into English are my own, as are any remaining errors.

Bibliography

Primary Sources

Alexandrov, Victor. *The Syntagma of Matthew Blastares: The Destiny of a Byzantine Legal Code among the Orthodox Slavs and Romanians 14–17 Centuries*. Frankfurt am Main: Löwenklau Gesellschaft, 2012.

Guboglu, Mihail, and Mustafa Mehmet, eds. *Cronici Turcești privind țările române*, vol. 1. Bucharest: Editura Academiei, 1955.

UK: Cambridge University Press, 2015), esp. chapter 2; and Vojvodić and Popović, eds., *Sacral Art of the Serbian Lands in the Middle Ages*, vol. 2. For an overview of the issues involved in the study of Byzantine art, see Antony Eastmond, "The Limits of Byzantine Art," in *A Companion to Byzantium*, ed. Liz James (Malden, MA: Wiley-Blackwell, 2010), pp. 313–22.

Panaitescu, Petre P., and Ion Bogdan. *Cronicile slavo-române din sec. XV–XVI*. Bucharest: Editura Academiei, 1959.

Repertoriul monumentelor și operelor de artă din timpul lui Ștefan cel Mare. Bucharest: Editura Academiei, 1958.

The "Painter's Manual" of Dionysius of Fourna: An English Translation, with Commentary, of Cod. Gr. 708 in the Saltykov-Shchedrin State Public Library, Leningrad, trans. Paul Hetherington. London: Sagittarius Press, 1974; rep. 1978, 1981, and 1989 by Oakwood Publications.

Secondary Sources

Balș, Gheorghe. *Bisericile lui Ștefan cel Mare*. Bucharest: Cartea Românească, 1926.

Balș, Gheorghe. *Bisericile și mănăstirile moldovenești din veacul al XVI-lea*. Bucharest: Cultura Națională, 1928.

Balș, Gheorghe. "Influence de l'art gothique sur l'architecture roumaine." *Bulletin de la section historique de l'Académie Roumaine* 15 (1929): 9–13.

Balș, Gheorghe. "Zugravi moldoveni." *Buletinul Comisiunii Monumentelor Istorice* 22 (1929): 141.

Balș, Gheorghe. "Influence du plan serbe sur le plan des églises roumaines." In *L'art byzantin chez les slaves: Les Balkans; Premier recueil dédié à la mémoire de Theodore Uspenskij*, 277–94. Paris: P. Geuthner, 1930.

Balș, Ștefan, and Corina Nicolescu. *Mănăstirea Moldovița*. Bucharest: Editura Academiei, 1958.

Batariuc, Paraschiva-Victoria. "Acoperișul bisericilor din Moldova: Secolele XV–XVI." *Ars Transilvaniae* 14/15 (2004–05): 35–50.

Bedros, Vlad. "Gheorghe din Trikkala." In *Allgemeines Künstlerlexikon: Die bildenden Künstler aller Zeiten und Völker* (AKL), 52:498. Leipzig and Munich: Saur, 2006.

Bedros, Vlad. "The Lamb of God in Moldavian Mural Decoration." *Revue des Etudes Sud-Est Européennes* 49 (2011): 53–72.

Beldiceanu, Nicoară. *La Moldavie ottomane à la fin du XVe siècle et au début du XVIe siècle*. Paris: Librairie Orientaliste Paul Geuthner, 1969.

Boeck, Elena N. *Imagining the Byzantine Past: The Perception of History in the Illustrated Manuscripts of Skylitzes and Manasses*. Cambridge, UK: Cambridge University Press, 2015.

Bogdanović, Jelena. "The Relational Spiritual Geopolitics of Constantinople, the Capital of the Byzantine Empire." In *Political Landscapes of Capital Cities*, ed. Jessica Joyce Christie, Jelena Bogdanović, and Eulogio Guzmán, 97–153. Boulder: University Press of Colorado, 2016.

Böker, Johann Josef. *Architektur der Gotik: Bestandskatalog der weltgrößten Sammlung an gotischen Baurissen (Legat Franz Jäger) im Kupferstichkabinett der Akademie der bildenden Künste Wien*. Vienna: Verlag Anton Pustet, 2005.

Bouras, Laskarina. "Working Drawings of Painters in Greece after the Fall of Constantinople." In *From Byzantium to El Greco: Greek Frescoes and Icons*, ed. Myrtalē Acheimastou-Potamianou, 54–56. Athens: Greek Ministry of Culture and Byzantine Museum of Athens, 1987.

Cazacu, Matei, and Ana Dumitrescu. "Culte dynastique et images votives en Moldavie au XVᵉ siècle." *Cahiers Balkaniques* 15 (1990): 13–102.

Cincheza-Buculei, Ecaterina. "Menologul de la Dobrovăț (1529)." *Studii și Cercetări de Istoria Artei, Seria Arte Plastice* 39 (1992): 7–32.

Cincheza-Buculei, Ecaterina. "Le programme iconographique des peintures murales de la chambre des tombeaux de l'église du monastère de Dobrovăț." *Cahiers Balkaniques* 21 (1994): 21–58.

Cincheza-Buculei, Ecaterina. "Programul iconografic al gropnițelor Moldovenești." In *Arta Românească, Arta Europeană. Centenar Virgil Vătășianu*, ed. Marius Porumb, 85–93. Oradea: Editura Muzeului Țării Crișurilor, 2002.

Cincheza-Buculei, Ecaterina. "Tema *Menologului* din pictura Bisericii Mănăstirii Neamț." In *Artă, istorie, cultură: Studii în onoarea lui Marius Porumb*, ed. Ciprian Firea and Coriolan Horațiu Opreanu, 135–42. Cluj-Napoca: Nereamia Napocae, 2003.

Ciobanu, Constantin Ion. *Stihia Profeticului: Sursele literare ale imaginii "Asediului Constantinopolului" și ale "Profețiilor" înțelepților antichității din pictura murală medievală Moldavă*. Chișinău: Institutul Patrimoniului Cultural, Academia de Științe a Moldovei, 2007.

Ciobanu, Constantin Ion. "L'iconographie de l'Hymne Acathiste dans les fresques de l'église St. Onuphre du monastère Lavrov et dans la peinture extérieure moldave au temps du premier règne de Petru Rareș." *Revue Roumaine d'Histoire de l'Art, Série Beaux-Arts* 47 (2010): 3–24.

Comărnescu, Petru. *Îndreptar artistic al monumentelor din nordul Moldovei, arhitectura și fresca în sec. XV–XVI*. Suceava: Casa Regională a Credinței Populare Suceava, 1961.

Crăciun, Casian. *Reprezentarea imnului Acatist în iconografia moldovă din secolul al XVI-lea*. Galați: Episcopia Dunării de Jos, 1999.

Crăciunaș, Irineu. "Acatistul Maicii Domnului in pictura exterioară din Moldova." *Mitropolia Moldovei și Sucevei* 48, no. 5–6 (1972): 297–340.

Ćurčić, Slobodan. "The Role of Late Byzantine Thessalonike in Church Architecture in the Balkans." *Dumbarton Oaks Papers* 57 (2003): 65–84.

Ćurčić, Slobodan. *Architecture in the Balkans from Diocletian to Süleyman the Magnificent*. New Haven: Yale University Press, 2010.

Diez, Ernst. "Moldavian Portrait Textiles." *Art Bulletin* 10, no. 4 (1928): 377–85.

Drăguț, Vasile. "Introducere. I. Arhitectura religioasă, pictură murală." In *Monumente istorice bisericești din Mitropolia Moldovei și Sucevei*, 9–22. Iași: Editura Mitropoliei Moldovei și Sucevei, 1974.

Eastmond, Antony. "The Limits of Byzantine Art." In *A Companion to Byzantium*, ed. Liz James, 313–22. Malden, MA: Wiley-Blackwell, 2010.

Fabini, Hermann. "Le chiese-castello della Transilvania ed i monasteri fortificati Ortodossi della Moldavia in Romania." *Castellum: Rivista dell'Istituto italiano dei castelli* 46 (2004): 7–22.

Firea, Elena. "Concepție dinastică în tablourile votive ale lui Petru Rareș." *Ars Transsilvaniae* 14/15 (2004): 143–61.

Florensky, Pavel. *Iconostasis* (1922), trans. Donald Sheehan and Olga Andrejev. Crestwood, NY: St. Vladimir's Seminary Press, 1996.

Gerstel, Sharon ed. *Thresholds of the Sacred: Architectural, Art Historical, Liturgical, and Theological Perspectives on Religious Screen, East and West*. Washington, DC: Dumbarton Oaks Research Library and Collection and Harvard University Press, 2006.

Giugea, Gheorghița Daniela. "The Last Judgment as Represented in the Sistine Chapel by Michelangelo and in the Romanian Byzantine Voroneț." *IJASOS—International E-Journal of Advances in Social Sciences* 3, no. 9 (December 2017): 1082–93.

Gorovei, Ștefan S. "Pacea moldo-otomană din 1486: Observații pe marginea unor texte." *Revista de Istorie* 35, no. 7 (1982): 807–21. Rep. *Ștefan cel Mare și Sfânt, 1504–2004: Portret în istorie*, 496–515. Putna: Sfânta Mănăstire Putna, 2003.

Gorovei, Ștefan S., and Maria Magdalena Székely. *Maria Asanina Paleologhina: O prințesă bizantină pe tronul Moldovei*. Putna: Sfânta Mănăstire Putna, 2006.

Grabar, André. "Les croisades de l'Europe orientale dans l'art." *Mélanges Charles Diehl*, 19–27. Paris: Ernest Leroux, 1930.

Henry, Paul. "L'arbre de Jessé dans les églises de Bukovine." In "Mélanges 1928," issue of *Extrait de la Bibliothèque de l'Institut Français de Hautes-Etudes en Roumanie* 2. (Bucharest: Cultura Națională, 1929): 1–31.

Herea, Gabriel. *Pelerinaj în spațiul sacru Bucovinean*. Cluj-Napoca: Patmos, 2010.

Himka, John-Paul. *Last Judgment Iconography in the Carpathians*. Toronto: Toronto University Press, 2009.

Iakouchev, Mikhaïl. *Vassili Grigorovich-Barski, Pérégrinations (1723–1747)*, trans. Myriam Odayski. Geneva: Les Syrtes, 2019.

Ilovan, Vasile. "Casa 'Ioan Zidarul' din Bistrița." *File de Istorie* 3 (1974): 190–96.

Katselaki, Andromachi-Maria Nanou. *Anthivola—The Holy Cartoons from the Chioniades at the Cathedral of Saint Alexander Nevski in Sofia*. Sofia: National Art Gallery, 2011.

Kaufmann, Thomas DaCosta. *Court, Cloister, and City: The Art and Culture of Central Europe, 1450–1800*. Chicago: Chicago University Press, 1995.

Lăpedatu, Alexandru. "Ioan Zidarul lui Petru-Vodă Rareș." *Buletinul Comisiunii Monumentelor Istorice* 5 (1912): 83–86.

Lidov, Alexei, ed. *The Iconostasis: Origins—Evolution—Symbolism*. Moscow: Progress-Tradition, 2000.

Mănăstirea Moldovița. Iași: Editura Mitropoliei Moldovei și Sucevei, 1971.

Marinescu, Florin. "Pictori greci în țările române." *Istorie și cultură* 44, no. 2 (2009): 690–95.

Mitric, Olimpia. "Nouveaux éléments concernant la datation des iconostases des monastères de Voroneț et de Moldovița." *Revue Roumaine d'Histoire de l'Art, Série Beaux-Arts* 41–42, no. 10 (2005): 103–6.

Mylonas, Pavlos. "Le plan initial du catholicon de la Grande-Lavra au Mont Athos et la genèse du type du catholicon athonite." *Cahiers archéologiques* 32 (1984): 89–112.

Nesterov, Tamara. "Bolta moldovenească: Aport original al meșterilor moldoveni la tezaurul arhitectural universal." *Akademos* 30, no. 3 (2013): 110–19.

Nicolescu, Corina. "Arta in epoca lui Ștefan cel Mare: Antecedentele și etapele de dezvoltare ale artei moldovenești din epoca lui Ștefan cel Mare." In *Cultura moldovenească în timpul lui Ștefan cel Mare*, ed. Mihai Berza, 259–362. Bucharest: Editura Academiei, 1964.

Nicolescu, Corina. *Mănăstirea Moldovița*. Bucharest: Meridiane, 1965. Trans. Elisa Madolciu. *Moldovița*. Bucharest: Sport-Turism, 1978.

Orășanu, Ana Maria. "Une maison patricienne de Bistriza au XVIe siècle 'La maison de Ion Zidaru.'" *Revue Roumaine d'Histoire* 15, no. 1 (1976): 57–69.

Ousterhout, Robert G. *Master Builders of Byzantium*. New Jersey: Princeton University Press, 1999; rep. Philadelphia: University of Pennsylvania Museum of Archaeology and Anthropology, 2008.

Ousterhout, Robert G. *Eastern Medieval Architecture: The Building Traditions of Byzantium and Neighboring Lands*. Oxford: Oxford University Press, 2019.

Palade, Mihaela. "Aspects of Mount Athos' Contribution to the Maintenance of the Triconchial Plan in Romanian Sacred Architecture." In *The Romanian Principalities and the Holy Places along the Centuries: Papers of the Symposium held in Bucharest, 15–18 October 2006*, ed. Emanoil Băbuș, Ioan Moldoveanu, and Adrian Marinescu, 145–56. Bucharest: Editura Sophia, 2007.

Peltomaa, Leena Mari. *The Image of the Virgin in the Akathistos Hymn*. Leiden: Brill, 2001.

Rossi, Maria Alessia. "Christ's Miracles in Monumental Art in Byzantium and Serbia (1280–1330)." PhD diss., Courtauld Institute of Art, 2017.

Rossi, Maria Alessia. "The Miracle Cycle between Constantinople, Thessaloniki, and Mistra." In *From Constantinople to the Frontier: The City and The Cities*, ed. Nicholas Matheou, Theofili Kampianaki, and Lorenzo Bondioli, 226–42. Leiden: Brill, 2016.

Sabados, Marina Ileana. "L'iconostase de Moldovița: Un repère dans l'évolution de l'iconostase moldave." *Series Byzantina* 6 (2008): 27–43.

Sinigalia, Tereza. "L'église de l'ascension du monastère du Neamț et le problème de l'espace funéraire en Moldavie aux XVe–XVIe siècles." *Revue Roumaine d'Histoire de l'Art: Série Beaux-Arts* 25 (1998): 19–32.

Sinigalia, Tereza. "Ctitori și imagini votive în pictura murală din Moldova la sfârșitul secolului al XV-lea și în prima jumătate a secolului al XVI-lea: O ipoteză." In *Arta istoriei, Istoria Artei: Academicianul Răzvan Theodorescu la 65 de ani*, 59–65. Bucharest: Editura Enciclopedică, 2004.

Spatharakis, Ioannis. *The Pictorial Cycles of the Akathistos Hymn for the Virgin*. Leiden: Alexandros Press, 2005.

Speake, Graham. *Mount Athos: Renewal in Paradise*. New Haven: Yale University Press, 2002.

Stănescu, Eugen. "Meșteri constructori pietrari și zugravi din timpul lui Ștefan cel Mare." *Studii și Cercetări de Istoria Artei* no. 1–2 (1955): 361–65.

Ștefănescu, Laura-Cristina. "Gift-Giving, Memoria, and Art Patronage in the Principalities of Walachia and Moldavia: The Function and Meaning of Princely Votive Portraits (14th–17th Centuries)." MA thesis, Utrecht University, 2010.

Stevović, Ivan. "Byzantine and Romanesque-Gothic Conceptions in Serbian Architecture and Sculpture in the 14th Century (till 1371)." In *Sacral Art of the Serbian Lands in the Middle Ages*, vol. 2, ed. Dragan Vojvodić and Danica Popović, 317–29. Belgrade: Serbian National Committee of Byzantine Studies; P.E. Službeni Glasnik: Institute for Byzantine Studies, Serbian Academy of Sciences and Arts, 2016.

Sullivan, Alice Isabella. "Western-Byzantine 'Hybridity' in the Ecclesiastical Architecture of Northern Moldavia." *Romanian Medievalia: Thraco-Dacian and Byzantine Romanity of Eastern Europe and Asia Minor* 12/13 (New York: Romanian Institute of Orthodox Theology and Spirituality, 2015): 35–37.

Sullivan, Alice Isabella. "Architectural Pluralism at the Edges: The Visual Eclecticism of Medieval Monastic Churches in Eastern Europe." In "Marginalia: Architectures of Uncertain Margins," special issue, *Studii de Istoria și Teoria Arhitecturii / Studies in History and Theory of Architecture* 4 (2016): 135–51.

Sullivan, Alice Isabella. "The Painted Fortified Monastic Churches of Moldavia: Bastions of Orthodoxy in a Post-Byzantine World." PhD diss., University of Michigan, 2017.

Sullivan, Alice Isabella. "Visions of Byzantium: *The Siege of Constantinople* in Sixteenth-Century Moldavia." *The Art Bulletin* 99, no. 4 (December 2017): 31–68.

Sullivan, Alice Isabella. "The Athonite Patronage of Stephen III of Moldavia, 1457–1504." *Speculum* 94, no. 1 (2019): 1–46.

Sullivan, Alice Isabella. "Byzantine Artistic Traditions in Moldavian Church Embroideries." In *L'évolution de la broderie de tradition byzantine dans la Méditerranée et le monde slave (1200–1800)*, ed. Elena Papastavrou and Marielle Martiniani-Reber. Paris: Presses d'Inalco, forthcoming.

Sullivan, Alice Isabella. Medieval Moldavian Tetraevangelia and their Afterlives: Preliminary Considerations. In *Fruits of Devotion: Essays in Honor of Predrag Matejic*, ed. M.A. Johnson and Sullivan. *Ohio Slavic Papers* 11, Columbus, OH: Department of Slavic and East European Languages and Cultures, 2020, forthcoming.

Székely, Maria Magdalena. "Mănăstirea Putna: Loc de memorie." *Studii și Materiale de Istorie Medie* 22 (2004): 73–99.

Taylor, Michael D. "Three Local Motifs in Moldavian Trees of Jesse, with an Excursus on the Liturgical Basis of the Exterior Mural Programs." *Revue des Études Sud-Est Européennes* 12 (1974): 267–75.

Taylor, Michael D. "A Historiated Tree of Jesse." *Dumbarton Oaks Papers* 34/35 (1980–81): 125–76.

Teodoru, Horia. "Contribuții la studiul originii și evoluției planului triconc în Moldova." *Buletinul Comisiunii Monumentelor Istorice* 31, no. 1 (1970): 31–33.

Todić, Branislav. *Serbian Medieval Painting: The Age of King Milutin*. Belgrade: Draganić, 1999.

Tronzo, William. *The Cultures of His Kingdom: Roger II and the Cappella Palatina in Palermo*. Princeton, NJ: Princeton University Press, 1997.

Vassilaki, Maria. *Working Drawings of Icon Painters after the Fall of Constantinople: The Andreas Xyngopoulos Portfolio at the Benaki Museum*. Athens: Peak Publishing, 2015.

Vătășianu, Virgil. "Bolțile moldovenești: Originea și evoluția lor istorică." *Anuarul Institutului de Istorie Națională*, no. 5 (1928–1930): 415–31.

Voinescu, Teodora. "Portretele lui Ștefan cel Mare în arta epocii sale." In *Cultura moldovenească în timpul lui Ștefan cel Mare*, ed. Mihai Berza, 463–78. Bucharest: Editura Academiei, 1964.

Vojvodić, Dragan, and Danica Popović, eds. *Sacral Art of the Serbian Lands in the Middle Ages*, vol. 2. Belgrade: Serbian National Committee of Byzantine Studies; P.E. Službeni Glasnik: Institute for Byzantine Studies, Serbian Academy of Sciences and Arts, 2016.

Voyatzis, Sotiris. "Evidence on the Building History of the Holy Monastery of the Great Lavra on Mount Athos: The Gateway in the Circuit Wall." *Deltion tes Christianikes Archaiologikes Hetaireias* 21, no. 4 (2000): 55–68.

Watson, Arthur. *The Early Iconography of the Tree of Jesse*. London: Oxford University Press, 1934.

Živković, Miloš. "Studenica: The Funerary Church of the Dynastic Founder—The Cornerstone of Church and State Independence." In *Sacral Art of the Serbian Lands in the Middle Ages*, vol. 2, ed. Dragan Vojvodić and Danica Popović, 193–209. Belgrade: Serbian National Committee of Byzantine Studies; P.E. Službeni Glasnik: Institute for Byzantine Studies, and Serbian Academy of Sciences and Arts, 2016.

CHAPTER 9

The Byzantine Tradition in Wallachian and Moldavian Embroideries

Henry David Schilb

The respective embroidery traditions of Wallachia and Moldavia were distinctive. The question of whether these differences parallel or illuminate differences in the social and political circumstances of the two principalities in the period immediately following the fall of Constantinople in 1453 is simply too broad to consider exhaustively in a brief essay and may be impossible to answer. My modest goal is to offer some evidence of difference between the embroidery traditions of two principalities that shared adjacent liminal conditions within the post-Byzantine sphere—liminal from an outside perspective, that is. From their own points of view, each was a center surrounded by Ottomans, Slavs, Hungarians, and each other. The art and architecture of Wallachia reveal stronger connections to artistic developments in regions of the Balkans, in part because of the principality's close proximity to Serbia and Bulgaria (with Byzantine models mediated through these Balkan regions north of the Danube), while Moldavia appears to have developed more direct connections to centers in the Byzantine cultural sphere, like Constantinople and Mount Athos, for example. These differences also reflect the different relations with Byzantium that the two principalities experienced, and their different responses to its legacy. In this way, visual and iconographic forms could reflect larger social, political, and even economic issues. I do not intend to argue that Wallachian donors and embroiderers were self-consciously differentiating themselves from their Moldavian counterparts, only that there are differences to consider once we recognize them among the details. Rather, I intend simply to demonstrate with a case study that there actually were such differences. I believe that it possible to attribute to Wallachian patronage an otherwise unattributed textile at the Eskenazi Museum of Art at Indiana University Bloomington. As I present a few of the differences between these closely linked post-Byzantine traditions in church embroidery in Wallachia and Moldavia, it should be understood that my goal is to bring into focus certain details of the art of embroidery in these two adjacent principalities during the period following the end of the Byzantine Empire in 1453.

1   Moldavian *Epitaphioi*

The corpus of Moldavian embroideries of the 14th through the 16th centuries is relatively large, thanks especially to the patronage of Stephen III of Moldavia (r. 1457–1504).[1] These embroideries have long attracted scholarly attention, some rather large *epitaphioi* not least among them. Focusing on just one or two details may help us to identify features that we can confidently associate with these Moldavian embroidered veils. In Orthodox Christian practice, the *epitaphios* is the liturgical veil carried in procession and displayed in the *naos* of a church on Good Friday and Holy Saturday.[2] The form and function of the *epitaphios* developed from the form and function of the *aër*, the veil that covers the Eucharistic elements on the altar.[3] It may be impossible to determine precisely when the *epitaphios* became a separate type of liturgical cloth distinct from the *aër*, but both types of textile invited complex iconography and long inscriptions.[4] Details can vary by region. On many *epitaphioi*, including a large *epitaphios* dated 1490 at the Putna Monastery (Fig. 9.1), each corner of the central panel is filled with one of the *zodia*, the four living creatures of the Apocalypse, which become the symbols of the evangelists in this context. We find them on the earliest extant Byzantine *epitaphioi*, dated to the beginning of the 14th century, such as the *epitaphios* of Emperor Andronicos Palaiologos (r. 1312–28).[5] As on this Byzantine example, Moldavian *epitaphioi* also typically surround each of the living creatures with a curved border. In Moldavia, however, we discover an innovation. Within the curved borders around the *zodia* on many Moldavian examples—including the *epitaphios* of Stephen III at Putna—are the Greek words ᾄδοντα, βοῶντα, κεκραγότα, καὶ λέγοντα, which are usually translated along the lines of "singing, crying, shouting,

---

1   See Alice Isabella Sullivan, "Byzantine Artistic Traditions in Moldavian Church Embroideries," in *L'évolution de la broderie de tradition byzantine dans la Méditerranée et le monde slave (1200–1800)*, ed. Elena Papastavrou and Marielle Martiniani-Reber (Paris: Presses d'Inalco), forthcoming.
2   *The Oxford Dictionary of Byzantium*, ed. Alexander P. Kazhdan (New York: Oxford University press, 1991), s.v. "epitaphios."
3   Ibid., s.v. "aër."
4   See Robert F. Taft, *The Great Entrance: A History of the Transfer of Gifts and Other Preanaphoral Rites of the Liturgy of St. John Chrysostom* (Rome: Pontificium Institutum Studiorum Orientalium, 1975), pp. 216–19.
5   See Helen C. Evans, ed., *Byzantium: Faith and Power (1261–1557)* (New Haven: Yale University Press, 2004), pp. 314–15.

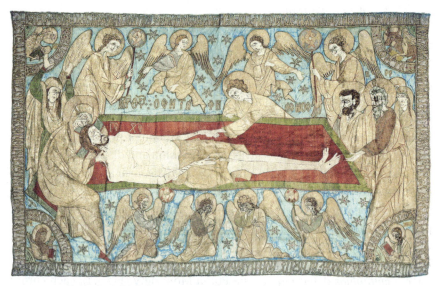

FIGURE 9.1 *Epitaphios* of Stephen III, 1490, 8 ft. 3 in. × 5 ft. 5 in. (252 × 166 cm). Putna Monastery, Romania
PHOTOGRAPH PROVIDED BY PUTNA MONASTERY

and saying."[6] As a string of participles, the whole phrase is spoken during the liturgy to introduce the Sanctus.[7] Irenaeus is credited with first associating the four beasts of Ezekiel 1:10 with the Evangelists, but it was in a text traditionally attributed to the 8th-century patriarch Germanos in which the four living creatures were first associated with this set of participles.[8] These words were paired with the *zodia* by the early 10th century in wall paintings in Cappadocia, where they were added to the iconography of Christ in Majesty, as at Haçlı Kilise.[9] However, it is only in Moldavia that we find this association of the participles with the *zodia*, or Evangelist symbols, on embroidered images of the Epitaphios Threnos.

---

6   The word κεκραγότα is sometimes translated as "proclaiming." Casimir A. Kucharek, *The Byzantine-Slav Liturgy of St. John Chrysostom: Its Origin and Evolution* (Allendale, NJ: Alleluia Press, 1971), pp. 578–87.

7   On these words in the liturgies of SS. Basil and James, see John R.K. Fenwick, *The Anaphoras of St. Basil and St. James: An Investigation into Their Common Origin* (Rome: Pontificium Institutum Orientale, 1992), pp. 88–95.

8   Irenaeus, "Adversus Hæreses," in *Patrologiae cursus completus: Series graeca*, ed. J.-P. Migne (Paris: 1857–66), 7:885–86. Germanos, "Historia ecclesiastica, et mystica contemplatio," in ibid., 98:429C–D.

9   On examples in manuscripts, see George Galavaris, *The Illustrations of the Prefaces in Byzantine Gospels* (Vienna: Verlag der Österreichischen Akademie der Wissenschaften, 1979).

Now let me turn your attention to the field of stars surrounding the figures on the Putna *epitaphios* of Stephen III. This type of field of stars can also be identified with a very specific source. Among the embroideries that have been attributed to the Serbian nun Jefimija, the widow of the despot Jovan Uglješa, is an *epitaphios* preserved in the collection of Putna Monastery (Fig. 9.2).[10] Similarities between the *epitaphios* of Jefimija and the *epitaphios* of Stephen III at Putna are unmistakable. Because it is preserved at Putna, the influence of Jefimija's *epitaphios* on Moldavian embroiderers was possibly direct, and because there is similar evidence of emulation on a Moldavian *epitaphios* dated to 1427/8—the *epitaphios* of the Metropolitan Macarie—it can be argued that Jefimija's embroidery had found its way to Moldavia already by the reign of Alexander I (r. 1400–32).[11] Whether due to direct emulation of Jefimija's embroidery, or to reliance on shared models, similar flowerlike stars decorate the space surrounding the figures on both of these *epitaphioi* at Putna. Also, the poses of some of the angels suggest that Stephen III's embroiderers were indeed acquainted with the Serbian embroidery. Regardless of the ultimate source, the use of this field of stars around the figures in this iconography remained a consistent feature of Moldavian *epitaphioi*.

One more feature of the *epitaphios* of Stephen III at Putna to consider is the lengthy inscription around the border. Here, in a dedication entirely displacing the liturgical hymns more typical of Byzantine *epitaphioi*, we read instead about the gift and the patron himself:

☦ Изволенїемъ ѡ(т)ца и съ пѡспешенїемъ с(ъі)на и съвръшенїемъ с(ве)т(а)гѡ д(оу)ха Iѡ(анна) Стефанъ воевода, б(о)жїею м(и)л(ос)тїю г(ос)п(ода)ръ земли Мѡ(л)давскѡи, с(ъі)нъ Богдана воеводи, и съ бл(а)гочестивою г(ос)п(о)жди его Марїи и съ възлюблен(н)ими дѣти Алеѯандра и Бѡгдана-Влада сътвѡриша съи аеръ въ монастири ѿ П8тнои, идеже ест(ь) 8спен(ї)е прѣс(ве)тиѧ б(огороди)ци и пр(ис)нод(ѣ)ви Марїѫ, в л(ѣ)тѡ ҂ѕЦЧӤ.

---

10 See Gabriel Millet, *Broderies Religieuses de Style Byzantin* (Paris: Presses Universitaires de France, 1947), pp. 99–102.

11 Ibid., p. 100. The *epitaphios* of the Metropolitan Macarie, formerly at the Żółkiew/Zhovkva Castle before it was moved to a museum in Lwów, has been missing since the Second World War. See also Émile Turdeanu, "La broderie religieuse en Roumanie: Les épitaphes moldaves aux XVe et XVIe siècles," *Cercetări Literare* 4 (1940): 173–76, 203–4; and Pauline Johnstone, *The Byzantine Tradition in Church Embroidery* (Chicago: Argonaut, 1967), pp. 83, 121–22.

FIGURE 9.2 *Epitaphios* of Jefimija, ca. 1405, 67 × 43–3/4 in. (170 × 111 cm).
Putna Monastery, Romania
PHOTOGRAPH PROVIDED BY PUTNA MONASTERY

With the will of the Father, the help of the Son, and the action of the Holy Spirit, John Stephen voivode, through God's grace prince of the land of Moldavia, son of Bogdan voivode, and with his devout wife Maria and with their beloved sons, Alexander and Bogdan-Vlad, had this *aër* made in Putna Monastery, dedicated to the Dormition of the Mother of God and pure virgin Mary, in the year 6998 (1490).

This dedication, which is similar to the inscriptions on the other *epitaphioi* of Stephen III, would become the template for inscriptions on later Moldavian *epitaphioi*.

2   Wallachian *Epitaphioi*

Compared to the wealth of extant Moldavian embroideries, Wallachia offers a more modest sample size. There are, nonetheless, details worth contemplating on the examples that we do have. An *aër* embroidered with an image of the Deposition and an inscription that includes the hymn "Noble Joseph" was given by Neagoe Basarab (r. 1512–21) to the Cathedral of the Dormition of the Mother of God at Curtea de Argeș, which he founded in the early 16th century.[12] The composition on this embroidered veil conflates the iconography of the Deposition with the iconography of the Epitaphios Threnos. We find a similar composition on a slightly later icon of the Deposition.[13] At the left side of the icon is Milița Despina (ca. 1485–1554), widow of Neagoe Basarab and regent of Wallachia from 1521 to 1522 on the behalf of her son Teodosie of Wallachia, whom she is shown holding in this image. Mixing the Deposition with the Epitaphios Threnos, as does the *aër* from Argeș, the icon also links the two lamenting mothers, Milița and Mary. Both the icon and the *aër* are thus "hybrid" images, conflating different iconographies in a single new compositional type. In a version of the iconography that is more like Western depictions of the pieta than is typical of Byzantine or post-Byzantine images of either the Deposition or the Epitaphios Threnos, the Virgin Mary here seems both to stand and to hold the dead body of Christ on her lap. Although both the embroidered image and the painted panel are recognizably in the Byzantine tradition, something has seeped in from Western models.

3   The Eskenazi Museum *Aër/Epitaphios*

Aspects of style and technique used in the *aër* of Neagoe Basarab (r. 1512–21) recur in a textile at the Eskenazi Museum of Art at Indiana University Bloomington (Fig. 9.3).[14] It is with this example that I intend to test whether I can convincingly attribute an embroidered veil to Wallachian work and patronage. The Eskenazi Museum textile is relatively small compared to the *epitaphios* of Stephen III. Perhaps this is due to the extensive and expensive use of gold-wrapped thread. In this regard, and in its embroidery technique, including couching patterns and a dramatic color palette, the Bloomington veil is very similar to the *aër* of Neagoe Basarab, although that textile is also much larger (81–3/4 × 63–3/8 in., or 207.5 × 161 cm) than the one in Bloomington. The

---

12   See Nataliia Andreevna Mayasova, *Medieval Pictorial Embroidery: Byzantium, Balkans, Russia; Catalogue of the Exhibition, XVIIIth International Congress of Byzantinists, Moscow, August 8–15, 1991*, trans. B.L. Fonkich (Moscow: Kremlin State Museum Publishers, 1991), p. 62.

13   See "Icon—The Descent from the Cross," at the website of the National Museum of Art of Romania, www.mnar.arts.ro/en/?option=com_content&view=article&id=283&catid=1 15&Itemid=258, accessed May 12, 2019. The inscription reads: "Our Lady, please hold the soul of your servant Voivode John Teodosie and take it to your judgment, Lady Despina."

14   Eskenazi Museum inv. no. 72.2.6. On this object, see also Henry Schilb, "Singing, Shouting, Crying, and Saying: Embroidered *Aëres* and *Epitaphioi* and the Sounds of the Byzantine Liturgy," in *Resounding Images*, ed. Susan Boynton and Diane Reilly (Turnhout: Brepols, 2015), pp. 167–87.

FIGURE 9.3 *Aër* or *Epitaphios* from Wallachia, 1535, 26–4/5 × 21–1/4 in. (68.1 × 54.1 cm). Burton Y. Berry Collection, Eskenazi Museum of Art, Indiana University Bloomington 72.2.6
PHOTOGRAPH BY KEVIN MONTAGUE

unusually extensive use of gold thread on both of these textiles is like the well-known *epitaphios* in the Museum of Byzantine Culture, Thessaloniki, although I make no claim for a link, either direct or indirect, between the Wallachian embroideries and the Thessaloniki *epitaphios*.[15]

A full discussion of the taxonomy of liturgical veils is beyond the scope of this essay, and the question of just when the *epitaphios* of Holy Week became distinct from the *aër* used in the Great Entrance processional of the Orthodox liturgy remains unresolved. With some confidence, however, we can describe the veil in the Eskenazi Museum as either an *aër* or an *epitaphios*, and it is not out of the question that such a veil could have served both functions. The textile in the Eskenazi Museum is inscribed with a hymn followed by the year 1535. The hymn is a truncated version of what would become the standard

15 Museum of Byzantine Culture, Thessaloniki inv. no. Βυφ 57. See Evans, *Byzantium: Faith and Power*, pp. 312–13; and Roland Betancourt, "The Thessaloniki *Epitaphios*: Notes on Use and Context," *Greek, Roman, and Byzantine Studies* 55, no. 2 (2015): 489–535.

replacement for the Cherubikon on Holy Saturday after the middle of the 16th century.[16] It is possible that inscribed hymns identify such a textile as either an *aër* or an *epitaphios*, since the choice of hymn embroidered on the textile may be interpreted as associating it either with the Great Entrance or with Holy Week.[17] Let me suggest, however, that we cannot definitively identify the textile in the Eskenazi Museum as one or the other—*aër* or *epitaphios*—because, even though it is embroidered with a hymn now associated with Holy Week, the relatively modest dimensions may suggest use as an *aër*. However, the dimensions of such veils ought not to be taken as sufficient evidence for identifying their functions.[18] Just as the relatively large size of one veil would not necessarily disqualify it from use as an *aër*—because it is perceived as too big to cover the gifts on the altar—so the relatively small size of another veil ought not to be taken as sufficient evidence that it was used only as an *aër*, especially in the case of a veil embroidered with the hymn for Holy Saturday. Nor will the iconography help us identify the function of this textile as specifically an *aër* or an *epitaphios*. Although it is far from conclusive, another piece of evidence worth noting is the fact that, on the textile in the Eskenazi Museum, as on many post-Byzantine *epitaphioi* I have examined, there appear to be drops of wax around the border. It would be necessary to analyze the material to be certain that it is wax rather than something else, but wax would be consistent with the liturgical function of an *epitaphios*. Candles are placed on the *epitaphios* during Holy Week, while an *aër* is less likely to have such drops of wax because of its use in covering the paten and chalice together on the altar. Given all the evidence, I refrain from identifying the intended function of the Eskenazi Museum textile. While I am certain that it functioned either as an *aër* or as an *epitaphios*—if not as both, as the occasion demanded—I choose to suspend judgment regarding the precise intended function of this veil.

The border inscription on the Eskenazi Museum textile records a Church Slavonic version of the hymn known in Greek as "Σιγησάτω πᾶσα σάρξ βροτεία" (Let all mortal flesh be silent), followed by the year 7043 (1535).

†Да оумлъчить вьсѣка плъть земльна и да стонть съ страхомь / и трепетомь ничтоже въ себе земльних / да помишлѣет[ь и] се бо [цр]

---

16 See Taft, *The Great Entrance*, pp. 76–77.
17 *The Oxford Dictionary of Byzantium* (1991), s.v. "epitaphios."
18 See Robert F. Taft's doubt concerning Pauline Johnstone's assertion regarding a veil's size affecting its use. Taft, *The Great Entrance*, p. 218; Johnstone, *The Byzantine Tradition in Church Embroidery*, p. 26.

ь црствоуецим[ь] х҃с б҃ъ нашь приходит / зак[лань]бити и датисе на ищѫ вѣрним в лѣт ҂зм҃г.[19]

Let all mortal flesh be silent and stand in fear and trembling and consider nothing of this earth for the king of kings himself Christ our God comes to be slaughtered and given as food to the faithful. In the year 7043 (1535).

The inscription in the border offers no other clues—no names of persons or places—only the hymn and the year.

If this *epitaphios* is Wallachian, then the date puts it within the successive reigns of two possible patrons. As I have proposed elsewhere, Vlad VII Vintilă (r. 1532–35) could have been the patron.[20] We know that Vlad VII had at least one other embroidery made, a *podea* at the Koutloumousiou Monastery at Mount Athos.[21] The Eskenazi Museum textile and the *podea* at Koutloumousiou are quite different in their figural styles, however, so the *podea* is not necessarily good evidence for attributing the textile in Bloomington to Vlad VII Vintilă's patronage. Another possibility, proposed by Emanuela Cernea and Iuliana Damian, is Radu VII Paisie (r. 1535–45).[22] A somewhat enigmatic figure, Radu VII was the successor and perhaps half-brother of Vlad VII. He was also possibly married to one of Neagoe Basarab's daughters and thus associated with the monastery of Curtea de Argeș.[23] Although the identity of the donor is likely to remain unresolved, the ability to make a plausible attribution to Wallachian patronage is what matters here. The question of whether the donor was Vlad VII or Radu VII is less important than the fact that we can identify at least two possible patrons in Wallachia in the year embroidered on the veil in the Eskenazi Museum.

Two documents among the papers of the collector Burton Y. Berry mention the textile that he gave to the Eskenazi Museum. Unfortunately, these

---

19   I thank the anonymous reader of this essay for guidance in correcting several transcription errors.

20   See Henry D. Schilb, "Byzantine Identity and Its Patrons: Embroidered *Aëres* and *Epitaphioi* of the Palaiologan and Post-Byzantine Periods" (PhD diss., Indiana University, 2009), pp. 141–42.

21   See Maria Theocharis, "Embroidery," in Θησαυροί τοῦ Ἁγίου Ὄρους [Treasures of the Holy Mountain] (Thessaloniki: Hellenic Ministry of Culture and the Museum of Byzantine Culture, 1997), p. 487.

22   I thank Emanuela Cernea and Iuliana Damian for bringing to my attention their alternative attribution.

23   Emanuela Cernea and Iuliana Damian, "La broderie de tradition byzantine en Roumanie (XIVe–XVIIe siècle)," in *Broderies de tradition byzantine en Roumanie du XVe au XVIIe siècle: Autour de l'Étendard d'Étienne le Grand* (Paris: In Fine, 2019), p. 21, n. 7.

documents take us back only to 1968, when Berry loaned the textile to Dumbarton Oaks.[24] Among Berry's papers at the Lilly Library at Indiana University Bloomington is a receipt dated November 14, 1968, and signed by John S. Thacher, director of Dumbarton Oaks at the time. The other document is a letter to Dumbarton Oaks dated November 11, 1968, discussing the loan of this textile and other objects for study. The textile was sent to Bloomington in 1972. Documents in the files of the Eskenazi Museum of Art do not add significant information other than the identity of the third party in whose name the donation to the museum was actually made. The dimensions recorded in the museum's files, 81.3 × 66 cm (32 × 26 in.), included a backing cloth that has since been removed by conservators. Berry's letter to Dumbarton Oaks recorded only the dimensions of the textile itself. The entry from Berry's papers reads, "A post-Byzantine embroidered church banner, roughly 65 by 55 cm, showing the placing of Christ in the Tomb, the picture surrounded by a border of an inscription in Greek letters. Cost to me $2500. (The embroidery is in exceptionally fine condition but on unpacking it needs to be flattened out before being rolled.)"[25] Judging by the little that Berry had to say about it in his own records, we can conclude that he had no idea what this textile actually was. He even mistook the Cyrillic letters in the inscription for Greek. With so little help from the collector, all that we can learn about the origin of the embroidered veil in Bloomington must be deduced from the object itself, the iconography, the inscription, and any other piece of evidence we can unravel.

We may start with the hymn embroidered in the border of the Eskenazi Museum textile. Although this hymn would become the standard hymn for Holy Saturday after the middle of the 16th century, that does not help us establish a *terminus post quem* because there are examples of this hymn on large embroidered veils that we may plausibly identify as *epitaphioi* dated before the middle of the 16th century.[26] This hymn also appears on a 14th-century *epitaphios* from Cozia Monastery, now in the National Museum of Art of Romania in Bucharest (MNAR 181/15.826) (Fig. 9.4).[27]

---

24   Burton Yost Berry Papers, Lilly Library, Indiana University Bloomington.
25   Ibid.
26   See Demetrios I. Pallas, "Der *Epitaphios*," in *Reallexikon zur byzantinischen Kunst*, vol. 5 (Stuttgart: Anton Hiersemann, 1995), p. 800.
27   For a transliteration and French translation of the inscription on the Cozia epitaphios, see Millet, *Broderies Religieuses*, pp. 104–5. See also Nikodim Pavlovich Kondakov, *Pamiatniki christianskago iskusstva na Athonje* (St. Petersburg: Izdanie Imperatorskoi Akademii Nauk, 1902), pp. 264–65; and Johnstone, *The Byzantine Tradition in Church Embroidery*, p. 122.

FIGURE 9.4 *Epitaphios* from the Cozia Monastery, 1396, 69–3/4 × 56–3/4 in. (177 × 144 cm). National Museum of Art of Romania, Bucharest
PHOTOGRAPH PROVIDED BY NATIONAL MUSEUM OF ART OF ROMANIA

†Да оумлъчитъ всѣка плть земнаа и да стоить страхом и трепетом се бо црь царствоуж/щимь и господь господствоуѧщимъ х҃с б҃ъ нашъ приходит заклатисѧ и даноу быти въ / пищѫ вѣрнымь прѣдварѣжт его лици ангельсти съ вьсѣми началы и власти многоочитаа хероу/вими и 8-крилата серафими лица накрываѧща и выпиѧща пѣснь ст ст ст в лѣт ҂ѕ҃ц҃д҃.

Let all mortal flesh be silent and stand in fear and trembling, for the King of kings and Lord of lords Christ our God comes to be slaughtered and given as food to the faithful. Before Him go the choirs of angels with all the principalities and powers, the cherubim with many eyes, and the six-winged seraphim covering their faces and crying the hymn Holy Holy Holy. In the year 6904 (1396).

The year at the end of this inscription is disputed because of different interpretations of the final numeral. Nicolae Iorga and Nikodim Kondakov read the date as 6904 (1396).[28] Gabriel Millet and Émile Turdeanu saw 6930 (1421/2).[29] As Pauline Johnstone pointed out, the confusion arises from the difficulty of discerning just what the final character is, a difficulty that Millet had also noted but dismissed as resolved in favor of 6930.[30] The date at the end of the inscription at the lower left corner of the border is either ҂ѕцл (6930) or ҂ѕцд (6904). Millet simply stated that one can read that the last figure is л rather than д despite the wear. Johnstone, while acknowledging that wear on the final character had led some scholars to read 6930 (1422), believed the year to be 6904 (1396). On close inspection, the year 6904 is easily confirmed, and so I agree with Iorga, Kondakov, and Johnstone that the date is 1396.

On the Eskenazi Museum textile (Fig. 9.3), the hymn in the border is truncated, possibly because of the limited space on this relatively small veil. The version embroidered here includes the phrase "considering nothing of this earth," which was omitted from the Cozia *epitaphios*, but the textile in Bloomington omits the phrase "Lord of lords." Otherwise, the variant of the hymn on the Eskenazi Museum textile is similar in its wording to the version on the Cozia *epitaphios*, while both inscriptions differ slightly from other Church Slavonic texts of the hymn, including embroidered examples. The Church Slavonic wording on the Cozia *epitaphios* and the Bloomington textile differs from Russian examples.[31] The Cozia *epitaphios* and the Bloomington textile both record versions of the same recension. The word "земльна" on the Bloomington textile is like the word "земнаа" in the same position on the Cozia *epitaphios*, using Church Slavonic words for "earthly" or "of the earth" respectively to translate the Greek word "βροτεία." On Russian embroideries, the usual word at this point is человѣча ("human" or "mortal"). Also compare the Bloomington textile's "на <п>ищѫ" to the word for "food" in this position on the Cozia *epitaphios*, "пищѫ." A different word again (снѣдь) appears in this place in Russian versions of this hymn.[32]

A dramatic version of the Epitaphios Threnos iconography, the composition of the central image of the veil in the Eskenazi Museum is another clue that might help us to determine just where this object was embroidered. In most

---

28   Nicolae Iorga and Gheorghe Balş, *Histoire de l'art roumain ancien* (Paris: E. de Boccard, 1922), p. 36; and Kondakov, *Pamiatniki christianskago iskusstva na Athonje*, p. 264.

29   Millet, *Broderies Religieuses*, p. 104; and Turdeanu, "La broderie religieuse en Roumanie," p. 171. The date 1421/22 is also accepted by Warren Woodfin, "Liturgical Textiles," in *Byzantium: Faith and Power (1261–1557)*, p. 601, n. 19.

30   Johnstone, *The Byzantine Tradition in Church Embroidery*, p. 122; and Millet, *Broderies Religieuses*, p. 104.

31   See Maria Engström, *Cheruvimskie pesnopenija v russkoj liturgičeskoj tradicii* [The Cherubika in the Russian liturgical tradition] (Stockholm: Almqvist och Wiksell International, 2004), p. 151.

32   Ibid., pp. 128–29, 151.

FIGURE 9.5 *Epitaphios Threnos*, 15th–16th century, 43–3/4 × 26–1/2 in. (111 × 67.5) cm.
National Museum of Art of Romania, Bucharest
PHOTOGRAPH PROVIDED BY NATIONAL MUSEUM OF ART OF ROMANIA

Moldavian *epitaphioi*—or, indeed, in most embroidered versions of the iconography, regardless of origin—the Epitaphios Threnos iconography presents an image of the dead Christ to which have been added the Virgin, John, and certain other figures. On the embroidered textile in Bloomington, however, the iconography is derived from the type of treatment of the Epitaphios Threnos that we are used to seeing in wall paintings or on painted icons, a narrative image with multiple figures acting within a landscape. The iconography on the Bloomington textile is very similar to the version in a wall painting of this iconography at the 14th-century Church of St. Nicholas at Curtea de Argeș in Wallachia.[33] It is closer still to an icon of the late 15th or early 16th century from Curtea de Argeș and attributed to a Wallachian workshop (Fig. 9.5).[34]

4 Conclusion

No resemblance would be sufficient to claim that one of the works discussed here copied the other, or even to attribute the two works to the same place—but the similarity is strong enough to suggest that the creators of both images

---

33 See Adela Văetiși, *Arta de tradiție bizantină în România* (Bucharest: NOI Media Print, 2008), p. 54.
34 Ibid., pp. 84–85.

FIGURE 9.6   *Epitaphios* of Șerban Cantacuzino, 1681, 74 × 51–1/4 in. (188 × 130 cm).
National Museum of Art of Romania, Bucharest
PHOTOGRAPH PROVIDED BY NATIONAL MUSEUM OF ART OF ROMANIA

were probably working from the same source material. In fact, so precise is the resemblance between the Eskenazi Museum textile and the icon from Curtea de Argeș that I am persuaded that the provenance of the icon corroborates my attribution of the embroidery to Wallachia. The poses of the *myrrophoroi* are particularly striking in this comparison. One figure in each work, icon and *epitaphios*, holds her right hand to her face and her left hand in the air. The figure next to her raises both arms and her face upward. The similarities continue in the poses of the Virgin Mary and John.

We find some of the same compositional features on an *epitaphios* associated with Șerban Cantacuzino (r. 1678–88) (Fig. 9.6).[35] Embroidered in 1679/80, this *epitaphios* is an unusual or even a unique example of the Deposition and the Epitaphios Threnos embroidered side by side, and the two scenes resemble the images on the *aër* of Neagoe Basarab and the textile in Bloomington. On the right is a version of the Epitaphios Threnos that deploys the figures in much the same was as we find on the icon from Curtea de Argeș and on the

---

35   See Victoria Gheorghiță, and Marina Vazaca, eds., *Romanian Medieval Art* (Bucharest: National Museum of Art of Romania, 2002), p. 88.

textile in the Eskenazi Museum. On the left is a conflation of the Deposition and the Epitaphios Threnos of the type that we recognize from the *aër* of Neagoe Basarab.

My goal in this essay has been admittedly modest: to take a small step toward a more detailed understanding of the art of the regions of Wallachia and Moldavia in the period after the fall of Constantinople. I have sought to demonstrate that it is possible to differentiate between some of the 14th and 15th-century embroideries of these two Romanian principalities, and to demonstrate that we can identify and enumerate distinctive characteristics of the respective Wallachian and Moldavian transformations of the Byzantine tradition in church embroidery.

Bibliography

Primary Sources

Germanos. "Historia ecclesiastica, et mystica contemplatio." In *Patrologiae cursus completus: Series graeca*, ed. J.-P. Migne, 98:429C–D. Paris: 1857–66.

Irenaeus. "Adversus Hæreses" In *Patrologiae cursus completus: Series graeca*, ed. J.-P. Migne, 7:885–86. Paris: 1857–66.

Secondary Sources

Berry, Burton Y. Papers. Lilly Library, Indiana University Bloomington.

Betancourt, Roland. "The Thessaloniki *Epitaphios*: Notes on Use and Context." *Greek, Roman, and Byzantine Studies* 55, no. 2 (2015): 489–535.

Cernea, Emanuela, and Iuliana Damian. "La broderie de tradition byzantine en Roumanie (XIVe–XVIIe siècle)." In *Broderies de tradition byzanien en Roumanie du XVe au XVIIe siècle: Autour de l'Étendard d'Étienne le Grand*, 20–25. Paris: In Fine, 2019.

Engström, Maria. *Cheruvimskie pesnopenija v russkoj liturgičeskoj tradicii* [The Cherubika in the Russian liturgical tradition]. Stockholm: Almqvist och Wiksell International, 2004.

Evans, Helen C., ed. *Byzantium: Faith and Power (1261–1557)*. New Haven: Yale University Press, 200.

Fenwick, John R.K. *The Anaphoras of St. Basil and St. James: An Investigation into Their Common Origin*. Rome: Pontificium Institutum Orientale, 1992.

Galavaris, George. *The Illustrations of the Prefaces in Byzantine Gospels*. Vienna: Verlag der Österreichischen Akademie der Wissenschaften, 1979.

Gheorghiță, Victoria, and Marina Vazaca, eds. *Romanian Medieval Art*. Bucharest: National Museum of Art of Romania, 2002.

Iorga, Nicolae, and Gheorghe Balş. *Histoire de l'art roumain ancien*. Paris: E. de Boccard, 1922.
Johnstone, Pauline. *The Byzantine Tradition in Church Embroidery*. Chicago: Argonaut, 1967.
Kazhdan, Alexander P., ed. *The Oxford Dictionary of Byzantium*. 3 vols. New York: Oxford University Press, 1991.
Kondakov, Nikodim Pavlovich. *Pamiatniki christianskago iskusstva na Athonje*. St. Petersburg: Izdanie Imperatorskoi Akademii Nauk, 1902.
Kucharek, Casimir A. *The Byzantine-Slav Liturgy of St. John Chrysostom: Its Origin and Evolution*. Allendale, NJ: Alleluia Press, 1971.
Mayasova, Nataliia Andreevna. *Medieval Pictorial Embroidery: Byzantium, Balkans, Russia; Catalogue of the exhibition, XVIIIth International Congress of Byzantinists, Moscow, August 8–15, 1991*, trans. B.L. Fonkich. Moscow: Kremlin State Museum Publishers, 1991.
Millet, Gabriel. *Broderies Religieuses de Style Byzantin*. Paris: Ernest Leroux 1939; Presses Universitaires de France, 1947.
National Museum of Art of Romania. "Icon—The Descent from the Cross." At http://www.mnar.arts.ro/en/?option=com_content&view=article&id=283&catid=115&Itemid=258, accessed May 12, 2019.
Pallas, Demetrios I. "Der *Epitaphios*." In *Reallexikon zur byzantinischen Kunst*, vol. 5, 789–806. Stuttgart: Anton Hiersemann, 1995.
Schilb, Henry. "Byzantine Identity and Its Patrons: Embroidered *Aëres* and *Epitaphioi* of the Palaiologan and Post-Byzantine Periods." PhD diss., Indiana University, 2009.
Schilb, Henry. "Singing, Shouting, Crying, and Saying: Embroidered *Aëres* and *Epitaphioi* and the Sounds of the Byzantine Liturgy." In *Resounding Images*, ed. Susan Boynton and Diane Reilly, 167–87. Turnhout: Brepols, 2015.
Sullivan, Alice Isabella. "Byzantine Artistic Traditions in Moldavian Church Embroideries." In *L'évolution de la broderie de tradition byzantine dans la Méditerranée et le monde slave (1200–1800)*, ed. Elena Papastavrou and Marielle Martiniani-Reber. Paris: Presses d'Inalco, forthcoming.
Taft, Robert F. *The Great Entrance: A History of the Transfer of Gifts and Other Preanaphoral Rites of the Liturgy of St. John Chrysostom*. Rome: Pontificum Institutum Studiorum Orientalium, 1975.
Theocharis, Maria. "Embroidery." In Θησαυροί τοῦ Ἁγίου Ὄρους [Treasures of the Holy Mountain], 441–89. Thessaloniki: Hellenic Ministry of Culture and the Museum of Byzantine Culture, 1997.
Turdeanu, Émile. "La broderie religieuse en Roumanie: Les épitaphes moldaves aux XVᵉ et XVIᵉ siècles." *Cercetări Literare* 4 (1940): 164–214.
Văetişi, Adela. *Arta de tradiţie bizantină în România*. Bucharest: NOI Media Print, 2008.
Woodfin, Warren. "Liturgical Textiles." In *Byzantium: Faith and Power (1261–1557)*, ed. Helen C. Evans, 295–98. New Haven: Yale University Press, 2004.

CHAPTER 10

Rethinking the Veglia Altar Frontal from the Victoria and Albert Museum and Its Patron

Danijel Ciković and Iva Jazbec Tomaić

1   Around 1358: (Re)Contextualizing the Veglia Altar Frontal

Among the many valuable textiles preserved at the Clothworkers' Centre for the Study and Conservation of Textiles and Fashion of the Victoria and Albert Museum is the Veglia Altar Frontal.

This object is the most valuable preserved Gothic altar frontal of Venetian provenance, originally made for the high altar of the Cathedral of the Assumption of the Blessed Virgin Mary in the town of Krk (on the island of Krk, in present-day Croatia). This is attested by a series of the Cathedral's inventory lists that mention the altar frontal, starting with the earliest, which dates to 1500. Archbishop Giovanni Robobello of Zadar recorded the following on that occasion as "Uno bello palio da Altaro grando in seta cremesina cum octo figure longe uno brazzo cum diversi Sancti lavorati cum lago de oro fino non roto" (One beautiful altar frontal in crimson silk for the high altar, with eight figures one arm long with various saints made in needlework with gold, fine, not damaged).[1] The altar frontal (Figs. 10.1 and 10.2) is made from a red tabby silk base embroidered with silver-gilt, silver, and polychrome silk threads.[2] Under a series of Gothic arcades, the central field shows the Coronation of the Virgin and a group of angels, while in the other niches, from left to right, appear the patron saint of the town and diocese, St. Quirinus of Sisak, St. Peter,

---

1   Archbishop Giovanni Robobello quoted in Dragutin Kniewald, "*Antependij* u Dobrinju na otoku Krku," *Godišnjak Sveučilišta Kraljevine Jugoslavije u Zagrebu* (1929/30–1932/33): 81; and Mato Polonijo, "Najstariji sačuvani inventar stolne crkve u Krku," *Croatia sacra* 13/14 (1937): 117.

2   On the red silk tabby ground, the composition is mainly made of silver-gilt and silver threads in underside couching technique (*punto affondato*), the same technique used on *opus anglicanum* examples. This is the technique by which the metal threads are drawn using the threads of other material through the ground fabric (silk and linen layer) and fixed on the back. The couching threads are not visible on the surface of the ground fabric. Silk threads are applied using satin stitch (*punto raso*) and split stitch (*punto spaccato*). The same underside couching technique and stitches were also used on the altar frontals from Zadar and Dobrinj.

RETHINKING THE VEGLIA ALTAR FRONTAL AND ITS PATRON   249

FIGURE 10.1   The Veglia Altar Frontal, ca. 1358, Victoria and Albert Museum, London, 2016
PHOTOGRAPH BY DANIJEL CIKOVIĆ, BY PERMISSION OF VICTORIA AND
ALBERT MUSEUM

FIGURE 10.2   The Veglia Altar Frontal at *The First Istrian Regional Exhibition*, 1910,
Koper, Civici Musei di Storia ed Arte di Trieste, inv. F77194
PHOTOGRAPH PROVIDED BY CIVICI MUSEI DI STORIA ED ARTE DI TRIESTE

St. John the Evangelist, St. John the Baptist, St. Paul, and St. Gaudentius, patron of the nearby Osor diocese. At the foot of the throne, to the right, the smaller figure of a donor dressed in pontifical vestments kneels with hands clasped in prayer (Fig. 10.3).

In the only monographic publication devoted to this exceptional artwork, from 1965, Donald King writes, "But in reality, by virtue of its superb design and splendid harmony of color, it still dominates the spectator with the authority of a great work of art."[3] Writing quite recently on the Zadar altar frontal now in Budapest, Silvija Banić concludes that the altar frontal from Krk is the most impressive example of 14th century Gothic Venetian embroidery preserved to date, taking into account not only its monumental dimensions, but also the number of embroidered figures and ornaments, and—most important—the skill with which they are executed.[4]

According to King, the altar frontal was made around 1330 after a preparatory drawing made by Paolo Veneziano, a theory that is still generally accepted.[5] It is necessary, however, to recall the opinion of Michelangelo Muraro, who assumes that the artwork was created between 1349 and 1358.[6] It seems that the compositional elements and figurative details that would place this artwork at the late stage of master Paolo's oeuvre are more convincing and more numerous, with some of them already noticed by King himself.[7] It is therefore advisable to stress some of the parallels with a few of Paolo's well-known paintings. In the figure's posture, and especially the way in which the vestment drapes collects, as well as the details of the feet, St. John the Evangelist on the altar frontal is very similar to the figure of St. Mark the Evangelist on the polyptych from Piran (1355), while the details of the head significantly correspond to the

---

3 Donald King, "A Venetian Embroidered Altar Frontal," *Victoria and Albert Museum Bulletin* 1, no. 4 (1965): 16.
4 Silvija Banić, "Zadarski gotički vezeni antependij u Budimpešti," *Ars Adriatica* 4 (2014): 90.
5 King, "A Venetian Embroidered Altar Frontal," pp. 22–24. On the altar frontal at the Victoria and Albert Museum and the most significant literature on the subject, see Banić, "Zadarski," p. 90.
6 Michelangelo Muraro, *Paolo da Venezia* (Milan: Istituto Editoriale Italiano, 1969), pp. 68, 120.
7 On Paolo Veneziano and accompanying literature, see Cristina Guarnieri, "Il passaggio tra due generazioni: Dal Maestro dell'Incoronazione a Paolo Veneziano," in *Il secolo di Giotto nel Veneto*, ed. Giovanna Valenzano and Federica Toniolo (Venice: Istituto Veneto di Scienze, Lettere ed Arti, 2007), pp. 153–201; and Cristina Guarnieri, "Per la restituzione di due croci perdute di Paolo Veneziano: Il leone marciano del Museo Correr e i dolenti della Galleria Sabauda," in *Medioevo adriatico: Circolazione di modelli, opere, maestri*, ed. Federica Toniolo and Giovanna Valenzano (Rome: Viella, 2010), pp. 133–58.

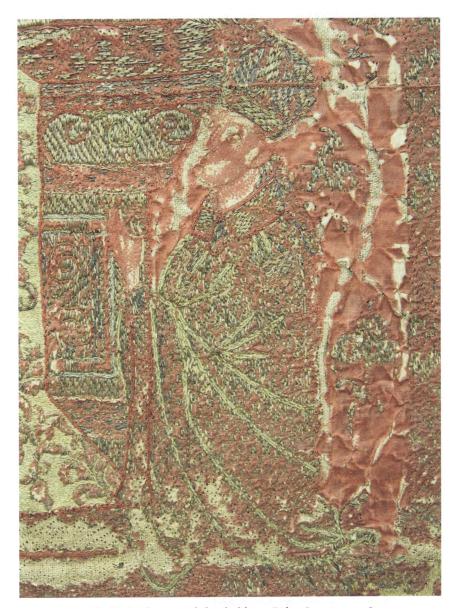

FIGURE 10.3　The Veglia Altar Frontal, detail of donor, Bishop Ivan II, ca. 1358, Victoria and Albert Museum, London, 2016
PHOTOGRAPH BY IVA JAZBEC TOMAIĆ, BY PERMISSION OF VICTORIA AND ALBERT MUSEUM

representation of St. Mark on the *Pala feriale* (1343–45).[8] The figure of St. Paul as a whole, and in details such as facial physiognomy, the diagonally placed index finger over the sword handle, the slight stepping out with the left foot, and the tunic that covers the feet almost to the toes, is analogous to the details and depictions of the same saint on Paolo's polyptychs in San Severino Marche (1358) and Museo Correr (ca. 1350).[9] The very specific gesture of St. Peter's right hand (Fig. 10.4) opened toward the viewer appears in several of Paolo's figures.

For example, it appears in the image of Christ in the Gethsemane Garden, as well as in the figures of saints in the Last Supper and Noli Me Tangere scenes on the famous polyptych of St. Clare.[10] The image of St. Quirinus is analogous to a series of depictions of bishops, like that of St. Hermolaus on the polyptych in Rab (ca. 1350) and St. Augustine on the polyptych in Museo Correr, while the detail of the right hand in blessing is identical to that of St. Nicholas on the *Pala feriale* and on the polyptych from Piran.[11] St. Gaudentius is manifestly reminiscent of St. Blaise, also from the Piran polyptych. One of the artistically most impressive segments is the image of the choir of angels (Fig. 10.5), the modeling of which perhaps most obviously betrays the influence of Byzantine artistic forms.

All of the above mentioned parallels indicate that Muraro's dating proposal is most likely correct.[12] Cristina Guarnieri probably most accurately describes

---

8   On the polyptych from Piran, see Luisa Morozzi, "28. Madonna in trono con Bambino e due angeli; Maria Maddalena, san Nicola di Bari, san Marco, san Giovanni Battista; san Giovanni evangelista, san Biagio, sant'Antonio abate, santa Caterina d'Alessandria," in *Il Trecento adriatico: Paolo Veneziano e la pittura tra Oriente e Occidente*, ed. Francesca Flores d'Arcais and Giovanni Gentili (Milan: Silvana Editoriale, 2002), pp. 158–61. On the *Pala feriale*, see Filippo Pedrocco, *Paolo Veneziano* (Milan: Alberto Maioli Editore, Società Veneta Editrice, 2003), pp. 170–73.

9   On the polyptych in San Severino Marche, see Alessandro Marchi, "31. Incoronazione della Vergine e santi Caterina d'Alessandria, Michele Arcangelo, Giovanni il Battista, Pietro, Severino Vescovo, Venanzio Martire, Pietro Martire, Paolo, Giovanni Evangelista, Domenico, Orsola, Tommaso d'Acquino, Tommaso Apostolo, Bartolomeo," in *Il Trecento adriatico*, pp. 166–67. On the polyptych at Museo Correr, see Francesca Flores d'Arcais, "32. Sant'Agostino, san Pietro, san Giovanni Battista; san Giovanni evangelista, san Paolo, san Giorgio," in *Il Trecento adriatico*, pp. 168–69.

10 On the polyptych of St. Clare, see Filippo Pedrocco, *Paolo Veneziano*, pp. 150–53.

11 On the polyptych in Rab, see Miljenko Domijan, "12. Raspeće i šest svetaca," in *Stoljeće gotike na Jadranu: Slikarstvo u ozračju Paola Veneziana*, ed. Biserka Rauter Plančić, exh. cat. (Zagreb: Galerija Klovićevi dvori, 2004), pp. 82–85.

12 On the altar frontal recently, see: Valentina Baradel, "Diramazioni adriatiche di botteghe veneziane. L'isola di Veglia (Krk), da Paolo Veneziano a Jacobello del Fiore," in *La Serenissima via mare*, ed. V. Baradel and C. Guarnieri (Padova: Padova University Press, 2019), pp. 70–72.

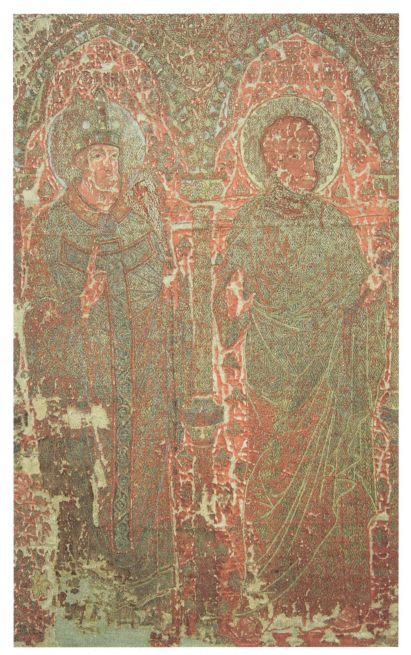

FIGURE 10.4   The Veglia Altar Frontal, detail of St. Quirinus and St. Peter, ca. 1358, Victoria and Albert Museum, London, 2016
PHOTOGRAPH BY IVA JAZBEC TOMAIĆ, BY PERMISSION OF VICTORIA AND ALBERT MUSEUM

FIGURE 10.5 The Veglia Altar Frontal, detail of the choir of angels, ca. 1358, Victoria and Albert Museum, London
PHOTOGRAPH BY DANIJEL CIKOVIĆ, BY PERMISSION OF VICTORIA AND ALBERT MUSEUM

this masterpiece of Venetian embroidery designed by the most important 14th-century Venetian artist as "L'opera ha lo stile, il tono e l'impostazione aulica delle opere di Paolo Veneziano" (The artwork shares the style, tone, and courtly setting of Paolo Veneziano's works).[13]

Redating the altar frontal to the sixth decade of the 14th century necessarily brings the question of the donor into focus. King's hypothesis that the donor of the altar frontal was a bishop named John (Ivan) seems acceptable, even very likely.[14] In the context of the preparatory drawing attributed to master Paolo, however, identification of the donor with Bishop Bonjohannes is less likely. The Benedictine Bonjohannes spent only one year in the bishop's seat at Krk Cathedral, in 1312, and not in 1326, as King states.[15] In that case, the preparatory drawing for the Krk altar frontal would be counted among Paolo's earliest

---

13   Cristina Guarnieri, *Lorenzo Veneziano* (Milan: Silvana Editoriale, 2006), p. 66.
14   King, "A Venetian Embroidered Altar Frontal," pp. 23–24.
15   On Bishop Bonjohannes, see Mihovil Bolonić and Ivan Žic-Rokov, *Otok Krk kroz vjekove* (Zagreb: Kršćanska sadašnjost, 1977), p. 108.

works, made only two years after the commission of *Ancona di San Donato* by the administrator of Murano Donato Memo.[16] Taking into account the seemingly more convincing assumption of a later dating for the altar frontal, and that the donor was a bishop by the name of John, it is possible to suggest another patron. The only other bishop with this name in Krk in the 14th century was first recorded in 1358, i.e., precisely the year in which the great Venetian master was last mentioned as still living. The bishop in question is Ivan II, whose episcopate lasted until 1389.[17] Bishop Ivan II is the best-documented bishop in 14th-century Krk and was recorded in four documents. In a letter written on Easter 1377, Pope Gregory XI invited him to consecrate the newly appointed Archbishop of Zadar, Petar de Matafaris. On April 22 of the same year, Duke of Krk Nikola III listed Bishop Ivan II as the executor of his will. On June 10, 1381, he consecrated the altar of St. John the Evangelist in the parish church in Dobrinj, and in 1387 he signed a document that he sent to the priests in Omišalj citadel. Based on the inscription on the Bishop's tombstone, we also learn that Ivan II was originally from the town of Krk.[18] Finally, the fact that the bishop's tombstone is located in a privileged position in the presbytery in front of the cathedral's high altar, as well as that the bishop was the executor of Duke Nikola III's will, indicates a real possibility that Bishop Ivan II was a member of Krk's noble family, from 1430 onward known as the Frankopans.[19] This reading allows for a much more convincing explanation of the bishop's sophisticated taste, as well as his financing of the certainly monumental commission of the luxurious altar frontal, whose purchase could have only been afforded by rare prelates. Everything therefore indicates that, at the beginning of his episcopate, Krk Bishop Ivan II commissioned the most famous Venetian artist of the time to design a luxurious altar frontal for the high altar of his cathedral, where he would be buried several decades later.

On the basis of scarce historical data around the middle of the 14th century, it is not possible to reconstruct exactly the circumstances of the commission of the altar frontal for the Krk Cathedral.[20] Additionally, the circumstances

---

16   See Cristina Guarnieri, "Il monumento funebre di Francesco Dandolo nella sala del capitolo ai Frari," in *Santa Maria Gloriosa dei Frari: Immagini di devozione, spazi della fede*, ed. Carlo Corsato and Deborah Howard (Padua: Centro Studi Antoniani, 2015), pp. 159–60.

17   See Bolonić and Žic-Rokov, *Otok Krk kroz vjekove*, p. 108; and Ivan Žic-Rokov, "Kompleks katedrala: Sv. Kvirin u Krku," *Rad JAZU* 360 (1971): 134.

18   Ibid.

19   On the tombstone of Bishop Ivan II, see Marijan Bradanović, *Grad Krk u srednjem vijeku* (Split: Muzej hrvatskih arheoloških spomenika, 2016), p. 29.

20   On the historical circumstances on the island of Krk around the middle of the century, see Ozren Kosanović, "Družine i potknežini knezova Krčkih na Krku (od 1260. do 1480.)," *Povijesni prilozi* 50 (2016): 253.

surrounding the commission of a similar frontal from the parish church in Dobrinj, on the same island, are equally unclear. The donor of the Dobrinj altar frontal was certainly inspired by the bishop's more luxurious donation, made earlier for the high altar of the cathedral. The commissions of the two artworks, in particular the one from Krk, should be considered in the context of Paolo's productive workshop after its projects for the Dandolo family, which were probably reflected on the eastern coast of the Adriatic through commissions such as those for Piran, Rab, and Dubrovnik.[21] The polyptych in Rab is believed to be the donation of Bishop Juraj II (Georg II) (Rab?, 1270/1–Rab?, before June 7, 1363), a member of the esteemed Rab family of Hermolaus educated at the University of Padua.[22] It is not difficult to imagine that, during the sixth decade of the 14th century, these important local church protagonists from neighboring dioceses—Bishop Ivan II and Juraj II—were personal acquaintances. There is no doubt that the four preserved altar frontals of this type (now in Budapest, Dobrinj, London, and Zadar) represent only modest fragments of the liturgical furnishing that equipped churches on the eastern Adriatic coast in the late Middle Ages. It is very plausible, therefore, that the case of "One crimson *cendal* altar cloth with its gilded figures" or "One red *cendal* cloth with figures" recorded by apostolic visitor Agostino Valier in Rab Cathedral in 1579, also implied similar luxurious altar frontals.[23]

---

21   On the Dubrovnik crucifix, see Igor Fisković, "23–25. Raspeće," in *Stoljeće gotike na Jadranu*, pp. 106–9. For an overview of recent information on Doge Andrea Dandolo and a bibliography of older literature, see Desi Marangon, "Il fascino delle forme greche a Venezia: Andrea Dandolo, l'arte e l'epigrafia," *Hortus Artium Medievalium* 22 (2016): 157–64.

22   On Bishop Juraj II Hermolaus, see Pejo Ćošković, "Hermolais, Juraj de (Ermolai, Ermolais; Georgio)," 2002, "Hrvatski biografski leksikon," available at http://hbl.lzmk.hr/clanak.aspx?id=7587, accessed January 14, 2019. On the polyptych in Rab and the most relevant older literature, see Donal Cooper, "Gothic Art and the Friars in Late Medieval Croatia, 1213–1460," in *Croatia: Aspects of Art, Architecture and Cultural Heritage*, ed. Jadranka Beresford-Peirse (London: Frances Lincoln, 2009), 84.

23   "Uno panno di altare di cendal cremesino con sue figure doratte ... Uno panno di cendalo rosso con figure." Vatican City, Archivio Segreto Vaticano, Congr. vescovi e regolari, Visita ap., 80 (d. Arbensis), fol. 21v–22r. See Tea Perinčić, "Rapska biskupija u vizitaciji Agustina Valiera 1579. godine" (MA thesis, University of Zagreb, 2004), p. 105; and Silvija Banić, "Prilog poznavanju sakralnih inventara otoka Raba: Najvrjedniji povijesni tekstili sačuvani na misnom ruhu i drugim dijelovima liturgijske opreme," in *Rapski zbornik II*, ed. (Rab: Ogranak Matice Hrvatske, 2012), p. 454.

The Italian term *cendal, cendale, cendalo, zendado,* or *zendale* stands for "light silk fabric." It is recorded in the late medieval documents from Tre Venezie as *cendatum* (829) and *cendalo* (867), in the Venetian sources in the form "de pannis et cendatis" (1219), and in sources from Aquileia as "duo cendalia deaurata" (1359). The term *zendado* occurs for the first time in a book of accounts from Pistoia dated 1245. See Michele A. Cortelazzo, Adriana da Rin, and Paola Frattaroli, "Glossario," in *Tessuti nel Veneto: Venezia e la Terraferma*, ed.

Looking at the wider historical context more closely, one can easily see the complex political situation that preceded the signing of the crucial Treaty of Zadar in 1358. In 1348, an eight-year armistice was signed between the Hungarian-Croatian King Louis I and the Venetian Republic, as a result of Louis's defeat before Zadar two years earlier. However, after abandoning the idea of joining the Kingdom of Naples and the Hungarian-Croatian Kingdom, in 1350 the king started preparing for a final confrontation with Venice, which indeed occurred immediately after the armistice's expiration in 1356.[24] The Venetian Republic could not resist Louis, and so on February 18, 1358, a peace treaty was signed in the sacristy of the monastery of St. Francis in Zadar. With the Treaty of Zadar, Venice renounced the entirety of Dalmatia, all the way to Durrës, while in practical terms Dubrovnik was already fully independent as a commune.[25]

Given the complex and dynamic political situation, it is almost impossible to make any reliable claims without new archival data, which would primarily give a more accurate dating for a series of artworks. However, the impression is that during the years-long tense political situation and perhaps even during intense military conflicts, patrons from the eastern Adriatic town-communes continued to acquire artworks in Venice. The eastern Adriatic coast, or rather the western Balkans, was for centuries a crossroad, a region of overlapping political, ecclesiastical, and cultural spheres, and thus the practice of commissioning artworks beyond the border would not have been exceptional in the 14th century.[26] However, this established practice of commissioning luxury

---

Giuliana Ericani and Paola Frattaroli (Verona: Banca Popolare di Verona, 1993), p. 32. For a comprehensive note on the term *cendà* or *cendal*, see Giuseppe Boerio, *Dizionario del dialetto veneziano* (Venice: Giovanni Cecchini, 1867), p. 158.

24 See Tomislav Raukar, "Arpadovići i Anžuvinci na hrvatskom prijestolju," in *Povijest Hrvata: Srednji vijek*, ed. Franjo Šanjek (Zagreb: Školska Knjiga, 2003), pp. 223–25.

25 "Toti Dalmacie a medietate scilicet Quarnerii usque ad confines Duracii." Ibid., pp. 225, 228.

26 As a paradigmatic example, it is possible to mention the import of silverware during the early modern period to the Istria region, an area which was for centuries divided between the Venetian Republic and the Habsburg Empire. Political boundaries, however, did not interfere with the commission of artworks by one state from the other's artistic centers. These results, as yet largely unpublished, were recently examined by Mateja Jerman as part of her doctoral research. They have been presented at several doctoral workshops. The thesis was first published in Mateja Jerman, "The Town of Boljun between the Lion and the Eagle: A Contribution to the Knowledge of Augsburg and Venetian Goldsmithing in Croatia," in *Istria in the Modern Period*, ed. Tatjana Bradara (Pula: Arheološki muzej Istre, 2017), pp. 339–63; and more comprehensively in Mateja Jerman, "Liturgijski predmeti od plemenitih metala od 1400. do 1800. godine na području nekadašnje Pulske biskupije" (PhD diss., University of Zadar, 2020).

artworks in the Adriatic metropolis of Venice, with the prior acceptance of the Krk altar frontal's redating to the sixth decade of the century, directly opens the question of Paolo's possible Dalmatian "intermezzo."[27] Igor Fisković pointed out that the place of the execution of Paolo's monumental crucifix for the Dubrovnik Dominicans ca. 1350 is uncertain. Due to the complexity of work that required collaboration between a group of skilled artisans and master Paolo himself, Fisković assumes that it is possible that the artwork was not made in Dubrovnik.[28] The realization of the altar frontal, like the one commissioned for the cathedral in Krk, geographically considerably closer to Venice than Dubrovnik, was at least equally demanding, if not even more complex. It is therefore justified to pose the question—could Paolo Veneziano, at the height of his fame, relatively easily move his accomplished painting workshop, and probably an associated embroidery workshop, from Venice to the eastern coast of the Adriatic Sea? It is certainly worth considering that in the middle of the 14th century, the plague was exceptionally devastating for the populaces of Zadar and Dubrovnik, the most important eastern Adriatic towns, as well as Venice, and so the argument that he was seeking refuge from the epidemic on the opposite side of the Adriatic should be rejected.[29] The hypothesis of Paolo's stay on the eastern Adriatic coast should therefore be reconsidered, focusing primarily on workshop practices.

2   Gothic Embroidered Altar Frontals and Eastern Adriatic Ecclesiastical Patrons

The decoration of the altar stipes with altar frontals made of precious metals or expensive fabrics for liturgical celebrations has a very long tradition.[30]

---

27   See Joško Belamarić, "La Dalmazia nella storia della pittura dal Duecento al Quattrocento," in *Il Trecento adriatico*, pp. 38–39; and Zoraida Demori Staničić, "Paolo Veneziano i trečento na Jadranu," in *Stoljeće gotike*, pp. 7, 9.

28   Fisković, "23–25. Raspeće," p. 106.

29   For more on the plague on the eastern Adriatic coast in the mid-14th century, see Gordan Ravančić, "Prilog proučavanju Crne smrti u dalmatinskom gradu (1348.–1353.): Raspon izvorne građe i stanje istraženosti na primjerima Dubrovnika, Splita i Zadra," *Povijesni prilozi* 26 (2004): 7–18.

30   Among numerous papers on this issue, see the following more recent titles: Jean-Pierre Caillet, "De l'*antependium* au retable: La contribution des orfèvres et émailleurs d'Occident," *Cahiers de civilisation medievale* 49 (2006): 3–20; Sible de Blaauw, "Altar Imagery in Italy before the Altarpiece," in *The Altar and Its Environment 1150–1400*, ed. Justin E.A. Kroesen and Victor M. Schmidt (Turnhout: Brepols, 2009), pp. 47–55; Andrea De Marchi, "La postérité du devant-d'autel à Venise: Retables orfévrés et retables peints,"

Luxurious, usually embroidered silks were also used to cover the walls of the apse, and according to Xavier Barral i Altet, they preceded the concept of the retable or altarpiece as early as the Romanesque period.[31] The oldest preserved examples of fabrics with figurative decoration intended to decorate the altar frontals are located in the treasury of the Cathedral of St. Mary in Girona (end of 11th or more likely the first quarter of the 12th century); at the Victoria and Albert Museum, which probably originates from the Cathedral of St. Mary in La Seu d'Urgell (12th century); in the Musées Royaux d'Art et d'Histoire, which originates from the Benedictine abbey in Rupertsberg (ca. 1220); in Heiningen Augustinian Abbey (ca. 1260); and at the Museo Archeologico Nazionale di Cividale del Friuli, attributed according to legend to the Blessed Dominican Benvenuta Boiani (Cividale del Friuli, 1254–Cividale del Friuli, 1292). Also noteworthy are five embroideries from the Premonstratensian Abbey at Altenberg an der Lahn (two from the 13th century, and three from the 14th), and the altar frontal of Jacopo di Cambio from the Dominican church of Santa Maria Novella in Florence, which is today kept in the Museo degli Argenti (1336).[32]

In the late Middle Ages, ecclesiastical patrons from the northwestern Balkans also furnished their sanctuaries in accordance with contemporary practice or,

---

in *The Altar and Its Environment*, pp. 57–86; Victor M. Schmidt, "Ensembles of Painted Altarpieces and Frontals," in *The Altar and Its Environment 1150–1400*, pp. 203–21; Aniello Sgambati, "La 'pala' di Pellegrino II nel Duomo di Cividale: Nuove considerazioni," *Forum Iulii: Annuario del Museo Archeologico Nazionale di Cividale del Friuli* 35 (2011): 85–105; Devis Valenti, *Le immagini multiple dell'altare: Dagli antependia ai polittici; Tipologie compositive dall'Alto Medioevo all'età gotica* (Padua: Il Poligrafo, 2012); Julian Gardner, "From Gold Altar to Gold Altarpiece: The *Pala d'Oro* and Paolo Veneziano," in *Encountering the Renaissance: Celebrating Gary M. Radke and 50 Years of the Syracuse University Graduate Program in Renaissance Art*, ed. Molly Bourne and A. Victor Coonin (Ramsey: WAPACC Organization, 2016), pp. 259–78; and Cristina Guarnieri, "Una pala ribaltabile per l'esposizione delle reliquie: Le *Storie di santa Lucia* di Jacobello del Fiore a Fermo," *Arte Veneta* 73 (2016): 9–35. See also the series of syntheses by Joseph Braun, which still represent a valuable catalogue of liturgical furnishings, for example, Braun, *Der christliche Altar in seiner geschichtlichen Entwicklung*, vols. 1–2 (Munich: Alte Meister Guenther Koch, 1924).

31 Xavier Barral i Altet, "Tessuti intorno all'altare: A proposito del ricamo del Victoria and Albert Museum di Londra con i fiumi del paradiso," *Hortus Artium Medievalium* 22 (2009): 273.

32 Ibid., pp. 273–76; Giuseppe Cantelli, *Storia dell'oreficeria e dell'arte tessile in Toscana dal Medioevo all'età moderna* (Florence: Banca Toscana, 1996), p. 42; Stefanie Seeberg, "Women as Makers of Church Decoration: Illustrated Textiles at the Monasteries of Altenberg/Lahn, Rupertsberg, and Heinigen (13th–14th c.)," in *Reassessing the Roles of Women as "Makers" of Medieval Art and Architecture*, vol. 1, ed. Therese Martin (Leiden/Boston: Brill, 2012), pp. 356–91; and Fiona J. Griffiths, *Nun's Priest's Tales: Men and Salvation in Medieval Women's Monastic Life* (Philadelphia: University of Pennsylvania Press, 2018), pp. 180–89.

FIGURE 10.6   The Zadar Altar Frontal, ca. 1340, Permanent Collection of Sacred Art (SICU), Zadar, 2009
PHOTOGRAPH BY NATALIJA VASIĆ

more specifically, in accordance with liturgical regulations and in step with the decorative trends of the period. As has already been mentioned, to date, four altar frontals dating to the 14th century have been almost entirely preserved, while a fifth is fragmentary. It seems that the oldest of them is the one exhibited in the Permanent Collection of Sacred Art (SICU) in Zadar (Fig. 10.6).

On red silk under three arches, representations of the Virgin and Child in the center, St. John the Baptist on the left, and St. John the Evangelist on the right are embroidered in silver-gilt and silk thread. At the foot of the throne, to the left of Mary's feet, the reduced figure of a kneeling donor with hands clasped in prayer is depicted. A label printed on a small rectangular segment that reads *PRES/BITE/RRAD/ONVS* reliably evidences his identity.[33] There is no doubt that the figure in question is the priest Radonja, who in 1337 commissioned the altar of St. John in Zadar's famous Benedictine church of St. Mary, and in 1349 compiled his will.[34] Archival data, as well as the iconography on the silk altar frontal, indicate that it was originally commissioned for the same

---

33   Banić, "Zadarski," p. 93.
34   Emil Hilje, "61. Vezeni Antependij," in *Stoljeće gotike na Jadranu*, pp. 188–89.

altar, and probably executed around 1340, according to the preparatory drawing of an artist from the circle of Paolo Veneziano.[35]

A similar altar frontal was made for another Benedictine church in Zadar, the famous male monastery of St. Chrysogonus. The altar frontal was probably in the church until the 19th century and is now held in the Museum of Applied Arts (*Iparművészeti Múzeum*) in Budapest. On a base of red silk taffeta in the form of a triptych, images of the Virgin and Child in the center, St. Chrysogonus on the left, and St. Benedict on the right, as well as smaller figures depicting St. Donatus, St. Gregory the Great, St. Catherine of Alexandria, and probably St. Margaret, are embroidered in silver-gilt thread.[36] Just as in the previous example, at the foot of the throne to the left of Mary's feet, the smaller figure of a kneeling donor dressed in a Benedictine habit with hands clasped in prayer is depicted. The iconographic program indicates that the altar frontal was originally embroidered for this abbey church, possibly for the altar in the southern apse devoted to St. Chrysogonus, one of the town's patron saints. The artwork was recently analysed by Banić, who argued for a dating of 1360, i.e., after the establishment of Anjou authority in Zadar in 1358. Among other arguments, Banić supports this dating by connecting the depictions of the mentioned female saints to the devastating plague epidemic of the mid-14th century. Especially convincing is the presumed identity of the presented donor, who is most likely John de Ontiac (Joannes de Onciache), a Benedictine from the Diocese of Lyon who was abbot of Zadar monastery from 1345 to 1377.[37] It was precisely during his time, after the destructive plague and then peace between the Venetian Republic and the Hungarian-Croatian King Louis I, that the monastery flourished. Banić, therefore, assumes that the altar frontal is an *ex voto* of then-abbot John, which was made about two decades after the one for the female Benedictine church in the same town.

The altar frontal made for the Church of St. Chrysogonus shows most similarities with the fourth example, the one kept in the Collection of Sacred Art in Dobrinj citadel on the island of Krk (Fig. 10.7).

The central field of this altar frontal shows the Coronation of the Virgin, with three angels holding the Cloth of Honor in the background. In the left niche is a depiction of St. Jacob, while on the right we see St. Stephen the

---

35 Silvija Banić has recently agreed with a number of scholars who date the altar frontal to around 1340, while Emil Hilje, in line with the thoughts of Vinko Zlamalik, believes that the author of the design is Menegelo Ivanov de Canali and that the artwork was executed at the end of the 14th century. For relevant literature, see Banić, "Zadarski," p. 93.
36 Ibid., p. 78.
37 Ibid., pp. 85–86.

FIGURE 10.7   The Dobrinj Altar Frontal, ca. 1360–70, Collection of Sacred Art of the Parish Church of St. Stephen, Dobrinj (Island of Krk), 2003
PHOTOGRAPH BY DAMIR KRIZMANIĆ

Martyr, patron saint of the citadel and the church's titular saint.[38] The altar frontal was first mentioned in the parish church in Dobrinj in 1579, in Agostino Valier's record of his apostolic visitation, on which occasion the following was written: "Pallium honorificum cum imaginibus asupiris ex auro sed est parum" (Honorable altar frontal with golden images, but small).[39] There is no reason to doubt that the artwork was originally commissioned for this church around the end of the sixth decade of the 14th century.[40]

---

38   See Nina Kudiš Burić, "62. Vezeni antependij s prizorom krunjenja Bogorodice i svecima Jakovom i Stjepanom," in *Stoljeće gotike na Jadranu*, pp. 190–91.

39   Vatican City, Archivio Segreto Vaticano, Congr. vescovi e regolari, Visita ap., 80 (d. Veglensis), fol. 53r; Bolonić and Žic-Rokov, *Otok Krk kroz vjekove*, p. 413; and Nina Kudiš Burić, "62. Vezeni antependij," pp. 190–91.

40   See Kudiš Burić, "62. Vezeni antependij," pp. 190–91. Enrica Cozzi quite recently considered that the Dobrinj altar frontal, as well as the two works executed in the workshop of Paolo Veneziano for the donors from island of Krk, was embroidered in the second quarter of the century. Cozzi, "Paolo Veneziano e bottega: Il polittico di Santa Lucia e gli *antependia* per l'isola di Veglia," *Arte in Friuli, Arte a Trieste* 35 (2016): 235.

Given the lack of a donor figure in the composition and of directly relevant archival insights, it is understandable that the question of the patron for the Dobrinj altar frontal has not been raised until now. However, it is now possible to propose a specific name. As was already mentioned, on June 10, 1381, the Bishop of Krk, Ivan II, consecrated the altar of St. John the Evangelist in the parish church of St. Stephen in Dobrinj.[41] It is a little-known fact that the altar was erected by a certain Ivan Richtar (Zuanne Rectar), who then also abundantly endowed it with all its mobile and immobile goods.[42] Considering the church's then-much-smaller dimensions and, of course, fewer altars, it is quite possible that the altar frontal was originally made for this altar. On the basis of stylistic analysis, Guarnieri believes that the altar frontal was woven in Venice between 1360 and 1370, according to a preparatory drawing by one of the followers of Paolo Veneziano.[43] It is possible, even more likely, that the altar was erected at least a few years prior to 1381, the year of its consecration, and that it was at that time already equipped with all the necessary liturgical furnishings. Especially interesting, and perhaps indicative, is information on the consecrator of the altar, Bishop Ivan II, who most probably commissioned a similar luxurious altar frontal some fifteen years earlier for the high altar of his Cathedral in Krk from the great master, then still alive.[44]

3   Opus Venetum

In the pivotal 1963 study *Il Ricamo nella storia e nell'arte*, Marie Schuette and Sigrid Müller-Christensen synthesized the activities of the most important medieval and early modern European production centers.[45] Particular attention was therefore devoted to analysis of the examples of *opus anglicanum*, *opus teutonicum*, and *opus fiorentinum* schools. Schuette states that the cities of Siena and Venice were particularly renowned for their high quality of production, but, well aware of the lack of research on the topic, she does not provide

---

41 Bolonić and Žic-Rokov, *Otok Krk kroz vjekove*, p. 108.
42 The contents of Ivan Richtar's will were not published *in extenso*. An 18th-century copy is in Venice, Archivio di Stato di Venezia, Cancelleria inferiore, Doge, Giurisdizioni, Veglia, Catastico di Veglia (bundle 221), fols. 178–81.
43 Guarnieri, *Lorenzo Veneziano*, p. 66.
44 See Danijel Ciković, "L'eredità artistica del medioevo nei documenti d'archivio della prima età moderna: Alcuni esempi quarnerini e istriani," *Mélanges de l'École française de Rome: Moyen Âge* 129, no. 1 (2017): 153–54.
45 Sigrid Müller-Christensen, "Materiale e tecnica," in *Il Ricamo nella storia e nell'arte*, ed. Marie Schuette and Müller-Christensen (Rome: Edizioni Mediterranee, 1963), pp. 7–12; Marie Schuette, introduction to *Il Ricamo*, pp. 15–24.

specific examples.[46] To some extent, such a selective approach to the subject can also be noted in later studies, while more concrete progress in the attempt to attribute and contextualize objects of 14th-century Venetian embroidery has been made only recently.[47]

Professional embroidery workshops most likely existed in Venice even earlier than 1271, when the embroiderers' organization *L'arte dei Ricamatori* is mentioned as part of the Venetian painters' guild.[48] It is also quite reasonable to assume that the guild of Venetian *battilori*, the manufacturers of the metal threads that were a key material for the embroiderers, already existed in the city in the second half of the 13th century.[49] The establishment of professional embroidery workshops in the context of Venice's growing silk industry in the 13th century is therefore not at all unexpected. A number of sources testify to the recognizability of Venetian products. One such source is the inventory list of St. Peter's in the Vatican of 1295, which mentions the fabrics *de Venetiis* and *de opere Venettico*. According to Ileana Chiappini di Sorio, this does not necessarily confirm the existence of local production, but rather determines the origin of the fabric.[50] In the 1361 inventory list of the same church, however, *opus Venetum* is once again differentiated from, for example, *opus Senese*, *opus Neapolitanum*, *opus Lucanum*, and *opus Romanum*.[51] Donald King is of the opinion that *opus Venetum* refers to objects made by Venetian embroidery workshops, stating that the same term is also mentioned in the 1245 and 1295 inventory lists of St. Paul's in London, as well as the 1343 inventory list of the papal court in Avignon.[52] Liturgical objects with embroidered decoration are

---

46 Ibid., p. 23.
47 For example, Banić, "Zadarski," pp. 75–94; Cozzi, "Paolo Veneziano e bottega," pp. 235–93; and Ciković, "L'eredità," pp. 143–59.
48 See Doretta Davanzo Poli, "Pietro e Marco nei ricami medievali," in *San Pietro e San Marco: Arte e iconografia in area adriatica*, ed. Letizia Caselli (Rome: Gangemi Editore, 2009), p. 202; and Doretta Davanzo Poli, "L'impiego dell'oro e dell'argento nei pizzi e ricami," in *Contributi per la storia dell'oreficeria, argenteria e gioielleria: Prima collana di studi sull'oreficeria*, ed. Piero Pazzi, vol. 1 (Venice: Biblioteca orafa di Sant'Antonio Abate, 1996), p. 247.
49 In 1264 there existed an office (or workshop) in Venice that was called Oro o foglia d'oro. See Luigi Brenni, *L'arte del battoloro ed i filati d'oro e d'argento: Cenni storico-tecnici e 18 illustrazioni* (Milan: Brenni, 1930), p. 47.
50 Ileana Chiappini di Sorio, "Le premesse storiche della tessitura a Venezia," in *Origine e sviluppo dei Velluti a Venezia: Il velluto allucciolato d'oro* (Venice: Università Internazionale dell'Arte, 1986), pp. 9–13.
51 Bernhard Degenhart and Annegrit Schmitt, *Corpus der italienischen Zeichnungen 1300–1450*, part 2, vol. 2, *Venedig 1300–1400; Addenda zu Süd- und Mittelitalien* (Berlin: Mann, 1980), p. 91.
52 King, "A Venetian Embroidered Altar Frontal," p. 12.

also mentioned in Venetian documents, the oldest of which is a record in the statute (*mariegola*) of the Venetian Scuola di San Teodoro, which states that in 1009 a light fabric of scarlet silk with figures embroidered in gold thread was placed on the altar of the Scuola.[53] Red embroidered fabrics (*pannum rubeum cositum ad agum*) are also mentioned in the 1283 inventory list of the Treasury of St. Mark.[54] Finally, the *pannos theutonicos*, made in 1335 by *pictor* Marco for the church of San Francesco in Treviso, can also be considered a Venetian work.[55]

Of the undoubtedly numerous objects produced by Venetian embroidery workshops in the 14th century, only a very small portion has been preserved. On the basis of stylistic and technical characteristics, it is possible to attribute a series of pieces with figurative embroidered decoration to 14th-century Venetian workshops. The Banner of St. Fosca, whose case inscription indicates that it was created in Venice in 1366, and which is today in the Museo Provinciale on Torcello, in that context also presents valuable evidence.[56] The embroidered frieze with vegetative ornaments and figures of saints under trefoil arches, today in the Keir Collection at the Dallas Museum of Art, and a similar fragment in the Museum of Applied Arts in Budapest are also of Venetian

---

53   See Franco Brunello, *Arti e mestieri a Venezia nel Medioevo e nel Rinascimento* (Vicenza: Neri Pozza Editore, 1981), p. 129.
54   Ibid., pp. 129–30.
55   Silk with embroidered decoration is often described in historical sources as *picti*, or "painted," since the workmanship of these pieces was reminiscent of the quality of painted works. See Brunello, *Arti e mestieri*, p. 130.

  The document further states that Marco had a brother named Paolo (*pictorem*) who made a drawing on paper after which, *ad modum Theotonicum*, a fabric decoration also for the monks in Treviso was executed. Muraro, *Paolo da Venezia*, pp. 86–87. The painter Paulus mentioned in this source is linked to none other than Paolo Veneziano, and the *panos ad modum Theotonicum* could be the monochrome linen fabrics with figurative decoration known as *opus teutonicum*. Zoraida Demori Staničić also noticed the link bethween *Opus theutonicum* and *pannos theutonicos*. See Zoraida Demori Staničić "Figuralni umjetnički vez obrednog ruha iz vremena renesanse u Dalmaciji i Istri", *Radovi Instituta za povijest umjetnosti* 32 (2008): 80. Although this technique is thought to have originated in a German-speaking region, it is well known that it was also produced in cities on the Apennine Peninsula, especially for the purpose of furnishing altars (*tovaglie d'altare*). Schuette, introduction to *Il ricamo*, p. 19. Franco Brunello assumes that the mentioned *pannos theutonicos* made by Marco could be analogous with the "Venetian fabric on which the death of the Virgin Mary is depicted" ("panno veneziano in quo est Virginis Mariae mortem designatam"), which Enrico Morosini donated to the monks of San Salvatore monastery in Venice in 1206. Brunello, *Arti e mestieri*, pp. 129–30.
56   See Davanzo Poli, "Pietro e Marco," p. 202.

production.[57] The Museum of Applied Arts in Budapest also houses the previously mentioned embroidered altar frontal originating from the church of St. Chrysogonus in Zadar.

On the eastern Adriatic coast, there are several objects belonging to this group: a frieze embroidered with saints' busts on the hems of a pair of bishop's gloves from the Treasury of the Cathedral of St. Domnius in Split,[58] the mitre of Bishop Nikola Kažotić from the Trogir Cathedral Treasury,[59] eight rectangular fragments with ornamental decoration and saints' busts from the Permanent Collection of Sacred Art (SICU) in Zadar,[60] an altar frontal fragment with an image of St. Peter from the Museum of Arts and Crafts (Muzej za umjetnost i obrt) in Zagreb,[61] and the previously mentioned altar frontals from the Permanent Collection of Sacred Art (SICU) in Zadar and the parish church of St. Stephen in Dobrinj.[62] We should take this opportunity to add to the list sixteen busts preserved on rectangular fragments sewn onto two dalmatics from the Cathedral Treasury in Korčula,[63] as well as the orphreys with figurative decoration from the Museum of Arts and Crafts in Zagreb,[64] and analogous orphreys that have been used as patches on the damaged spots of the London altar frontal.[65]

Certainly, the most monumental preserved example of 14th-century Venetian embroidery is the altar frontal originally from Krk Cathedral, now at the Victoria and Albert Museum. Although very little is known about the

---

57   See Banić, "Zadarski," p. 92, n. 28; and Monique King and Donald King, *European Textiles in the Keir Collection 400 BC to 1800 AD* (London: Faber and Faber, 1990), p. 92.

58   Banić, "Zadarski," p. 92, n. 28; Joseph Braun, *Die liturgische Gewandung im Occident und Orient nach Ursprung und Entwicklung: Verwendung und Symbolik* (Darmstadt: Wissenschaftliche Buchgesellschaft, 1964), p. 374; and Deša Diana, Nada Gogala, and Sofija Matijević, *Riznica splitske katedrale* (Split: Muzej Grada Splita, 1972), p. 133.

59   Banić, "Zadarski," pp. 90–91, n. 13; Zoraida Demori Staničić, "Prilozi o srednjovjekovnom tekstilu u Trogiru: Prijedlozi za lokalnu vezilačku radionicu," in *Prilozi povijesti umjetnosti u Dalmaciji* 40 (2003–04): 113–47; and Davanzo Poli, "Pietro e Marco," pp. 195–202.

60   Banić, "Zadarski," pp. 82–83.

61   Jelena Ivoš, *Liturgijsko ruho iz zbirke tekstila Muzeja za umjetnost i obrt*, exh. cat. (Zagreb: Muzej za umjetnost i obrt, 2010), pp. 44–45; and Banić, "Zadarski," pp. 84–85.

62   Banić, "Zadarski," pp. 83–84.

63   Damir Tulić and Nina Kudiš, *Opatska riznica, katedrala i crkve grada Korčule* (Korčula: Župa sv. Marka, 2014), pp. 133–34.

64   Ivoš, *Liturgijsko ruho*, pp. 45–46.

65   It must be pointed out that the current appearance of the artwork is not entirely original and that new layers of fabric have been added due to incurred damage. The patch applied on the upper edge of the frontal is actually a reused Renaissance orphrey from the second half of the 16th century, and the patches around the figures' faces and in the lower right corner are also from the 14th century.

practice of 14th-century embroidery workshops in Venice, it is certain that there existed so-called serial production of less complex and repetitive compositions, such as bands with figurative decoration designed to decorate orphreys.[66] The designs after which such compositions were made were surely kept in workshops and then modified and adapted depending on the commission, as evidenced by the preserved examples.[67] Exceptionally rare and particularly valuable are those objects outside the framework of serial production, those that were made as exclusive commissions after designs created by renowned painting workshops. The execution of such complex and prestigious projects had to be entrusted to the professional embroidery workshops, and special attention was paid to the process of transferring the design to the silk base. The design, which preceded the execution of the embroidered composition, could be drawn directly onto a silk base or onto a piece of paper that would then be transferred to the fabric.[68] A key source of information on the techniques of making and transmitting the design onto the fabric is the late 14th-century treatise of the Florentine painter Cennino Cennini (ca. 1370–1427), *Il Libro dell'Arte*. In section 164, under the title "How to draw on canvas or silk designs that are to be embroidered" (Come si dee disegnare in tela o in zendado per servigio de'ricamatori), Cennini describes drawing in charcoal directly on a taut silk fabric where the embroidery will be made.[69] The back of the fabric would then be moistened with a wet sponge, after which shading

---

66 See Cristina Borgioli, "Tessuti e ricami: Progettualità ed esecuzione tra Medioevo e Rinascimento," in *Chirurgia della creazione: Mano e arti visive*, vol. 3 of Predella (2011), ed. Annamaria Ducci (Ghezzano: Felici Editore, 2011), pp. 59–72.

67 The figures of St. Agnes from the fragment in Korčula and St. Lucy from the fragment in Zadar, for example, are based on the same design. See Tulić and Kudiš, *Opatska riznica*, p. 134.

68 There exist only a few known drawings that can be considered preparatory studies or, rather, cartoon designs for embroidered works. Noteworthy are the perforated drawings attributed to Raffaellino del Garbo (ca. 1466–1524), a pupil of the painter Filippino Lippi, drawn in charcoal and ink. They depict the Virgin, St. John the Baptist, and the angel of the Annunciation, and are today held by the Metropolitan Museum of Art, New York. The drawing of Mary Magdalene from the National Gallery of Denmark (Staatens Museum for Kunst) in Copenhagen is also a cartoon for an embroidered work. See Borgioli, "Tessuti e ricami," p. 62.

69 The ground fabric on which the Krk altar frontal is embroidered consists of three layers. The upper layer consists of three pieces of red taffeta (*zendado*) joined lengthwise, of which the central piece is preserved in its full width (range within 17-1/2 and 17-5/8 in., or 44.4 and 44.8 cm). Beneath the layer of red taffeta is a piece of paper to strengthen the composition, as well as a base of firm linen canvas. The composition was executed with silk and metal threads (paired silver and silver-gilt *filé* threads). The silver and metal threads used for the embroidery penetrate all the layers (silk taffeta, paper, and linen).

would be done on the front side of the fabric.[70] Lisa Monnas believes that the drawing, which can be seen on the red silk taffeta base of the Krk altar frontal in the places where the original embroidered layer of silk threads has been lost, was made in precisely this way.[71] However, before drawing on the silk surface, a sketch would most likely have been made, or rather a study that preceded the execution of a final preparatory drawing after which the embroiderers could work. It can therefore be assumed that Paolo Veneziano's sketch for the Krk altar frontal did not differ much from the well-known sketch depicting *The Madonna della Misericordia with Saints John the Baptist and John the Evangelist, the Circumcision, and the Presentation of the Virgin*, attributed to Lorenzo Veneziano (Venice, active 1356–72), and dated to around 1370.[72]

4 The 15th-Century Fabric Patronage Tradition in the Western Balkans

Compared to the relatively small number of silk fabrics and embroidery preserved in the western Balkan region originating in the 14th century, a significantly larger number of fabrics related to certain local legends or testamentary donations date to the 15th century. However, the authenticity of the patronage behind these well-preserved examples cannot be determined with any certainty or probability, as is the case with the previously mentioned examples of Venetian embroidered frontals from the 14th century. One exception, albeit older, is a chasuble from the treasury of Zagreb Cathedral tailored from Byzantine lampas derived from the mantle belonging to King (Saint) Ladislaus I of Hungary (r. 1077–95). The mantle was, in fact, a gift from the Hungarian-Croatian King Charles I Robert (Naples, 1288–Visegrád, 1342) to the Bishop of Zagreb, (The Blessed) Augustin Kažotić (Trogir, 1260–Lucera, 1323) at the beginning of the 14th century and has been venerated as a relic since Ladislaus was canonized.[73]

---

70 Cennino Cennini, *Knjiga o umjetnosti: Il libro dell'arte*, trans. Katarina Hraste and Jurica Matijević, ed. Milan Pelc (Zagreb: Institut za povijest umjetnosti, 2007), p. 137.

71 Lisa Monnas, *Merchants, Princes and Painters. Silk Fabrics in Italian and Northern Paintings 1300–1550* (London: Yale University Press, 2008), p. 42.

72 The drawing (5-3/4 × 10-3/8 in., or 14.6 × 26.3 cm) is at the Metropolitan Museum of Art, New York. For a photograph, see https://www.metmuseum.org/art/collection/search/459179, accessed February 10, 2020. See also Guarnieri, *Lorenzo Veneziano*, p. 67; and Banić, "Zadarski," p. 85.

73 See Mechthild Flury-Lemberg, "87. Bell-shaped Chasuble of St. Ladislaus of Hungary," in *Textile Conservation and Research: A Documentation of the Textile Department on the Occasion of the Twentieth Anniversary of the Abegg Foundation* (Bern: Abegg Stiftung,

Among the most significant examples of 15th-century textile patronage in the western Balkans is the case of Bosnian Queen Katarina Kosača Kotromanić (b. 1425–Rome, 1478). On October 20, 1478, in her home near the church of St. Mark's in Rome, she wrote her will. Listing numerous testamentary donations, the Queen included, among other things, the following: "Item voluit et legavit dicte ecclesie sancte Marie de Araceli palium seu suum Regale mantellum de panno aurato" (And to the aforementioned church of Santa Maria in Aracoeli she leaves in her will her royal mantle of golden fabric)."[74] As her final resting place, Queen Katarina chose none other than the Franciscan church of Santa Maria in Aracoeli, where she was buried in front of the high altar. She endowed the church with a series of testamentary donations, among which stands out her royal mantle embroidered with gold thread. Through the centuries, the figure of the queen acquired almost mythical status, and she is still worshipped as Blessed, even Holy, by the Bosnian people.[75] It appears that, with the strengthening of the queen's cult, especially among the Franciscan Order, her alleged donations multiplied. According to local tradition, Queen Katarina donated to the Franciscan monastery of St. Mary in Zaostrog (Croatia) a set of liturgical vestments that comprised a chasuble, stole, and maniple. The vestments were said to derive from the mantle of Katarina's husband, the Bosnian King Stjepan Tomašević Kotromanić (b. 1438–Jajce, 1463), although they are actually

---

1988), pp. 176–78, 498; and Igor Fisković, "37. King Ladislav's Cloak," in *The First Five Centuries of Croatian Art*, ed. Biserka Rauter Plančić, exh. cat. (Zagreb: Galerija Klovićevi dvori, 2006), pp. 174–75.

74 Augustin Theiner, *Epistolae Sixti PP. IV., DCLXXXIII: Catherinae reginae Bosniae testamentum, per quod, nisi Sigismundus et Catherina eius filii ad christianam fidem redirent, Romanam ecclesiam instituit haeredem; Ex Cencio Camerario* fol. 347, Vetera Monumenta Slavorum Meridionalium historiam illustrantia, vol. 1 (Rome: Typis Vaticanis, 1863), p. 510. The contents of Queen Katarina's will, which has in the past caused much controversy of an often political character, are known from a transcript kept in the Archivio Segreto Vaticano, not from the original document. It is important therefore to point out the existence of another transcript of the will contained in the I Codici Minucciani fund, kept in the Deutsches Historisches Instituts in Rome. Rome, Archivio dell'Istituto Storico Germanico, I Codici Minucciani (bundle 7), fols. 94r–98r. For a detailed inventory of this fund, see Alexander Koller, Pier Paolo Piergentili, and Gianni Venditti, eds., *I Codici Minucciani dell'Istituto Storico Germanico: Inventario* (Rome: Deutsches Historisches Institut in Rom, 2009), p. 21.

75 For more on Bosnian Queen Katarina Kosača Kotromanić, with a list of relevant literature, see Esad Kurtović, "Prilog bibliografiji radova o bosanskoj kraljici Katarini Kotromanić (1425–1478)," *Bosna franciscana* 22 (2005): 201–11; and Luka Špoljarić, "Bosanska kraljica Katarina i humanisti, dio prvi: Leonardo Montagna i njegovi epigrami," *Zbornik Odsjeka za povijesne znanosti Zavoda za povijesni i društvene znanosti, HAZU* 36 (2018): 61–80.

made from an Ottoman lampas from the second half of the 16th century.[76] According to another, similar legend, the queen also donated a chasuble she had embroidered herself to the Franciscan church in Kraljeva Sutjeska (Bosnia and Herzegovina).[77] It is possible that these deeply rooted local legends are inspired by the aforementioned donation to the church of Santa Maria in Aracoeli or, more likely, by the queen's testamentary donation of a relic to a Franciscan church in Jajce (Bosnia and Herzegovina).[78] To date, however, it has not been possible to identify any preserved fabric as Katarina's donation.

The Bosnian queen's testamentary donations of liturgical attire to Franciscan churches are no exception. It is well known that noble garments, mostly dresses made of precious silk fabrics, were for centuries considered valuable family assets and were thus often used as substitutes for cash pledges, or as diplomatic gifts. They were additionally considered valuable inheritances, whose fate was determined through a will after the death of the owner. The donation of garments made of precious silk as pledges to churches and monasteries was a common practice for members of the aristocracy.[79] From the asset list of Barbara Frankopan (d. 1508), the wife of the Serbian despot Vuk Grgurević Branković (1440–1485), composed in 1505, we can discern much about the quantity and quality of items in the wardrobe of the Balkans nobility.[80] According to the list, we can assume that Barbara Frankopan had in her ownership at that time: a gilded tunic, a scarlet dress decorated with gold hems, a gilded velvet dress decorated with gold ties, a satin gilded shirt with pearl decoration, a red scarlet shirt with pearls, a belt with pearls, a silver belt, a veil with gold beads, and two hats decorated with gold, pearls, and jewels.[81] Only a narrow circle of customers could have afforded these silken garments. When compared with similar asset lists of noblewomen from Western European courts, it is evident that Barbara Frankopan's wardrobe was much more modest, but her manner of dressing did not differ significantly. For example, a dress made of velvet with a pattern embroidered in metal threads is included in the asset list of Lucrezia Borgia (Subiaco, 1480–Ferrara, 1519), drawn up in 1502.[82] Barbara Frankopan

---

76 See Silvija Banić, "O misnom ornatu od 'Jelisavetina plašta' u župnoj crkvi u Novigradu," in *Novigrad nekad i sad*, ed. Slobodan Kaštela (Zadar: Sveučilište u Zadru, 2016), p. 306.
77 Ibid.
78 See Augustin Theiner, *Epistolae Sixti*, p. 510.
79 See Sara Piccolo Paci, *Storia delle vesti liturgiche: Forma, immagine e funzione* (Milan: Àncora editrice, 2008), pp. 178–79.
80 See Arijana Koprčina, "Barbara Frankapan i zlatarske narudžbe oko 1500. godine," *Radovi Instituta za povijest umjetnosti* 37 (2013): 65.
81 Ibid.
82 See Lisa Monnas, *Renaissance Velvets* (London: Victoria and Albert Museum, 2012), p. 20; and Carole Collier Frick, *Dressing Renaissance Florence: Families, Fortunes, and Fine Clothing* (Baltimore: Johns Hopkins University Press, 2002), pp. 113–14.

made a series of well-known donations to churches and Franciscan monasteries, so it is quite reasonable to assume that some of them are related to the luxurious silk fabrics from which the pieces in her wardrobe were made.[83] The practice of testamentary donation among the prominent Croatian noble Frankopan family is also evident from another document, the will of Duke Ivan Frankopan VII (b. 1434–Zákány, 1486), written on March 2, 1453.[84] Among the testamentary donations, of which several also went to the then-ubiquitous Franciscans, the young Duke Ivan wished for the following:

> Item ordinavit et legavit, quod si eum ante sue vite decessum de suis bonis mobilibus, ut puta de pecuniis, equis, argenteriis, vestimentis vel aliis huiusmodi mobilibus bonis alicui ecclesie vel monasterio vel cuivis pio loco.

> He bequeaths after his death those movable goods that were his during his lifetime, such as money, horses, silver, clothing, or other movable goods of this kind, to a church or a monastery or another holy place.[85]

Silvija Banić recently noted that "local stories which tell of the 'royal' origin of certain valuable fabrics are not rare."[86] In addition to the aforementioned examples, we are reminded of a few more from the western Balkans, also associated with prominent members of ruling dynasties. In Novigrad, near Zadar, a widely accepted and deeply rooted local story tells of Elizabeth's Chasuble (*Jelisavetina planita*) kept in the parish church. According to legend, a chasuble, a stole, and a maniple of the same silk were made from the mantle of Elizabeta Kotromanić (Bobovac or Srebrenik, 1340–Novigrad, 1387), the wife of the Hungarian-Croatian King Louis I (Visegrád, 1326–Trnava, 1382). Moreover, it has been argued that the liturgical vestments were tailored by the queen

---

83   See Mateja Jerman, Iva Jazbec Tomaić, and Danijel Ciković, "Frankapanski zagovori u zlatu i svili," in *Putovima Frankopana*, ed. Ines Srdoč-Konestra and Saša Potočnjak (Rijeka: Primorsko-goranska županija, Filozofski fakultet Sveučilišta u Rijeci, 2018), p. 233. For the donations of Barbara Frankopan, see Koprčina, "Barbara Frankapan."

84   Vjekoslav Klaić, *Krčki knezovi Frankapani: Od najstarijih vremena do gubitka otoka Krka (od god. 1118. do god. 1480.)* (Zagreb: Matica Hrvatska, 1901), p. 237.

85   Šime Ljubić, "Commissiones et relationes Venetae (Annorum 1433–1527)," vol. 1, *Giurisdizione antica di Veglia: Relazione di Antonio Vinciguerra 1481*, Monumenta spectantia historiam Slavorum meridionalium 6 (Zagreb: Ex officina Societatis Typographicae, 1876), p. 100. In the context of textile donations to Franciscan churches on the eastern Adriatic coast, see also Ana Marinković, "John Capistran's Mantle and the Early Propaganda of Franciscan Observant Cults in Dubrovnik," in *Genius Loci—Laslovszky 60*, ed. Dóra Mérai et al. (Budapest: Archaeolingua, 2018), pp. 171–74.

86   Banić, "O misnom," p. 306.

herself during her captivity in Novigrad, shortly before she was executed. However, the vestments are actually made of velvet woven in the third quarter of the 17th century, most likely of Genoese manufacture.[87] In the Chest of St. Simeon in Zadar, made between 1377 and 1380, there is a linen covering for the head, but Banić notes that the motifs on the covering show "striking similarity" with those on a Venetian samite in the Victoria and Albert Museum that dates to the 13th century.[88] Furthermore, the mantle in the Franciscan monastery of the Holy Spirit in Fojnica (Bosnia and Herzegovina) is considered a gift from Sultan Mehmed II (Edirne, 1432–Hünkar Çayırı, 1481) to the monastery's guardian, Fr. Anđelo Zvizdović in 1463, but it seems that it is actually made of silk, probably created not before the late 15th or early 16th century.[89] Finally, the somewhat later chasuble known as Hasan's Mantle (*Hasanov plašč*) in the National Museum of Slovenia in Ljubljana is also noteworthy. According to legend, the chasuble and accompanying maniple were tailored from the mantle of the Beylerbey of the Eyalet of Bosnia, Hasan Pasha Predojević (b. ca. 1530–Sisak, 1593), who drowned in the river Kupa after the defeat of the Ottoman army at the Battle of Sisak in 1593.[90] The chasuble was made of *saten liseré broché* dating to the second half of the 16th century, which may have been woven in Venice, so it is not possible to completely reject this idea about its origin.

5 Conclusion

Given the complexity and high quality of execution of the Veglia altar frontal, it is possible to assume that master Paolo himself supervised the realization of this exclusive commission. Hélène Papastavrou is of the opinion that the work was created through close cooperation between embroiders and painters. She also points out the differences in the quality of specific parts, which supports the theory of a clear division of labor within the workshop.[91] Additionally, the differences in execution within the group of 14th-century Venetian

---

87   Ibid., p. 310.
88   On the Chest of St. Simeon and relevant older literature, see Nikola Jakšić, "Od hagiografskog obrasca do političkog elaborata: Škrinja Sv. Šimuna, zadarska *arca d'oro*," Ars Adriatica 4 (2014): 95–124. On the head covering, see Silvija Banić, "Gotički lampas u relikvijarima za glave Sv. Asela i Sv. Marcele u Ninu," Ars Adriatica 3 (2013): 88.
89   Banić, "O misnom," p. 306.
90   See Barbara Ravnik-Toman et al., "Turški mašni plašč," in *Narodni muzej Slovenije: Zgodovinske in umetnostne zbirke; Stalna razstava*, ed. Maja Lozar Štamcar (Ljubljana: Narodni muzej Slovenije, 2011), pp. 20–21.
91   Hélène Papastavrou, "À propos d'un voile brodé vénitien du XIVe siècle à Zadar," Zograf 32 (2008): 99.

embroidery examples indicate the serial production of embroidered orphreys, as well as production of sophisticated compositions for exclusive commissions. Although the number of preserved examples of 14th-century Venetian embroidery is modest, the pieces do point to very high production standards. Further research on the London altar frontal, as a masterpiece of 14th-century Venetian embroidery, will surely result in an even greater understanding of the production process, as well as a reevaluation of the *opus venetum* in the broader context of late medieval embroidery schools. The suggested later dating and the context in which the London altar frontal was commissioned also open up a new perspective on patronage and the transmission of ideas among prominent members of society on the eastern Adriatic coast.[92]

Acknowledgments

This research has been supported in part by the Croatian Science Foundation under the project IP-2016-06-1265, ET TIBI DABO: Commissions and Donors in Istria, Croatian Littoral, and North Dalmatia from 1300 to 1800. For their help in researching and writing this paper, we would like to thank most sincerely Nina Kudiš, Marijan Bradanović, Ivana Čapeta Rakić, Dean Krmac, Elisa Concini, Mateja Jerman, Damir Krizmanić, Sarah Sharpe, and Ruiha Smalley, as well as Alice Isabella Sullivan, Maria Alessia Rossi, and the anonymous reviewers for their careful reading of our essay and their valuable suggestions. Unless otherwise noted the translations in the essay are made by the authors.

Bibliography

Primary Sources

Rome, Archivio dell'Istituto Storico Germanico, I Codici Minucciani (bundle 7), fols. 94r–98r.

Vatican City, Archivio Segreto Vaticano, Congr. vescovi e regolari, Visita ap., 80 (d. Arbensis), fol. 21v–22r.

---

92 On potential future research on Paolo Veneziano's art and especially the patronage of his works, it is essential to highlight the recent and for the most part unpublished research of Christopher W. Platts. In the context of this essay, we await his potentially important contribution in his article Christopher W. Platts, "Establishing the International Patronage of Paolo Veneziano: New Case Studies from France and Croatia," in *Trecento Forum* 2, forthcoming.

Vatican City, Archivio Segreto Vaticano, Congr. vescovi e regolari, Visita ap., 80 (d. Veglensis), fol. 53r.

Venice, Archivio di Stato di Venezia, Cancelleria inferiore, Doge, Giurisdizioni, Veglia, Catastico di Veglia (bundle 221), fols. 178–81.

Secondary Sources

Banić, Silvija. "Prilog poznavanju sakralnih invenatra otoka Raba: Najvrjedniji povijesni tekstili sačuvani na misnom ruhu i drugim dijelovima liturgijske opreme." *Rapski zbornik II* (2012): 461–98.

Banić, Silvija. "Gotički lampas u relikvijarima za glave Sv. Asela i Sv. Marcele u Ninu." *Ars Adriatica* 3 (2013): 85–102.

Banić, Silvija. "Zadarski gotički vezeni antependij u Budimpešti." *Ars Adriatica* 4 (2014): 75–94.

Banić, Silvija. "O misnom ornatu od 'Jelisavetina plašta' u župnoj crkvi u Novigradu." In *Novigrad nekad i sad*, ed. Slobodan Kaštela, 302–17. Zadar: Sveučilište u Zadru, 2016.

Baradel, Valentina. "Diramazioni adriatiche di botteghe veneziane. L'isola di Veglia (Krk), da Paolo Veneziano a Jacobello del Fiore." In *La Serenissima via mare*, ed. V. Baradel and C. Guarnieri, 70–72. Padova: Padova University Press, 2019.

Barral i Altet, Xavier. "Tessuti intorno all'altare: A proposito del ricamo del Victoria and Albert Museum di Londra con i fiumi del paradiso." *Hortus Artium Medievalium* 22 (2009): 273.

Belamarić, Joško. "La Dalmazia nella storia della pittura dal Duecento al Quattrocento." In *Il Trecento adriatico: Paolo Veneziano e la pittura tra Oriente e Occidente*, ed. Francesca Flores d'Arcais and Giovanni Gentili, 168–69. Milan: Silvana Editoriale, 2002.

Boerio, Giuseppe. *Dizionario del dialetto veneziano*. Venezia: Giovanni Cecchini, 1867.

Bolonić, Mihovil, and Ivan Žic-Rokov. *Otok Krk kroz vjekove*. Zagreb: Kršćanska sadašnjost, 1977.

Borgioli, Cristina. "Tessuti e ricami: Progettualità ed esecuzione tra Medioevo e Rinascimento." In *Chirurgia della creazione: Mano e arti visive*, vol. 3 of Predella (2011), ed. Annamaria Ducci, 59–72. Pisa: Felici Editore, 2011.

Bradanović, Marijan. *Grad Krk u srednjem vijeku*. Split: Muzej hrvatskih arheoloških spomenika, 2016.

Braun, Joseph. *Der christliche Altar in seiner geschichtlichen Entwicklung*, vols. 1–2. Munich: Alte Meister Guenther Koch, 1924.

Braun, Joseph. *Die liturgische Gewandung im Occident und Orient nach Ursprung und Entwicklung: Verwendung und Symbolik*. Darmstadt: Wissenschaftliche Buchgesellschaft, 1964.

Brenni, Luigi. *L'arte del battoloro ed i filati d'oro e d'argento: Cenni storico-tecnici e 18 illustrazioni*. Milan: Brenni, 1930.

Brunello, Franco. *Arti e mestieri a Venezia nel Medioevo e nel Rinascimento*. Vicenza: Neri Pozza Editore, 1981.

Caillet, Jean-Pierre. "De l'*antependium* au retable: La contribution des orfèvres et émailleurs d'Occident." *Cahiers de civilisation medievale* 49 (2006): 3–20.

Cantelli, Giuseppe. *Storia dell'oreficeria e dell'arte tessile in Toscana dal Medioevo all'età moderna*. Florence: Banca Toscana, 1996.

Cortelazzo, Michele A., Adriana da Rin, and Paola Frattaroli. "Glossario." In *Tessuti nel Veneto: Venezia e la Terraferma*, ed. Giuliana Ericani and Paola Frattarol, Verona: Banca Popolare Di Verona, 1993.

Cennini, Cennino. *Knjiga o umjetnosti. Il libro dell' arte*, trans. Katarina Hraste and Jurica Matijević, ed. Milan Pelc. Zagreb: Institut za povijest umjetnosti, 2007.

Chiappini di Sorio, Ileana. "Le premesse storiche della tessitura a Venezia." In *Origine e sviluppo dei Velluti a Venezia: Il velluto allucciolato d'oro*, 9–13. Venice: Università Internazionale dell'Arte, 1986.

Ciković, Danijel. "L'eredità artistica del medioevo nei documenti d'archivio della prima età moderna: Alcuni esempi quarnerini e istriani." *Mélanges de l'École française de Rome: Moyen Âge* 129, no. 1 (2017): 153–54.

Collier Frick, Carole. *Dressing Renaissance Florence: Families, Fortunes, and Fine Clothing*. Baltimore, Maryland: Johns Hopkins University Press, 2002.

Cooper, Donal. "Gothic Art and the Friars in Late Medieval Croatia, 1213–1460." In *Croatia: Aspects of Art, Architecture and Cultural Heritage*, ed. Jadranka Beresford-Peirse, p. 84. London: Frances Lincoln, 2009.

Ćošković, Pejo. "Hermolais, Juraj de (Ermolai, Ermolais; Georgio)." In *Hrvatski biografski leksikon*. Available at http://hbl.lzmk.hr/clanak.aspx?id=7587, accessed January 14, 2019.

Cozzi, Enrica. "Paolo Veneziano e bottega: Il polittico di Santa Lucia e gli *antependia* per l'isola di Veglia." *Arte in Friuli, Arte a Trieste* 35 (2016): 235.

Davanzo Poli, Doretta. "L'impiego dell'oro e dell'argento nei pizzi e ricami." In *Contributi per la storia dell'oreficeria, argenteria e gioielleria: Prima collana di studi sull'oreficeria* ed. Piero Pazzi, vol. 1, 246–49. Venice: Biblioteca orafa di Sant'Antonio Abate, 1996.

Davanzo Poli, Doretta. "Pietro e Marco nei ricami medievali." In *San Pietro e San Marco: Arte e iconografia in area adriatica*, ed. Letizia Caselli, 185–203. Rome: Gangemi Editore, 2009.

De Blaauw, Sible. "Altar Imagery in Italy before the Altarpiece." In *The Altar and Its Environment 1150–1400*, ed. Justin E.A. Kroesen and Victor M. Schmidt, 47–55. Turnhout: Brepols, 2009.

De Marchi, Andrea. "La postérité du devant-d'autel à Venise: Retables orfévrés et retables peints." In *The Altar and Its Environment 1150–1400*, ed. Justin E.A. Kroesen and Victor M. Schmidt, 57–86. Turnhout: Brepols, 2009.

Degenhart, Bernhard, and Annegrit Schmitt. *Corpus der italienischen Zeichnungen 1300–1450*, part 2, vol. 2, *Venedig 1300–1400; Addenda zu Süd- und Mittelitalien*. Berlin: Mann, 1980.

Demori Staničić, Zoraida. "Prilozi o srednjovjekovnom tekstilu u Trogiru: Prijedlozi za lokalnu vezilačku radionicu." *Prilozi povijesti umjetnosti u Dalmaciji* 40 (2003–04): 113–47.

Demori Staničić, Zoraida. "Paolo Veneziano i trečento na Jadranu." In *Stoljeće gotike na Jadranu: Slikarstvo u ozračju Paola Veneziana*, ed. Biserka Rauter Plančić, 7–9. Zagreb: Galerija Klovićevi dvori, 2004.

Demori Staničić, Zoraida. "Figuralni umjetnički vez obrednog ruha iz vremena renesanse u Dalmaciji i Istri." *Radovi Instituta za povijest umjetnosti*, 32 (2008): 69–86.

Deša, Diana, Nada Gogala, and Sofija Matijević. *Riznica splitske katedrale*. Split: Muzej Grada Splita, 1972.

Domijan, Miljenko. "12. Raspeće i šest svetaca." In *Stoljeće gotike na Jadranu: Slikarstvo u ozračju Paola Veneziana*, ed. Biserka Rauter Plančić, exh. cat., 82–85. Zagreb: Galerija Klovićevi dvori, 2004.

Fisković, Igor. "23–25. Raspeće." In *Stoljeće gotike na Jadranu: Slikarstvo u ozračju Paola Veneziana*, ed. Biserka Rauter Plančić, 106–9. Zagreb: Galerija Klovićevi dvori, 2004.

Fisković, Igor. "37. King Ladislav's Cloak." In *The First Five Centuries of Croatian Art*, ed. Biserka Rauter Plančić, 174–75. Exh. cat. Zagreb: Galerija Klovićevi dvori, 2006.

Flores d'Arcais, Francesca. "32. Sant'Agostino, san Pietro, san Giovanni Battista; san Giovanni evangelista, san Paolo, san Giorgio." In *Il Trecento adriatico: Paolo Veneziano e la pittura tra Oriente e Occidente*, ed. Francesca Flores d'Arcais and Giovanni Gentili, 168–169. Milan: Silvana Editoriale, 2002.

Flury-Lemberg, Mechthild. "87. Bell-Shaped Chasuble of St. Ladislaus of Hungary." In *Textile Conservation and Research: A Documentation of the Textile Department on the Occasion of the Twentieth Anniversary of the Abegg Foundation*, 176–78, 498. Bern: Abegg Stiftung, 1988.

Gardner, Julian. "From Gold Altar to Gold Altarpiece: The *Pala d'Oro* and Paolo Veneziano." In *Euncountering the Renaissance: Celebrating Gary M. Radke and 50 Years of the Syracuse University Graduate Program in Renaissance Art*, ed. Molly Bourne and A. Victor Coonin, 259–78. Ramsey: WAPACC Organization, 2016.

Griffiths, Fiona J. *Nun's Priest's Tales: Men and Salvation in Medieval Women's Monastic Life*. Philadelphia: University of Pennsylvania Press, 2018.

Guarnieri, Cristina. *Lorenzo Veneziano*. Milan: Silvana Editoriale, 2006.

Guarnieri, Cristina. "Il passaggio tra due generazioni: Dal Maestro dell'Incoronazione a Paolo Veneziano." In *Il secolo di Giotto nel Veneto*, ed. Giovanna Valenzano and Federica Toniolo, 153–201. Venice: Istituto Veneto di Scienze, Lettere ed Arti, 2007.

Guarnieri, Cristina. "Per la restituzione di due croci perdute di Paolo Veneziano: Il leone marciano del Museo Correr e i dolenti della Galleria Sabauda." In *Medioevo adriatico: Circolazione di modelli, opere, maestri*, ed. Federica Toniolo and Giovanna Valenzano, 133–58. Rome: Viella, 2010.

Guarnieri, Cristina. "Il monumento funebre di Francesco Dandolo nella sala del capitolo ai Frari." In *Santa Maria Gloriosa dei Frari: Immagini di devozione, spazi della fede*, ed. Carlo Corsato and Deborah Howard, 159–60. Padua: Centro Studi Antoniani, 2015.

Guarnieri, Cristina. "Una pala ribaltabile per l'esposizione delle reliquie: Le *Storie di santa Lucia* di Jacobello del Fiore a Fermo." *Arte Veneta* 73 (2016): 9–35.

Hilje, Emil. "61. Vezeni Antependij." In *Stoljeće gotike na Jadranu: Slikarstvo u ozračju Paola Veneziana*, ed. Biserka Rauter Plančić, 188–89. Zagreb: Galerija Klovićevi dvori, 2004.

Ivoš, Jelena. *Liturgijsko ruho iz zbirke tekstila Muzeja za umjetnost i obrt*. Exh. cat. Zagreb: Muzej za umjetnost i obrt, 2010.

Jakšić, Nikola. "Od hagiografskog obrasca do političkog elaborata: Škrinja Sv. Šimuna, zadarska *arca d'oro*." *Ars Adriatica* 4 (2014): 95–124.

Jerman, Mateja. "The Town of Boljun between the Lion and the Eagle: A Contribution to the Knowledge of Augsburg and Venetian Goldsmithing in Croatia." In *Istria in the Modern Period*, ed. Tatjana Bradara, 339–63. Pula: Arheološki muzej Istre, 2017.

Jerman, Mateja, Iva Jazbec Tomaić, and Danijel Ciković. "Frankapanski zagovori u zlatu i svili." In *Putovima Frankopana*, ed. Ines Srdoč-Konestra and Saša Potočnjak, 229–46. Rijeka: Primorsko-goranska županija, Filozofski fakultet Sveučilišta u Rijeci, 2018.

Jerman, Mateja. "Liturgijski predmeti od plemenitih metala od 1400. do 1800. godine na području nekadašnje Pulske biskupije." PhD diss., University of Zadar, 2020.

King, Donald. "A Venetian Embroidered Altar Frontal." *Victoria and Albert Museum Bulletin* 1, no. 4 (1965): 14–25.

King, Monique, and Donald King. *European Textiles in the Keir Collection 400 BC to 1800 AD*. London: Faber and Faber, 1990.

Klaić, Vjekoslav. *Krčki knezovi Frankapani: Od najstarijih vremena do gubitka otoka Krka (od god. 1118. do god. 1480.)*. Zagreb: Matica Hrvatska, 1901.

Kniewald, Dragutin. "*Antependij* u Dobrinju na otoku Krku." *Godišnjak Sveučilišta Kraljevine Jugoslavije u Zagrebu* (1929/30–1932/33): 81.

Koller, Alexander, Pier Paolo Piergentili, and Gianni Venditti, eds. *I Codici Minucciani dell'Istituto Storico Germanico: Inventario*. Rome: Deutsches Historisches Institut in Rom, 2009.

Koprčina, Arijana. "Barbara Frankapan i zlatarske narudžbe oko 1500. godine." *Radovi Instituta za povijest umjetnosti* 37 (2013): 65.

Kosanović, Ozren. "Družine i potknežini knezova Krčkih na Krku (od 1260. do 1480.)." *Povijesni prilozi* 50 (2016): 253.

Kudiš Burić, Nina. "62. Vezeni antependij s prizorom krunjenja Bogorodice i svecima Jakovom i Stjepanom." In *Stoljeće gotike na Jadranu: Slikarstvo u ozračju Paola Veneziana*, ed. Biserka Rauter Plančić, 190–91. Zagreb: Galerija Klovićevi dvori, 2004.

Kurtović, Esad. "Prilog bibliografiji radova o bosanskoj kraljici Katarini Kotromanić (1425–1478)." *Bosna franciscana* 22 (2005): 201–11.

Ljubić, Šime. "Commissiones et relationes Venetae (Annorum 1433–1527)." Vol. 1. *Giurisdizione antica di Veglia: Relazione di Antonio Vinciguerra 1481*. Monumenta spectantia historiam Slavorum meridionalium 6. Zagreb: Ex officina Societatis Typographicae, 1876.

Marangon, Desi. "Il fascino delle forme greche a Venezia: Andrea Dandolo, l'arte e l'epigrafia." *Hortus Artium Medievalium* 22 (2016): 157–64.

Marchi, Alessandro. "31. Incoronazione della Vergine e santi Caterina d'Alessandria, Michele Arcangelo, Giovanni il Battista, Pietro, Severino Vescovo, Venanzio Martire, Pietro Martire, Paolo, Giovanni Evangelista, Domenico, Orsola, Tommaso d'Acquino, Tommaso Apostolo, Bartolomeo." In *Il Trecento adriatico: Paolo Veneziano e la pittura tra Oriente e Occidente*, ed. Francesca Flores d'Arcais and Giovanni Gentili, 166–67. Milan: Silvana Editoriale, 2002.

Marinković, Ana. "John Capistran's Mantle and the Early Propaganda of Franciscan Observant Cults in Dubrovnik." In *Genius loci—Laslovszky 60*, ed. Dóra Mérai et al., 171–74. Budapest: Archaeolingua, 2018.

Monnas, Lisa. *Merchants, Princes and Painters. Silk Fabrics in Italian and Northern Paintings 1300–1550*. London: Yale University Press, 2008.

Monnas, Lisa. *Renaissance Velvets*. London: Victoria and Albert Museum, 2012.

Morozzi, Luisa. "28. Madonna in trono con Bambino e due angeli; Maria Maddalena, san Nicola di Bari, san Marco, san Giovanni Battista; san Giovanni evangelista, san Biagio, sant'Antonio abate, santa Caterina d'Alessandria." In *Il Trecento adriatico: Paolo Veneziano e la pittura tra Oriente e Occidente*, ed. Francesca Flores d'Arcais and Giovanni Gentili, 158–61. Milan: Silvana Editoriale, 2002.

Müller-Christensen, Sigrid. "Materiale e tecnica," in *Il Ricamo nella storia e nell'arte*, ed. Marie Schuette and Sigrid Müller-Christensen, 7–12. Rome: Edizioni Mediterranee, 1963.

Muraro, Michelangelo. *Paolo da Venezia*. Milan: Istituto Editoriale Italiano, 1969.

Papastavrou, Hélène. "À propos d'un voile brodé vénitien du XIVe siècle à Zadar." *Zograf* 32 (2008): 91–99.

Pedrocco, Filippo. *Paolo Veneziano*. Milan: Alberto Maioli Editore, Società Veneta Editrice, 2003.

Perinčić, Tea. "Rapska biskupija u vizitaciji Agustina Valiera 1579. godine." MA thesis. Sveučilište u Zagrebu, 2004.

Piccolo Paci, Sara. *Storia delle vesti liturgiche: Forma, immagine e funzione*. Milan: Àncora editrice, 2008.

Platts, Christopher W. "Establishing the International Patronage of Paolo Veneziano: New Case Studies from France and Croatia." In *Trecento Forum* 2, forthcoming.

Polonijo, Mato. "Najstariji sačuvani inventar stolne crkve u Krku." *Croatia sacra* 13/14 (1937): 117.

Raukar, Tomislav. "Arpadovići i Anžuvinci na hrvatskom prijestolju." In *Povijest Hrvata: Srednji vijek*, ed. Franjo Šanjek, 223–28. Zagreb: Školska Knjiga, 2003.

Ravančić, Gordan. "Prilog proučavanju Crne smrti u dalmatinskom gradu (1348.–1353.): Raspon izvorne građe i stanje istraženosti na primjerima Dubrovnika, Splita i Zadra." *Povijesni prilozi* 26 (2004): 7–18.

Ravnik-Toman, Barbara, et al. "Turški mašni plašč." In *Narodni muzej Slovenije: Zgodovinske in umetnostne zbirke; Stalna razstava*, ed. Maja Lozar Štamcar, 20–21. Ljubljana: Narodni muzej Slovenije, 2011.

Schmidt, Victor M. "Ensembles of Painted Altarpieces and Frontals." In *The Altar and Its Environment 1150–1400*, ed. Justin E.A. Kroesen and Victor M. Schmidt, 203–21. Turnhout: Brepols, 2009.

Schuette, Marie. Introduction to *Il Ricamo nella storia e nell'arte*, ed. Marie Schuette and Sigrid Müller-Christensen, 15–24. Rome: Edizioni Mediterranee, 1963.

Seeberg, Stefanie. "Women as Makers of Church Decoration: Illustrated Textiles at the Monasteries of Altenberg/Lahn, Rupertsberg, and Heinigen (13th–14th c.)." In *Reassessing the Roles of Women as "Makers" of Medieval Art and Architecture*, vol. 1, ed. Therese Martin, 356–91. Leiden/Boston: Brill, 2012.

Sgambati, Aniello. "La 'pala' di Pellegrino II nel Duomo di Cividale: Nuove considerazioni." *Forum Iulii: Annuario del Museo Archeologico Nazionale di Cividale del Friuli* 35 (2011): 85–105.

Špoljarić, Luka. "Bosanska kraljica Katarina i humanisti, dio prvi: Leonardo Montagna i njegovi epigrami,"*Zbornik Odsjeka za povijesne znanosti Zavoda za povijesne i društvene znanosti*, HAZU 36 (2018): 61–80.

Theiner, Augustin. *Epistolae Sixti PP. IV., DCLXXXIII: Catherinae reginae Bosniae testamentum, per quod, nisi Sigismundus et Catherina eius filii ad christianam fidem redirent, Romanam ecclesiam instituit haeredem; Ex Cencio Camerario* fol. 347. Vetera Monumenta Slavorum Meridionalium historiam illustrantia, vol. 1. Rome: Typis Vaticanis, 1863.

Tulić, Damir, and Nina Kudiš. *Opatska riznica, katedrala i crkve grada Korčule*. Korčula: Župa sv. Marka, 2014.

Valenti, Devis. *Le immagini multiple dell'altare: Dagli antependia ai polittici; Tipologie compositive dall'Alto Medioevo all'età gotica*. Padua: Il Poligrafo, 2012.

Žic-Rokov, Ivan. "Kompleks katedrala—Sv. Kvirin u Krku." *Rad JAZU* 360 (1971): 134.

Indices

Preliminary Notes: In the *Biblical Index*, Old Testament books are arranged according to the Septuagint (MT indications have been added as needed). In the *Index of Names, Titles and Selected Realia*, Emperors, Kings and other rulers and their wives have been usually indexed under their first names. Proper names have been qualified in English (e.g. 'Apostle', 'Bishop', 'saint', etc.). The *Index of Repositories: Archives, Libraries and Museums* does not include churches and monasteries unless they have a repository or museum section. Popular names of manuscripts have been added within parentheses whenever it was deemed expedient.

1   Biblical Index

Old Testament	21, 84, 220	*Ezekiel*	
		1:10	234
Genesis	143, 222		
		Matthew	
Exodus		24:31	156
33:13	31	25:4	45
33:20	31	25:35–36	45
33:22–23	31	25:40	45
Psalms		*Luke*	
40 (41):1–2	45	19:1–10 (encounter with	
103 (104):15	31	Zacchaeus)	128–31
111 (112):5	45	19:5	129
148	17	19:8	129
149	17	19:9	132, 137
150	17		
		John	
Wisdom		1:1	30
7:15	30	2:1–12 (Marriage at Cana)	133–35
		4:4–26 (Samaritan woman)	128–29, 137
Proverbs		5:1–18 (Healing of the	
9:1	22	paralytic)	126–29, 137
9:3	22	9:1–34 (Healing of the man	
9:4	22	born blind)	126–27
9:5	22, 31	20:17 (*Noli me Tangere*)	252
Zechariah		*Acts*	
4:10	27	1:10–11	156
Isaiah		*Romans*	
11:1–2	27	12:5	110

1 Corinthians
1:30	30
2:10	31
12:27	110
14:3–5	29
14:26	29

11 Corinthians
9:6	45

Colossians
2:9	27

1 Thess.
5:11	29

Apocalypse (Revelation)   233
4:2–5:10	156

2   Index of Names, Titles and Selected Realia

Abraham, bishop of Kolomna   62
Acheimastou-Potamianou, Myrtalē   220
Adriatic Sea (area, coast, region)   7–8, 92, 96, 100–1, 106, 114, 143–66, 172, 256–58, 261, 266, 271, 273
Adriaticus   178
aër (epitaphios)   233–46
Agallona, Moschos's son, Constantinopolitan layman   78
Agnes, saint   267
Agnus Dei (Lamb of God)   215, 218
Agoritsas, Demetrios K.   74
Ahl, Diane Cole   162
Ahsmann, Mark   15
Akathistos Hymn   143, 219, 221
Al Purković, Miodrag   160
Albania   4, 106
Alef, Gustav   37, 41
Aleksei Mikhailovich Romanov, Tsar   46–47, 62
Alexander I, Moldavian ruler (Alexandru cel Bun)   235
Alexandrov, Victor   204
Allegory of Wisdom   14–35
Altenberg an der Lahn, Premonstratensian Abbey   259
ambo   54, 64
Ambrose, Kirk   6
Amiroutzes, George   81
Anastasios Sinaites   24
Anderson, Jeffrey   60
Andrea Dandolo, Doge   256
Andreaš, Church   174
Andrejev, Olga   210

Andronicos Dioscurides, Eparchos   78
Andronicos II Palaiologos, Emperor   72–75, 119, 137
   chrysobull (February 1321)   73, 75
   chrysobull (June 1321)   73
   epitaphios   233
Andronicos III Palaiologos, Emperor   73–74
   chrysobull (June 1321)   73
Androshchuk, Fedir   42
Angelos Demetrios   78
angels   21–22, 31, 110, 155–56, 215, 218, 235, 248, 252, 254, 261, 267
Anichini, Guido   91
Anjou dynasty   261
Annunciation   121, 267
Antelami, Benedetto   157
anthivolon   190, 220
Antonius de Roxellis   79
Anzy-le-Duc, Priory church   155
Apulia   101
Aquileia   256
Arabs   221
Arbore, Beheading of St. John the Baptist (church)   214
Arezzo, Santa Maria della Pieve (church)   158
Argyropoulos, John   75–79
Arilje, St. Achillius (church)   101, 103, 109–10, 112
Aristotle   220
Arrian (Arrianus)   83
Arsenii (Ivashenko), Bishop   25
Asia, Central   37–38, 50
Aspile, amolunte, aphthore (prayer)   64

INDICES

Athanasios of New Patras, saint 178–79, 181
Augustine, saint 252
Augustus Caesar 50
Austria 97
Avars 221
Avignon, Papal Treasury 264
Axion estin (hymn, *Dostoinno est*) 63

Babić, Gordana 107, 124, 126, 146
Băbuș, Emanoil 210
Bacci, Michele 17, 190
Baert, Barbara 127
Baia (Suceava) 212
Bakalova, Elka 12, 17
Balkans 1–4, 6–7, 9, 11–12, 32, 36, 71, 106, 111, 167–68, 172–73, 175, 179, 191–92, 207–8, 217, 221, 224, 232, 257, 259, 268–71
Balș, Gheorghe (Georges) 175, 205, 208, 211–12, 215, 223, 243
Balș, Ștefan 205
Baltic Sea (area) 37
Bandini, Angelo-Maria 84
Banić, Silvija 250, 256, 260–61, 264, 266, 268, 270–72
Banjska, St. Stefan (church) 124, 154
Bar—Council (1199) 96
Baradel, Valentina 252
Barber, Charles 32
Bari, San Nicola (church; St. Nicholas). Icon donated by Queen Jelena 96–100
  enamel with St. Nicholas crowning Roger II 105–6
barmy of Monomakh 43, 45–46, 48–49, 51, 62, 64–65
Barral i Altet, Xavier 259
Barsov, Elpidifor Vasilievich 52–53, 55, 60
Bartholomew de Sancta Sophia, jr 79
Bartusis, M.C. 14
Basian, bishop of Tver 62
Basil the Great, saint 22
  Liturgy of Saint Basil 234
Batariuc, Paraschiva-Victoria 212
Battaglia, Salvatore 99
Battaglini, Fabiano 83
Bauer, Franz Alto 185
Bayezid I, Sultan 53
Bazilevich, Konstantin Vasilievich 41
Beatillo, Antonio (A. da Bari) 97–99

Bedros, Vlad 215, 218
Begunov, Iu.K. 25
Bekker, Immanuel 80–81
Belamarić, Joško 258
Beldiceanu, Nicoară 203
Belgrade 112
  Diocese 132
Beloozero 38
Belting, Hans 101
Benedict, saint 261
Benedictines 154, 254, 259–61
Bentchev, Ivan 122
Beresford-Peirse, Jadranka 256
Berry, Burton Y. 240–41
Bertonière, Gabriel 129, 132
Berza, Mihai 214
Bessarion, Cardinal—poetry for him 83
Betancourt, Roland 238
Bibikov, M.V. 26
Birchler-Argyros, Urs Benno 74
Bistrița (Transylvania) 212
Blaauw, Sible de 258
Black Sea (area) 38, 201, 214
BLAGO Fund 26, 130, 133–35
Blaise, saint 252
Blanche, daughter of Philip I of Taranto 160
Blastares, Matthew, *Syntagma Canonum* 204
blessing of water 186
Bodnar, Edward W. 82
Boeck, Elena N. 224
Boerio, Giuseppe 257
Bogatyrev, Sergei 44, 48, 58
Bogdanović, Dimitrije 186
Bogdanović, Jelena 8–9, 167–200, 225
Bogoje, Prince and Family 177–78, 192
Boiadzhiev, Stefan 18
Boiani, Benvenuta, Dominican, blessed 259
Bojović, Boško 96
Böker, Johann Josef 212
Boldura, Oliviu 208
Bolonić, Mihovil 254–55, 262–63
Boltunova, Ekaterina 50
Bondioli, Lorenzo 120, 217
Boniface VIII, Pope 95
Bonjohannes, Bishop of Krk, Benedictine 254
Borgia, Lucrezia 270

Borgioli, Cristina 267
Bošković, Djurdje (Georges M.) 121, 143, 146, 150–51, 153–56
Bosnia and Herzegovina (Bosnians) 4, 112, 150, 269
Bosnic, Dragan 83
Boudon-Millot, Véronique 78
Bouras, Laskarina 220
Bourdieu, Pierre 43
Bourne, Molly 259
boyars 44, 58, 64–65
Boynton, Susan 237
Bradanović, Marijan 255, 273
Bradara, Tatjana 257
Braničevo, Diocese (Branichevo) 132
Branković, George Vuk 82, 86
Branković, Mara 186
Braun, Joseph 259, 266
Brenni, Luigi 264
Briusova, V.G. 24–25
Brookline, Holy Cross Orthodox College, Mary Jaharis Center for Byzantine Art and Culture 13, 32, 138, 193, 225
Brooks, Sarah T. 110
Brunello, Franco 265
bubonic plague (14th century; Black Death) 258, 261
Bucossi, Alessandra 30
Bulgaria 4, 6, 9–10, 12, 14, 27, 156, 175, 204, 207, 214, 217, 224, 232
Bushkovitch, Paul 39

Cacoulide, Eleni 73, 75
Caillet, Jean-Pierre 258
Cameron, Averil 30
Čanak-Medić, Milka 143, 148, 150–51, 153–54, 156, 158
Canali, Menegelo Ivanov de 261
Cannadine, David 41
Cantelli, Giuseppe 259
Čapeta Rakić, Ivana 273
Cappadocia 234
Carile, Maria Cristina 189
Carpathian Mountains (area) 1–4, 6, 8, 10–11, 175, 200, 208, 221–22, 224
Cartelazzo, Michele A. 256
Casarino, Cesare 25–26
Caselli, Letizia 264

Caspian Sea 38
Cataldi Palau, Annaclara 73, 80
Catherine of Alexandria, saint 261
Cazacu, Matei 217
cendal (*cendale, cendalo, cendatum, zendado, zendale*) 256
Cennino Cennini, Florentine painter 267–68
censer 96
Cernea, Emanuela 240
Cetatea Albă. Fortress 201
Chaadaev, Piotr J. 37
Charles I Robert, Hungarian-Croatian King 112, 268
Charles II of Anjou, King of Naples 160
Chatterjee, Paroma 106–7
Chernigov region 38
Chernova, O.A. 25
Cherubikon (hymn) 239
Chiappini di Sorio, Ileana 264
Chichurov, Igor Sergeevich 42
Chilia Fortress 201, 212
Chinggisid Dynasty 37
Chirban, John T. 120
Chiriță, Cristian 183
chiton 92
choros (candle holder) 143
Chortasmenos, John 76–77, 79, 82, 86
 Letter 36 82
 Letter 38 82
Christ, W. 24
Christe, Yves 156
Christidou, Anna 104, 106
Christie, Jessica Joyce 185, 200
chrysobull 73–76
Chrysochoides, Criton 82
Chrysogonus, saint 261
Ciković, Danijel 8, 11, 248–80
Cincheza-Buculei, Ecaterina 215
Ciobanu, Constantin Ion 220–21
Ćirković, Sima 53, 161
Clare, Edward G. 102
Colonna family 103–4, 106
Comărnescu, Petru 205
commons 6, 24, 26–27
Concini, Elisa 273
Constantin Brâncoveanu, Wallachian ruler 177, 179

Constantine Dejanović Dragaš 81
Constantine I, the Great 91–92
Constantine IX, Monomachos, Emperor 48, 50, 62
  see also *barmy* of Monomakh; *shapka Monomakha*
Constantine XI Palaiologos Dragases, Despot 82, 84
Constantinople (Istanbul) 2, 7, 12, 18–19, 25, 27, 32, 39, 52–53, 55, 65, 71–72, 80, 82, 111, 123, 167–68, 172–73, 180, 182, 190–92, 214, 216, 232
  fall (1453) 1, 8, 10, 36, 71, 76, 80, 84, 167, 175, 191, 201, 217–19, 221, 224, 232, 246
  fire (September 17, 1305) 74
  Latin conquest (1204) 160
  recapture of 1261 87
  Aetius's cistern 73
  Blachernae 73
  Chora monastery 80, 123–24, 127, 129, 182
  Constantine Lips monastery 182
  Gate of the Hunters 74
  Hagia Sophia (St. Sophia; church) 54, 212
  Monastery of Christ Pantokrator (Zeyrek camii) 161, 182
  Opaine 74
  Pammakaristos monastery 182
  St. John Prodromos en Petra (monastery) 73–74, 79–81, 86
  Xenon of the Kral 71, 73–82, 86–87
Coonin, Victor (A. Victor) 259
Cooper, Donal 256
Cormack, Robin 3
Corsato, Carlo 255
Ćošković, Pejo 256
Coxe, Henry Octavius 75, 78
Cozia Monastery 189
  epitaphios 241–43
  Holy Trinity Church 176–78, 180, 182–84, 187
Cozzi, Enrica 262, 264
Crăciun, Casian 221
Crăciunaș, Irineu, Bishop of Suceava 221
Cracraft, James 50
Cristea, Gherasim 179
Cristea, Ovidiu 9
Croatia 4, 8, 10–11, 248, 269

Cronica Moldo-Germană (Moldo-German Chronicle) 201
Cross of the Crucifixion (True Cross; feast; relic) 48, 97, 185–87, 203–4
Crummey, Robert Oliver 58
Crusade 111
  IV (1204) 71
Čubrović, Zorica 154
Čučaković, Aleksandar A. 189
Čučer, St Nikita (church) 121–24, 127, 129, 131, 134
Ćuk, Ruža 96
Ćurčić, Slobodan 9, 107, 119, 121, 124, 126, 147, 149–50, 167–70, 174–75, 178–80, 182–85, 188–90, 213, 218
Curta, Florin 4, 9
Curtea de Argeș Monastery 237, 240, 245
  Cathedral of the Dormition of the Mother of God 236
  Saint Nicholas (church) 176, 244
Cvetković, Branislav 108
Cyprian, Franciscan envoy 111
Cyriacus of Ancona 82
Cyrillic alphabet (writing) 92, 100, 241

D'Amico, Rosa 91–92, 95, 111
Da Rin, Adriana 256
Dalmatia (Dalmatian coast; Sclavonia) 111, 150, 257–58
Damasus I, Pope, saint 92
Damian, Iuliana 240
Dandolo family 256
Daničić, Đuro (Djuro; Djura) 96, 147
Danilo II, Archbishop 74, 108, 121, 147–48, 162
  Biography of Uroš II 76
  Vita of Queen Jelena 97, 112
  Životi Kraljeva i Arhiepiskopa Srpskih (Life of the Serbian Kings and Archbishops) 97, 146–47
Danube River 4, 8–10, 169, 175, 232
Daskalov, Roumen 36
Davanzo Poli, Doretta 264–66
David, King of Israel 21, 51
Davidescu, Mișu 176
Davidov, Dinko 95
Davit' v Narin, King of Georgia 110
De Marchi, Andrea 258

Dečani Monastery   22, 129, 143–66, 220
  Christ Pantokrator *katholikon*   7, 19, 26,
    143–66
  St. Demetrios (chapel)   143, 148
  St. Nicholas (chapel)   148
Dečani Bistrica (Bistrica)   153
Decembrists   37
Degenhart, Bernhard   264
Dekanski   178
della Valle, Mauro   120
Demetrios Lascaris Leontares, notary, *oikeios*
  of Manuel II Palaiologos   84–86
Demori Staničić, Zoraida   258, 265–66
Demosthenes   79
Deroko, Aleksandar   107–8, 168
Devič, Church   173
Deževo—Council (1282)   112
Diana, Deša   266
Diels, Hermann-Alexander   79
Diez, Ernst   204
Dijkstra, Roald   92
Dimitrova, Margaret   12
Diodorus Siculus   83
Dionysius of Fourna, *Hermeneia*   123, 217
Djordjević, Ivan   146
Djurić, Srdjan   185
Djurić, Vojislav J.   127, 143, 146–47, 185
Dmitrii Donskoi of Moscow   38
  testament   49
Dmitrii Ivanovich, Grand Prince of
  Muscovy—inauguration (1498)   36–70
Dmitrii Konstantinovich of Tver   38
dodekaorton   122–23
Domentijan, *Život Svetoga Save*   52, 96–97,
  186
  Život Svetoga Simeuna   52, 96–97, 186
Domijan, Miljenko   252
Dominicans   258–59
Donatus, saint   261
Đorđevič, Ivan M.   22
Doronin, Andrei   48
Dragović, Magdalena S.   189
Drăguţ, Vasile   212
Dragutin, King of Serbia, King of Mačva *see*
  Stefan Dragutin, King of Serbia, King of
  Mačva
Drpić, Ivan   11–12

Dubrovnik (Ragusa)   82, 256–58
  Benedictine cloister   154
  Cathedral of St. Mary   154
  Dominikanski samostan i crkva
    (Dominican monastery),
    Crucifix   256, 258
Ducas, *Historia Byzantina*   80
Ducci, Annamaria   267
Dufrenne, Suzy   124, 126
Dujčev, Ivan   79
Dumitrescu, Ana   217
Dunning, Chester   50
Đurađ Branković, Despot of Serbia (George
  Vulcos)   81
Durand, Jannic   185
Đurđević, Marko   98
Đurić, Ivan   112
Durrës   257
Dvornik, Francis   37, 42, 51

eagle (double-headed)   58
Easter   129, 218, 255
Eastmond, Antony   3, 96, 110, 119, 138, 186,
  225
*Ecthesis Chronica and Chronicon
  Athenarum*   81
Efrosini Palaiologina Leontarina   86
Egypt   38
Elizabeta Kotromanić   271–72
  see also Jelisavetina planita (Elizabeth's
    Chasuble)
Elizabeth II, Queen of the United
  Kingdom—Coronation (1953)   57
embroidery (textile)   3–4, 8, 10–11, 95–96,
  204, 232–48, 250, 254, 258–59, 264–70,
  272–73
enamel   99, 105–6
Enev, Mikhail   17
Engström, Maria   243
enkainia (church dedication)   24–25
Ephrem, Bishop of Rădăuţi   210
Epirus   168
Epitaphios Threnos   233–37, 241–46
Erdeljan, Jelena   11–12, 153, 185
Ericani, Giuliana   257
Eudocia Palaiologina, empress-dowager of
  Trebizond   72

Euthymius, bishop of Sarai 62
evangelists 19, 151, 233
Evans, Helen C. 167, 233, 238
Evdokiia, daughter of Dmitrii
 Konstantinovich of Tver 38
Evseeva, L.M. 25
Eyice, Semavi 167
Eyler, Joshua 120

Fabini, Hermann 211
Failler, Albert 72, 119
Featherstone, Michael 50
Felmy, Karl Christian 19
Fenwick, John R.K. 234
Feron, Ernest 83
Filelfo, Francesco 80
Filioque 30
Filippino Lippi, painter 267
Fine, John V.A. 50, 119
Firea, Ciprian 216
Firea, Elena 217
Fisković, Cvito 154
Fisković, Igor 256, 258, 269
Flier, Michael 40, 50
Florence, Museo degli Argenti 259
 Santa Maria Novella (church) 259
Florensky, Pavel 210
Flores d'Arcais, Francesca 252
Florescu, Radu 179
Flury-Lemberg, Mechthild 268
Flusin, Bernard 185
Fojnica, Franciscan monastery of the Holy
 Spirit 272
Fonkich, Boris L. 237
Franciscans (Franciscan Order) 106, 111,
 269–72
Franklin, Simon 56
Frankopan (Croatian family) 255, 271
Frankopan, Barbara, wife of Vuk Grgurević
 Branković 270–71
Frattaroli, Paola 256–57
fresco 27, 217
Frick, Carole Collier 270
Frolow, Anatole 186
Frost, Robert 38

Galavaris, George 234
Gamillscheg, Ernst 79–80

Gardner, Julian 103–5, 259
Gardthausen, Victor 79
Gaudentius, saint 250, 252
Gaul, Niels 30
Gavrić, Gordana 108
Gavrilović, Zaga 157, 185
Geanakoplos, Deno 160
Gelasios, hieromonk, patron at Lapušnja
 182, 192
Gelat'i Monastery 110
Genoa (Genoese) 52, 272
Gentili, Giovanni 252
George, saint 156
George Branković, Prince of Smederevo 84
George Chrysococces 79
George from Trikala, painter 218
George Kantakouzenos Palaiologos 82,
 84–86
 letter to Constantine Palaiologos
  (1431) 82
 funeral oration for him 82
 Library 71, 81–86
Georgia 204
Georgievska-Juhas, Ljiljana 96–97
Gergina, Joupan 177–78, 192
German language 210, 265
Germanos I, patriarch of Constantinople,
 *Historia ecclesiastica, et mystica
 contemplatio* 234
Germany, southern 176, 212
Gerstel, Sharon 211
Getcha, Job 126, 129
Gethsemane Garden 252
Gheorghiță, Victoria 245
Gilles, Pierre 80
Girolamo d'Ascoli, Franciscan 111
Girona, Cathedral of St. Mary 259
Giugea, Gheorghița Daniela 222
Gjuzelev, Vasil 12
Glass, Dorothy F. 157
Gogala, Nada 266
Golden Horde 38
Golovkova, D.S. 22
Gonneau, Pierre 57
González de Clavijo, Ruy 73–74
Good Friday 233
Goodich, Michael 120
Gorovei, Ștefan S. 203–4

Gorskii, Anton Anatolevich   38
Gortan, Veljko   98
Gothic art (influence)   7, 11, 144–45, 147–48, 154–55, 158–59, 187, 205, 211–12, 214, 223, 225, 248, 250, 258
Gouma-Peterson, Thalia   120
Govora Monastery, Church of the Assumption of the Mother of God   177–79
Grabar, André   218
Grabar, Oleg   188
Gračanica Monastery, Church of the Annunciation / Dormition (Church of the Virgin; *katholikon*)   19, 120–21, 123–24, 127, 129–30, 133–37, 150, 216, 220
Gradac Monastery, Church of St. Nicholas   108
Grashchenkov, Vladimir N.   57
Greece (Greek influence; Greeks)   4, 9, 11, 137, 145, 233, 239
Greek language (alphabet)   80, 86, 126, 215, 233, 241, 244
Gregory I, the Great, Pope, saint   261
Gregory X, Pope   95–96
Gregory XI, Pope, letter written on Easter 1377   255
Gregory Nazianzos, saint   22
Griffiths, Fiona J.   259
Grigorije Camblak (Gregory Tsamblak), Metropolitan of Kiev   29, 147
   Homily on the Birth of the Bogoroditsa   29
   Žitije Stefana Dečanskog (Life of Stefan Dečanski)   147
Grigorovich-Barsky, Vasil, Russian monk and traveler   218
Grković, Milica   146
Guarino da Verona   80
Guarnieri, Cristina   250, 252, 254–55, 259, 263, 268
Guboglu, Mihail   201, 203
Guzmán, Eulogio   185, 200

Habsburg Empire   257
Haçlı Kilise   234
Hadjitryphonos, Evangelia   189
Hafner, Stanislaus   73–74, 76, 112
Hajdu, Ada   36

Haldon, John F.   3
Hannan, Joe   33, 193, 225
Harlfinger, Dieter   79
Harris, Jonathan   84
Hasan Predojević, Beylerbey of Bosnia   272
Hasan's Mantle (*Hasanov plašč*)   272
Haury, Jacob   84
Haustein-Bartsch, Eva   19
Hazard, Harry W.   160
Healing of the Paralytic at Bethesda (John 5:1–18)   126–29, 137
Heiningen, Augustinian Abbey   259
Helena Dragaš, Manuel II's wife, empress (Helena Palaiologina; Jelena Dragaš)   52–53, 55, 58, 81
Hellenism (classical tradition)   3, 50
Henry, Paul   219
Herea, Gabriel   187, 215
Herkov, Zlatko   98
Hermolaus (family)   256
Hermolaus, saint   252
Herodotus   83
Herzegovina *see* Bosnia
Herzen, Aleksander Ivanovich   37
Hetherington, Paul   123, 217
Hilje, Emil   260–61
Hilsdale, Cecily J.   92, 95–96
himation   92
Himka, John-Paul   222
Hippolytus (of Rome), *Commentarii in Proverbia*   24
Historia Politica et Patriarchica Constantinopoleos   81
Hlaváček, Ivan   4
Ho euschemon Ioseph (hymn; *Noble Joseph*)   236
Hobsbawm, Eric   41
Hoffmann, Annette   186
Hoffmann, Lars M.   20
Homer   79
Honorius II, Pope   160
Honorius III, Pope   96
Horologion   60
Hosios Loukas (church)   218
Howard, Deborah   255
Hraste, Katarina   268
Hrelja, protosebastos (Stefan Hrelja Dragovol; Chrelja)   14, 18

humanists 80
Humor Monastery 214
Hungary (Hungarians; Hungarian-Croatian Kingdom) 4, 112, 175–76, 212, 232, 257
Hunger, Herbert 72, 76, 82
Hunt, Priscilla 21, 25
Huskinson, Janet M. 94

Iacobini, Antonio 120
Iagaris (around 1460) 81
Iakouchev, Mikhaïl 218
Iaroslavl 38
Ibar, river 112
icon 4, 7, 22, 91–118, 210, 215, 237, 244–46
iconostasis 143, 150, 210–11
Ignatios, Bishop of Panion 27
Ignatius of Smolensk, *Choždenie* 44, 51–55
Ilovan, Vasile 212
India 38
Ioan Zidarul (John the Mason) 212
Ioanikius, Archbishop in Sopoćani 158
Iorga, Nicolae 1–3, 36, 56, 180, 242–43
Irenaeus of Lyons, *Adversus Hæreses* 234
Irene Kantakouzene, wife to George Branković 81–82, 84
Iron Curtain 4–5
Islam 167, 191
Istanbul *see* Constantinople
Istria 257, 273
Italians 46, 80
    colonies on the Black Sea 38
Italy (Apennine Peninsula) 71, 79–80, 84, 92, 96, 102, 106, 153–54, 156–57, 186, 265
Italy, Southern 100–1
Iurevich, Mikhailko 52
Iurii Ivanovich, Prince son of the Grand Prince 62, 65
Ivan, son of Ivan III Vasilevich 63
Ivan Frankopan VII, Duke 271
Ivan I, Kalita, Prince of Moscow, Grand Prince of Vladimir—Testament 49
Ivan II—Testament 49
Ivan III Vasilevich, Grand Prince 39–49, 51, 55, 57–58, 62–63
    inauguration (1440) 41
Ivan IV, the Terrible, Czar 51, 57
    Testament 50

Ivan II, bishop of Krk (John) 251, 254–56, 263
Ivanov, Sergei 37
ivory 98
Ivoš, Jelena 266

Jacopo di Cambio 259
Jagić, Vatroslav 97
Jajce, Franciscan church 270
Jakšić, Nikola 272
James the Elder, Apostle, saint 101–2
James, Bishop of Jerusalem 261
    Liturgy 234
James, Liz 3, 225
Janin, Raymond 74
Jazbec Tomaić, Iva 8, 11, 248–80
Jeffreys, Elizabeth M. 3, 39, 185
Jefimija, nun, widow of Jovan Uglješa 235–36
Jelena, Bulgarian Queen, sister of Uroš III Dečanski 152
Jelena of Anjou, Queen of Serbia 91–92, 95–100, 103, 106–9, 111–14
Jelisavetina planita (Elizabeth's Chasuble) 271
Jerman, Mateja 257, 271, 273
Jesse, David's father 220
    see also Tree of Jesse
Jesus Christ 92, 110, 114, 122, 126, 135, 137, 155–56, 216–17, 219, 244, 252
    Ascension 156–58, 176–77
    Baptism 156–58
    Crucifixion 158
    – *see also* Cross of the Crucifixion; Stations of the Cross
    Deposition (pietà) 236–37, 245–46
    genealogy 220
    miracles 7, 119–20, 122–23, 143, 217; *see also* Index 1
    Passion 157
    Resurrection 158
    Transfiguration 14, 178, 181
    as Pantokrator 17, 146, 156, 222–23, 234
Jevtić, Ivana 11–12
John, evangelist, saint 244–45, 250, 255, 260, 263
John the Baptist, saint 156–57, 250, 260, 267
John Chrysostom, saint 22

John de Ontiac (Joannes de Onciache),
    Benedictine, abbot of Zadar
    monastery 261
John of Rila, saint 17
John Panaretos, physician 78
John V Palaiologos, Byzantine Emperor,
    chrysobull (December 1342) 76
John VI Kantakouzenos, Byzantine
    Emperor 18, 81, 110
John VIII Palaiologos, Byzantine
    Emperor 79
Johnson, Mark J. 12, 21, 159, 189, 205
Johnstone, Pauline 235, 239, 241, 243
Jones, Larry Paul 127
Jones, Lynn 186
Jones, Michael 38
Jovanović, Jelena 169
Jovanović, Tomislav 96
Judelson, Katharine 25
Juraj II (Georg II Hermolaus), Bishop of
    Rab 256

Kažotić, Augustin, Bishop of Zagreb 268
Kažotić, Nikola, Bishop 266
Kalabaka, Great Meteoron Monastery,
    katholikon 178–81, 190
Kalavryta region 82
Kaldellis, Anthony 3
Kalenić Monastery 134, 137
Kalić, Jovanka 53
Kampianaki, Theofili 120, 217
Kandić, Olivera 108
Kantakouzenos family 81
Kantakouzenos, Matthew 81
Kasić, Dušan 132
Kaštela, Slobodan 270
Kastoria, Omorphokklesia (church) 123
Katalina Crnojević, Princess of Zeta 177–78,
    192
Katarina Kosača Kotromanić, Bosnian
    Queen—will 269
Kataxioson Kurie (prayer) 60
Kaufmann, Thomas DaCosta 213
Kavala 72
Kazamia-Tsernou, Maria 127
Kazhdan, Alexander P. 72, 233
Kelly, Aileen 37
Kidonopoulos, Vassilios 74
Kiev (Kievan Rus) 3, 36–37, 42, 48

Kiev, St. Sophia 43
King, Donald 250, 264, 266
King, Monique 266
Kirin, Asen 14, 17, 20
Kitzinger, Beatrice 32
Kivelson, Valerie 41
Klaić, Vjekoslav 271
Klaniczay, Gábor 4
Kleimola, Ann 48
Klein, Holger A. 123, 185–86
Klenina, Elena Ju. 189
Kloss, Boris Mikhailovich 40
Knežević, Branka 178, 182
Kniazevskaia, Tatiana B. 57
Kniewald, Dragutin 248
Koester, Craig R. 127
Koller, Alexander 269
Kollmann, Nancy Shields 38–39, 41, 58
Komnene (family, dynasty; Komnenian) 30
Konchul, Diocese 132
Kondakov, Nikodim Pavlovich 241–43
Konstantin Vsevolodich 43
    enthronement (1206) 42
Koprčina, Arijana 270–71
Korablev, Boris 73
Korać, Dušan 146
Korać, Vojislav 150, 153, 155
Korčula, Cathedral Treasury 266–67
Kormchaia Kniga 51
Korpela, Jukka 38
Kosanović, Ozren 255
Kosmas the Hymnographer, *Ode for Great
    Thursday* 24
Kosovo 4, 143
Kostof, Spiro 189
Kostomarov, Nikolay 37
Kostrenčić, Marko 98
Kostroma 38
Kotor 148
    Cathedral of St. Tryphun 154
Kouzes, Aristotle P. 79
Kovijanić, Risto 148
Kraljeva Sutjeska, Franciscan church 270
Krautheimer, Richard 189
Kremlin 58
    Cathedral of the Dormition
        (Assumption) 39, 43–44, 46, 50, 62,
        65
    Church of the Annunciation 62, 65

INDICES

Church of the Archangel Michael
    62, 65
Kresten, Otto   72
Krizmanić, Damir   262, 273
Krk (Veglia), Cathedral of the Assumption of
    the Blessed Virgin Mary   8, 248, 254–55,
    258, 263, 266
    Altar Frontal   248–80
Krk (island; Veglia)   255, 261–62
Krmac, Dean   273
Kroesen, Justin E.A.   258
Krsmanović, Bojan   160
Krstić, Ivan   170, 178, 183, 193
Kruševac, St. Stephen (Lazarica church)
    169–70, 176–78, 180, 182–84, 187
Kučevište Monastery   170
Kucharek, Casimir A.   234
Kudiš Burić, Nina   262, 266–67, 273
Kulikovo Field—Battle (1380)   38
Kupa, river   272
Kurbinovo, St. George (church)   218
Kuršumlija, St. Nicholas (church)   107
Kurtović, Esad   269
Kyrie, eleison (invocation; Have mercy on us,
    o Lord)   64

Ladislaus I, Hungarian-Croatian King (Louis I
    of Anjou), saint   8, 257, 261, 268, 271
Laiou, Angeliki E.   71, 119, 134
lampas   268, 270
Lampros, Spyridon P.   75, 79–82
Langlois, Ernest   106, 111
Lăpedatu, Alexandru   212
Lapušnja Monastery, St. Nicholas
    (church)   176–80, 190–93
Last Judgment   156–58, 222
Latin (language, alphabet)   11, 99–100, 108
Laurent, Vitalien   119
Lawrence, saint   95–96, 101–2
Lazar Branković Kantakouzenos, Despot of
    Serbia   81
Lazar Hrebeljanović, Serbian Prince *see*
    Stefan Lazar Hrebeljanović
Lazarev, Victor N.   25
Lazarica—*see* Kruševac, St. Stephen
    (Lazarica church)
Lazić, Miroslav P.   87
Le Strange, Guy   73

Lecaque, Patrick   17
Lemerle, Paul   76
Lenhoff, Gail   48
Lent   129
Leo Atrapes   79
Leonard of Limoges   101–2
Leonardo da Pistoia   92, 100
Leonardo de Rosio, *podestà*   52
Leontaris family   86
Letopisețul anonim al Moldovei (Anonymous
    Chronicle of Moldavia)   201
Lidov, Alexei   186–87, 189, 210
Lifshits, Lev I.   19
Lipanj, Diocese   132
Lithuania, Grand Duchy   4, 38
Litsevoi Svod   52
Ljubić, Šime   271
Ljubostinja Monastery   171, 184, 187
London, Courtauld Institute of Art, Conway
    Library   105
    Victoria and Albert Museum,
        Clothworkers' Centre for the Study
        and Conservation of Textiles and
        Fashion   248
Lønstrup Dal Santo, Gitte   92
Loparev, Khrisanf Mefodievich   55
Lorenzo Veneziano, *Madonna della
    Misericordia with Saints John the Baptist
    and John the Evangelist, the Circumcision,
    and the Presentation of the Virgin*   268
loros   62, 94, 108
Lozar Štamcar, Maja   272
Lucca, Basilica of S. Frediano   155
Lucy, saint   267
Lur'e, Iakov Solomonovich   40, 49
Lviv (Lwów)   235
Lyons, Diocese   261
    Council (1274)   94–95, 111

Mačva (Machva), Diocese   112, 132
Mabi Angar   119
Macarie, Metropolitan of Moldavia   235
Macedonia   168, 217, 224
    Republic of North Macedonia   4, 10
Madariaga, Isabel de   57–58
Madolciu, Elisa   205
Magdalino, Paul   25
Maglič Castle   147

Maglovski, Janko 154
Majeska, George 40, 42–44, 49, 52–55
Major, Randall A. 143, 146
Makhan'ko, M.A. 25
Makris, Georgios 78
Maksimović, Jovanka 151, 154, 158
Maksimović, Ljubomir 153, 160, 186
Maksymovych, Mykhailo 37
Mamai, Khan 38
Mamaloukos, Stavros 173, 189
Mamluks 38
Mamytzona, village 75
Man Born Blind (John 9:1–34) 126–27, 129, 137
Manasija *see* Ravanica
Mango, Cyril 175, 180
maniakia 94, 108
Manuel, Constantinopolitan layman (?) 78
Manuel II Palaiologos, Byzantine Emperor 53, 55, 74, 81
  coronation (1392) 44, 52–55
maphorion 94
Marangon, Desi 256
marble 143, 146, 150, 153–54, 161
Marchi, Alessandro 252
Marciniak, Przemsław 37
Marco, painter in Venice 265
Margaret, saint 261
Margaret, Queen of Sicily 111
Maria of Hungary, daughter of Stephen V of Hungary 160
Maria of Mangup (Maria Asanina Palaiologina) 204
Maria Palaiologina, wife of Stefan Uroš III 80, 146, 152, 160
Marin, Franciscan envoy 111
Marinescu, Adrian 210
Marinescu, Florin 218
Marinis, Vasileios 159
Marinković, Čedomila 189
Marinković, Ana 271
Marinković, Radmila 186
Marinov, Tchavdar 36
Marjanović-Dušanić, Smilja 52–53, 112, 152, 160
Mark, evangelist, saint 250, 252
Markova Sušica, Markov Manastir, *katholikon* 20–21, 24, 170
Marković, Miograd 122

Maroules, Constantinopolitan layman (?) 78
Marriage at Cana (John 2:1–12) 133–34, 136–37
Martin, Bishop of Tours, saint 101–2
Martin, Janet 38
Martin, Russell 50
Martin, Therese 259
Martiniani-Reber, Marielle 204, 233
Mary, Virgin 29, 63, 126, 217, 219–21, 237, 244–45, 261, 265, 267
  Assumption (Dormition) 121, 177
  Coronation 248, 261
  Eleousa icon 63
  icon of the Burning Bush 22
  life of the Virgin 216
  Platytera icon 17
  with Child 218, 260–61
Mary Magdalene, saint 267
Matei Basarab, Wallachian ruler 177, 179
Matejče Monastery (Matejič, Matejić) 170, 173, 220
Matheou, Nicholas 120, 217
Matijević, Jurica 268
Matijević, Sofija 266
Matka Monastery 170, 173–74
Mattiello, Andrea 6, 12
Mavromatis, Leonidas 95, 119
Mayasova, Nataliia Andreevna 237
Mediterranean Sea (basin, area) 10–11, 36, 188, 214, 224
Mehmed II, Sultan 86, 272
Mehmet, Mustafa 201, 203
Meletius, Abbot of St. John Prodromos Monastery 74
Memo, Donato, administrator of Murano 255
Menologium (Menologion) 126, 215–16
Mérai, Dóra 271
Mesley, Matthew M. 120
metatorion 54
Methodius, apostle of the Slavs, saint 91
Metohija region 143
Metsikosta, Theotekne 179
Metzler, Irina 120
Meyendorff, Jean 19, 24–25
Meyïer, Karel Adriaan de 84
Michael VIII Palaiologos, Emperor 72, 80, 95–96

Michael Apostoles 79
    address to his teacher John
        Argyropoulos 75
Michael Astrapas 121–22, 125, 128, 131
Mihajlovic-Shipley, Marija 7, 11–12, 91–118, 138
Mihaljević, Marina 189
Mikić, Ana 87
Miklosich, Franciscus 81, 86
Mileševa Monastery 156
Milica Hrebeljanović (née Nemanjić) 171, 185, 187
Milița Despina, wife of Neagoe Basarab 237
military saints 217
Miljković, Bojan 96, 99–100, 103
Miller, David 50
Miller, Timothy S. 73–74, 76
Millet, Gabriel 21, 120, 149, 167–70, 173–75, 180, 235, 241, 243
Milosević, Desanka 121
Mioni, Elpidio 78
Milutin, King of Serbia *see* Stefan Uroš II Milutin
Mircea I, Wallachian ruler 176–77, 183
Mirković, Lazar 147
Miroslav, Prince 91
Mishkova, Diana 36
Mitric, Olimpia 211
Mitrović, Katarina 95–96, 108
Modrište, Church 173
modus Theotonicus 265
Moldavia (principality, region) 2, 8–11, 175–76, 187, 200, 217–18, 220–25, 232–47
Moldova 4, 200
Moldoveanu, Ioan 210
Moldovița Monastery 207–8, 210, 212–13, 215, 217–18, 221, 225
    Church of the Annunciation 201–2, 205–6, 209, 211, 216, 219, 221–24
Molinier, Émile 95–96, 98–99
Monchizadeh, Anuscha 20
Mondrain, Brigitte 78
Mongols (Mongol Empire) 7, 37–39, 41, 48, 50, 56, 62
Monnas, Lisa 268, 270
Montague, Kevin 238
Montenegro 4, 148, 150
Morača, Chapel of St. Nicholas 107–8

Morava School (architectural style) 168–69, 172–76, 180, 183–84, 191
Morava Valley 168, 170, 172, 176, 180, 187, 192
Morosini, Enrico 265
Morozzi, Luisa 252
Moscow 36–39, 42, 55, 62–63, 65
    Epiphany Ritual (1558) 50
    Sieges (1368, 1370, 1382) 38
    as Third Rome 39, 57
    see also Kremlin
Mount Athos (Athonite) 2, 9, 14, 73, 122, 167, 170, 172–73, 180, 187–88, 190–92, 204, 207–10, 220, 232
    Great Lavra 174, 207, 209
    Hilandar Monastery (Chilandari) 129, 147, 160, 170, 181–82, 184
    – *pyrgos* 122
    – abbot 75
    Koutloumousiou Monastery 178, 181, 187, 240
    – *katholikon* 179
    Panteleimonos Monastery 76
    Protaton Monastery 123–24, 127
    – *katholikon* 123
    Vatopedi monastery 186
Muffel, Nikolaus 92
Müller, Ioseph 81, 86
Müller-Christensen, Sigrid 263
Murad II, Sultan 84
Muraro, Michelangelo 250, 252, 265
Murzaleev, Il'nur Midkhatovich 49
Muscovy (Moscow) 7, 11, 36–37, 39–41, 43, 48, 50–51, 54, 56, 58, 62, 204
Mylonas, Pavlos M. 123, 173–74, 179, 210
myrrophoroi 245
Mystra 82, 84
    Brontochion Monastery of the Virgin Hodegetria 123
    Metropolis 123

Nairn, Tom 57
Nanou Katselaki, Andromachi-Maria 220
Naples, Kingdom 257
Năstăsoiu, Dragoș 187
Nathanael, monk and physician at the Xenon 76
Naupara Monastery 187
Neagoe Basarab, Wallachian ruler 236–37, 240, 245–46

Necipoğlu, Nevra   71
Negrău, Elisabeta   175
Negri, Antonio   26
Nelson, Janet   43
Nelson, Robert   4, 25, 132
Nemanjić dynasty (period; Nemanjids)   52, 96–97, 107–8, 110, 146, 152–54, 156–57, 161–62, 168, 220
Németh, András   56
Nenadović, Slobodan   150, 188, 190
Neophytos Prodromenos, monk   79
Nesterov, Tamara   211
New York, International Center of Medieval Art (ICMA)   1
Nicephorus Gregoras (Nikephoros)   83, 119
Nicholas IV, Pope   91, 94, 99, 103–6, 111
   letters   111
Nicholas of Bari (N. of Myra), saint   98, 101–4, 106–8, 110, 114, 252
   iconography   97–101, 105–7
Nickel, Heinrich L.   176, 187
Nicol, Donald M.   71, 81–82, 119, 136
Nicolae Alexandru, Wallachian ruler   178–79
Nicolescu, Corina   205, 214
Nifont, bishop of Suzdal   62
Nikodemos (Nikodim), Athonite monk   176, 189, 192
Nikodim I, Archbishop of Peć   126
Nikola III, Duke of Krk   255
Nikolajević, Ivanka   154, 156, 158
Nikovskaia letopis' (Patriarchal/Nikon Chronicle)   40, 43, 46, 49, 53, 58–65
Nizhny Novgorod   38
Northern Coalition   38
Novaković, J.   169
Novgorod (Old Novgorod)   37–38, 42–43, 63
   Church of the Dormition on Volotovo Field   19
   St. Sophia (church)   42
Novi Pazar, Tracts of St. George (church)   112, 131
Novigrad, Parish church   271–72

Obolensky, Dimitri   1–3
Odayski, Myriam   219
Ohrid (Ochrid), Perivleptos (church)   123, 129
   St. Sophia (church)   19
   Metropolitanate   132, 217

Oka river   38
Old Church Slavonic   54, 147, 158, 203, 210, 215, 239, 243
Oldjira, Meseret   137
Olympos Mount, H. Dionysios monastery   188
Omišalj, Citadel   255
Opreanu, Coriolan Horațiu   216
opus anglicanum   248, 263
opus fiorentinum   263
opus Lucanum   264
opus Neapolitanum   264
opus Romanum   264
opus Senese   264
opus teutonicum   263, 265
opus Venetum   264, 273
Orășanu, Ana Maria   212
orphrey   266
Osnova (periodical)   37
Osor, Diocese   250
Ossa Mount, Monastery of H. Demeterios   188
Ostrogorsky, George   57
Ostrowski, Donald   37, 41, 49–50, 62
Ottoman Empire (Ottomans)   9, 36, 38, 71, 80, 167–68, 175, 179, 191, 201, 203, 205, 214, 221, 224, 232, 270, 272
   conquest of the Balkans   71
   see also Turks
Ousterhout, Robert G.   10, 25, 123, 148, 159, 188–89, 200, 210–11

Pachymeres, George, *Historia Romana*   72, 74, 119, 134
Padua, University   79, 256
Palade, Mihaela   210
Palaiologans (dynasty, family, period)   1, 7, 11, 20, 32, 58, 71–90, 119, 122, 129, 204, 221
Palamar, Petru   187
Palamism   27
Pallas, Demetrios I.   241
Palmieri, Nicoletta   78
Panaite, Viorel   9
Panaitescu, Petre P.   201
pannus theutonicus   265
Pan-Slavism   37
Pantelić, Bratislav   124, 143, 147–48, 150
Paolo Veneziano   8, 250, 252, 254–56, 258, 261–63, 265, 268, 272–73

Ancona di San Donato 255
Crocifisso di Ragusa 256, 258
Pala feriale 252, 254
Polittico di Santa Chiara 252
Papademetriou, George A. 72
Papadrianos, Ioannes A. 82
Papalexandrou, Amy 159, 189
Papastavrou, Elena (Hélène) 204, 233, 272
Parani, Maria 134–35
Paranikas, M. 24
Parenti, Stefano 60
Parma, Baptistery 157
Parppei, Kati 38
Pasi, Silvia 120
Patlagean, Évelyne 120
Pătrăuți Monastery, Church of the Holy Cross 187, 203, 215
patronage 4, 7–8, 13–14, 72, 97, 103, 121, 146–48, 167–69, 172, 180, 200, 204–5, 213, 216–17, 220, 224, 232–33, 235, 240, 255, 257–63, 268–72
Patschovsky, Alexander 4
Paul, Apostle, saint 91–92, 94, 98, 101–2, 105, 250, 252
Paul II, Pope 58
Pavlov, Andrei 57
Pavlović, Leontje 97–98
Pavlović, Paul 126, 132
Pax Mongolica 37–38
Peć, Metropolitanate 217
  Church of the Holy Apostles 147
  monastery 220
Peccioli, San Verano (church). Icon of St. Nicholas 106
Pedrocco, Filippo 252
Pelc, Milan 268
Peloponnese 82
Peltomaa, Leena Mari 221
Pentekostarion 129
Pera, Genoese colony, Account book 52
Perinčić, Tea 256
Perm 38
Perrie, Maureen 40, 57
Persians 221
Petar de Matafaris, Archbishop of Zadar 255
Peter, Apostle, saint 91–92, 94, 98, 105, 248, 252–53, 266
Peter of Bua, scribe 83

Peter Rareș, Prince (Petru) 200, 205, 207, 212, 217, 224
Petersen, Erik 87
Petit, Louis 73
Petkov, Kiril 12
Petković, Vladimir R. 121, 143, 146, 151
Petrou, Elias 7, 12, 71–90
phiale 186
Philip, Prince I of Taranto 160
Philotheos Kokkinos, Patriarch of Constantinople 6, 14–35
Piccolo Paci, Sara 270
Piergentili, Pier Paolo 269
Piguet-Panayotova, D. 17
Pilat, Liviu 9
Piran polyptych 250, 252, 256
Pirivatrić, Srdjan 153
Pistoia—book of accounts 256
Pitarakis, Brigitte 123
Plato 79, 220
Platoneum Publishing 144–45, 151, 155, 157, 159, 162
Platts, Christopher W. 273
Pleshchev, Mikhailko 65
Plokhy, Serhii 37
podea 240
Poe, Marshall 39
Poland 4, 37
Polonijo, Mato 248
Popov, G.V. 17
Popović, Danica 11, 22, 97, 112, 119, 150, 152–53, 158, 169, 186, 207, 216, 225
Popović, Marko 147
Popović, Miroslav 100, 111
Popović, Pera J. 121
Popovich, Ljubica D. 185
Poppel, Sanne van 92
Porumb, Marius 215
Potočnjak, Saša 271
Prashkov, Liuben 14, 16–18, 20, 22, 28
prayer 46, 54–55, 62–65, 99, 156, 207, 250, 260–61
Preradović, Dubravka 169
Price, Simon 41
Prilep 192
Princeton University, Michigan-Princeton-Alexandria Expeditions to Mount Sinai 102, 104

Prizren 172
　Church of the Holy Archangels 152, 154
　Church of the Virgin of Ljeviška 150
Procopius, *De bello Gothico* 83–84
Prokhorov, G.M. 25
Prolović, Jadranka 185
Protasius, bishop of Riazan 62
Pseftogas, B.S. (Pseftonkas) 25, 27–31
Pskov 37
Ptolemaeus 83
Puchsbaum, Hanns, architect 213
punto affondato 248
punto raso 248
punto spaccato 248
Putna Monastery 204, 233–36
Pyropoulos, Antonius, physician 78
Pyropoulos, Manuel, son of Jacob 78
Pyropoulos, Marc 78

Quirinus of Sisak, saint 248, 252–53

Rab Cathedral, polyptych 252, 256
Rădăuți 212
Radojčić, Svetozar 19, 146
Radonja, priest 260
Radovanović, Janko 110
Radu IV cel Mare, Wallachian ruler 177–79, 192
Radu VII Paisie, Wallachian ruler 240
Raffaellino del Garbo 267
Raffensperger, Christian 3
Ranger, Terrence 41
Rascia region 149–50
Raška (Rascia) School (style) 124, 149–50, 168
Raukar, Tomislav 257
Rauter Plančić, Biserka 252, 269
Ravančić, Gordan 258
Ravanica Monastery 171, 177–78, 183–84
　Mausoleum of Lazar Hrebeljanović 176
Ravnik-Toman, Barbara 272
Regensburg, Regensburger Bauhüttentagung (1459) 213
Reilly, Diane 237
Reinert, Stephen 52–53
relic 48, 74, 97, 99, 102, 146, 173, 185–86, 268, 270
Renaissance 188, 266
Resava Church (Manasija) 171, 185
Restle, Marcell 17

Reynolds, M. 20
Richard, Marcel 24
Richtar, Ivan (Zuanne Rectar) 263
Rila, Monastery of Saint John of Rila (Mother of God Osianovitsa) 14
　Hrelja's Tower 14–35
Rila mountains 14
Ristić, Lj. P. 169
Ristić, Vladislav 169–70, 183
rituals 55
Robobello, Giovanni, Archbishop of Zadar 248
Roger II, King of Sicily 106
Romanesque art 7, 124, 144–45, 147, 150, 152–55, 158–59, 161, 259
Romania (Romanians) 4, 10, 36, 200, 210
　see also Moldavia (principality, region); Wallachia (principality; region)
Rome (Roman) 50, 52, 58, 96
　S. Marco (church; St. Mark) 269
　S. Maria in Aracoeli (church) 104, 269–70
　S. Maria Maggiore apse 94, 103, 105
　sack (1527) 92
Ronchey, Silvia 39
Rossi, Maria Alessia 1–13, 32–33, 119–42, 193, 217, 225, 273
Rovine—Battle (1395) 81
Rowell, Stephen Christopher 38
Rowland, Daniel 39, 50
Rubik, Savior Church 106
Rupertsberg, Benedictine abbey 259
Rus 36–39, 42–43, 46, 48, 50–52, 54–57, 62, 221
　chronicles (Rus/Muscovite chronicles) 43, 62
Russia (Russian) 2–4, 6, 10, 36–37, 41, 243
Russkii Khronograf 40
Rybakov, B.A. 24

Sabados, Marina Ileana 211
Sabas (Savva), saint, *Typikon* 126
Saint-Guillain, Guillaume 119
Sakellion, Ioannes 86
sakkoi 94, 108
Saltykov, A.A. 22
samite 272
Samuel, prophet 63
San Severino Marche, polyptychs 252
Šanjek, Franjo 257

INDICES

Sarabianov, Vladimir D. 19
Sarai 38
sarcophagus 146, 152, 158
Saul, King of Israel 51
Sava, Archbishop of Peć, saint 52, 96
  see also Domentijan, *Život Svetoga Save*;
  Teodosije, *Žitija Svetoga Save*
Savva, Vladimir 37, 55
Saxon colonies in Transylvania 212
Schartau, Bjarne 84
Schilb, Henry David 8, 10, 232–47
Schilbach, Erich 20
Schmidt, Victor M. 258–59
Schmitt, Annegrit 264
Scholtz, Cordula 78
Schopen, Ludwig 119
Schreiner, Peter 53
Schroeder, Rossitza 120
Schuette, Marie 263, 265
Seeberg, Stefanie 259
Șerban Cantacuzino, Wallachian ruler 245
Serbia (Serbian Kingdom) 4, 7–12, 18, 36,
  52–54, 71–90, 94, 96, 98, 100–1, 107–8,
  112–13, 119–66, 170, 178, 186, 190, 204,
  207, 214, 217, 220, 224, 232, 235
  Ottoman conquest (1459) 168, 175
Serbian Orthodox Church 137
  autocephaly (1219) 132
Serbo-Byzantine School 168
La Seu d'Urgell, Cathedral of St. Mary 259
Ševčenko, Nancy 106–7
Sgambati, Aniello 259
Shakespeare, William 57
Shakko 46
shapka Monomakha (cap / crown of
  Monomakh) 41, 43, 45, 48–51, 56, 59, 62,
  64–65
Sharpe, Sarah 273
Sheehan, Donald 210
Shepherd, William R. 2
Sicily 224
Sidorova, T.A. 19, 25
Siena 263
Sigesato pasa sarx (hymn) 239
Sigismundus de Polcastris 79
silk 95–96, 248, 259, 264
  see also samite
Silk Road 38
Simeon, monk, saint see Stefan Prvovenčani

Simeon, Metropolitan of All Rus 44–46, 51,
  54, 60, 62–64
Simić-Lazar, Draginja 134
Simonis, Queen 72–73, 80, 87, 119, 121, 135–36
Sinai, Saint Catherine's Monastery 101–3,
  123
  Icon depicting St. Nicholas 101
  Triptych depicting St. Nicholas 104
Singelenberg, Pieter 127
Sinigalia, Tereza 208–9, 217
Sinkević, Ida 7, 11–12, 143–66, 186, 193
Siret 212
Sisak—Battle (1593) 272
Šiševo, Church 173–74
Skadar, St. Nicholas (church) 108
Skazanie o kniaz'iakh vladimirskikh (Tale of
  the Princes of Vladimir) 50
Skopje 72, 170, 176, 191
  Diocese 132
  St. Niketa (church) 218
Skopje area 172–75
Slavophiles 37
Slavonic see Old Church Slavonic
Slavs (Slavic) 8, 11–12, 19, 24–25, 52, 145, 232
  see also Old Church Slavic
Slootjes, Daniëlle 92
Slovenia 4
Smalley, Ruiha 273
Smederevo 71, 84, 86
  Jerinina Kula (Tower of Irene) 82–83
  Public Enterprise Smederevo Fortress
  company 87
Smythe, Dion 37
Sode, Claudia 52, 119
Sofia, daughter of Vytautas, wife of Vasilii I
  Dmitrievich 38, 49
Sofronov, Pimen 91–92
Sokol, Razvan 178
Solomon, King of Israel 21–22, 28
  see also Allegory of Wisdom
Solovjev, Aleksandar 52
Sopoćani Monastery 97, 107–8
  katholikon 19
Spatharakis, Joannis 75, 221
Speake, Graham 9, 204
Špehar, Olga 169
Spenning, Lorenz 212–13
Spišský Štvrtok 212
Split, St. Domnius (cathedral), Treasury 266

Špoljarić, Luka 269
Spremić, Momčilo 96
Srdoč-Konestra, Ines 271
Stachowiak, Dominik 189
Stănescu, Eugen 215
Stanković, Nebojša 159
Stanković, Vlada 119
Staro Nagoričino, St. George (church) 120–21, 123–25, 127–29, 137, 150, 216
Stathakopoulos, Dionysios 119
Stations of the Cross 186
Stefan Dragutin, King of Serbia, King of Mačva 91–92, 95, 97–98, 101, 109, 111–13
Stefan Lazar Hrebeljanović, Serbian Prince 169–71, 176–77, 183–85, 187
  mausoleum at Ravanica 176
Stefan Lazarević, Prince and Despot of Serbia 171, 185
Stefan of Perm, saint—*Life* 38
Stefan Prvovenčani (First Crowned; St. Simeon, monk; Stefan Nemanja), King of Serbia 52, 91, 107, 109, 153, 156, 160–61, 207
  see also Domentijan, *Život Svetoga Simeuna*
Stefan Uroš I, King of Serbia 95, 97–98, 109, 112
Stefan Uroš II Milutin, King of Serbia 72–73, 80, 91–92, 95, 97–98, 111–13, 119, 121–22, 124, 126, 132, 134–37, 147, 150, 154, 161, 216
Stefan Uroš III, Dečanski 80–81, 143, 146–47, 150, 152, 156, 160–62
  Monastic Charter for Dečani 146
Stefan Uroš IV Dušan, Tsar of Serbia 14, 18, 53, 143, 146–148, 150, 152, 154, 162
Stefan Vukanović, Prince (Nemanja's grandson) 107
Ştefănescu, Laura-Cristina 217
Stefanovich, Piotr 48
Stefec, Rudolf S. 84
Stepennaia Kniga (Book of Degrees) 48
Stephanos, *skeuophylax* 79
Stephanus de Doctoribus 79
Stephen, First Martyr, saint 101–2, 261
Stephen III, Moldavian ruler, the Great 167, 187, 200–1, 203–5, 214, 217, 233, 235–37
  Epitaphios 233–34
Stevenson, Henry M. 84

Stevović, Ivan 11–12, 134, 150, 153–54, 169, 218
Stjepan Tomašević Kotromanić, Bosnian King 269
Stoikov, Georgi 16
Stroe, Andrei 178
Studenica Monastery 107, 153–54, 207
  Church of the Virgin 153
  Icon of St. Nicholas 107
Studenica Typikon 107
Subotić, Gojko 95, 108
Suceava 187
  St. Demetrios (church) 212
  Archbishopric of Suceava and Rădăuți 225
Sullivan, Alice Isabella 1–13, 21, 32–33, 107, 138, 167, 175–76, 179, 187, 190, 193, 200–31, 233, 273
Suzdal 38
Sviatoslav, *Sbornik of 1073* 24
Sylvester, Pope 91
Symeon Uroš Palaiologos, King of Serbia (monk Ioannis-Ioasaph) 80–81, 178–79, 181
Székely, Maria Magdalena 204

Taft, Robert F. 233, 239
Takacs, Sarlota 52
Tantsis, Anastasios 173
Tatars 48
Tatić-Djurić, Mirjana 91–92
Taylor, Michael D. 219
Teoctist I, Metropolitan of Moldavia 217
Teodoru, Horia 209
Teodosie, Wallachian ruler 237
Teodosije, *Žitija Svetoga Save* 186
Terebenin, Vladimir 47
Thacher, John S. 241
Theilmann, John M. 105
Theiner, Augustin 269–70
Theocharides, George 75
Theocharis, Maria 240
Theoctistos, monk of the monastery of Hodegon in Constantinople, scribe 72
Theodor, hieromonk, patron at Lapušnja 182, 192
Theodora, Bulgarian princess 160
Theodora Palaiologina—poetry for her 83
Theodore Teron, saint 122

Thessalonica 72–73, 81, 172, 190, 204
  Prophet Elias (church) 188
  St. Euthymios (church) 123
  St. Nicholas Orphanos (church) 216
Thessaly 168
Thomais Comnena Angelina Orsini 80–81
Thomas Kantakouzenos Palaiologos 82
Thracia 72
Tikhon, archbishop of Rostov 62
Tismana Monastery, Church of the
  Dormition of the Virgin at 176
Todić, Branislav 22, 95, 121–24, 143, 146, 148, 150, 216
Tolochko, Oleksiy Petrovich 42
Tomeković, Svetlana 120
Tomić Đurić, Marka 24
Tomin, Svetlana 97, 108, 112
Toniolo, Federica 250
Torriti, Jacopo 105
translatio imperii 36–37
Transylvania 10, 176, 212
  Saxon colonies 212
Trapp, Erich 27, 72
Tre Venezie (region) 256
Trebinje 112
Trebnik (Synodal Ritual) 52–55
Tree of Jesse 126, 219–21
Tree of Life 158–59
Treptow, Laura 1
Treska, St. Andrew (church) 173–74
Treviso, San Francesco (church) 265
Triantaphyllès (printer in Venice) 25
Triconch churches 167–99
Triodion 132
Trisagion (Trisviatoe; hymn) 63
Trogir, Cathedral Treasury 266
Tronzo, William 224
troparion 63
Tulić, Damir 266–67
Turdeanu, Émile (Emil) 235, 243
Turks 80, 121, 167
Tursun Beg 201–2
Tver 38

Ukraine 4, 37
Underwood, Paul A. 120, 123, 127
United Nations peacekeeping force (UNMIK) 143
Uroš I–IV (Kings of Serbia) *see* Stefan Uroš I–IV

Văetişi, Adela 10, 244
Vafeiades, Konstantinos M. 179
Vaida, Gamaliil 176
Vaiophoros, George 79–80
Valeeva-Suleimanova, Guzel'
  Fuadovna 48–49
Valenti, Devis 259
Valenzano, Giovanna 250
Valier, Agostino, apostolic visitor 256, 262
Vanev, Ivan 21, 23
Varangians 48
Vardar River 168
Vasić, Natalija 260
Vasilii I Dmitrievich, grand prince of
  Moscow 38
  Testament 49
Vasilii II, grand prince of Moscow 57
  Testament 43, 49
Vasilii III, grand prince of Moscow 49
Vassilaki, Maria 190, 220
Vătăşianu, Virgil 211
Vatican City, St. Peter (church), St. Peter's
  tomb 96
  Tesoro di San Pietro—Inventory of
    1295 96, 98
  – Panel of St. Peter and St. Paul 7, 91–118
Vazaca, Marina 245
Veglia *see* Krk (city); Krk (island)
Veglia altar frontal 248–80
Velbužd (Kiustendil) – battle (1330) 156
Velmans, Tania 21
Venditti, Gianni 269
Venetian Republic 8, 257, 261
Venice (Venetians) 82, 96, 248, 250, 254, 256–58, 263–65, 267–68, 272–73
  Arte dei Ricamatori 264
  Guild of *battilori* 264
  inventory list of the Treasury of St.
    Mark 265
  Painters' guild 264
  San Salvatore (monastery) 265
  Scuola di San Teodoro, statute
    (*mariegola*) 265
Venjamin, *hegoumenos* 121
Vienna, Chapel of Saint Maria
  Magdalene 212
  Stephansdom 212–13
  Ottoman siege (1529) 205
Visoki Dečani *see* Dečani
Vita, Franciscan friar 147–48, 162

Vlad VII Vintilă, Wallachian ruler 240
Vladimir area 62
Vladimir Monomakh, Prince of Kiev 48–50, 53, 62–63
  see also *barmy* of Monomakh; *shapka Monomakha*; Moscow, Kremlin, *Zolotaia palata* (Golden Palace), Throne Room (throne of Monomakh) (Index 3)
Vladislav, son of Stefan Prvovenčani 156
Vladislav Vlaicu, Wallachian ruler 178–79
Vodiţa Monastery 176
Vogel, Marie 79
Voinescu, Teodora 217
Vojvodić, Dragan 11, 95, 109, 119, 146, 150, 160, 162, 169, 207, 216, 225
Volbach, Wolfgang Fritz 91, 95, 99
Volk, Otto 73–75, 79
Vologda 38
Voroneţ Monastery 214, 222
Voskressenskii Chronicle 40, 48–49, 59
Voyatzis, Sotiris 207
Vranas, physician, son of Protomastoros of the Kral 78
Vsevolod Iurevich, Prince of Vladimir 42
Vujičić, Dušan 162
Vuk Grgurević Branković, Serbian despot 270
Vukan, son of Stefan Nemanja 96
Vukovich, Alexandra 6–7, 11, 36–70
Vulović, Branislav 183
Vychegda 38

Walker, Alicia 1
Wallachia (principality; region) 2, 7–10, 167, 169, 175–76, 178, 180, 187, 190, 204, 217, 232–47
Walter, Christopher 19
Walther, Rainer 72
Watson, Arthur 219
Weitzmann, Kurt 101
Wiedmann, Gerhard 92
Wikimedia Commons 2, 15, 46
Wilkinson, Catherine 189
Willson, Justin L. 6, 12, 14–35
Wilson, Louise E. 120
Wisdom (iconography and allegory) 22, 27, 29, 31

Wolf, Gerhard 186
Woodfin, Warren 10, 243
World War I 168
World War II 235
Wortman, Richard 46–48

Xu, Tianling (Rusty) 178, 183–84, 193

Yota, Élisabeth 42

Zacchaeus, publican (Luke 19:1–10) 127–32, 137
Zadar 248, 256–58, 261, 271
  Chest of St. Simeon 272
  St. Chrysogonus (church), altar frontal 250, 260–61, 266–67
  St. Francis (monastery) 257
  St. Mary (Benedictine church), altar of St. John 260
  Treaty of 1358 257
Zagreb, Cathedral, treasury 268
  Croatian Science Foundation 273
Zahumlia 150
Zaostrog, Franciscan monastery of St. Mary 269
zendado 256, 267
Zenkovsky, Betty Jean 62
Zenkovsky, Serge 62
Zeta (Diokletia) 150
Zeta (Zetska Država) 112, 161
Žic-Rokov, Ivan 254–55, 262–63
Žiča Monastery 156
Zimin, Aleksandr Aleksandrovich 49
Zinsmeister, Erika 193
Živković, Branislav 108, 121, 154
Živković, Miloš 153, 207
Živkovic, Zdenka 93
Živojinović, Mirjana 74
Zlamalik, Vinko 261
zodia, the four living creatures of the Apocalypse 233–34
Zoe/Sofiia Palaiologina 39, 58
Žokva (Żółkiew; Nesterov) Castle 235
Zupka, Dušan 9
Zvizdović, Anđelo, Franciscan 272

3   Index of Repositories: Archives, Libraries and Museums

Athens, Benaki Museum, Neohellenic Architecture Archives   210
Athens, National Library
    1075   86

Belgrade, National Museum   93
Bloomington, Bloomington Indiana University, Eskenazi Museum of Art   232, 237, 239, 241, 243–46
    Eskenazi Museum of Art, Burton Y. Berry Collection 72.2.6 (*Aër/Epitaphios*)   237–38, 243
    Lilly Library, Burton Yost Berry Papers   241
Brussels, Musées Royaux d'Art et d'Histoire   259
Bucharest National Museum of Art of Romania   237, 242, 244–45
    MNAR 181/15.826   241
    MNAR 14 888/37   218
Budapest Museum of Applied Arts (*Iparművészeti Múzeum*)   250, 256, 261, 265–66

Cairo, Patriarchal Library
    gr. 35   82
Cividale del Friuli, Museo Archeologico Nazionale   259
Copenhagen, Det Kongelige Bibliothek (Royal Danish Library)
    GkS 6,2   84–85, 87
Copenhagen, National Gallery of Denmark (Staatens Museum for Kunst)   267

Dallas Museum of Art, Keir Collection   265
Dobrinj, St. Stephen (church), Collection of Sacred Art, Altar Frontal   248, 255–56, 261–63, 266

Firenze, Biblioteca Medicea Laurenziana
    55,47   84

Genoa, Archivio di S. Giorgio
    Cartolario della Masseria di Pera   52

Kalabaka, Varlaam Monastery
    151   72

Leiden, Universiteitsbibliotheek
    Voss. Gr. F. 42   84
Ljubljana, National Museum of Slovenia   272
London, St. Paul's Cathedral, Inventory lists   264
London, Victoria and Albert Museum
    Veglia altar frontal   248–80

Moscow, State Historical and Cultural Museum and Heritage Site   45
Moscow, Kremlin, *Zolotaia palata* (Golden Palace), Throne Room (throne of Monomakh)   50
Mount Athos, Dionysiou Monastery, archives   220
Mount Athos, Hilandar Monastery, archives
    58 (February 1321)   75
    60 (June 1321)   75
    61 (June 1321)   75
    82 (August 1, 1322)   74–75

New York, Metropolitan Museum of Art   267–68

Oxford, Bodleian Library
    Barocci 87   75–77, 87

Paris, Bibliothèque nationale de France
    grec 139 (Paris Psalter)   19
    grec 1242   110
    latin 5180 (Tesoro di San Pietro— Inventory of 1295)   95, 264
Paris, Louvre   10
Princeton University, Index of Medieval Art   1, 138

Rome, Archivio dell'Istituto Storico Germanico, Codici Minucciani 7   269

Saint Petersburg, State Hermitage Museum   47
Saint Petersburg, Rossijskaja nacional'naja biblioteka
    Gil'ferding 54   96
Sergei Posad, Trinity Lavra of St. Sergius
    MS 304.I. Služebnik i Trebnik (1474)   52, 60

Smederevo, Fortress Museum 87

Thessaloniki, Museum of Byzantine Culture
   inv. no. Βυφ 57 238
Torcello, Museo Provinciale
   Banner of St. Fosca 265
Trieste, Civici Musei di Storia ed Arte
   inv. F77194 249

Vatican City, Archivio Apostolico Vaticano
   (Archivio Segreto Vaticano) 269
   Congr. vescovi e regolari, Visita ap., 80 (d.
     Arbensis) 256
   Congr. vescovi e regolari, Visita ap., 80 (d.
     Veglensis) 262
Vatican City, Biblioteca Apostolica Vaticana
   Ottob. gr. 67 83
   Pal. gr. 278 84
   Vat. gr. 537 73
   Vat. gr. 564 73
   Vat. gr. 1301 83

Venice, Archivio di Stato di Venezia
   Cancelleria inferiore, Doge, Giurisdizioni,
     Veglia, Catastico di Veglia, 221 263
Venice, Biblioteca Nazionale Marciana
   Class. v, 9 77–78
Venice, Gallerie dell'Accademia
   Polittico di Santa Chiara 252
Venice, Museo Correr 252
   polyptych 252
Vienna, Akademie der Bildenden Künste,
   Graphic Collection 212
Vienna, Österreichische
   Nationalbibliothek 77, 87
   Med. gr. 1 76–77, 79
   Slav. 57 96
   Theol. gr. 138 72

Zadar, Permanent Collection of Sacred Art
   (SICU) 260, 266
Zagreb, Muzej za umjetnost i obrt (Museum
   of Arts and Crafts) 266